Mel Bay Presents

Parking Lot Picker's Songbook

By Gerald Jones & Dix Bruce

FIDDLE EDITION

Cover photos by Gerald Jones except lower right by Dix Bruce.

A collection of over 200 great Bluegrass, Old Time, Country, and Gospel standards. Melodies are presented with standard notation along with lyrics and chords. The two CDs include recordings of EVERY song in the book.

Learn to play songs written and recorded by the giants of traditional American music: Bill Monroe, The Stanley Brothers, Flatt & Scruggs, Ralph Stanley, The Osborne Brothers, Jimmy Martin, Doc Watson, and many more.

Also included: Step-by-step instruction on how to transpose any song to any key!

Special thanks to Marjorie McWee for her excellent proofing and editing suggestions.

MEL BAY

1 2 3 4 5 6 7 8 9 0

Visit us on the Web at www.melbay.com — E-mail us at email@melbay.com

Table of Contents

Introduction

The Parking Lot Picker's Songbook is an all-in-one sourcebook for musicians to help build their bluegrass repertoire and more effectively play with others in jam sessions and in bands.

Bluegrass and old time music is unlike most other types of music. Aside from the obvious differences in sound, bluegrass fans are usually players in addition to being listeners. Bluegrass fans typically bring their instruments to concerts and festivals and spend as much time swapping songs and jamming as they do watching the headline acts. Everybody picks: young and old, male and female, beginner to professional. It's a wonderfully communal, world-wide group that welcomes like-minded strangers who pack a guitar, banjo, mandolin, fiddle, or a voice to sing with.

The shared repertoire is what brings them all together and it's a powerful phenomenon. You can go to a bluegrass get-together in Tokyo, Buenos Aires, Paris, Reykjavik, or anywhere else in the world, and the local players will know the same Bill Monroe and Stanley Brothers songs and fiddle tunes that you know. You'll be able to break musical bread and communicate with strangers no matter what the local language is. *The Parking Lot Picker's Songbook* is our attempt to collect a large number of these songs in one place and present them to you with melody, lyrics, chords, tablature, and a recording of each individual song. *The Parking Lot Picker's Songbook* provides easy access to much of this core repertoire and is a great resource for both the newcomer and the more experienced player who is looking to expand his or her song repertoire.

So, what's a "parking lot picker"?

The term "parking lot picker" grew out of the early bluegrass festivals where fans would stand around in parking lots adjacent to festival or concert sites and jam or "pick." These days you're likely to find assorted groups of parking lot pickers jamming, swapping tunes and licks, and sharing their love of the music at any bluegrass event you attend. Parking lot pickers play music together at every opportunity. If you have an interest in playing and singing bluegrass music with others — no matter what your experience or ability level — then you are a "parking lot picker" and this book is for you!

What songs are included in this book?

Many of the most loved and important songs in traditional American music are collected in the *Parking Lot Picker's Songbook*, including many traditional favorites from gospel music. We love every one of them! We've heard many of them all of our lives, around home, at school and in church. Each represents a favorite theme, artist, or period in the history of American bluegrass, country, gospel, and old time music. It is our hope that you too will love these songs and use this book at jam sessions and performances sharing great music with friends and family.

In compiling this anthology we combed though our LPs and CDs, song books, and set lists. We paid special attention to the works of the pioneers of bluegrass and American old time music: Bill Monroe, the Stanley Brothers, Flatt & Scruggs, Ralph Stanley, the Osborne Brothers, Jimmy Martin, Doc Watson, along with many other important artists. You'll find them strongly represented, both with traditional pieces that were part of their repertoires and with songs they composed themselves. Over 100 years of American music is contained in these pages. From Stephen Foster's tragic "Hard Times" to Dean Webb and Mitch Jayne's "Old Home Place," to the traditional-turned-jam band favorite "I Know You Rider." You're bound to encounter many of your favorites as well as discover new songs that you'll want to add to your repertoire. Of course we had to leave out hundreds more. Maybe someday there'll be a *Parking Lot Picker's Songbook Volume Two*!

Most of these songs have been recorded again and again by bluegrass, country, gospel, and old time artists. We've listed the names of some of them on each song. If we left out your favorite artist, we apologize. Our aim was to give you a representative artist for each song rather than a comprehensive or all-inclusive list. We did lean toward the pioneers of the styles mentioned above. We also included some personal favorites that we wanted you to know about. We mentioned a few of our own recordings.

It's important that you seek out and listen to these seminal recordings. We didn't name specific CDs the songs can be found on since collections, titles, and availability are constantly changing. Anything we might have included would likely be out of date within a month or two. Since the advent of box sets, compilations by the great artists are widely available. These days you can also search for instantly downloadable versions of your favorite songs on the internet. iTunes and other downloading services are convenient and reasonably priced and seem to be the wave of the future.

Some of the songs are more obscure and may not have been recorded widely. Still they are special favorites of ours that we hope you will enjoy both in the book and on the accompanying CDs.

How do I use the Parking Lot Picker's Songbook?

The songs are listed alphabetically and we've designed this book to minimize page turns. Song titles are shown centered at the top of each page. Composer information, if known, is shown on the upper right. CD and track locations are shown on the upper left under key designation. For example, the recording of "Are You From Dixie?" is on CD number one, track six. Most song titles are shown in the "Notes on Selected Songs" section on page 256 where alternate titles are listed. This section includes any short notes there may be on many of the individual songs. Following that you'll find the Index by Artist.

Most of these songs are based on traditional sources and as such can be heard with a variety of versions, melodies and lyrics. we went with the versions we were most familiar with. Feel free to do the same and substitute your favorite chords, lyrics, and melodies as the mood strikes you.

Standard Notation vs. Tab

Fiddle, unlike most of the other bluegrass instruments, has no one standard form of tablature. This isn't a problem because standard notation works like tab for the fiddle. It's all in the way you visualize it.

Reading music for fiddle/violin is not all that hard. Little kids all over the world can read music and so can you. The great thing about standard notation is that there are thousands upon thousands of tunes written in it. It's almost as simple as tab and a lot faster to read after you get the hang of it. Standard notation has a five line staff. Let's look at where to place your first three fingers in first position.

You are probably familiar with the phrase "Every Good Boy Does Fine" used to help you remember the names of the notes each line represents, E G B D F from the lowest line to the highest. For the spaces the names of the notes are F A C E, which spells "FACE." This is great but even in first position the fiddle has notes both lower and higher than this. To represent the lowest note on the fiddle we need to add two more lines below the staff. For the highest note in first position using only the first three fingers we add one line. The short lines above and below the staff are called ledger lines. The example below shows where each finger is placed on each string. You place each finger according to the scale key you are in. If you can play G, A, C and D scales you will cover most tunes.

Starting from the space below the second ledger line is your open G string. The second space up from the G is your open D string. Skip a space and you have the open A string, etc.

The second line below the staff is an A note using your first finger on the G string. Every other line is your first finger on the next string up. This same system goes for your next two fingers. When I see the line second from the top of the staff (not the ledger lines) I don't think "Hey that's a D note!" I just put my 3rd finger on the 2nd string.

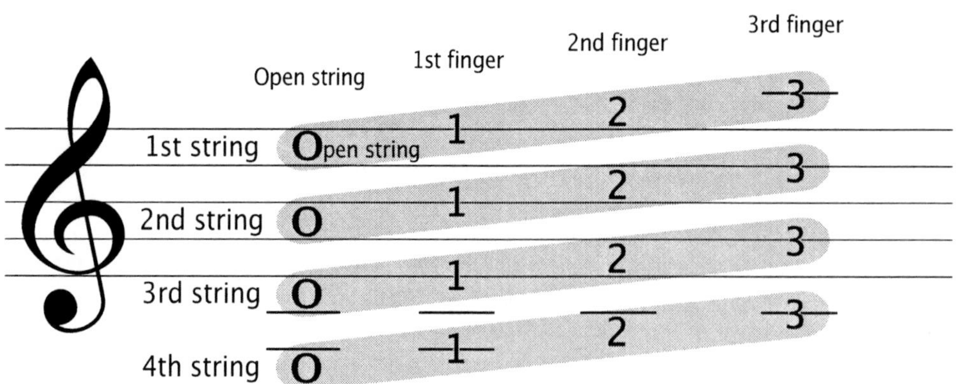

Open string
1st finger
2nd finger
3rd finger
1st string
Open string
2nd string
3rd string
4th string
O
1
2
3

In the example above I put a grey bar on the notes for each string to help you visualize which notes are played on each string with what finger. Below is a chart of the actual notes.

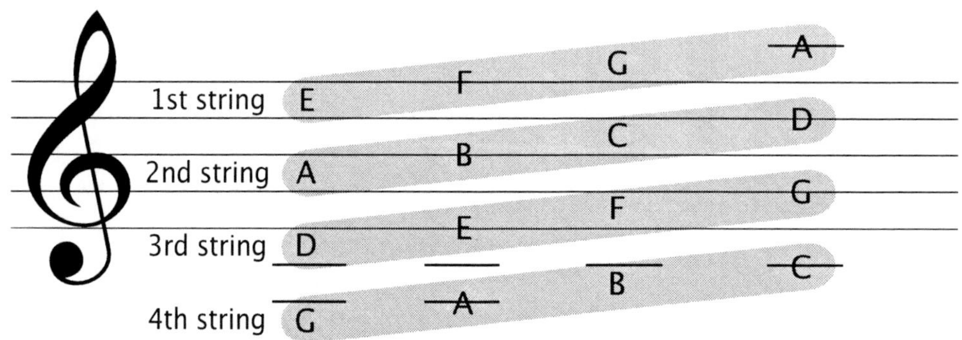

1st string E F G A
2nd string A B C D
3rd string D E F G
4th string G A B C

Performance Keys and Transposing

Typical performance keys for both male and female voices are shown in the upper left corner of each song. We used our own voice as a starting point. We have fairly typical male voices, not too low, not too high. We have found that if we sing a song in the key of G, a typical female voice will sing the same song in the key of C or D, a fourth or fifth higher than where we sing it. This is reflected in the notation:

M: G
F: C or D

"M" stands for "male voice," which will sing the song in the key of "G," *"F"* stands for "female voice," which will sing the song in the key of "C" or "D." Of course there will be cases when these suggested keys might not fit your voice, whether you are a male or a female. Never fear, we'll learn to transpose the songs to any key.

Most of the songs are pitched in the keys of G and C. There are several reasons for this. G and C are probably the most popular keys for bluegrass, gospel, and old time music, and many of the "original" recordings of these songs are in G or C. G and C are also relatively easy keys to play in. However, most of the songs fit well into other keys too. Don't be afraid to move songs around. You'll discover all sorts of tonal characteristics unique to different keys.

What's the best way to learn a song?

It's a good idea to listen to the recorded version of the song first to get an idea of how it goes. CD and track numbers are listed under the key designations on each page. Short representative excerpts of **all** the songs have been recorded with fiddle, guitar, mandolin, banjo, and vocals on the CDs accompanying this book. Dix played mandolin and guitar and sang the vocals. Gerald played the fiddle parts. Banjo parts were recorded by Bill Evans. Dix also wrote the mandolin and guitar versions of *The Parking Lot Picker's Songbook.* They're just like this fiddle edition except that they include tablature. Bill Evans wrote the banjo version of this book. It includes chords, lyrics, melodies in standard notation, plus banjo tablature. Dix and Stacy Phillips wrote the Dobro version. All books are identical to this and include the same songs, chords, lyrics, with melodies in standard notation and tablature.

As you listen to a song, follow along with the lyrics and music. Then play along. Try singing with the recording to determine if the song is pitched in your key.

As mentioned above, we've found that a typical female range is usually a fourth or fifth musical interval above the male key. Key designations on each song reflect this. Of course everybody's voice is a little different and we're looking at this rule only as a starting point. So, if a song is written here in the key of D, to back up a female voice, you'd start by transposing the chords of the song from the key of D to the key of G or A, a fourth or fifth above the key of D. More about the process of transposing below.

How can I change the key of a song to better fit my voice or instrument?

Let's say the suggested keys don't work for your voice or for how you want to play the violin. It's a simple process to transpose the chord progression to other keys. It's a bit more involved to change the melodies and write them out, but the same principles apply.

Let's look at "Amazing Grace" on page 13. It's presented here in the key of G, noted in the upper left hand corner of the page. Again, *"M: G"* means that a typical male voice would sing "Amazing Grace" in the key of G. To accommodate a typical female voice we need to change the chords to a different key, C or D. The ***Scale and Transposition Chart*** on page 6 will make the process of transposing easier.

Photo by Gerald Jones

One of Gerald's young students, an aspiring Parking Lot Picker.

Scale and Transposition Chart

	Key signature	***Major scale***	***1***	***2***	***3***	***4***	***5***	***6***	***7***	***8 (1)***
Key	***#/b***		**I**	**ii**	**iii**	**IV**	**V**	**vi**	**vii°**	**I**
C	none	C	C	Dm	Em	F	G	Am	B°	C
F	1 - ♭	F	F	Gm	Am	B	C	Dm	E°	F
B♭	2 - ♭	B♭	B♭	Cm	Dm	E	F	Gm	A°	B
E♭	3 - ♭	E♭	E♭	Fm	Gm	A	B	Cm	D°	E
A♭	4 - ♭	A♭	A♭	B♭m	Cm	D♭	E♭	Fm	G°	A
D♭	5 - ♭	D♭	D♭	E♭m	Fm	G♭	A♭	B♭m	C°	D♭
G♭	6 - ♭	G♭	G♭	A♭m	B♭m	C♭	D♭	E♭m	F°	G♭
C♭	7 - ♭	C♭	C♭	D♭m	E♭m	F♭	G♭	A♭m	B♭°	C♭
C♯	7 - ♯	C♯	C♯	D♯m	E♯m	F♯	G♯	A♯m	B♯°	C♯
F♯	6 - ♯	F♯	F♯	G♯m	A♯m	B	C♯	D♯m	E♯°	F♯
B	5 - ♯	B	B	C♯m	D♯m	E	F♯	G♯m	A♯°	B
E	4 - ♯	E	E	F♯m	G♯m	A	B	C♯m	D♯°	E
A	3 - ♯	A	A	Bm	C♯m	D	E	F♯m	G♯°	A
D	2 - ♯	D	D	Em	F♯m	G	A	Bm	C♯°	D
G	1 - ♯	G	G	Am	Bm	C	D	Em	F♯°	G

The chart above shows the scales, chords, and key signature (number of sharps or flats) that identify each key. If you look in the key of G line at the bottom of the chart, you'll see in the second column ("key signature") that the key of G has one sharp in its key signature. If you read across to the right you'll see "G Am Bm C D Em F#°." These are the chords of the key of G and all are made up using only the notes of the G major scale. Songs in the key of G can have other chords as well, like E or A7, but to make these chords we need to use notes from outside of the G major scale. If you remove all the "m" (minor) and "°" (diminished) chord designations, you'll come up with the G scale, which is "G A B C D E F#." Be sure to leave the sharps and flats shown or the scale changes. So, how do we use this to transpose?

Going back to "Amazing Grace," we see that the chord progression to the first line of the song is G—C—G. Since "Amazing Grace" is written here in the key of G (noted in the upper left hand corner of the page, *"M: G"*) let's see where these chords occur in the "key of G" line in the chart. The G chord is in the "I" (upper case Roman numeral one) column. The G chord in the key of G is a "one" chord. The C chord is in the "IV" column and is a "four" chord. We need to know where these chords fit numerically in order to transpose them. All chords are identified by Roman numerals, upper case for majors (I, IV, V) lower case for minors (ii, iii, vi) and the lone diminished chord which has a little circle as part of the chord name (vii°).

Let's transpose "Amazing Grace" from the male key of G to the first suggested female key of C. We'll be transposing it to a higher key, which will be to a key "later" in the musical alphabet (A, B, C, D, E, F, G) like C, D, E, etc. (That might be a little confusing but keep in mind that the musical alphabet continues to the right and left, like a keyboard: A, B, C, D, E, F, G, A, B, C, D, E, F, G, A, B, C, D, E, F, G. If you start in the middle on a G, you can get to an A by going either left or right, "later" or "earlier" in the musical alphabet. For our purposes here, let's say that "later" in the musical alphabet is toward a higher key, "earlier" is toward a lower key.)

Let's start with the first chord of the original key, the G chord, in the "I" column. Follow up in the "I" column to the key of C row. The I chord in the key of C is an C chord. Write a "C" in everywhere you see a G chord on the music to "Amazing Grace." (We suggest that you write in pencil in case your voice changes!)

The next chord in the original key of G version of "Amazing Grace" is a C. The C chord is in the IV column of the key of G row. Follow that column up to the key of C row and you'll find the new chord is an F. Write an "F" in everywhere you see a C chord in the music to "Amazing Grace."

There's one more chord in the key of G version of "Amazing Grace" and that's the D. Once again, find the D in the key of G row. It's in the "V" column and is a "five" chord. Follow up in the V column to the key of C row and you'll find a G chord. Write a "G" in everywhere you see a D chord in the music to "Amazing Grace." Now you've changed every G chord to an C, every C to an F, and every D to a G, transposing the chord progression from the key of G to the key of C.

You may need a key higher than C for "Amazing Grace." If that's the case, go through the same procedure and try transposing from the key of G to the key of D. In the key of D your new chords will be D, G, and A. What if "Amazing Grace" is pitched too high to sing in the key of G? You will need to transpose it to a lower key, which will be to a key "earlier" in the musical alphabet (A, B, C, D, E, F, G) like F, E, etc. Try transposing "Amazing Grace" to the key of E. Start with the first chord of the original key, the G chord, in the "I" column. Follow up in the "I" column to the key of E row. The I chord in the key of E is an E chord. Write an "E" in everywhere you see a G chord on the music to "Amazing Grace." Do the same procedure as before. Your new chords in the key of E will be E, A, and B.

Transposing other songs

Some songs are in kind of nebulous keys like "I Know You Rider," "Shady Grove," "Rain and Snow," and "Wayfaring Stranger." The first three are sometimes described as "modal," the last as "minor." In cases like this, it may not be clear to you which key row to use. If you match the number of sharps or flats in the key signature of the song to the second column ("#/b") of the chart, you can't go wrong. Just make sure that you follow up or down in the correct column.

There will be times when the exact chord you're transposing can't be found on the chart. In "Wayfaring Stranger" there's an "A7" chord but there's no "A7" in the key of F row, only an "Am" in the "iii" column. **You can still use this column as long as you maintain the original "quality" of the chord as you transpose.** For example, if the original is a seventh, the transposed chord needs to be a seventh. If the original chord is a minor, the transposed chord needs to be a minor also. Let's transpose "Wayfaring Stranger" from the given key of F/Dm up to G/Em. The first chord is a Dm. Find the Dm in the key of F row. It's in the "vi" column. Follow the "vi" column down to the key of G row and you'll find an Em. Pencil in an Em everywhere you see Dm in "Wayfaring Stranger." Find the next chord, the Gm in the key of F row, in the "ii" column. Follow the "ii" column down to the key of G row where you'll see Am. Write Am in the music where you see Gm. The next chord in the original key of F is Bb. Find the Bb in the "IV" column of the key of F row. Follow this down to the key of G row, where you'll find a C. Pencil it in. Do the same with the original F chord changing it to G. Finally, find the A in the iii column, where it's listed as Am. The original chord is an A7. Follow down in the iii column until you get to the key of G row. There you'll find a Bm, which you'll change to a B7 to preserve the dominant seven quality of the original. That's all there is to it, you've transposed the chords of "Wayfaring Stranger" from the key of F to the key of G.

A similar thing happens in "Little Maggie." It's printed in the key of G and the second chord is an F. However, there's no F chord in the key of G row, only an F# in the "vii" column. F# is one half step higher in pitch than F natural. All you have to do is take that into account in the transposed key. Let's transpose "Little Maggie" to the key of D. The first chord of the original key is a G. The G chord is in the I column of the key of G row. Follow this up in the I column to the key of D row and our first chord is transposed to a D chord. Now go back to the key of G row and the "vii" column, which is still an F#. Lower it one half step to get the F chord from the song in the original key of G. Follow up in the vii column to the key of D row. You'll find a C#. Since we lowered our original F# one half step to F natural, we'll need to do the same here and lower the C# one half step to C natural. So, the first two chords in the key of D version of "Little Maggie" are D and C. For more about music theory and transposing, check out Dix's *Guide to Capo, Transposing, & the Nashville Numbering System* from Mel Bay. Although the capo section applies to guitarists, the theory will work with any instrument.

More on transposing: why the violin is way cooler than the guitar or banjo

The violin is tuned in fifths, so the musical interval between two neighboring strings is a perfect fifth. The interval between the E (string one) and the A (string two) is a perfect fifth. The interval between the A (string two) and the D (string three) is a perfect fifth, and so on. This, friends, makes all the difference in the world!

Because of this symmetrical tuning, we can move melodies and chord progressions "across" and up and down the violin fingerboard to different keys with relative ease. Guitars are tuned in fourths and a third which makes certain types of transposition very difficult. A guitar picker always has to take into account that interval of a third between strings two and three.

Look at the first song in *The Parking Lot Picker's Songbook*, "All the Good Times," on page 12. As played in the key of G, you'll see that all the notes fall on either the second or third strings. (Note: string one, the highest pitched string, is tuned to E; string two, the second highest pitched, is tuned to A; string three is tuned to D; string four, the lowest pitched, is tuned to G.) Because of the violin's symmetrical tuning, we can move this melody, lock, stock, and barrel, "over" one string to a new key. Instead of playing the first note with the first finger on the second string, play it with the first finger on the third string. Here's the first line of the new key to get you started.

C
F
C
1. I wish to the Lord I'd nev-er been born, Or died when
Cho: All the good times are past_ and gone,_ All the good
2. Don't you_ see that tur - tle dove, That flies from
3. Come back, come_ back my own_ true love, And stay a -

As you try to move the melody over one string, keep your fingering in the same basic position you use when you play "All the Good Times" in the original key of G.

By moving the melody in this way you've transposed it to the key of C, which is the first suggested female key. It is a little odd to think that we moved the melody down in pitch to move it to a higher key. And you will have to pitch your voice correctly to sing along in the new key.

If you are the genius that most of us violin players are, you are already thinking, "If I can move the melody **down** from the original to string three, can I also move it **up** one string to start the melody on string one?" The answer is yes!

Look again at the original version of "All the Good Times" in the key of G. This time move the melody **up** one string so that your first note is played with the first finger on the first string.

By moving the melody in this way you've transposed it to the key of D, which is the second suggested female key. Is this great, or what? Of course, if the melody spans three strings, you'll only be able to move it one way and to one other key. You can move the melody the other way, you just may have to move a few notes around that aren't automatically playable.

D
G
D
1. I wish to the Lord I'd nev-er been born, Or died when
Cho: All the good times are past_ and gone,_ All the good
2. Don't you_ see that tur - tle dove,That flies from
3. Come back, come_ back my own_ true love, And stay a -

Learning Chords is Important!

Unfortunately many fiddlers don't know much about the chords of the tune they are playing and sometimes even the key. If you don't know at least a few chords and how to use them you are missing a valuable tool to improvise and to support the other players in a jam. I recommend getting a mandolin and learning the basic open and closed positions.

Here is a simple example of how this can help. Try to visualize frets on your fiddle. Below is a G chord double stop on the first two strings. Move your fingers over one string and it becomes C chord. Move over once more and you have a F chord. You can drone or "chop" with these two notes to provide a rhythm accompaniment. In this position the higher note is the root or 1 of the chord and the lower note is the 3rd. Place the 1 of the chord on any note with this fingering and you have the chord of the same name. In the next example I used a simple barre to make an A chord. This time the 1 is on the lower string. By moving it to different pairs of strings you are able to play A, E or B chord. These positions can be moved anywhere on the fingerboard to give you any chord you need.

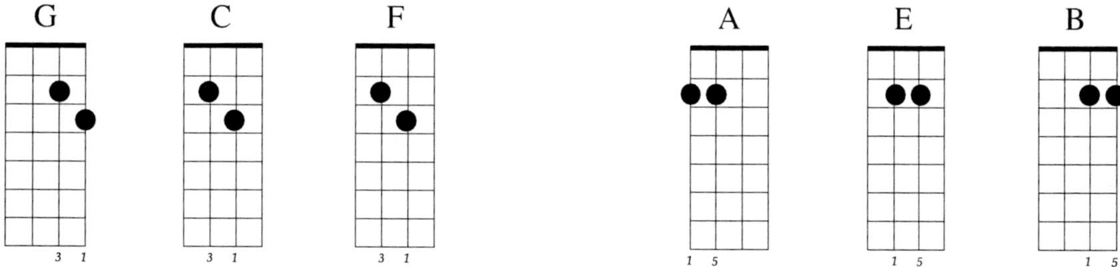
G
C
F
A
E
B
3 1
3 1
3 1
1 5
1 5
1 5

Below are a few mandolin chord positions. On the fiddle you can play double stops on any two adjacent strings and that will work as an accompaniment. This gives you something to do when you aren't playing the lead besides standing around looking pretty...

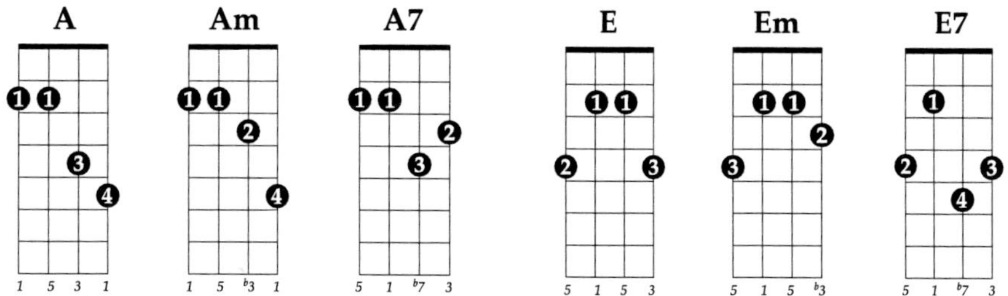
A
Am
A7
E
Em
E7
1 5 3 1
1 5 b3 1
5 1 b7 3
5 1 5 3
5 1 5 b3
5 1 b7 3

In addition, one can move these sets of closed position chords up and down the fingerboard. For example, if you move the original key of A chords up two "frets," you'll transpose the song to the key of B. Move them down two imaginary frets from the original key of A position and you'll transpose the song to the key of G. The "Transposer Wheel" on page 253 will also be helpful in transposing. The small numbers below the chord diagrams tell what part of the chord (1-3-5-v7) each note supplies.

When looking for melody notes it's important to remember that musical phrases usually start and almost always end on one of the notes of the chord. Most tunes with a strong melody will mainly be chord tones. A good example is Red River Valley. In the key of G the first notes are: D G B B B B A B A G. ("From this valley they say you are going") The G chord consists of G B and D notes. Out of the first ten notes in this phrase eight are chord tones and the first and last notes are chord tones too! When the song changes chords the most likely notes of the melody change to the notes of the new chord. For the second phrase the notes are: D G B G B D C B A ("I will miss your bright eyes and sweet smile.") Seven out of these nine notes are G chord tones and the last note is in the D chord. By knowing the chords of a tune you also know the most likely places to find the melody notes.

This book is intended to provide lyrics, chords, and melody to many great tunes. You may find that you would like to spice up the fiddle part beyond playing just the melody. There are many ways to do this by adding licks and phrases that may have little to do with the actual melody of the song. My favorite way to build fiddle solos is to scat sing the song, varying the phrasing and adding extra notes and licks. I then try play what I sang on the fiddle. I recommend that you learn to sing along with your fiddle tunes. If you can sing what you play, eventually you will be able to play what you sing. To help you learn to create solos we have provided a few examples at: http://TheGeraldJones.com/ PLP

Of course there are several other fascinating ways to move melodies, chords and progressions around on the fingerboard. These exercises just scratch the surface. The best part is that you just can't do it this easily on either the guitar or the banjo. Violin rules! For a full examination of the subject of using chords and solos, check out Dix's *Getting into Bluegrass Mandolin* book/CD set from Mel Bay Publications. No home should be without a copy!

Here's hoping you enjoy this collection of great songs! Visit us online at **TheGeraldJones.com** or **www.musixnow.com**. Lots of music, tablature and MP3s to download and learn. Or email us at:

Gerald Jones: gerald@TheGeraldJones.com
Dix Bruce: dix@musixnow.com

— Gerald Jones and Dix Bruce, Spring 2009

Gerald Jones *is well known in Texas music circles as a multi-instrumentalist. His group, Acoustic Plus, showcases his wide range of talents on banjo, guitar, mandolin and fiddle. He began teaching almost from the time he started playing. He has taught private lessons since 1972 and taught at many music camps since the 1980s. In 2007 he founded Acoustic Music Camp (http://AcousticMusicCamp.com) featuring great artists and teachers of acoustic music. His special topic seminars such as "Jam Session Survival Skills" are very popular.*

Gerald has played or recorded with many fiddle greats like Jim "Texas Shorty" Chancellor, Mark O'Connor, Benny Thomasson, Dale Morris, Ricky Soloman, Randy Elmore, and others. Gerald picked up the fiddle later in life and his experience has given him a unique insight into fiddling, especially in how it relates to the older beginner.

Gerald was always known for being the guy who knew all the cool licks. While most North Texas banjo players were playing in a Scruggs/Stanley inspired approach, Gerald was listening to everything and incorporating it into his style. Prince, disco, fusion jazz. . . The 1970s were experimental years for bluegrass with groups such as New Grass Revival, Red White and Bluegrass, The II Generation, Seldom Scene, The New Deal String Band, High Country, Country Gazette, and Country Cooking. Gerald soaked it all in and more. Charlie Christian, Jean-Luc Ponty and Charlie Parker records all found a place in Gerald's record collection while the licks found their way into his playing. In these years, Gerald was playing music full time and worked with a variety of groups including Roanoke (Bluegrass with Dan Huckabee, Mike Anderson and Joe Carr), Lazy River (formerly Bluegrass Alliance), Spats (80s soul/pop/fusion), and Texas country singers Will Barnes, and Red Stegall. He also appeared with Michael Martin Murphy, Hank Thompson, John Hartford, Mark O'Connor, LuLu Roman, Peter Noone, Bucky Pizzarelli, and R&B artists Al "TNT" Braggs, and Johnnie Taylor. He has also performed for the Dallas Lyric Opera, Dallas Metropolitan Ballet, and many musicals. Gerald is Vice-President of the Allegro Guitar Society (http://GuitarSociety.org) presenting classical guitar greats in Dallas, Fort Worth, and Las Vegas.

During this period, Gerald recorded on numerous projects including recordings featuring Dan Huckabee, Country Gazette and an unreleased project of Jazz/fusion banjo with Mark O'Connor, Sam Bush, and Jerry Douglas. This material foreshadowed the later work of Bela Fleck. During the country-rock crazed 1980s, Gerald worked regularly as a lead electric guitarist and an occasional banjo picker. He developed and marketed the first good sounding electric pickup for banjo called the Jones/Acoustic Plus used by Earl Scruggs, Bela Fleck, Alan Munde, and many others. Gerald also edits Mel Bay's http://www.BanjoSessions.com website.

Photo by Leigh Taylor

Gerald Jones

__Dix Bruce__ is a musician and writer from the San Francisco Bay Area. He has authored over fifty books, recordings, and videos for Mel Bay Publications. Dix performs and does studio work on guitar, mandolin, and banjo and has recorded two LPs with mandolin legend Frank Wakefield, eight big band CDs with the Royal Society Jazz Orchestra, his own collection of American folk songs entitled "My Folk Heart" on which he plays guitar, mandolin, autoharp and sings, and a CD of string swing and jazz entitled "Tuxedo Blues." He contributed two original compositions to the soundtrack of Harrod Blank's acclaimed documentary film "Wild Wheels." He has released four CDs of traditional American songs and originals with guitarist Jim Nunally, most recently a collection of "brother duet" style recordings entitled "Brothers at Heart." Dix arranged, composed, and played mandolin on the soundtracks to four different editions of the best selling computer game "The Sims."

Books and instructional DVDs: (For song lists and full details, as well as info on new books, CDs and DVDs, contact Musix, e-mail: info@musixnow.com)

The Parking Lot Picker's Songbooks for Guitar, Mandolin, Bass, Dobro (with Stacy Phillips), & Banjo (with Bill Evans).
You Can Teach Yourself Country Guitar book & CD, DVD or video set.
You Can Teach Yourself Mandolin book & CD, DVD or video set.
Getting into Bluegrass Mandolin book & CD.
First Lessons Mandolin book, CD, & DVD set.
Swing & Jazz Mandolin: Chords, Rhythm & Songs DVD everything you need to know to get up and swinging on the mandolin.
BackUp Trax: Old Time Fiddle Tunes Vol. I book & CD set. Jam all night long with the band on old time and fiddle tunes.
Gypsy Swing & Hot Club Rhythm for Guitar and Mandolin book & CD set
Gypsy Swing & Hot Club Rhythm II for Guitar and Mandolin book & CD set. Learn chords, melodies, lyrics, how to play rhythm and more on 12 great standards recorded by Django Reinhardt and Stephane Grappelli. Learn while jamming with the recorded band!BackUp Trax: Swing & Jazz Vol. I book & CD set. Jam all night long with a great band. You play all the leads and the band never gets tired!
BackUp Trax: Traditional Jazz & Dixieland book & CD set. Jam all night long with the band on the basic Dixieland repertoire.
BackUp Trax: Early Jazz & Hot Tunes book & CD set. Jam all night long with the band on more traditional jazz standards.
Basic Swing Guitar (DVD). Learn swing chord comping on the classics of the genre.
Basic Country Flatpicking Guitar (DVD). Explores easy Carter-style solos.

Recordings:
Brothers at Heart by Dix Bruce & Jim Nunally. Brother duet-style songs, & hot guitar picking (FGM CD 111).
From Fathers to Sons by Dix Bruce & Jim Nunally. Folk, bluegrass, & hot guitar picking (Musix CD/C 104).
In My Beautiful Dream by Dix Bruce & Jim Nunally. Great new songs & old classics by the duo. (Musix CD 106).
The Way Things Are by Dix Bruce & Jim Nunally. More hot picking & great new songs by the duo. (Musix CD 105).
My Folk Heart by Dix Bruce, solo & small group, traditional American folk music (Musix CD/C101). With Jim Nunally, Tom Rozum, and John Reischman.
Tuxedo Blues by Dix Bruce, string swing & jazz (Musix CD/C102). With Bob Alekno on mandolin, David Balakrishnan on violin, Mike Wollenberg on bass.

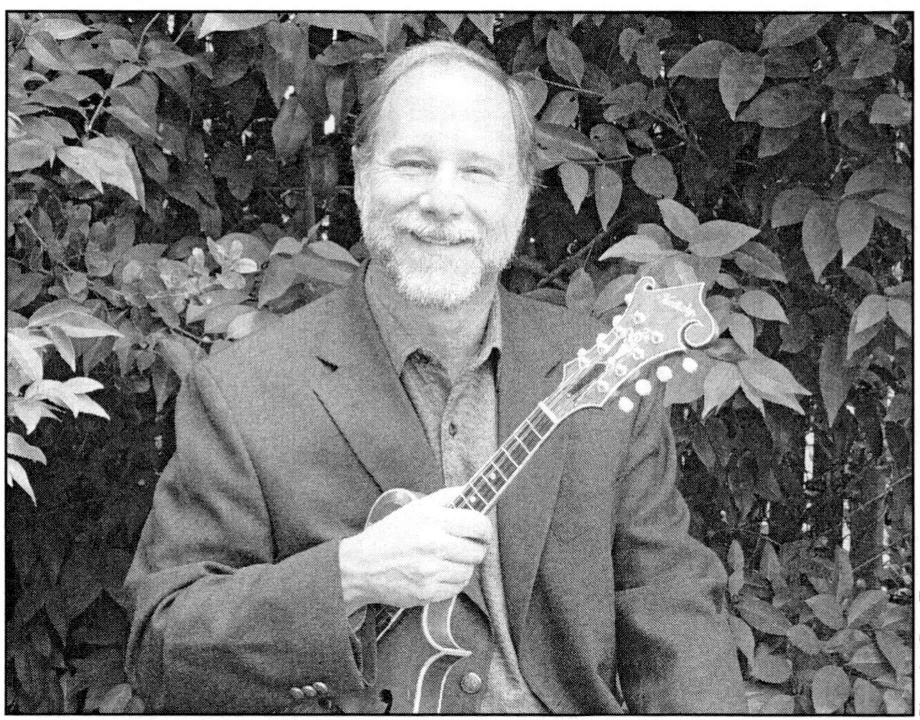
Photo by Gene Tortora

Dix Bruce

All the Good Times

M: G; F: C or D
CD 1-Track 1

Traditional

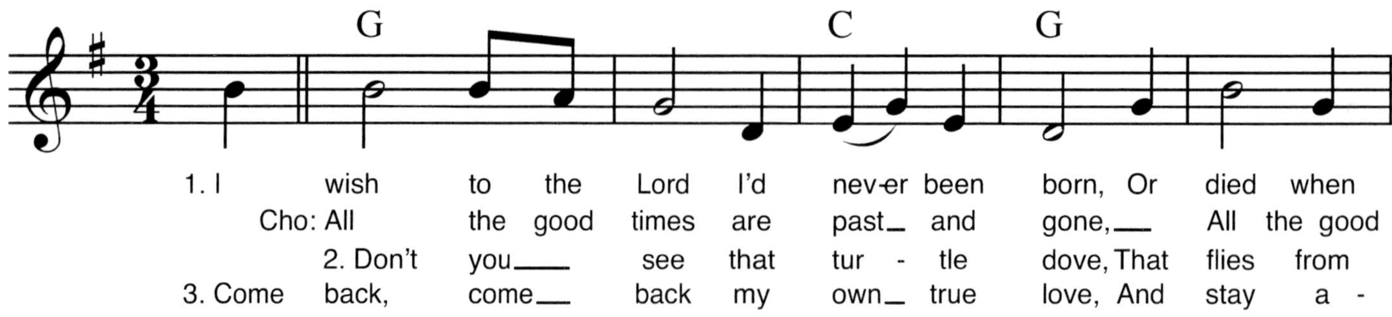
G
C
G
1. I wish to the Lord I'd nev-er been born, Or died when
Cho: All the good times are past_ and gone,_ All the good
2. Don't you_ see that tur - tle dove, That flies from
3. Come back, come_ back my own_ true love, And stay a -

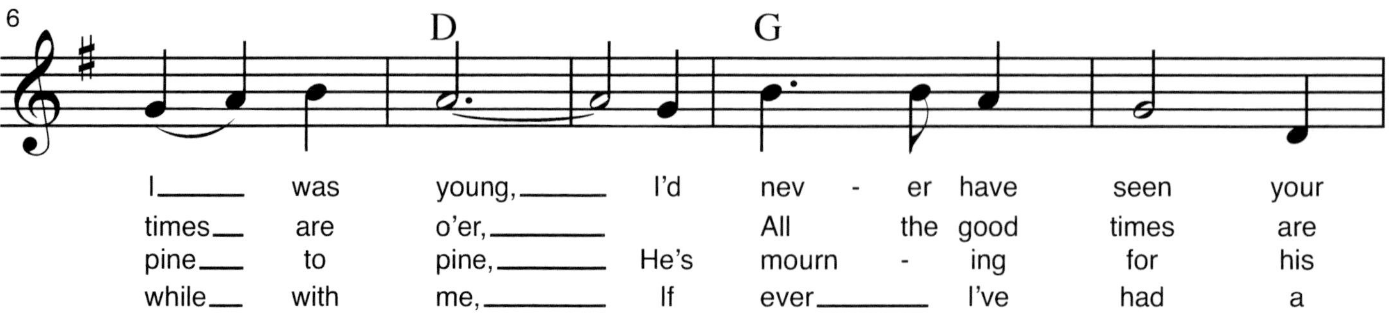
6
D
G
I_ was young,_ I'd nev - er have seen your
times_ are o'er,_ All the good times are
pine_ to pine,_ He's mourn - ing for his
while_ with me,_ If ever_ I've had a

11
C
G
D
G
spar - kling blue eyes, Or heard your ly - ing tongue.
past_ and gone, Little darling don't you weep_ no more._
own_ true love, Just like I mourn_ for mine._
friend in this world, You've been that friend_ to me._

B. Monroe, Monroe Bros., Flatt & Scruggs, R. Allen & F. Wakefield, Ken. Colonels, J. Martin

Amazing Grace

M: G; F: C or D
CD 1-Track 2

John Newton, ca. 1779

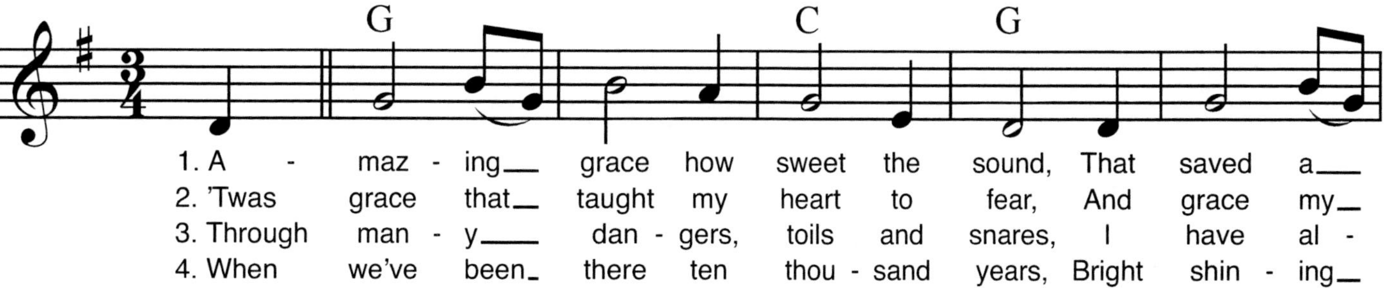

G C G
1. A - maz - ing grace how sweet the sound, That saved a
2. 'Twas grace that taught my heart to fear, And grace my
3. Through man - y dan - gers, toils and snares, I have al -
4. When we've been there ten thou - sand years, Bright shin - ing

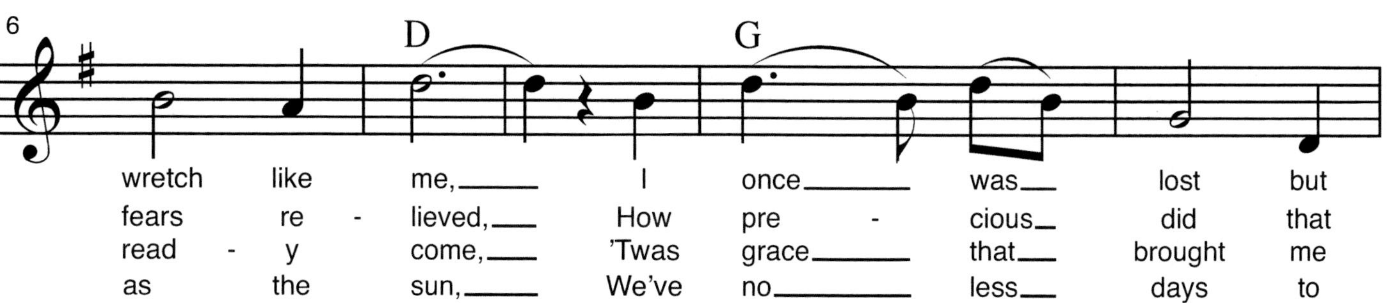

6
D G
wretch like me, I once was lost but
fears re - lieved, How pre - cious did that
read - y come, 'Twas grace that brought me
as the sun, We've no less days to

11
C G D G
now I'm found, Was blind but now I see.
grace ap - pear, The hour I first be - lieved.
safe thus far, And grace will lead me home.
sing God's praise, Then when we first be - gun.

D. Watson, R. Stanley, Osborne Bros., Lewis Family, J. Garcia & D. Grisman

Angel Band

M: G; F: C or D
CD 1-Track 3

Hascall & Bradbury, ca. 1860

G C G D G
1. My lat - est sun is sink - ing fast, My race is near - ly run,
2. Oh, bear my long - ing heart to Him, Who bled and died for me.
3. I know I'm nearing the ho - ly ranks, Of friends and kin - dred dear.
4. I've al - most gained my heaven - ly home, My spir - it loud - ly sings,
8
G C G
My strong - est trials now are past, My tri - umph
Whose blood now cleans - es from all sin, And gives me
I've brushed the dew on Jor - dan's banks, The cross - ing
Thy ho - ly ones, be - hold, they come, I hear the
14
D G D G
has be - gun.
vic - tor - y.
must be near.
noise of wings.
Cho: Oh come an - gel band,
21
D G C G
Come and a - round me stand, Oh bear me a - way on your snow-white
28
D G C
wings, To my im - mor - tal home, Oh bear me a -
34
G D G
way on your snow - white wings, To my im - mor - tal home.

Stanley Bros., R. Stanley, Flatt & Scruggs, Old & in the Way

Angelina Baker

M: C; F: F or G
CD 1-Track 4

Stephen Foster, 1850

C
G7
1. Way down on the old plan - ta - tion, There's where I was born, I
Then I work and then I sing, So hap - py all the day,

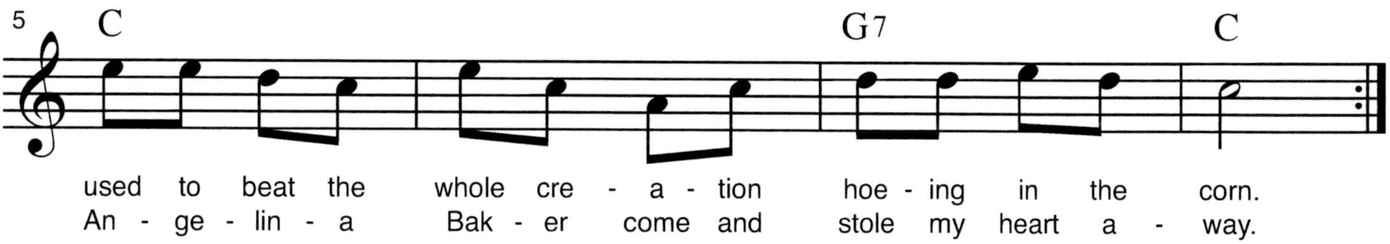

5
C
G7
C
used to beat the whole cre - a - tion hoe - ing in the corn.
An - ge - lin - a Bak - er come and stole my heart a - way.

9
C
G7
An - ge - lin - a Bak - er, An - ge - lin - a Bak - er's gone, She

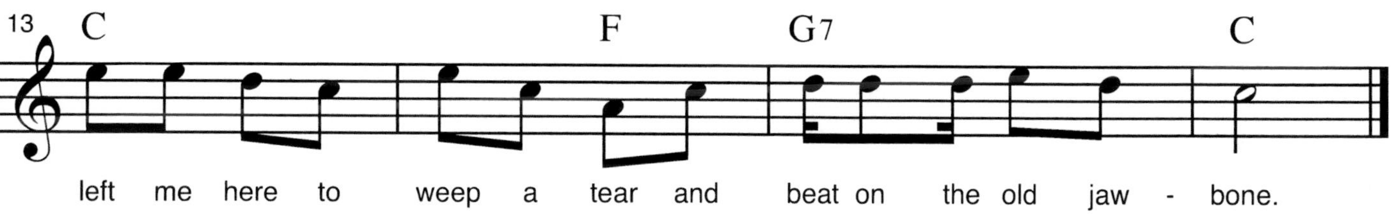

13
C
F
G7
C
left me here to weep a tear and beat on the old jaw - bone.


```
C                               G7
2. I've seen my Angelina in the Springtime and the Fall,
   C                                  G7              C
I've seen her in the cornfield and I've seen her at the ball,
        C                              G7
And every time I met her she was smiling like the sun,
    C                                      G7         C
But now I'm left to weep a tear cause Angelina's gone.
```

3. Angelina is so tall, she never sees the ground,
She has to take a wellumscope to look down on the town.
Angelina likes the boys, as far as she can see 'em,
She used to run old master 'round, to ask him for to free 'em.

4. Early in the morning of a lovely summer day,
I asked for Angelina, and they say "she's gone away."
I don't know where to find her, 'cause I don't know where she's gone,
She left me here to weep a tear, and beat on the old jawbone.

Dry Branch Fire Squad, Alan Senauke

Angels Rock Me To Sleep

***M:** G; **F:** C or D*
CD 1-Track 5

Traditional

G C G
1. My heart is sad, My soul is wear - y,
2. There is no earth - ly friend to guide me,
3. At last the har - bor I am near - ing,
A D G
While sail - ing on life's rug - ged plain, The clouds are dark,
No one to call to heav - en's goal, But Christ the sav -
I see the lights a - long the shore, I hear my friends
C G
The day is drear - y,
ior stands be - side me,
and loved ones cheer-ing,
It seems all earth -
To cheer and com -
I'll soon be safe
D G G
ly help is vain.
fort my poor soul.
for ev - er more.
Cho: An - gels rock me to sleep
C G Em
in the cra - dle of love, bear me o - ver the deep,
A D G
to hea - ven a - bove, When sha - dows shall fall,
C G
and the sav - ior shall call, An - gels rock me to sleep,
Em D G
In the cra - dle of love.

B. Monroe

ARE YOU FROM DIXIE?
('CAUSE I'M FROM DIXIE, TOO!)
WORDS BY
JACK YELLEN
MUSIC BY
GEORGE L. COBB
WRITERS OF
"IT'S ALL A DREAM,"
"JUST FOR TO-NIGHT," ETC.
M. WITMARK & SONS
NEW YORK CHICAGO SAN FRANCISCO LONDON
ALSO PUBLISHED
AS A
ONE
STEP

Dix collects old sheet music and this is the original 1915 cover "Are Your From Dixie?"

Are You From Dixie?

M: *C;* ***F:*** *F or G*
CD 1-Track 6

Cobb & Yellin, 1915

C
1. Hel - lo there stran - ger, how do you do? There's some - thing I'd like
2. It was a way back in old eigh - ty nine, When first I crossed that
7
G7
to say to you, You seem sur - prised, I re - co - gnize,
Mas - on Dixon line, Gee! but I've yearned, longed to re - turn,
13
D7
G7
C
I'm no de - tect - ive but I just sur - mised. You're from a place I'm
To all the good folks I left be - hind. My home is way down in
19
long - ing to be, Your smil - ing face seems to say to me,
old Al - a - bam, On a plan - ta - tion near Bir - ming - ham,
25
G7
D7
G7
You're from my own land, my sun - ny home - land, Tell me, can it be?
And there's one thing cer - tain, I'm sure - ly flir - tin', With those south bound trains.
32
C
F
C
Chorus: Are you from Dix - ie? I said from Dix - ie! Where the fields of

Blue Sky Boys, B. Clifton

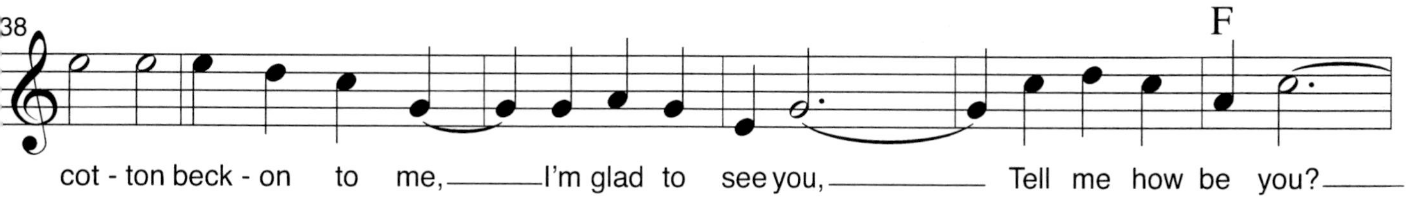
38
F
cot - ton beck - on to me, I'm glad to see you, Tell me how be you?

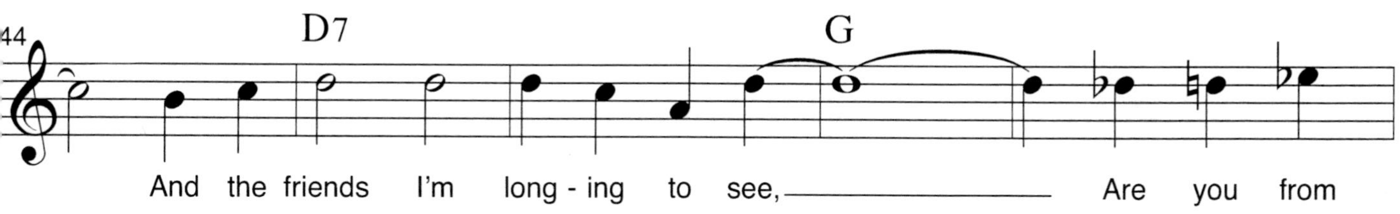
44
D7
G
And the friends I'm long - ing to see, Are you from

49
C7
Al - a - bam - a, Tenn - ess - ee, or Car - o - line,

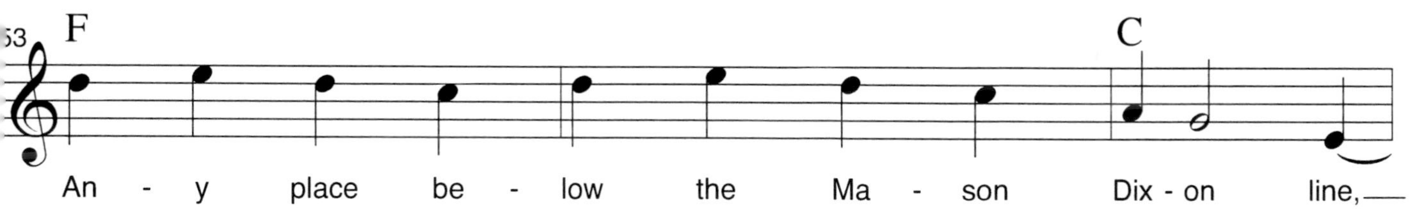
53
F
C
An - y place be - low the Ma - son Dix - on line,

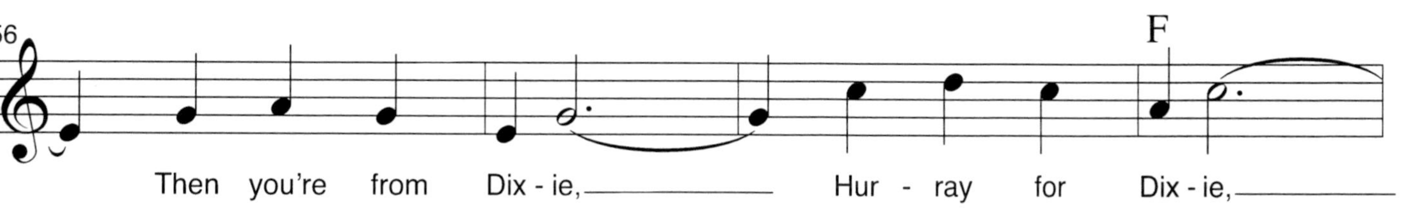
56
F
Then you're from Dix - ie, Hur - ray for Dix - ie,

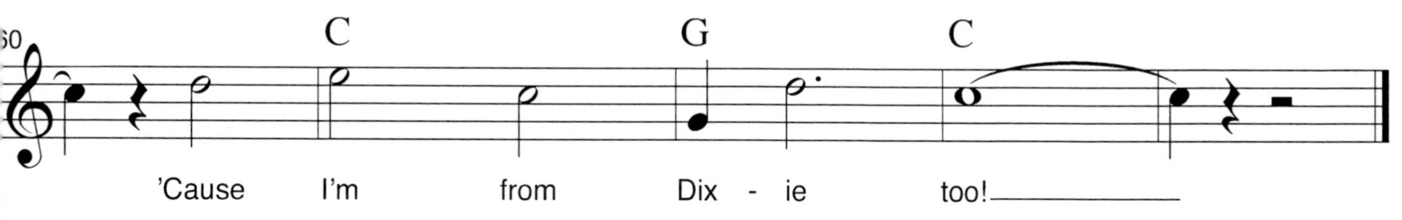
60
C
G
C
'Cause I'm from Dix - ie too!

Are You Washed in the Blood of the Lamb?

M: G; F: C or D
CD 1-Track 7
Elisha A. Hoffman, 1878
G C G
1. Have you been to Je - sus for the cleans - ing power? Are you
2. Are you walk - ing dai - ly by the Sav - ior's side? Are you
3
D G
washed in the blood of the Lamb? Are you ful - ly trust - ing in His
washed in the blood of the Lamb? Do you rest each mo - ment in the
6
C G D
grace this hour? Are you washed in the blood of the
Cruc - i - fied? Are you washed in the blood of the
8
G G C
Lamb? Cho: Are you washed, in the blood, In the
Lamb?
11
G D G
soul cleans - ing blood of the Lamb? Are your gar - ments spot - less, are they
14
C G D G
white as snow? Are you washed in the blood of the Lamb?

3. When the bridegroom cometh will your robes be white? (G, C)
Are you washed in the blood of the Lamb? (G, D)
Will your soul be ready for the mansions bright, (G, C)
And be washed in the blood of the Lamb? (G, D, G)

4. Lay aside the garments that are stained with sin,
And be washed in the blood of the Lamb;
There's a fountain flowing for the soul unclean,
O be washed in the blood of the Lamb!

Stanley Bros., R. Allen & F. Wakefield

Arkansas Traveller

M: G; F: C or D
CD 1-Track 8

Traditional

G D
1. Oh, once up - on a time in Ark - an - sas, An old man sat in his
4
G
lit - tle cab - in door, And he fidd - led at a tune that he liked to hear, A
7
D G G C
jol - ly old tune that he played by ear. It was rain - ing hard but the
10
G D G C G D
fidd - ler did - n't care, He sawed a - way at the pop - u - lar air, Though his
13
G C G D G D G
roof top leaked like a wat - er fall, It did - n't seem to both - er that man at all.

G
2. A traveller was riding by that day,
D
And stopped to hear him a-practicing away.
G
The cabin was afloat and his feet were wet,
D G
But still the old man didn't seem to fret.
G C G D
So the stranger said: "Now the way it seems to me,
G C G D
You'd better mend your roof," said he.
G C G D
But the old man said, as he played away:
G D G
"I couldn't mend it now, it's a rainy day."

3. The traveller replied: "That's all quite true,
But this, I think, is the thing for you to do;
Get busy on a day that is fair and bright,
Then pitch the old roof till it's good and tight."
But the old man kept on a-playing at his reel,
And tapped the ground with his leathery heel:
"Get along," said he, "for you give me a pain;
My cabin never leaks when it doesn't rain."

:. White, New Lost City Ramblers (NLCR)

Aunt Dinah's Quilting Party

M: *A;* ***F:*** *D or E*
CD 1-Track 9

Kyle & Fletcher, 1856

A
1. In the sky the bright stars glitt - ered, On the
5
D A
bank the pale moon shone, It was from Aunt Din - ah's
11
D E A
quilt - ing par - ty, I was see - ing Nell - ie home. Cho: I was
17
A D A D
see - ing Nell - ie home, I was see - ing Nell - ie
23
A D
home, It was from Aunt Din - ah's quilt - ing
28
E A
par - ty, I was see - ing Nell - ie home.

2. On my arm a soft hand rested, (A)
Rested light as ocean foam, (D, A)
And 'twas from Aunt Dinah's quilting party, (D)
I was seeing Nellie home. *(Chorus)* (E, A)

3. On my lips a whisper trembled,
Trembled 'til it dared to come,
And 'twas from Aunt Dinah's (etc., chorus)

4. On my life new hopes were dawning,
And those hopes have lived and grown,
And 'twas from Aunt Dinah's (etc., chorus)

Country Gentlemen, John Lawless, Osborne Bros.

Away in a Manger

M: G; F: C or D
CD 1-Track 10

Luther & Muller

G C

1. A - way in a man - ger no crib for his
2. The cat - tle are low - ing the poor ba - by
3. Be near me, Lord Je - sus, I ask you to

4 G D7

bed, The lit - tle Lord Je - sus lay
wakes, But lit - tle Lord Je - sus no
stay, Close by me for - ev - er and

7 G

down his sweet head.___ The stars in the
cry - ing He makes.___ I love thee Lord
love me I pray,___ Bless all the dear

10 C G

sky___ looked down where he lay, the
Je - sus look down from the sky, and
chil - dren in thy ten - der care, and

13 D7 G D7 G

lit - tle Lord Je - sus a - sleep on the hay.
stay by my cra - dle 'til morn - ing is nigh.
take us to hea - ven to live with you there.

mmylou Harris, Larry Sparks, Louvin Bros.

Banks of the Ohio

M: *D;* ***F:*** *G or A*
CD 1-Track 11

Traditional

D A7
1. I asked my love to take a walk, Just to walk
2. I held a knife a - gainst her breast, As deep in - to
6
D
a lit - tle ways, As we walked, and as we
my arms she pressed, She cried, "Oh Willie, don't mur - der
11
G D A7 D
talked, All a - bout our wed - ding day.
me, I'm un - pre - pared for e - ter - ni - ty."
16
D A7
Cho: On - ly say that you'll be mine,
20
D
In our home we'll hap - py be.
24
G
Down be - side where the wat - ers flow,
28
D A7 D
On the banks of the O - hi - o.

3. I took her by her lily white hand, (D, A7)
Led her down that bank of sand, (D)
There I pushed her in to drown, (G)
And watched her as she floated down. (D, A7, D)

4. I started home 'tween twelve and one,
Crying "God, what have I done?
I've killed the girl I love you see,
Because she would not marry me."

5. Next morning was about half a past four,
The sheriff knocked upon my door,
Says "Young man, come go with me,
Down be side the deep blue sea."

B. Monroe, Monroe Bros., T. Rice, D. Watson, D. Grisman, C. White, J.D. Crowe, Country Gentlemen, Stanley Bros., Blue Sky Boys

A Beautiful Life

M: G; F: C or D
CD 1-Track 12

Wm. Golden, 1918

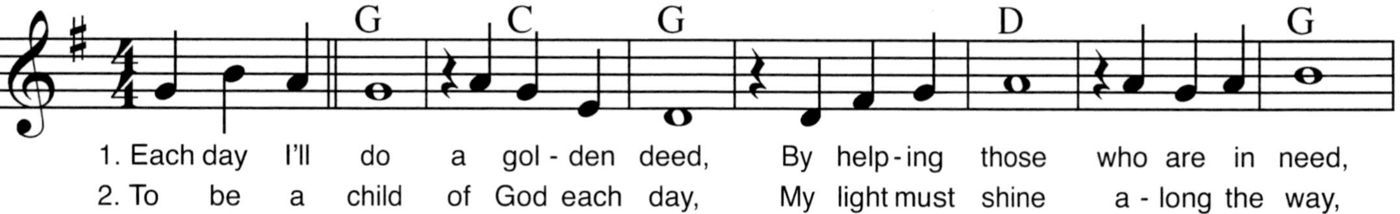
G C G D G
1. Each day I'll do a gol - den deed, By help-ing those who are in need,
2. To be a child of God each day, My light must shine a - long the way,

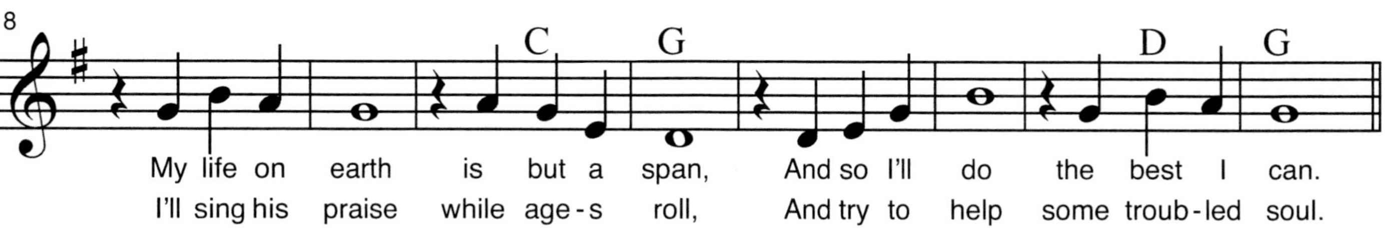
8
C G D G
My life on earth is but a span, And so I'll do the best I can.
I'll sing his praise while age-s roll, And try to help some troub-led soul.

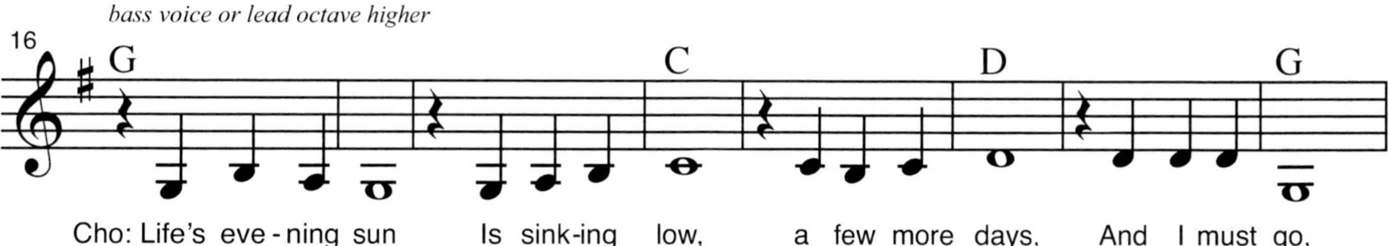
bass voice or lead octave higher
16
G C D G
Cho: Life's eve-ning sun Is sink-ing low, a few more days, And I must go,

lead voice
24
C G D G
To meet the deeds that I have done, Where there will be no sett-ing sun.

G C G
3. The only life that will endure,
D G
Is one that's kind and good and pure,
C G
And so for God I'll take my stand,
D G
Each day I'll lend a helping hand.

4. While going down life's weary road,
I'll try to lift some traveler's load,
I'll try to turn the night to day,
Make flowers bloom along the way.

B. Monroe, J. Martin, Stanley Bros., Ken. Colonels, Country Gentlemen, Doyle Lawson

Beautiful Star of Bethlehem

***M:** D; **F:** G or A*
CD 1-Track 13

Boyce & Pace

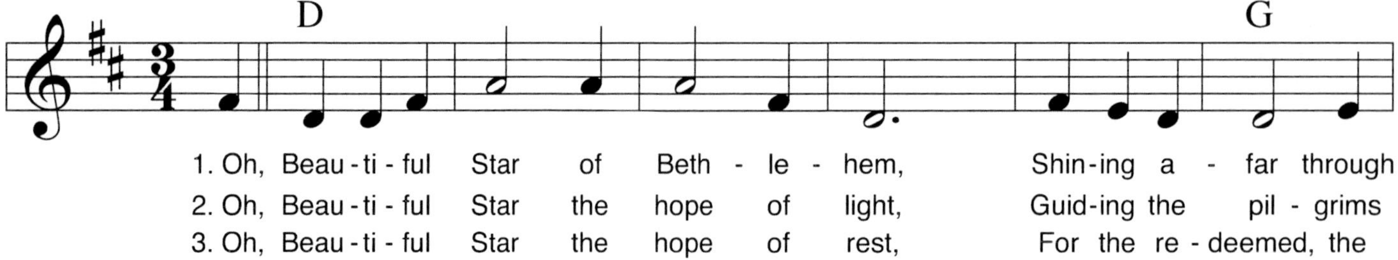
D
G
1. Oh, Beau - ti - ful Star of Beth - le - hem, Shin-ing a - far through
2. Oh, Beau - ti - ful Star the hope of light, Guid-ing the pil - grims
3. Oh, Beau - ti - ful Star the hope of rest, For the re - deemed, the

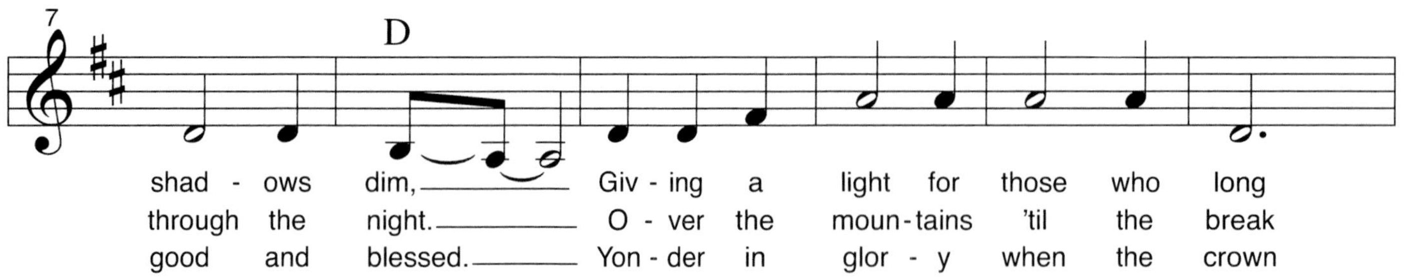
7
D
shad - ows dim, Giv - ing a light for those who long
through the night. O - ver the moun-tains 'til the break
good and blessed. Yon - der in glor - y when the crown

13
A
E
A
D
have gone, And guid-ing the wise men
of dawn, In - to the light of
is won, For Je - sus now that

19
G
D
on their way, Un - to the place where Je - sus lay,
per - fect day, It will give out a love - ly ray, Oh,
star di - vine, Bright-er and bright - er he will shine, Oh,

Stanley Bros., R. Stanley, Larry Sparks, Patty Loveless

25
E A D G
Beau - ti - ful Star of Beth - le - hem, shine on. Cho: Oh,
Beau - ti - ful Star of Beth - le - hem, shine on.
Beau - ti - ful Star of Beth - le - hem, shine on.

33
D
Beau - ti - ful Star of Beth - le - hem,

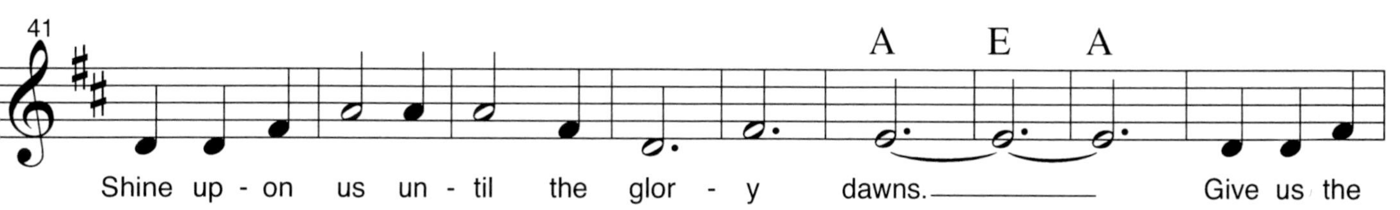
41
A E A
Shine up - on us un - til the glor - y dawns. Give us the

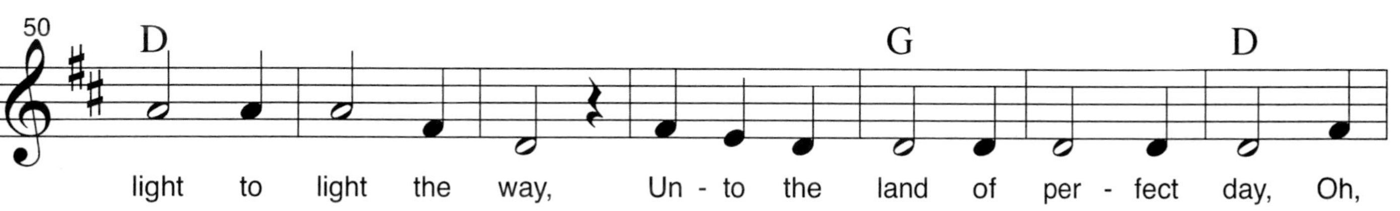
50
D G D
light to light the way, Un - to the land of per - fect day, Oh,

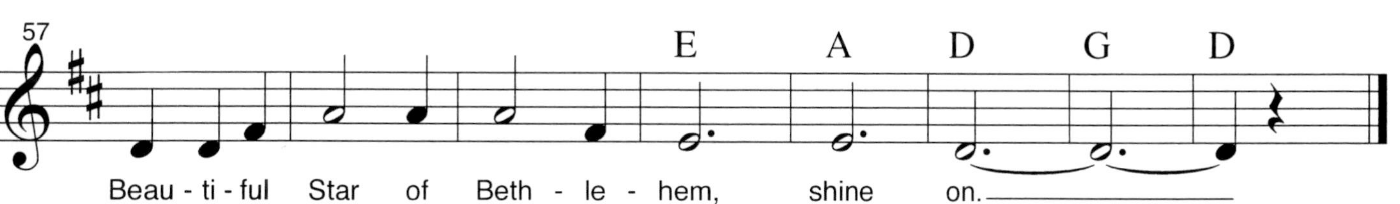
57
E A D G D
Beau - ti - ful Star of Beth - le - hem, shine on.

Bile Them Cabbage Down

M: G; F: C or D
CD 1-Track 14, medley pt. 1

Traditional

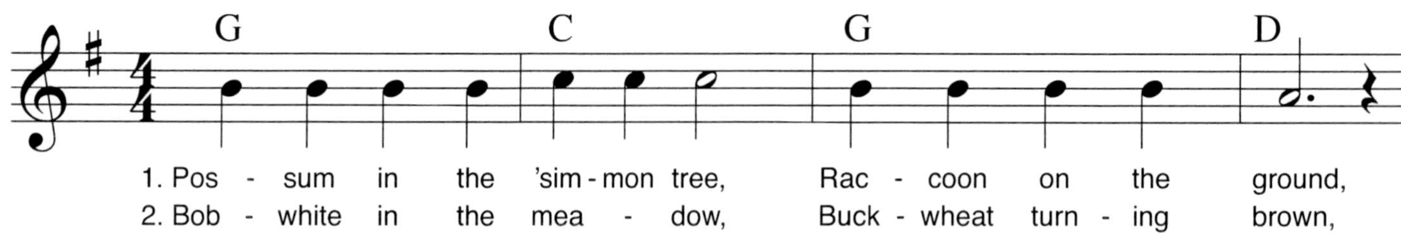
G C G D
1. Pos - sum in the 'sim - mon tree, Rac - coon on the ground,
2. Bob - white in the mea - dow, Buck - wheat turn - ing brown,

5
G C G D G
Rac - coon said, "You orn' - ry cuss, Shake them 'sim - mons down."
Bro - ther pos - sum, fat and fine, Bile the cab - bage down.

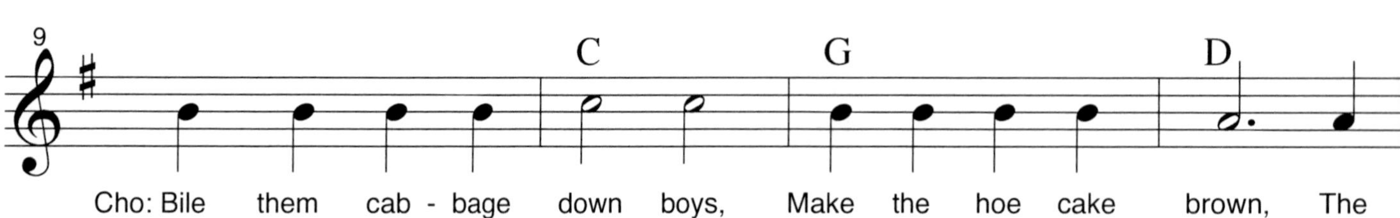
9
C G D
Cho: Bile them cab - bage down boys, Make the hoe cake brown, The

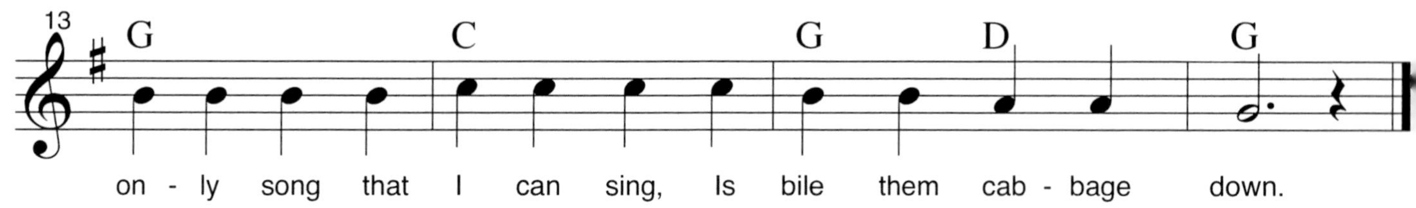
13
G C G D G
on - ly song that I can sing, Is bile them cab - bage down.

5. I bought my gal a bicycle,
She learned to ride it well,
She ran into a telephone pole,
And broke it all to pieces.

6. Grandpa had a muley cow,
She was muley when she was born,
It took the jaybird forty years,
To fly from horn to horn.

7. Grandpa had a setting hen,
He set her as you know,
Set her on three buzzard eggs,
Hatched out one old crow.

Stover-Lilly-Anthony, Bluegrass Band, Skillet Lickers

Black Eyed Susie

M: *G;* ***F:*** *C or D*
CD 1-Track 14, medley pt. 2

Traditional

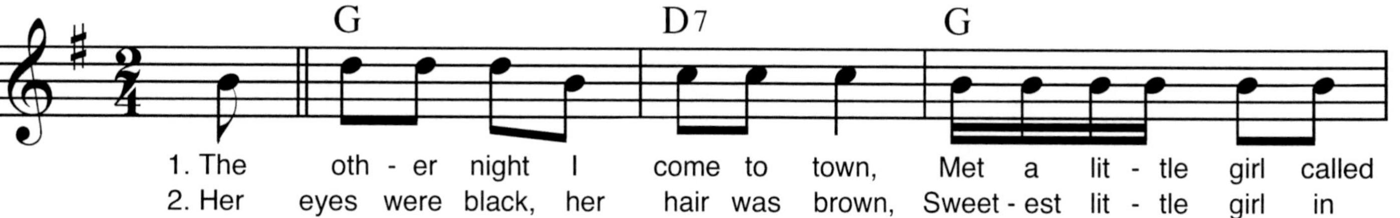
G
D7
G
1. The oth - er night I come to town, Met a lit - tle girl called
2. Her eyes were black, her hair was brown, Sweet - est lit - tle girl in

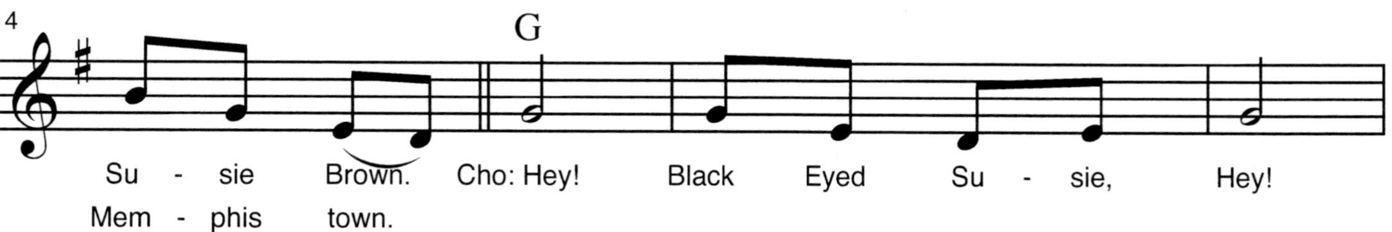
4
G
Su - sie Brown. Cho: Hey! Black Eyed Su - sie, Hey!
Mem - phis town.

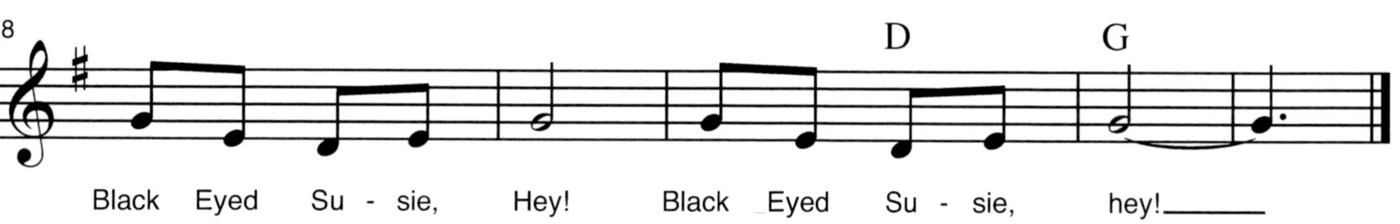
8
D
G
Black Eyed Su - sie, Hey! Black Eyed Su - sie, hey!

G D
3. All I need to make me happy
G
Two little boys to call me pappy,

(Chorus)
G
Hey! Black Eyed Susie,
Hey! Black Eyed Susie,
D7 G
Hey! Black Eyed Susie, hey!

4. One named Paul and the other one Davey,
One loves ham and the other one gravy. (Chorus)

5. Some got drunk and some got woozy,
I went home with Black Eyed Susie. (Chorus)

6. I fell in love with her that night,
Sent for the preacher and the preacher was tight. (Chorus)

7. We said "I do" by the lantern light,
Promised that preacher we'd never fight. (Chorus)

Holy Modal Rounders, Fiddlin' Doc Roberts, Skillet Lickers, Vern Williams, Mac Martin, Bill Evans

Blue Ridge Mountain Blues

M: G; F: C or D
CD 1-Track 15

Cliff Hess

G D
1. When I was young and in my prime,
2. I see a win - dow with a light,

G
I left my home in Car - o - line, Now all I do is sit and
I see two heads of snow - y white, I seem to hear them both

D
pine, For all those folks I left be -
recite, "Where is my wan - dering boy to -

G G D
hind. Cho. 1: I've got those Blue Ridge Moun - tain blues, Want to
night?"

G
hear those hound dogs bay, I want to hunt the pos - sum when the

C D7 G
corn tops blos - som, In that Blue Ridge far a - way.

```
G                      D
3. I'll always do right by my Ma,
                       G
I'll always do right by my Pa,
                        D
I'll hang around that cabin door,
                       G
No work, no worry anymore.
```

```
        G                                    D
Cho. 2: I've got those Blue Ridge Mountain blues,
                                   G
I want to stand right here and say,
                                            C
My grip is packed to travel and I'm scratching gravel
          D7           G
To the Blue Ridge far away.
```


B. Monroe, Jim & Jesse, Flatt & Scruggs, D. Watson, Bill Clifton

The Bluebirds are Singing for Me

M: C; F: F or G
CD 1-Track 16
Mac Wiseman
C
1. Though to - night I'm far, from the Blue Ridge
Cho: There's a blue - bird singing, in the Blue Ridge
2. There was a girl, I loved so
3. When I reached home, I was so
3
F
G
moun - tains, Far from my home,
moun - tains, Call - ing me,
dear - ly, She lived a - way,
lone - ly, For the one I loved,
6
C
a - cross the hills, I'm go - ing back,
back to my home. I can hear,
back in the hills, When the blue - bird sings,
had gone a - way, That sad news,
10
F
to the Blue Ridge moun - tains, These mem - o -
those blue - birds call - ing, Call - ing
I miss my dar - ling, She loves me I
came from her moth - er, . She's sleep - ing
13
G
C
ries, they haunt me still.
me, back to my home.
know, and she al - ways will.
there, be - neath the clay.

Bound to Ride

M: G; F: C or D
CD 1-Track 17

Traditional

C
G
1. Com - ing down from Tenn - es - see rid - ing that blind,
2. Rid - ing on the street - car look - ing over town,
3. Work - ing on the rail - road sav - ing all I can,
4. If I die a rail - road man bury me 'neath the ties, So

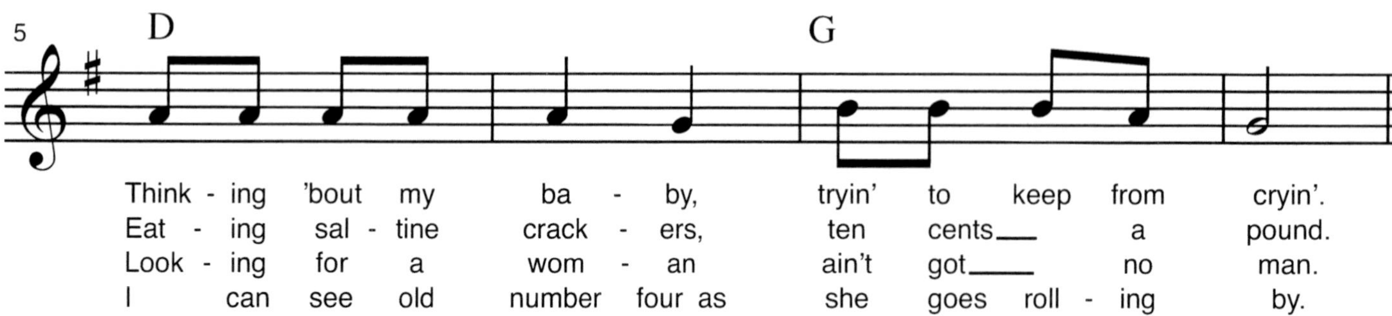
5
D
G
Think - ing 'bout my ba - by, tryin' to keep from cryin'.
Eat - ing sal - tine crack - ers, ten cents a pound.
Look - ing for a wom - an ain't got no man.
I can see old number four as she goes roll - ing by.

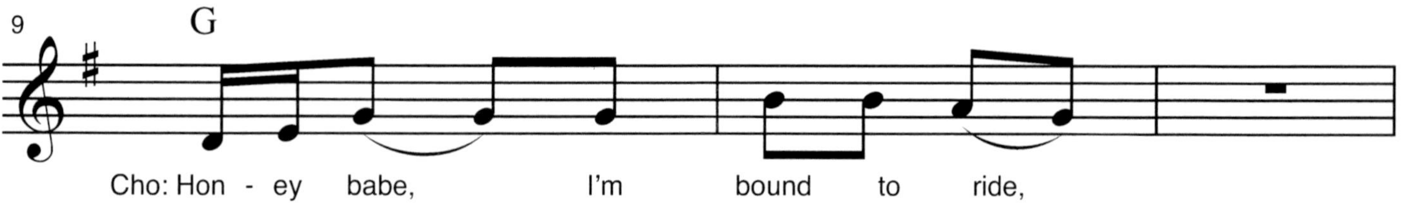
9
G
Cho: Hon - ey babe, I'm bound to ride,

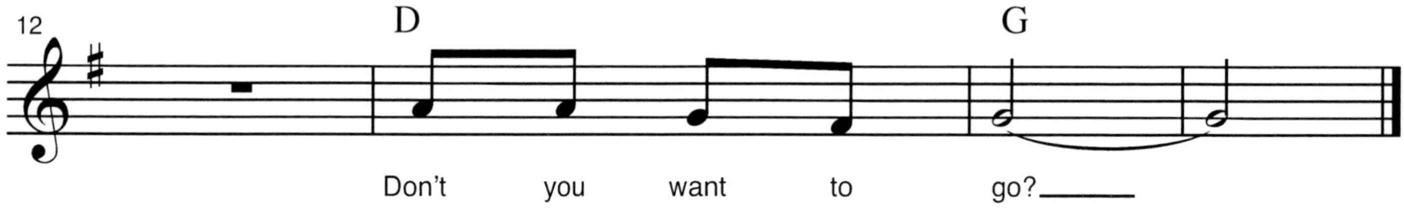
12
D
G
Don't you want to go?

Stanley Bros., Flatt & Scruggs, R. Stanley

Bright Morning Stars

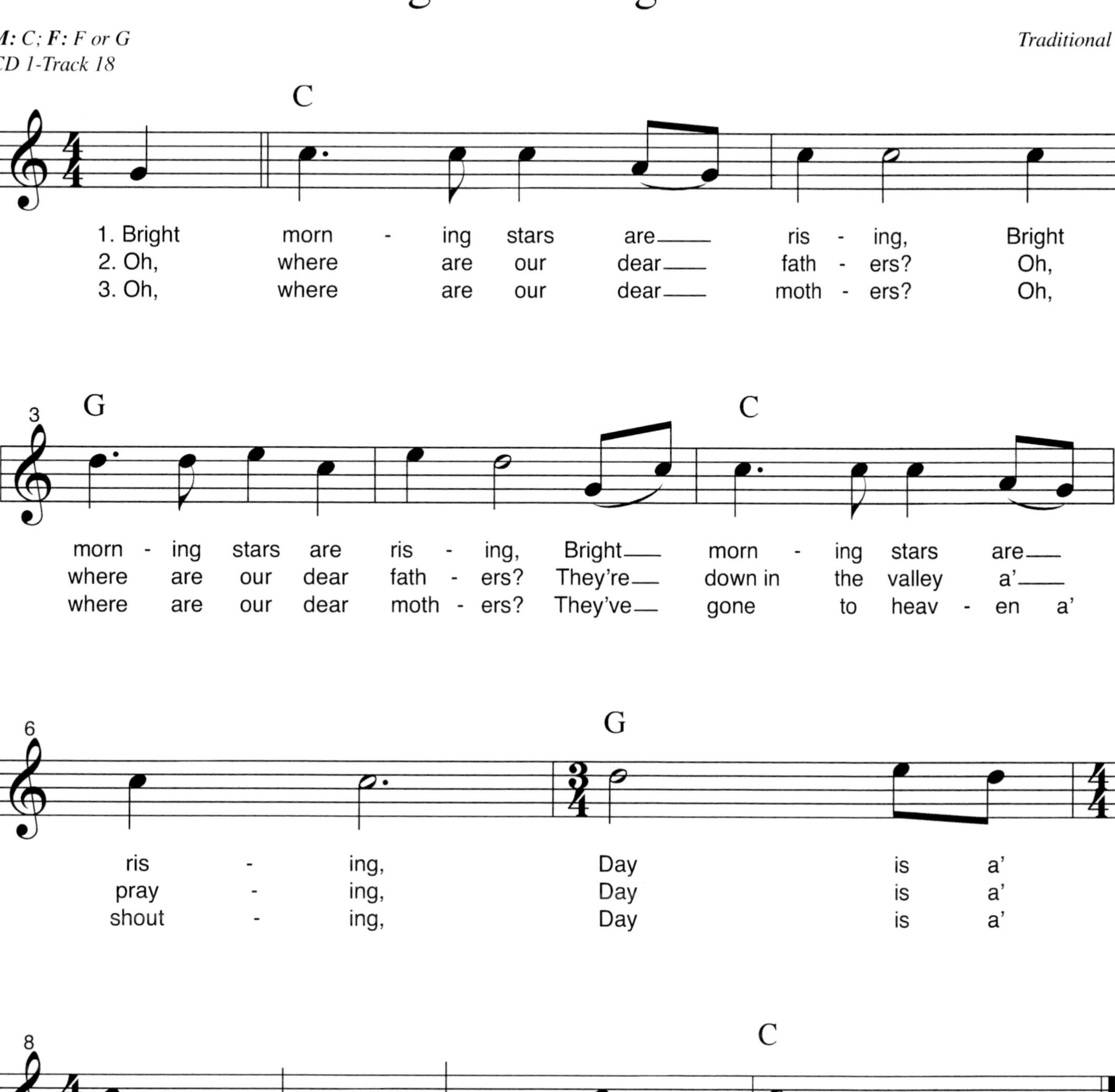
M: C; F: F or G
CD 1-Track 18
Traditional
C
1. Bright morn - ing stars are ris - ing, Bright
2. Oh, where are our dear fath - ers? Oh,
3. Oh, where are our dear moth - ers? Oh,
G C
morn - ing stars are ris - ing, Bright morn - ing stars are
where are our dear fath - ers? They're down in the valley a'
where are our dear moth - ers? They've gone to heav - en a'
G
ris - ing, Day is a'
pray - ing, Day is a'
shout - ing, Day is a'
C

break - ing in my soul!
break - ing in my soul!
break - ing in my soul!

Stanley Bros.

Bring Back to Me My Wandering Boy

M: G; F: C or D
CD 1-Track 19

Traditional

G C G
1. Out in the cold world and far a - way from home,
2. Out in the hall - way, there stands a va - cant chair,
3. Well I re - mem - ber those part - ing words he said,
5
D
Some moth - er's boy is wand - ering all a - lone,
And an old pair of shoes that he used to wear,
"We'll meet up yonder, where tears are nev - er shed,
9
G C G
No one to guide him or keep his foot - steps right,
Emp - ty is the cra - dle he used to love so well,
In that land of sun - shine a - way from toil and care,
13
D G
Some moth - er's boy is home - less to - night.
Oh, how I miss him no tongue can tell.
When life is over, I'll meet you up there."
17
G C G
Cho: Oh, bring back to me my wan - der - ing boy, There is no
23
D G
oth - er that's left to give me joy, Tell him his moth - er with
28
C G D G
fad - ed cheeks and hair, Is at the old home a - wait - ing him there.

B. Monroe, Flatt & Scruggs, Blue Sky Boys, Carter Fam., J. Val

Buffalo Gals

M: C; F: F or G
CD 1-Track 20

Traditional

C
G7
1. As I was walk - ing down the street, Down the street,
4 C
Down the street, A pret - ty girl I chanced to meet, Oh,
7 G7
C
C
she was fair to see. Cho: Buff - a - lo gals won't you come out to - night,
11 G7
C
Come out to - night, Come out to - night, Buff - a - lo gals won't you
14
G7
C
come out to - night, And dance by the light of the moon.

C
2. I danced with a gal with a hole in her stockin',
G7 C
Her heel kept a-rockin', her knees kept a-knockin',
I danced with a gal with a hole in her stockin',
G7 C
We danced by the light of the moon.

(Chorus after each verse)

3. I asked her if she'd like to talk, (like to talk 2X)
Her feet took up the whole sidewalk,
Oh, she was fair to see.

4. I asked her if she'd have a dance, (have a dance 2X)
I thought that I might have a chance,
To shake a foot with her.

5. I asked her if she'd be my wife, (be my wife 2X)
Then I'd be happy all my life,
If she'd marry me.

The Bully of the Town

M: G; F: C or D
CD 1-Track 21

Unknown, 1895

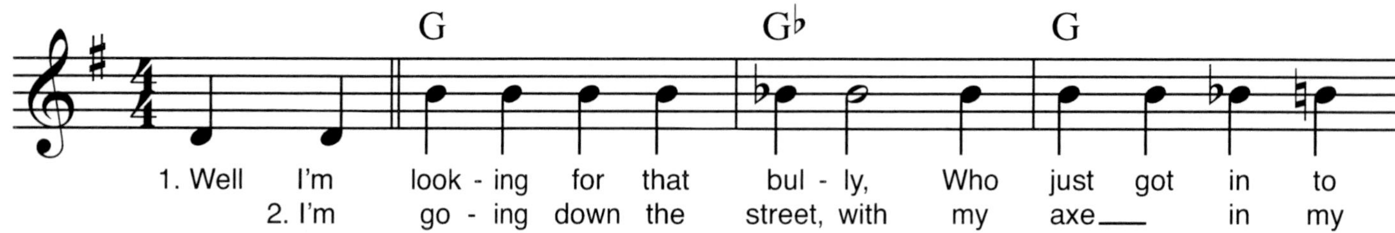

G
G♭
G
1. Well I'm look - ing for that bul - ly, Who just got in to
2. I'm go - ing down the street, with my axe in my

4
E7
C
town, I'm look - ing for that bul - ly, You know he can't be
hand, I'm look - ing for that bul - ly and I'll sweep him off this

8
A7
D7
G
found, And I'm look - ing for that bul - ly of the town.
land, I'm look - ing for that bully to make him stand.

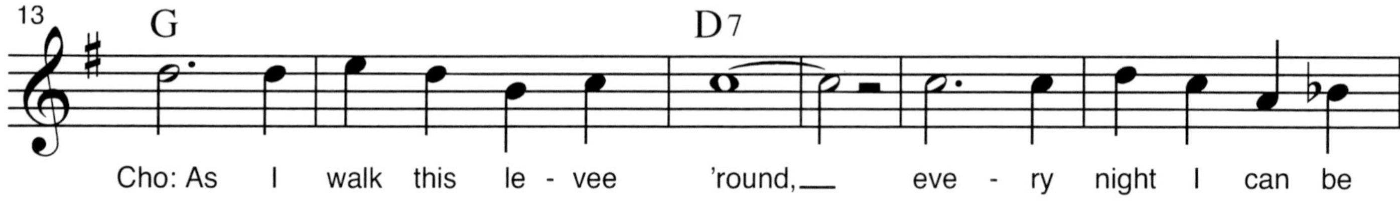

13
G
D7
Cho: As I walk this le - vee 'round, eve - ry night I can be

19
G
C
found, As I walk this le - vee 'round, I'm

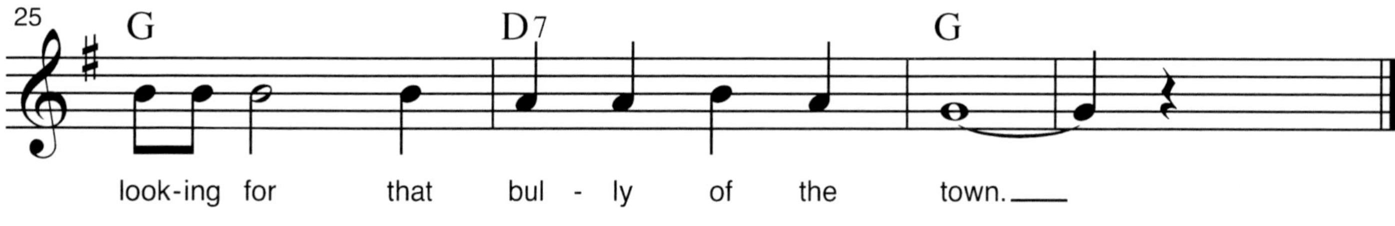

25
G
D7
G
look-ing for that bul - ly of the town.

H. M. Rounders, B. Keith, Fiddlin' John Carson, Skillet Lickers, Stanley Bros, Alan Munde, Allen Shelton, Doug Dillard

G Gb G
3. I'll take my long razor, I'm going to carve him deep,

E7 C A7
And when I see that bully, I'll lay him down to sleep,

D7 G
I'm looking for that bully to make him weep.

4. I went a winging, down at Parson Jones',
Took along my trusty blade to carve that fellow's bones,
Just a'looking for that bully to hear his groans.

5. I walked in the front door, the men were prancing high,
For that levee fella, I skinned my foxy eye,
Just a'looking for that bully and he wasn't nigh.

6. I asked Miss Pansy Blossom, if she would wing a reel,
She says, "Laws, Mr. Johnson, how high you make me feel,"
Then you ought to see me shake my sugar heel.

7. I rose up like a black cloud and took a look around,
There was that new bully, standing on the ground,
I've been looking for you fella and I've got you found.

8. When I got through bully, a doctor and a nurse,
Were no good to that man, so they put him in a hearse,
A cyclone couldn't have torn him up much worse.

9. You don't hear about that fella, that treated folks so free,
Go down upon the levee and his face you'll never see,
There's only one boss bully and that is me.

10. When you see me coming, hoist your windows high,
When you see me going, hang your heads and cry,
I'm looking for that bully and he must die.

11. My madness is a rising, and I'm not going to get left,
I'm getting so bad that I'm scared of myself,
I was looking for that bully now he's on the shelf.

Bury Me Beneath the Willow

M: D; F: G or A
CD 1-Track 22
Traditional
D G D
1. My heart is sad and I am lone - ly, For the
2. To - mor - row was to be our wed - ding, God, oh
3. She told me that she did not love me, I could
4. Place on my grave a snow white li - ly, To prove my
6 A D G
on - ly one I love, When shall I see her oh no
God where can she be? She's gone a' court - ing with an -
not be - lieve 'twas true, Un - til an an - gel soft - ly
love for her was true, To show the world I died of
12 D A D D
nev - er, 'Til we meet in hea - ven a - bove. Cho: So bur - y
oth - er, And no lon - ger cares for me.
whis - pered, "She no lon - ger cares for you."
griev - ing, For her love I could not win.
18 G D A
me be - neath the wil - low, Un - der the weep - ing wil - low tree,
24 D G D
When she hears that I am sleep - ing, Then per -
30 A D
haps she'll weep for me.

Carter Fam., Rice and Skaggs, C. White, W. Guthrie, Ken. Colonels

C-H-I-C-K-E-N

M: C; *F:* F or G
CD 1-Track 23

Perrin & Slater, 1902

In a lit - tle coun - try school house, Where the child - ren used to go, There
day the teach - er called his class to spell one sort of bird, That

5 was a lit - tle round - er, By the name of "Rag - time" Joe. Now
kind of bird was chick - ens, and they could not spell the word. So the

9 when it came to spell - ing, His rag - time brain worked fast, He's the
teach - er called on Rag - time Joe to spell that word to them, He

13 on - ly well - learned schol - ar, That holds down his whole class. One
did - n't hes - i - tate a bit, this is how he be - gan:

17 Cho: "C," that's the way to be - gin, "H," that's the next let - ter in, "I,"

22 that is the third, "C," that's to "cea - son" the word, "K," that's a'

26 fill - ing in, "E," I'm near the end, "C - H - I - C -

30 K - E - N," that's the way to spell "chick - en."

Greenbriar Boys, Sam McGee, Kathy Kallick

Can't You Hear Me Callin'?

M: D; F: G or A
CD 1-Track 24
Bill Monroe
D
D
G
D
G
D
G
A7
D
1. The days are long the nights are lone - ly, Since you've left me all a - lone, I loved you so my lit - tle dar - ling, I've wor - ried so since you've been gone.
Cho: Sweet - heart of mine, can't you hear me call - ing? A mil - lion times, I loved you Bess, I mis - treated you, Lord, and I'm sor - ry, Come back to me, is my re - quest.
2. I re - mem - ber now the night we part - ed, A big mis - take has caused it all, If you'll re - turn, sun - shine will fol - low, To stay a - way would be my fall.
3. The days are dark, my lit - tle dar - ling, Oh, how I need your sweet em - brace, When I a - woke the sun was shin - ing, When I looked up, I saw your face.

B. Monroe, Country Gentlemen, V. Williams

Careless Love

M: F; F: Bb or C
CD 1-Track 25

Traditional

F
C7
F
Cho: Love, oh love, oh Care - less Love,
1. I love my Momma and Pop - pa too,

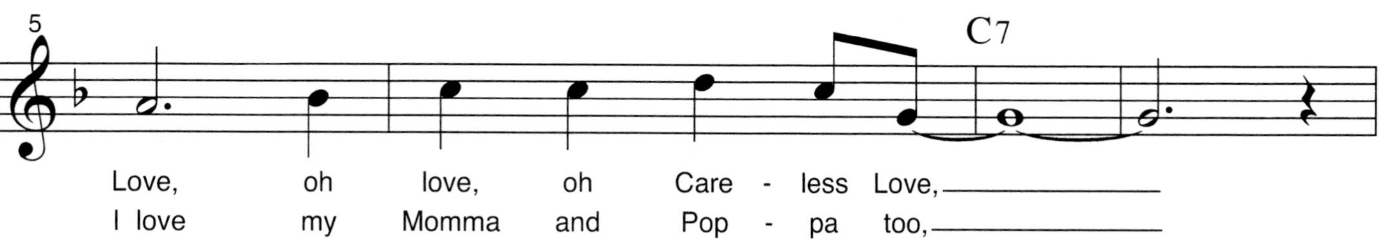

5
C7
Love, oh love, oh Care - less Love,
I love my Momma and Pop - pa too,

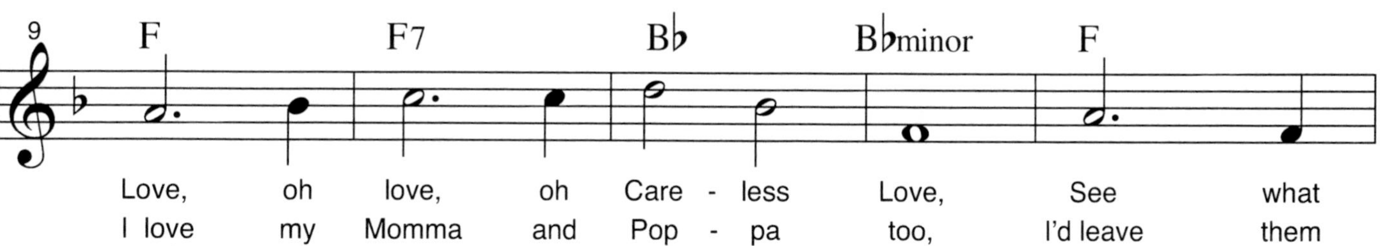

9
F
F7
B♭
B♭minor
F
Love, oh love, oh Care - less Love, See what
I love my Momma and Pop - pa too, I'd leave them

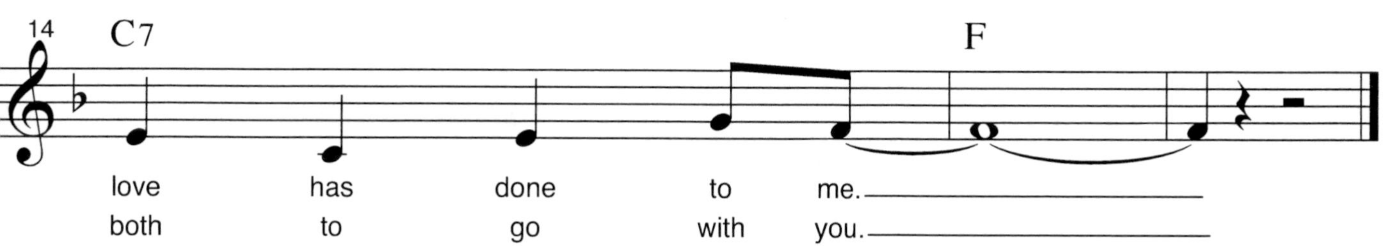

14
C7
F
love has done to me.
both to go with you.


```
  F      C7            F
2. Sorrow, sorrow to my heart,
                         C7
Sorrow, sorrow to my heart,
F        F7       Bb    Bbm
Sorrow, sorrow to my heart,
F           C7              F
Since we two have been apart.
```

3. What, oh what will Momma say? (3X)
When she learns I've gone astray?

4. Once I wore my apron low, (3X)
Scarcely keep you from my door.

5. Now my apron strings don't pin, (3X)
You pass my door and you don't come in.

. Monroe, Flatt & Scruggs, Stanley Bros., M. Seeger, E. Taylor

Children Go Where I Send Thee

***M:** D; **F:** G or A*
CD 1-Track 26

Traditional

D
Child - ren go where I send thee, How shall I

4
G
D
send thee? I'm a gon - na send thee one by one,
two by two,
three by three,

7
1st X, no repeat, go on: 2nd X, repeat, go on;
3rd X, repeat twice, go on; etc.
One for the lit - tle bit - ty ba - by was born,
Two for Jos - eph and Ma - ry,
Three for the three old wise men,

10
G
D
A7
D
born, born in Beth - le - hem.

Four for the four who stood at the door,

Five for the Hebrew children,

Six for the six who didn't get fixed,

Seven for the seven who couldn't get to heaven,

Eight for the eight who didn't get straight,

Nine was the nine that stood in the line,

Ten for the ten commandments.

Stanley Bros., R. Stanley, R. Skaggs

The Church in the Wildwood

M: A; F: D or E
CD 1-Track 27

Wm. Pitts, ca. 1850s

A E

1. There's a church in the val - ley by the wild - wood, No
2. How sweet on a clear Sab - bath morn - ing, To
3. There, close by the church in the val - ley, Lies
4. There, close by the side of that loved one, 'Neath the

3 A D

love - li - er place in the dale, No spot is so dear to my
listen to the clear ring - ing bell, It's tones so sweet - ly are
one that I loved so well, She sleeps, sweet - ly sleeps, 'neath the
trees where the wild flow - ers bloom, When the fare - well hymn shall be

6 A E A

child - hood, As the lit - tle brown church in the vale. Cho: Oh,
cal - ling, Oh, come to the church in the vale.
wil - low, Dis - turb not her rest in the vale.
chant - ed, I shall rest by her side in the tomb.

9 A E A

come to the church by the wild - wood, Oh, come to the church in the dale, No

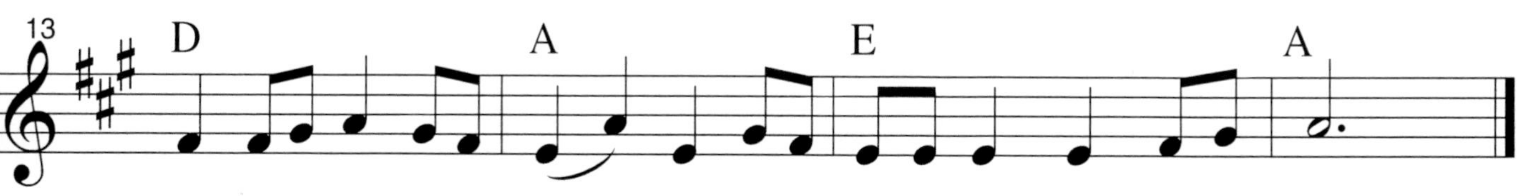
13
D
A
E
A

spot is so dear to my child - hood, As the lit - tle brown church in the vale.

Cindy

M: G; F: C or D
CD 1-Track 28

Traditional

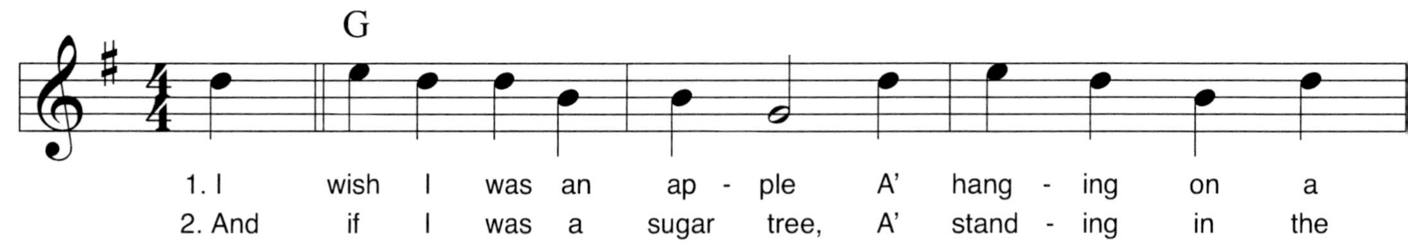

G
1. I wish I was an ap - ple A' hang - ing on a
2. And if I was a sugar tree, A' stand - ing in the

4
D G
tree, And ev - ery time that Cin - dy passed, She'd
town, Ev - ery time my Cin - dy passed, I'd

7
D G
take a big bite out of me. Cho: Get a - long
shake some sug - ar down.

9
C G
home, Cin - dy, Cin - dy, Get a - long home, Get a - long

13
C G D G
home, Cin - dy, Cin - dy, I'll mar - ry you some day.

G
3. The first time I saw Cindy,
D
She was standing in the door,
G
Her shoes and stockings in her hand,
D G
Her feet all over the floor.

4. She took me to her parlor,
She cooled me with her fan,
She said I was the prettiest thing,
In the shape of mortal man.

5. She kissed me and she hugged me,
She called me "Sugar Plum,"
She throwed her arms around me,
I thought my time had come.

6. Oh, Cindy is a pretty girl,
Cindy is a peach,
She threw her arms around my neck,
And hung on like a leech.

7. If I had a thread and needle,
Fine as I could sew,
I'd sew that gal to my coat tails,
And down the road I'd go.

Columbus Stockade Blues

M: G; **F:** C or D
CD 1-Track 29

Traditional

G
1. Way down in Co - lum - bus Geor - gia,
2. Last night as I lay sleep - ing, I
5
D7
G
Want to be back in Ten - nes - see. Way
dreamed I held you in my arms. When I a -
9
D7
down in Co - lum - bus stock - ade, my friends have
woke, I was mis - tak - en, I was
14
G
turned their backs on me. Cho: You can
peep - ing through the bars.
17
C
G
C
go a - way and leave me if you wish to, Nev - er
22
D7
G
let it cross your mind. In your heart,
26
D7
you love an - oth - er, Leave me lit - tle
30
G
dar - ling I don't mind.

B. Monroe, Ken. Colonels, W. Guthrie, B. Clifton, D. Watson, N. Blake

Cotton-Eyed Joe

M: G; F: C or D
CD 1-Track 30

Traditional

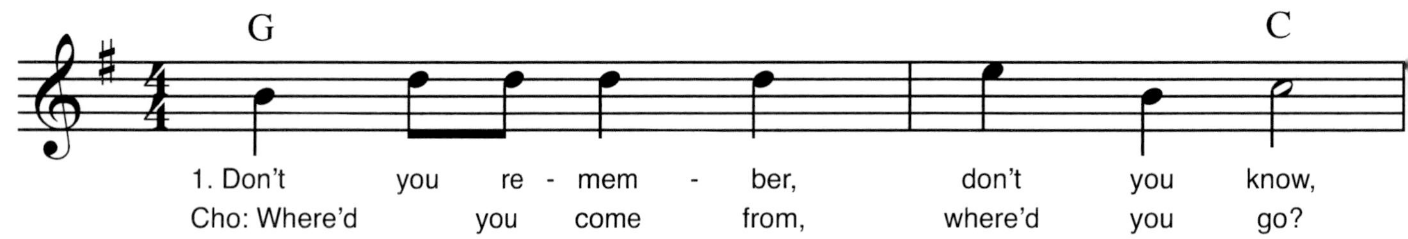
G
C
1. Don't you re - mem - ber, don't you know,
Cho: Where'd you come from, where'd you go?

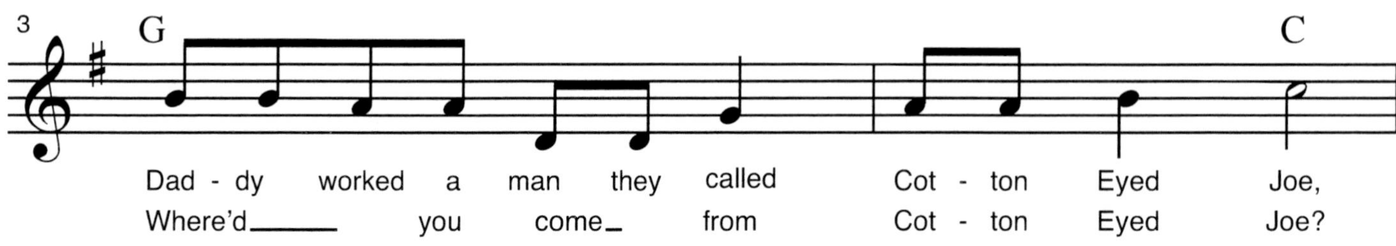
3
G
C
Dad - dy worked a man they called Cot - ton Eyed Joe,
Where'd you come from Cot - ton Eyed Joe?

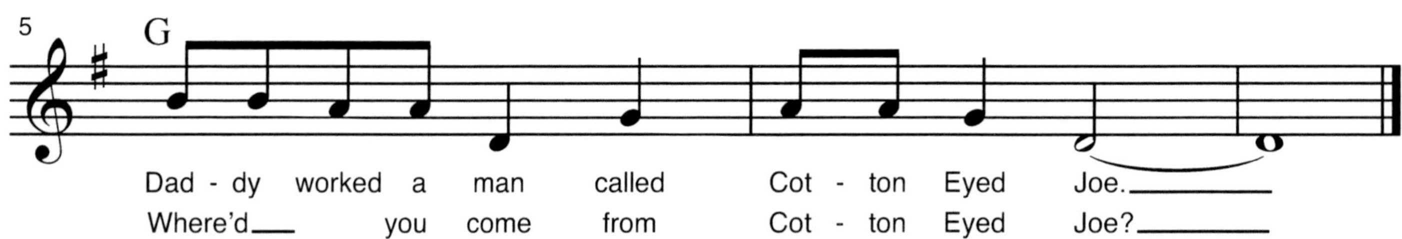
5
G
Dad - dy worked a man called Cot - ton Eyed Joe.
Where'd you come from Cot - ton Eyed Joe?

G C
2. Had not been for Cotton-Eyed Joe,
G C
I'd a'been married a long time ago,
G
I'd a'been married a long time ago.

3. Down in the cotton patch, way down low,
Everybody singing the Cotton-Eyed Joe. (2X)

4. I know a gal lives down below,
I used to go to see her but I don't no more. (2X)

5. I fell down and stubbed my toe,
Call for the doctor, Cotton Eyed Joe. (2X)

C. White, D. Watson, Fiddlin' John Carson, M. Seeger, Ken. Colonels, NLCR, E. Taylor, Skillet Lickers, K. Hall, D. Reno & R. Smiley, Kathy Kallick

Cowboy Jack

M: C; F: F or G
CD 1-Track 31

Traditional

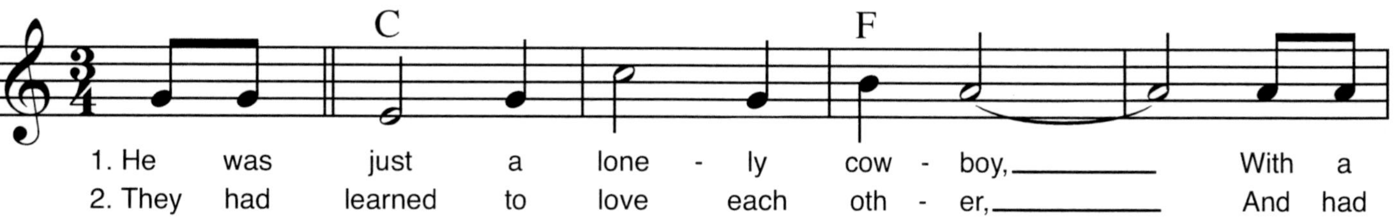

C F
1. He was just a lone - ly cow - boy, With a
2. They had learned to love each oth - er, And had

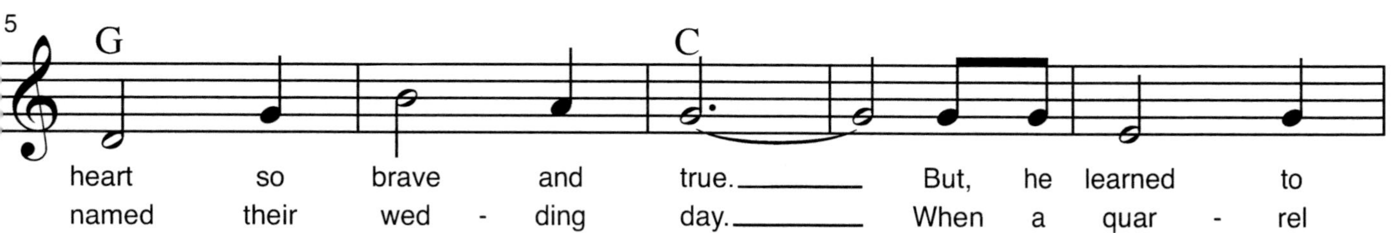

G C
heart so brave and true. But, he learned to
named their wed - ding day. When a quar - rel

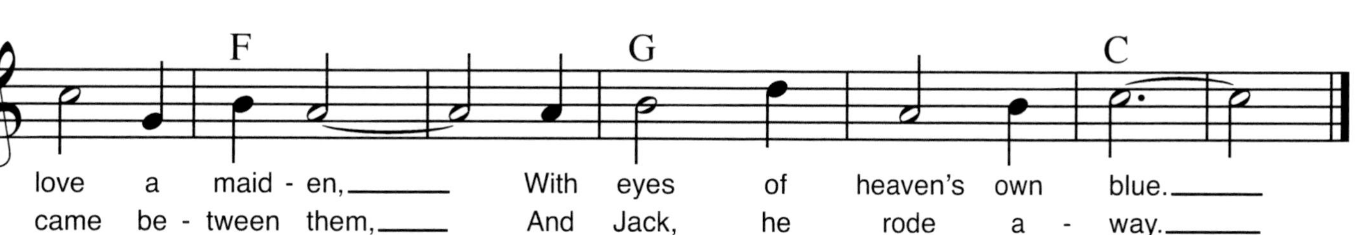

F G C
love a maid - en, With eyes of heaven's own blue.
came be - tween them, And Jack, he rode a - way.

C F
3. He joined a band of cowboys,
G C
And tried to forget her name.
F
But, out on the lonely prairie,
G C
She waits for him the same.

4. Your sweetheart waits for you, Jack,
Your sweetheart waits for you.
Out on the lonely prairie,
Where the skies are always blue.

5. One night as the work was finished,
Just at the close of day.
Someone said, "To sing a song, Jack,
T'will drive dull care away."

6. When he began his singing,
His mind it wandered back.
For he sang of a maiden,
Who waited for her Jack.

7. Jack left the camp next morning,
He was breathing his sweetheart's name.
He says, "I'll ask forgiveness,
For I know that I'm to blame."

8. But, when he reached the prairie,
He found a new made mound.
And his friends they sadly told him,
They had laid his loved one down.

9. They said as she was dying,
She breathed her sweetheart's name.
And asked them with her last breath,
To tell him when he came.

10. "Your sweetheart waits for you, Jack,
Your sweetheart waits for you.
Out on the lonely prairie,
Where the skies are always blue."

Carter Fam., Country Gentlemen, V. Williams

The Crawdad Song

M: G; F: C or D
CD 1-Track 32

Traditional

G
Cho: You get a line and I'll get a po - le hon - ey,
1. Set on the bank 'til my feet got co - ld hon - ey,

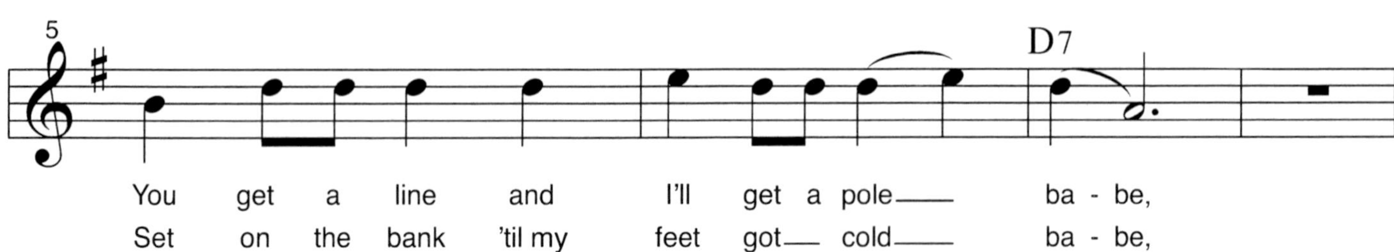
5
D7
You get a line and I'll get a pole ba - be,
Set on the bank 'til my feet got cold ba - be,

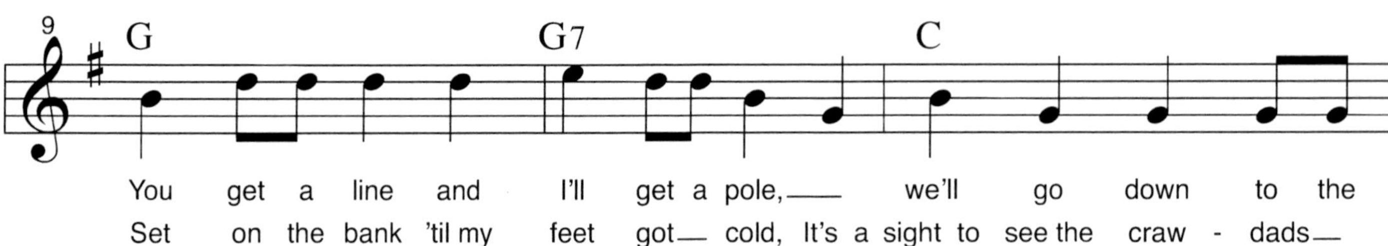
9
G
G7
C
You get a line and I'll get a pole, we'll go down to the
Set on the bank 'til my feet got cold, It's a sight to see the craw - dads

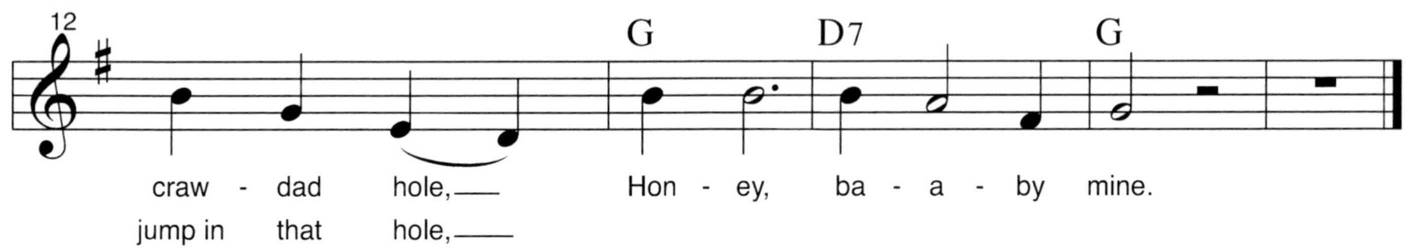
12
G
D7
G
craw - dad hole, Hon - ey, ba - a - by mine.
jump in that hole,

G D7
2. Yonder come a man with a sack on his back honey, Yonder come a man with a sack on his back babe,
G G7 C G D7 G
Yonder come a man with a sack on his back, He's got more crawdads than he can pack, Honey, baby mine.

3. He fell down and he broke that sack honey, He fell down and he broke that sack babe,
He fell down and he broke that sack, Was a sight to see the crawdads backing back, Honey, baby mine.

4. What did the hen duck say to the drake honey? What did the hen duck say to the drake babe?
What did the hen duck say to the drake, "There ain't no crawdads in that lake," Honey, baby mine.

D. Watson, F. Wakefield, D. Bruce & J. Nunally, Kathy Kallick, W. Guthrie

Cripple Creek

M: A; *F:* D or E
CD 1-Track 33

Traditional

A D A
1. Girls on Crip - ple Creek 'bout half grown,
Rolled my britch - es up to my knees, I'll
3
E A
Jump on a man like a dog on a bone.
wade old Cripple Creek when ever I please.
5
A
Cho: Go - in' up Crip - ple Creek, Go - in' in a run,
Go - in' up Crip - ple Creek, Go - in' in a whirl,
7
E A
Go - in' up Crip - ple Creek to have a lit - tle fun.
Go - in' up Crip - ple Creek to see my girl.

A D A
2. Cripple Creek's wide and Cripple Creek's deep,
E A
I'll wade old Cripple Creek before I sleep.
A D A
I got a girl and she loves me,
E A
She's as sweet as sweet can be.

3. I went down to Cripple Creek,
To see what them girls had to eat.
I got drunk and fell against the wall,
Old corn likker was the cause of it all.

4. I got a girl and she loves me,
She's as sweet as she can be.
She got eyes of baby blue,
Makes my gun shoot straight and true.

Monroe Bros., Flatt & Scruggs, R. Stanley, Jimmy Martin, C. White, D. Watson, Fiddlin' Doc Roberts, K. Hall, A. Munde, Country Gentlemen, John McEuen

Crying Holy

***M:** G; **F:** C or D*
CD 1-Track 34

Traditional

G
Chorus: Cry - ing, "Ho - ly un - to the Lord," Cry - ing,
1. Sin - ners run and hide your face, Sin - ners
2. Lord I ain't no stran - ger now, Lord I
3. Lord I ain't no sin - ner now, No I

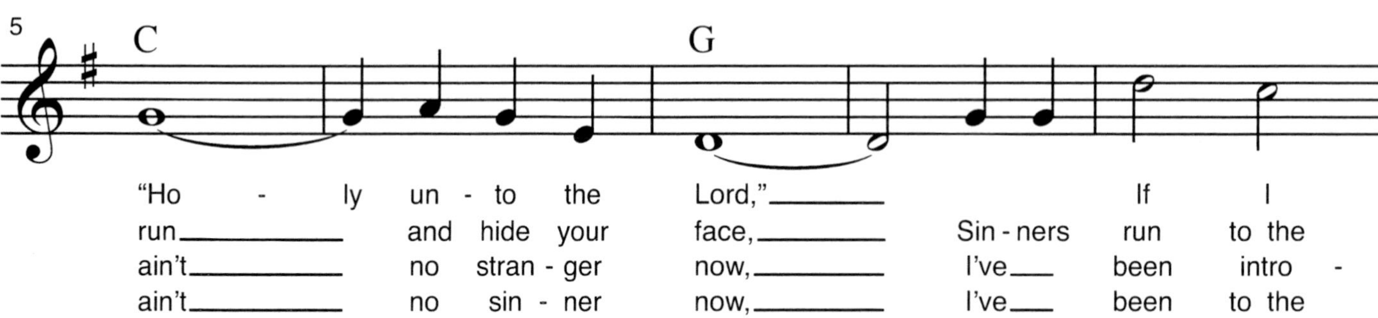
5
C
G
"Ho - ly un - to the Lord," If I
run and hide your face, Sin - ners run to the
ain't no stran - ger now, I've been intro -
ain't no sin - ner now, I've been to the

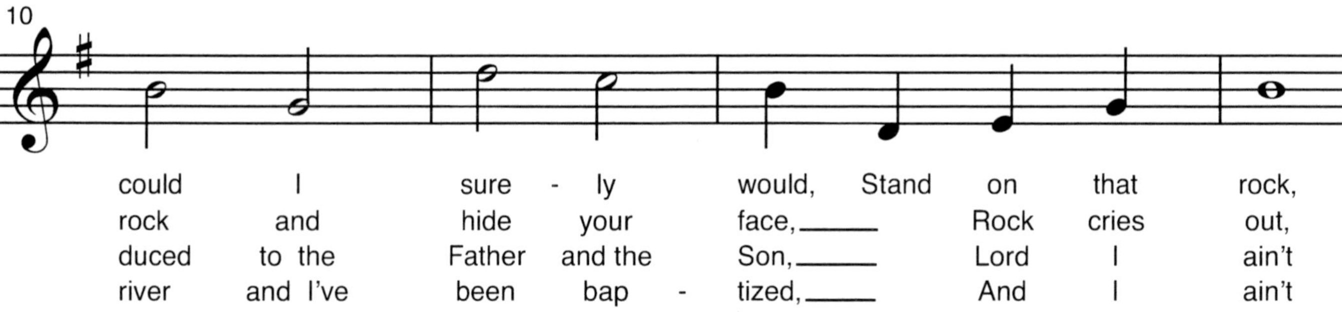
10
could I sure - ly would, Stand on that rock,
rock and hide your face, Rock cries out,
duced to the Father and the Son, Lord I ain't
river and I've been bap - tized, And I ain't

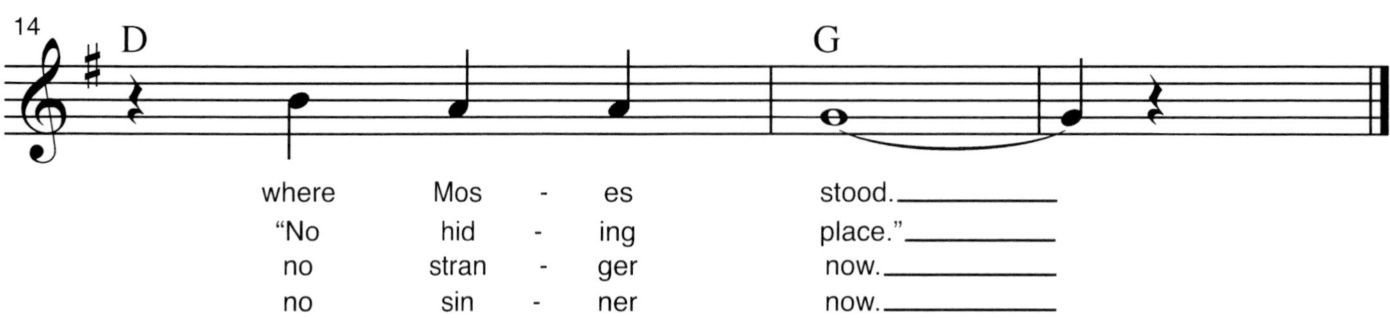
14
D
G
where Mos - es stood.
"No hid - ing place."
no stran - ger now.
no sin - ner now.

B. Monroe, Flatt & Scruggs, Carter Fam., J.D. Crowe, Country Gentlemen, J.E. Mainer

The Cuckoo

M: Dm; F: Gm or Am *Traditional*
CD 1-Track 35

Dm
1. Oh the cuck - oo, she's a pretty bird,
2. Jack of Dia - monds, Jack of Dia - monds,

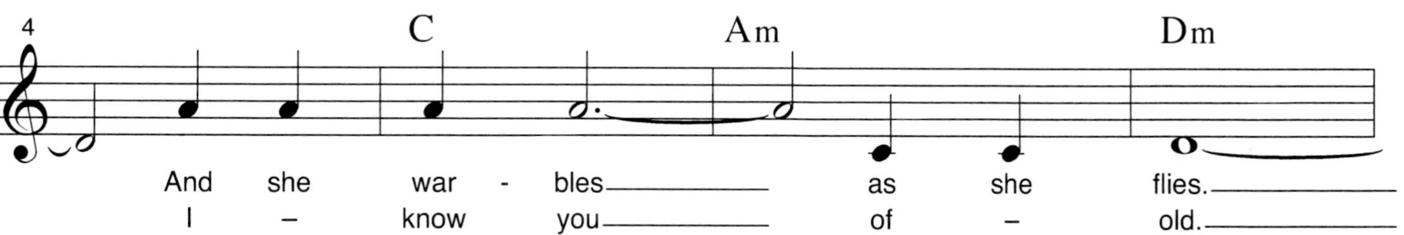
4
C
Am
Dm
And she war - bles as she flies.
I – know you of – old.

8
And she nev - er, says "cuck - oo,"
You – robbed my poor pock - ets,

12
C
Am
Dm
'til the fourth day, of Ju - ly.
of my sil - ver and my gold.

Dm
3. I've played cards in England,
C Am Dm
I've played cards in Spain,
I'll bet you ten dollars,
C Am Dm
I'll beat you next game.

4. My horses ain't hungry,
They won't eat your hay,
I'll drive on a little further,
I'll feed 'em on the way.

5. Gonna build me log cabin,
On a mountain so high,
So I can see Willie,
When he goes on by.

6. Oh the cuckoo, she's a pretty bird,
I wish that she was mine.
She never drinks water,
She always drinks wine.

Osborne Bros., C. Ashley, D. Watson, M. Seeger, D. Bruce, Dry Branch Fire Squad

Daniel Prayed

***M:** G; **F:** C or D*
CD 1-Track 36

Traditional

G
1. I heard a - bout a man one day who wast - ed not his
2. They cast him in the li - on's den be - cause he would not
3. Oh broth - er let us watch and pray, Like Dan - iel, live from

4
D G
time a - way, He prayed to God, ev - ery morn - ing,
hon - or men, He prayed to God, ev - ery morn - ing,
day to day, He prayed to God, ev - ery morn - ing,

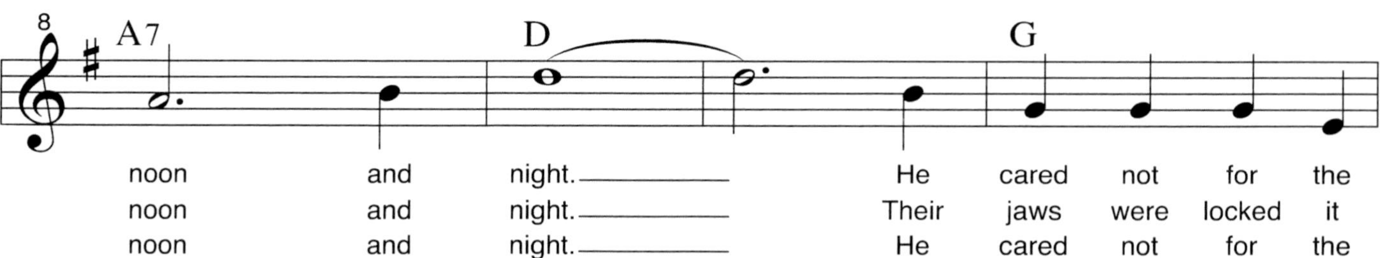
8
A7 D G
noon and night. He cared not for the
noon and night. Their jaws were locked it
noon and night. He cared not for the

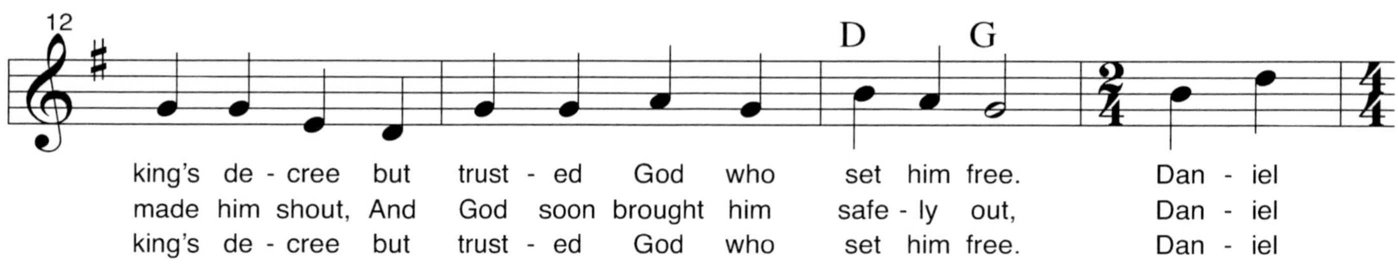
12
D G
king's de - cree but trust - ed God who set him free. Dan - iel
made him shout, And God soon brought him safe - ly out, Dan - iel
king's de - cree but trust - ed God who set him free. Dan - iel

16
D G
prayed, ev - ery morn - ing, noon and night.
prayed, ev - ery morn - ing, noon and night.
prayed, ev - ery morn - ing, noon and night.

D. Watson, Stanley Bros., R. Stanley, Boone Creek

20
G
Cho: Dan - iel served the liv - ing God while here up - on this

24
D
G
earth he trod, He prayed to God,
ev - ery morn - ing,

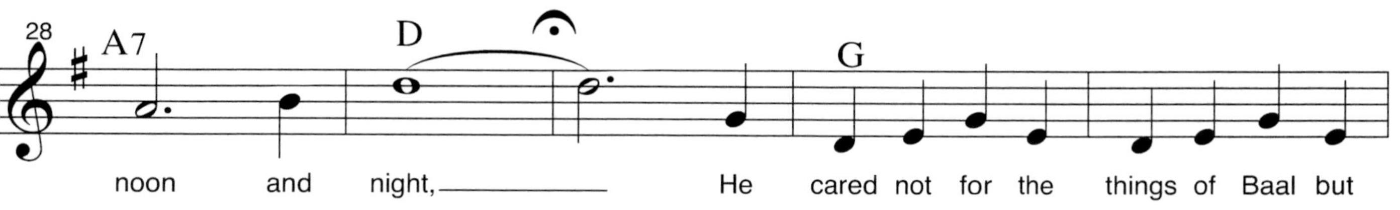
28
A7
D
G
noon and night,
He cared not for the things of Baal but

33
D
G
trust - ed God who nev - er failed, He prayed to God

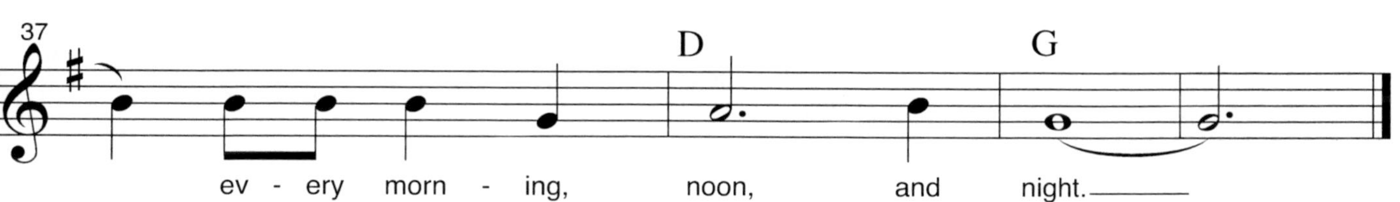
37
D
G
ev - ery morn - ing, noon, and night.

Danny Boy

M: C; F: F or G
CD 1-Track 37

Traditional

C F C
1. Oh, Dan - ny boy, the pipes, the pipes are call - ing, From glen to glen and
2. But when ye come when all the flowers are dy - ing, If I am dead, as
6
D7 G C F
down the moun - tain side, The sum - mer's gone and all the ros - es fall - ing,
dead I well may be, Ye'll come and find the place where I am sleep - ing,
12
C G C C
1. Oh, 'Tis you, 'tis you must go and I must bide. But come ye back when
And kneel and say an 'A - ve' there for me. And I shall hear, though
18
F C Am F
sum - mer's in the mead - ow, Or when the val - ley's hushed and white with
soft you tread a - bove me, And all my dreams will warm and sweet - er
23
D7 G C F C Am
snow, 'Tis I'll be here in sun - shine or in sha - dow, Oh Dan - ny
be, For you will bend and tell me that you love me, And I shall
29
C A7 F G C
boy, oh Dan - ny boy, I love you so!
sleep in peace, un - til you come to me.

B. Monroe, Jim Hurst, Butch Waller

Darling Corey

M: C; F: F or G
CD 1-Track 38, medley pt. 1

Traditional

C
1. Wake up, wake up dar - ling Cor - ey, What
Cho: Dig a hole, dig a hole in the mea - dow, Dig a

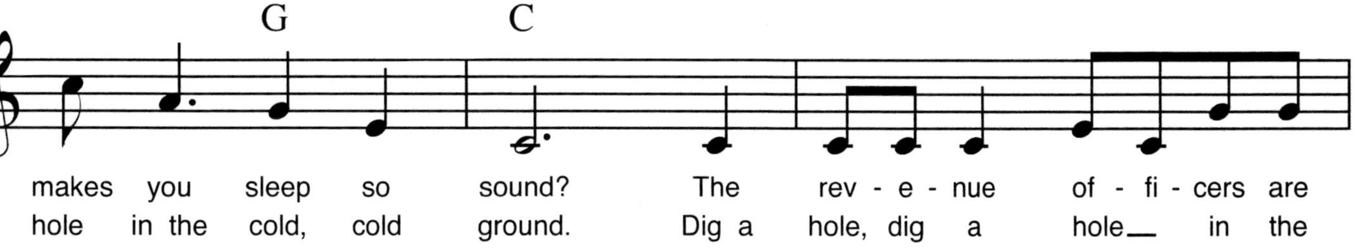
3
G
C
makes you sleep so sound? The rev - e - nue of - fi - cers are
hole in the cold, cold ground. Dig a hole, dig a hole in the

6
G
C
com - ing, Gon - na tear your still - house down.
mea - dow, Gon - na lay darling Cor - ey down.

C
3. Well, the first time I saw darling Corey,
G C
She was sittin' on the banks of the sea,
Had a forty-four around her body,
G C
And a banjo on her knee.

4. Go away, go away darling Corey,
Quit hanging around my bed.
Bad liquor has ruined my body,
Pretty women gone to my head.

5. Can't you hear those bluebirds a'singing?
Don't you hear that mournful sound?
They're preaching darling Corey's funeral,
In some lonesome graveyard ground.

6. Wake up, wake up darling Corey,
Go and get my gun,
I ain't no man for trouble,
But I'll die before I'll run.

Monroe Bros., B. Monroe, Flatt & Scruggs, D. Watson, Country Gazette, NLCR, Seldom Scene, Gibson Bros.

Darling Nellie Gray

M: *C;* ***F:*** *F or G*   *B.R. Hanby, 1856*

CD 1-Track 38, medley pt. 2

C
1. There's a low green___ valley on the old Ken-tuck-y shore, Where I've wiled man-y hap-py hours a-way, A___ sit-ting and a sing-ing by the lit-tle cab-in door, Where___ lived my dar-ling Nell-ie Gray.
2. When the moon had climbed the moun-tain, And the stars were shin-ing too, Then I'd take___ my dar-ling Nell-ie Gray, And we'd float___ down the riv-er in my lit-tle red ca-noe, With my ban-jo, sweet-ly I would play.
F C G C F C G7 C G7 C G C F C G7 C
Cho: Oh my poor Nell-ie Gray, they have tak-en her a-way, And I'll nev-er see my dar-ling an-y-more, I'm sit-ting by the riv-er, and I'm weep-ing all the day, For she's gone from the old Ken-tuck-y shore.

Stanley Bros., Goose Island Ramblers, B. Clifton, M. Wiseman, D. Bruce & J. Nunally

C   F
3. My canoe is under water and my banjo is unstrung,
C   G
Lord, I'm tired of living anymore,
C   F
My eyes shall look downward, my songs shall be unsung,
C   G7   C
While I stay on the old Kentucky shore.

4. One night I went to see her, "She's gone," the neighbors say,
The white man bound her with his chain,
They have taken her to Georgia, for to wear her life away,
As she toils in the cotton and the cane.

5. My eyes are growing blinded and I can not see my way,
Hark, there's someone knocking at the door.
I hear the angels calling, and I see my Nellie Gray,
Farewell, to the old Kentucky shore.

Last chorus: Oh, my darling Nellie Gray, up in heaven, there they say,
That they'll never take you from me anymore.
I'm a'coming, coming, coming, as the angels clear my way,
Farewell, to the old Kentucky shore.

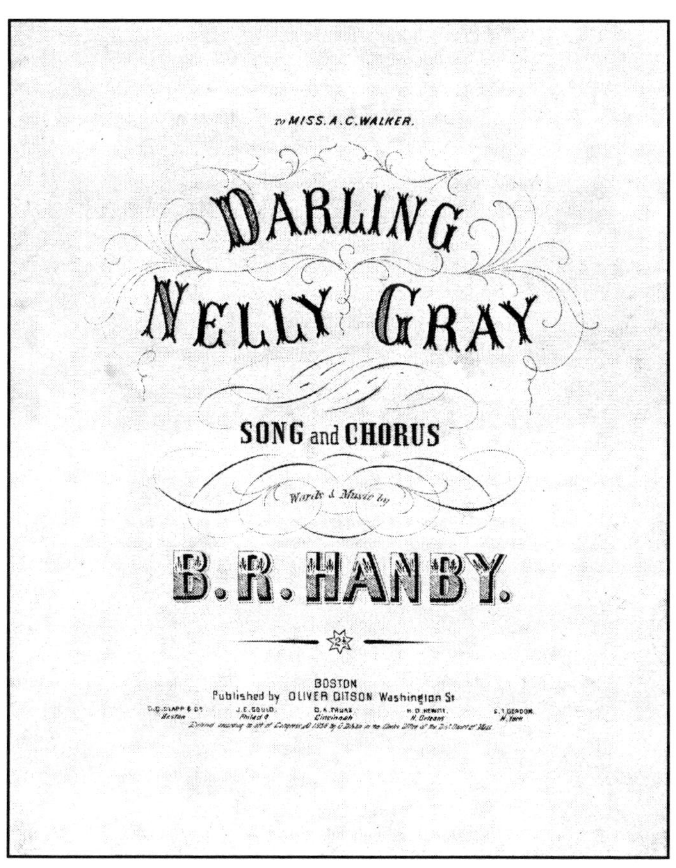
To MISS. A. C. WALKER.
DARLING NELLY GRAY
SONG and CHORUS
Words & Music by
B. R. HANBY.
BOSTON
Published by OLIVER DITSON Washington St

Original sheet music cover page, 1856.

Darling Will You Ever Think of Me?

M: D; F: G or A
CD 1-Track 39

Dix Bruc

D G D
1. When the sun shines in the gar - den, un - der - neath the sway - ing
As you lin - ger in the moon - light, With some - one new now you'll

A7 D G Em
trees, As the leaves all start to shim - mer, Dar - ling
be, As he holds you ev - er clos - er, Dar - ling

A7 D 1 2 G
will you think of me?
will you think of me?
Tenor: Will you think of
Lead: Will you think of me in the

D A7 D
me? Will you think of me?
morn - ing - light? Will you think of me deep in the

G D
Will you think of me?
mid - night? Will you think of me when your new love is near?

Em A7 D
Dar - ling will you ev - er think of me?
Dar - ling will you ev - er think of me?

D G
2. With the scent of summer fading,
D A7
From the gentle autumn breeze,
D G
As you pause in reflection,
Em A7 D
Darling will you think of me?
I will love you in September,
As in summer I will be,
Ever loving through December,
Darling will you think of me? (Chorus)

3. Worlds away my heart is beating,
Always lost in revery,
Pleading though the night won't answer,
Darling will you think of me?
Can I ever find escape love,
From your tender memory?
Need I ask and be heartbroken,
Darling will you think of me? (Chorus)

Deep Elem Blues

M: C; F: F or G
CD 1-Track 40

Traditional

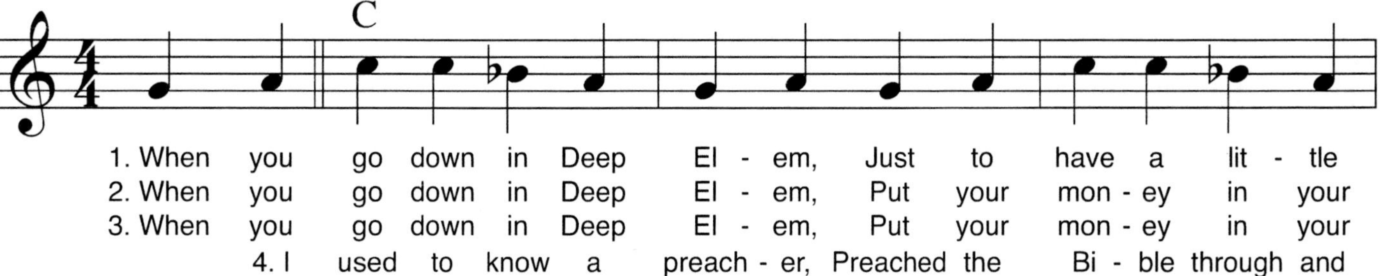
C
1. When you go down in Deep El - em, Just to have a lit - tle
2. When you go down in Deep El - em, Put your mon - ey in your
3. When you go down in Deep El - em, Put your mon - ey in your
4. I used to know a preach - er, Preached the Bi - ble through and

4
fun, Bet - ter have fif - teen dol - lars when that po - lice - man runs.
pants, Those good look - ing wo - men, Won't give a man a chance.
socks, Those Deep El - em wom - en, They will throw you on the rocks.
through, He come down in Deep El - em, Now his preachin' days are through.

9
F
C
Cho: Oh, sweet ma - ma, Dad - dy's got them Deep El - em blues.

14
G
C
Oh, sweet ma-ma, Dad - dy's got them Deep El - em blues.

C. Wakefield, R. Allen & F. Wakefield

Diamonds in the Rough

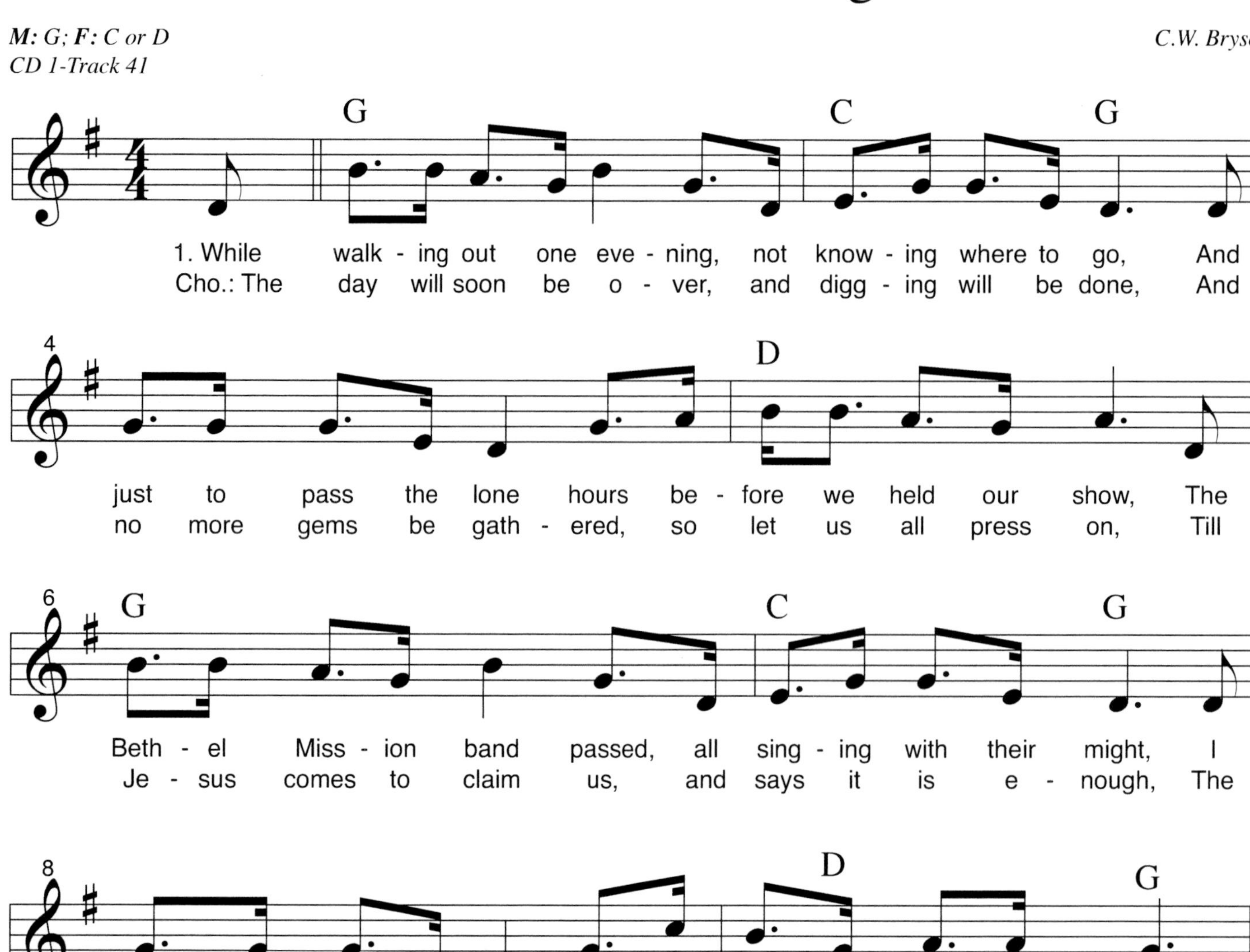
M: G; F: C or D
CD 1-Track 41
C.W. Bryson
G C G
1. While walk - ing out one eve - ning, not know - ing where to go, And
Cho.: The day will soon be o - ver, and digg - ing will be done, And
D
just to pass the lone hours be - fore we held our show, The
no more gems be gath - ered, so let us all press on, Till
G C G
Beth - el Miss - ion band passed, all sing - ing with their might, I
Je - sus comes to claim us, and says it is e - nough, The
D G
gave my heart to Je - sus, and left the show that night.
dia - monds will be shin - ing, no lon - ger in the rough.

```
G                               C            G
2. I used to dance the polka, the schottische and the waltz,
                           D
I also loved the theater, its glitter vain and false,
     G             C                           G
And Jesus, when He found me, He found me very tough,
                                          D      G
But praise the Lord, He saved me, a diamond in the rough.
```

3. One day, my precious comrades, you, too, were lost in sin,
When some one sought your rescue, and Jesus took you in,
When you are tried and tempted, by sinners' stern rebuff,
Don't turn away in anger, they're diamonds in the rough.

4. While reading through the Bible, some wondrous sights I see
I read of Peter, James, and John, by the sea of Gallilee,
And when the Savior called them, their work was rude enough,
Yet they were precious diamonds, He gathered in the rough.

5. Now keep your lamps all burning, the lamps of holy love,
And unto every sinner point out the way above,
The dying love of Jesus, will help you love the tough,
He'll polish into beauty, the diamond from the rough.

Carter Fam., N. Blake, Alan Senauke, Nitty Gritty Dirt Band

Do Lord

M: A; F: D or E
CD 1-Track 42

Traditional

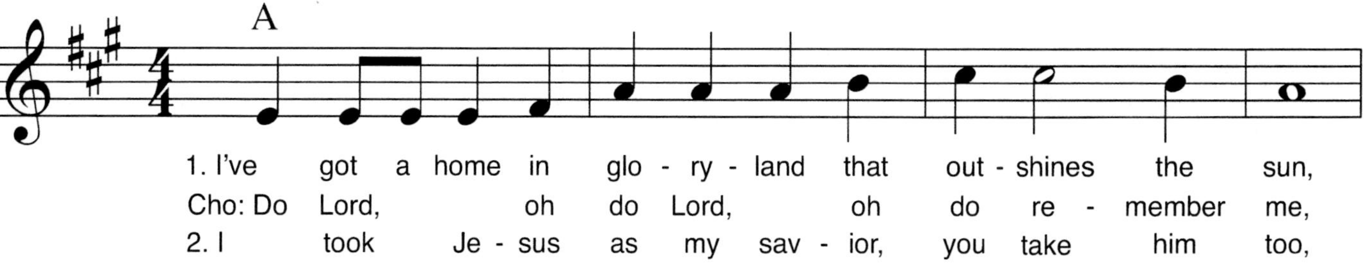

A
1. I've got a home in glo - ry - land that out - shines the sun,
Cho: Do Lord, oh do Lord, oh do re - member me,
2. I took Je - sus as my sav - ior, you take him too,

5
D
A
I've got a home in glo - ry - land that out - shines the sun,
Do Lord, oh do Lord, oh do re - member me,
I took Je - sus as my sav - ior, you take him too,

9
(C♯7)
(F♯m)
I've got a home in glo - ry - land that out - shines the sun, Look a -
Do Lord, oh do Lord, oh do re - member me, Look a -
I took Je - sus as my sav - ior, you take him too,

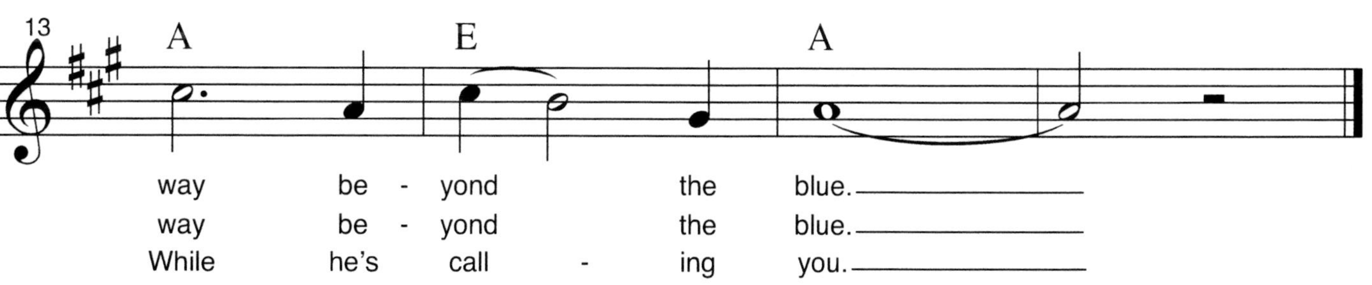

13
A
E
A
way be - yond the blue.
way be - yond the blue.
While he's call - ing you.

Don't Let Your Deal Go Down

M: G; F: C or D — *Traditional*
CD 1-Track 43

E7 A7 D7
1. Well I've been all a - round this whole wide world, I've done most
2. When I left my love be - hind, She was stand - ing
3. Now who's gon - na shoe your pretty little feet? And who's gonna
4. Pa - pa will shoe my pretty little feet, And Mama will
5. Where'd you get them high top shoes, The dress you
6 G E7 A7
ev - ery thing, I've played cards with the king and the queen, The
in the door, She threw her arms a - round my neck said,
glove your hand? Who's gonna kiss your ru - by lips?
glove my hand. You can kiss my red ru - by lips,
wear so fine? Got them shoes from an en - gin - eer, Got th
13 D7 G
ace and the deuce and the trey.
"Daddy, please don't go."
Who's gon - na be your man?
When you get back a - - - gain.
dress from a driver in the mine.
17 E7 A7 D7
Cho: Don't let your deal go down, Don't let your deal go
23 G E7 A7
down, Don't let your deal go down,
28 D7 G
'Til the last gold dol - lar is gone.

Flatt & Scruggs, NLCR, C. Poole, Ken. Colonels,
D. Watson, B. Keith, Fiddlin' John Carson, M. Wiseman

Don't This Road Look Rough and Rocky?

*: D; **F:** G or A*
D 1-Track 44

Traditional

D G D
1. Dar - ling I have come to tell— you,— Though it
2. Don't you hear the night birds cry - ing,— On some
3. One more kiss be - fore I leave you,— One more
A7 D G
al - most breaks my heart,— That be - fore the morn - ing
dark and lone - ly sea,— While of oth - ers you are
kiss be - fore we part.— You have caused me lots of
D A7 D D7
dar - ling,— We'll be man - y miles a - part.—
think - ing,— Won't you some - times think of me?—
trou - ble,— Dar - ling, you have broke my heart.—
G D
Cho: Don't this road look rough and rock - y?—
A7
Don't that sea look wide and deep?—
D G D A7
Don't my ba - by look the sweet - est,— When she's
D
in my arms a - sleep?—

Don't You Hear Jerusalem Moan?

M: G; F: C or D
CD 1-Track 45
Traditiona
G
1. Well, I got a home on the oth - er shore, Don't you
2. Well, the Bap - tist preacher you can tell him by his coat, Don't you
3. Well, the Holy Roll - er preacher sure is a sight, Don't you
4. Well, the Presby - te - rian preacher he lives in town, Don't you
3
hear Je - ru - sa - lem moan? I know I'll live there for
hear Je - ru - sa - lem moan? With a bottle in his pocket he can
hear Je - ru - sa - lem moan? He gets them all a' rolling, and he
hear Je - ru - sa - lem moan? Neck's so stiff he can
6
D
G
ev - er more, Don't you hear Je - ru - sa - lem moan? Cho: Don't you
hard - ly tote, Don't you hear Je - ru - sa - lem moan?
kicks out the light, Don't you hear Je - ru - sa - lem moan?
hardly look a - round, Don't you hear Je - ru - sa - lem moan?
9
G
hear Je - ru - sa - lem moan? Don't you hear Je - ru - sa - lem
12
moan? Thank God there's a heav - en with a ring - ing in my ear, And my
15
D
G
soul set free, Don't you hear Je - ru - sa - lem moan?

F. Wakefield, Skillet Lickers, Jody Stecher, Nitty Gritty Dirt Banc

Down Among the Budded Roses

1: C; F: F or G
D 1-Track 46

Traditional

C
G7
1. Lit - tle sweet - heart we have part - ed,
But I can't for - get the pro - mise,
Cho: Down a - mong the budd - ed ros - es,
5
C
From each oth - er we must go,
That you made me in the lane,
I am noth - ing but a stem,
9 F
C
Man - y miles may sep - a - rate us,
When you said we'd be to - geth - er,
I have part - ed from my dar - ling,
13 G
C
In this world of care and woe.
When the ros - es bloom a - gain.
Nev - er more to meet a - gain.

C G7 C
2. Now this parting gives me sorrow, And it almost breaks my heart,

F C G7 C
Tell me darling will you love me, When we meet, no more to part.

G7 C
Or will this parting be forever, Will there be no coming day,

F C G7 C
When our hearts will be united, And all sorrows pass away?

3. Darling, meet me up in heaven, That's my true and earnest prayer,
If you love me here on earth dear, Then I'm sure you'll love me there.
There our hearts will be united, Free from every pain and care,
In the land of life eternal, In that city bright and fair.

oose Island Ramblers, V. Williams, Keith Little, Bob Paisley

Down in the Valley to Pray

***M:** G; **F:** C or D*
CD 1-Track 47

Traditional

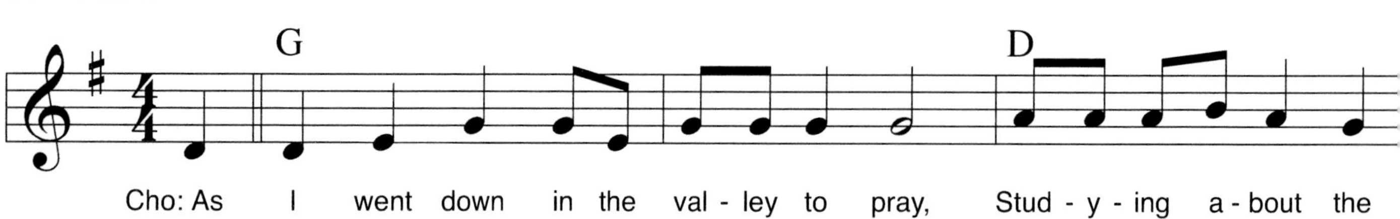

G
D
Cho: As I went down in the val - ley to pray, Stud - y - ing a - bout the

4
G
D C G
good old way and who will wear the star - ry crown? Oh, Lord, show me the way.

9
D G C G
1. Oh, child - ren let's go down,___ Come on down, Don't you want to go down?___
2. Oh, moth - er let's go down,___ Come on down, Don't you want to go down?___

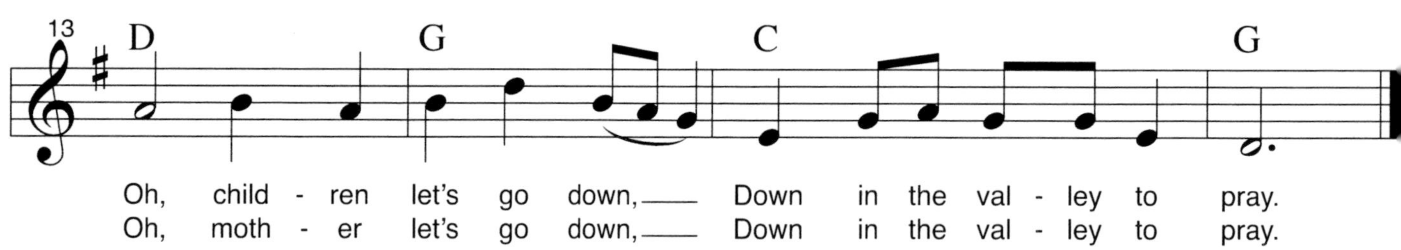

13
D G C G
Oh, child - ren let's go down,___ Down in the val - ley to pray.
Oh, moth - er let's go down,___ Down in the val - ley to pray.

Additional verses:
Oh, brother, father, etc.

D. Watson, A. Krauss, Scruggs/Watson/Skaggs, Dry Branch Fire Squad

Down in the Willow Garden

M: E; F: A or B
CD 1-Track 48
Traditional
E C♯m E
1. Down in the wil - low gar - den, where me and my
2. I drew my sa - ber through her, which was a
3. Now he sits by his cabin door, a' wip - ing his
6 C♯m E C♯m
love did meet, And there we sat a - court - ing, my
blood - y knife, I threw her in to the riv - er, which
tear - brimmed eyes, Mourn - ing for his only son, out
13 E B E E7 A E C♯m
love fell off to sleep. I had a bot - tle of bur - glar's wine, which
was a dread - ful sight. My fa - ther of - ten told me, that
on the scaf - fold high. My race is run be - neath the sun, the
21 E C♯m E
my true love did not know, And there I poi - soned that
money would set me free, If I would mur - der that
devil is wait - ing for me, For I did mur - der that
27 C♯m E B E
dear lit - tle girl, down by the banks be - low.
dear lit - tle miss, whose name was Rose Connel - ly.
dear lit - tle girl, whose name was Rose Connel - ly.

. Monroe, R. Allen & F. Wakefield, D. Grisman, NLCR,
. Hall, Everly Brothers, Osborne Bros., Lonesome River Band

Down the Road

***M:** G; **F:** C or D*
CD 1-Track 49

Traditional

G Em
1. Now down the road a - bout a mile or two,
2. Now any - time___ you___ want to know,

3 G D G
Lives a lit - tle girl named Pear - ly Blue,
Where___ I'm___ heading it's down the road,

5 Em
About so high and her hair is brown,
Got my girl___ on the line, You'll

7 G D G
Pret - ti - iest thing, boys, in this town.___
find___ her there most any old time.___

```
         G                            Em
3. Now every time I get the blues,
  G                        D       G
I walk the soles right off my shoes,
                                  Em
I don't know why I love her so,
       G                 D         G
That gal of mine lives down the road.
```

4. Now everyday and Sunday too.
I go to see my Pearly Blue,
Before you hear that rooster crow,
You'll see me headed down the road.

5. Now old man ___ * he owned a farm,
From the hog lot to the barn,
From the barn to the rail,
He made his living by carrying the mail.

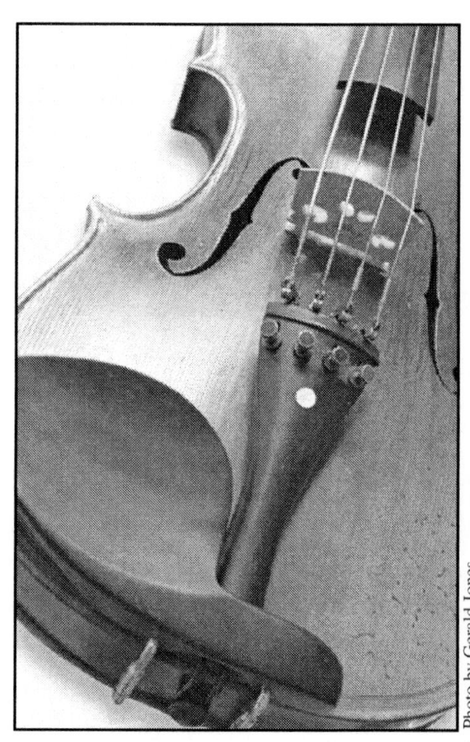

Photo by Gerald Jones

* *your name here*

Flatt & Scruggs, Greenbriar Boys, D. Watson, Country Gentlemen, BG Album Band

Drifting Too Far From the Shore

1: G; F: C or D
D 1-Track 50

Chas. Moody

G D G
1. Out on the per - il - ous deep, Where
2. To - day the temp - est rolls high, And
3. Why meet a ter - ri - ble fate? Mer -
3 D G
dan - gers si - lent - ly creep, And storms so vio - lent - ly
clouds over - shad - ow the sky, Sure death is hov - er - ing
cies a - bun - dant - ly wait, Turn back be - fore it's too
6 C G D G
sweep, You're drift - ing too far from the shore.
nigh, You're drift - ing too far from the shore.
late, You're drift - ing too far from the shore.
9 C G D
Cho: Drift - ing too far from the shore, You're drift - ing too far from the
12 G G7 C
shore, Come to Je - sus to - day, let him show you the way, You're
15 G D G
drift - ing too far from the shore.

Ionroe Bros., B. Monroe, Blue Sky Boys, Country Gentlemen,
oone Creek, Grisman-Garcia-Rice, Stanley Bros., Seldom Scene,
ld & in the Way, IIIrd Tyme Out

East Virginia Blues

M: E; F: A or B
CD 1-Track 51

Traditional

E
1. I was born in East Vir - gin - ia,
2. Oh, her hair was dark and cur - ly,
3. Moll - y dear, go ask your moth - er,

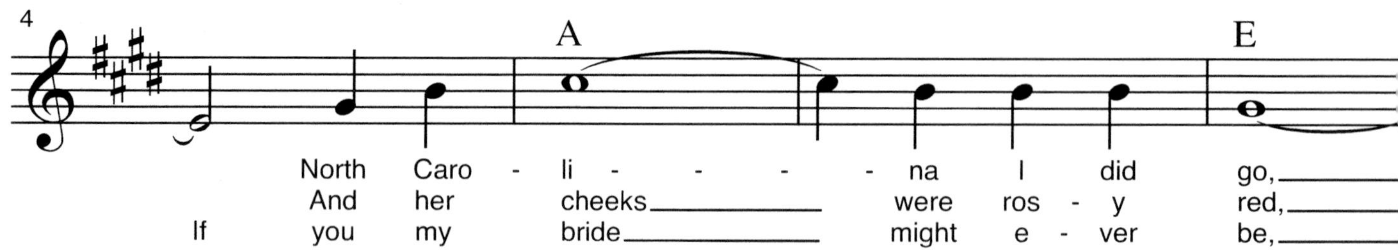

4
A
E
North Caro - li - - - - na I did go,
And her cheeks were ros - y red,
If you my bride might e - ver be,

8
A
E
There I met a fair young maid - en,
On her breast she wore white lin - en,
If she says no, come back and tell me,

12
B7
E
Though her age, I did not know.
Where I longed to lay my head.
And I'll run a - way with thee.


```
E
4. No I'll not go ask my mother,
         A                   E
Where she lies on her bed of rest,
        A                  E
For at her side she holds a dagger,
        B7              E
To kill the one that I love best.
```

5. I don't want your green back dollar,
I don't want your watch and chain,
All I want is your heart darling,
Say you'll take me back again.

6. The ocean's deep and I can't wade it,
And I have no wings to fly,
I'll just get some blue-eyed boatman,
For to row me over the tide.

7. I'll go back to East Virginia,
North Carolina ain't my home,
I'll go back to East Virginia,
Leave old North Carolina alone.

8. Oh, you know I'd like to see you,
At my door you're welcome in,
At my gate I'll always greet you,
For you're the girl I tried to win.

Carter Fam., Flatt and Scruggs, Stanley Bros., R. Stanley, J.D. Crowe, Country Gentlemen, Kathy Kallick, NLCR

Fair and Tender Ladies

M: *D;* ***F:*** *G or A*
CD 1-Track 52

Traditional

D
1. Come all ye fair and ten - der la - dies,
2. They'll tell to you some lov - ing stor - ies,
3. I wish I was a lit - tle spar - row,
4. Oh, love is hand - some, love is charm - ing,
4
A7
Take warn - ing how you court young men,
They'll tell you that they love you well,
And I had wings and I could fly,
Love is pret - - - ty while it's new,
8
Em
D
They're like a star of a sum - mer's morn - ing,
Then a - way they'll go and court some oth - er,
Then a - way I'd go to my false true lov - er,
But love grows cold as love grows old - er,
12
Em
A7
D
They'll first ap - pear and then they're gone.
And leave you here in grief to dwell.
And when he'd ask I would de - ny.
And fades a - way like morn - ing dew.

Fathers Have a Home Sweet Home

M: G; F: C or D
CD 1-Track 53

Traditional

G
C
G
D
G
1. Fa - thers have a home sweet home, fa - thers have a home sweet home, Fa - thers have a home sweet home, Lord I want to join the an - gels, Beau - ti - ful home.
Cho: Beau - ti - ful home sweet home, Beau - ti - ful home sweet home, Beau - ti - ful home sweet home, Lord I want to join the an - gels, Beau - ti - ful home.

Additional verses:

Mothers, brothers, sisters, etc.

Feast Here Tonight

M: D; F: G or A
CD 1-Track 54
Traditional
D
1. There's a rab - bit in the log and I ain't got my dog,
2. I'll build me a fire and I'll roast that old hare,
3. I'm go - ing down the track with my coat ripped up my back,
5
A D
How will I get him? I know, I'll get me a briar and I'll
Roll him in the flames to make him brown, Have a feast here to - night while the
Soles on my shoes are nearly gone, Just a lit - tle ways a - head there's a
11
A D
twist it in his hair, That way I'll get him I know. I
moon is shin - ing bright, Just find me a place to lie down. To lie
farm - er's shed, That's where I'll rest my weary bones. Weary
17
G D A
know, I know, That way I'll get him I know, I'll
down, to lie down, Find me a place to lie down, Have a
bones, weary bones, That's where I'll rest my weary bones, Just a
25
D
get me a briar and I'll twist it in his
feast here to - night while the moon is shin - ing
lit - tle ways a - head there's a farm - er's
28
A D
hair, That way I'll get him I know.
bright, Find me a place to lie down.
shed, That's where I'll rest my weary bones.

Monroe Bros., B. Monroe, R. Stanley, Stanley Bros.,
D. Grisman, Lilly Bros., Scruggs/Watson/Skaggs

The Foggy Mountain Top

***M:** G; **F:** C or D*
CD 1-Track 55

Traditional

G C G D G C G D G
3 5 7
1. If I was on some fog - gy moun - tain top, I'd sail a - way to the West, I'd sail all a - round this whole wide world, To the girl I love the best.
2. Now if you see that girl of mine, There's some - thing you must tell her, She need not to fool her time a - way, To court some oth - er feller.
3. She caused me to weep, she caused me to mourn, She caused me to leave my home, To the lone - some pines and the good old times, I'm on my way back home.
4. If I had listened to what my ma - ma said, I would not be here to - day, Just ly - ing a - round this old jail - house, A' weep - ing my poor life a - way.

Verse 1 often used as chorus

Carter Fam., Monroe Bros., B. Monroe, Flatt & Scruggs, NLCR, E. Taylor, D. Grisman, The Bluegrass Band, W. Guthrie

Footprints in the Snow

1: C; F: F or G
CD 1-Track 56

Harry Wright, ca. 1880

C F G C F G C
1. Some folks like the sum - mer time, When they can walk — a - bout,
2. I dropped in to see — her, There was a big — round moon, Her
3. Now she's up in heav - en, She's with an an - gel band, I
Stroll - ing through the mea - dow green, It's pleas - ant there's no doubt.
moth - er said she just went out, She would be re - turn - ing soon. I
know I'm going to see — her, — in that prom - ised land.
But give me the win - ter - time, when the snow is on the ground, For I
found her lit - tle foot - prints, and I traced them through the snow, I —
Eve - ry time the snow — falls, It — brings back mem - o - ries, Oh, I
found her when the snow was on the ground. Cho: I
found her when the snow was on the ground.
found her when the snow was on the ground.
traced — her lit - tle foot - prints in the snow, I found — her lit - tle
foot - prints in the snow, Lord — I bless that hap - py day, When Nel - lie — lost her
way, I found her when the snow was on the ground.

The Girl I Loved in Sunny Tennessee

M: G; F: C or D
CD 1-Track 57, medley pt. 1
Braisted & Carter,
ca. 1899
G
1. On one morn - ing bright and clear, To my
2. It was but a few short years since I'd
3. As the train drew up at last, Old fa -
4. As I whis - pered, "Moth - er dear, Where is
3
C
D7
old home I drew near, Just a vill - age down in
kissed a - way her tears, As I left her at my
mil - iar scenes I passed, And I kissed my moth - er
Mar - y, she's not here!" All the world seemed lost, and
6
G
sun - ny Ten - nes - see. I was speed - ing on a
dear old moth - er's side. And each day we've been a -
at the sta - tion door. But as old friends gath - ered
sad - ness came to me. For she point - ed to the
10
C
train, that would car - ry me back a - gain, To my
part, she's grown dear - er to my heart, Than the
'round, tears on ev - er - y face I found. And I
spot, in the lit - tle church yard lot. Where my
13
D7
G
sweet - heart who was wait - ing there for me.
day I asked of her to be my bride.
missed the one that I'd been long - ing for.
sweet - heart sleeps in sun - ny Ten - nes - see.

Goose Island Ramblers, D. Watson, C. Poole, Fiddlin' J. Carson, Dixon Bros., B. Clifton, N. Blake

16
G
Cho: We could hear the old folks sing - ing, As she

21
C
G
bid fare - well to me. Far a - cross the fields of

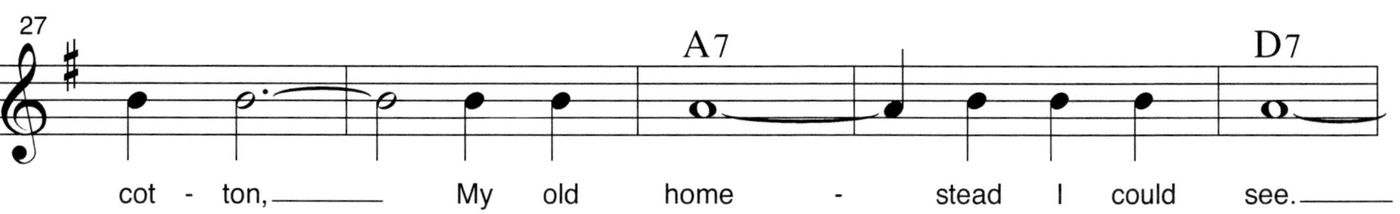
27
A7
D7
cot - ton, My old home - stead I could see.

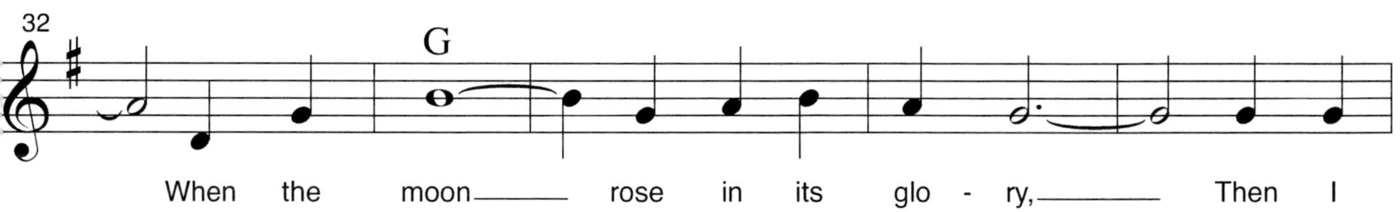
32
G
When the moon rose in its glo - ry, Then I

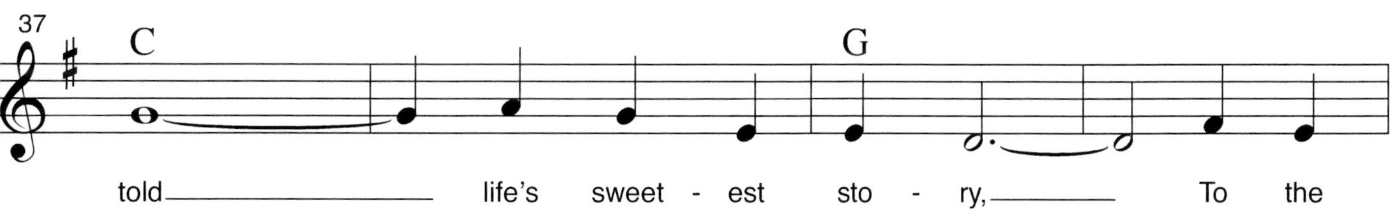
37
C
G
told life's sweet - est sto - ry, To the

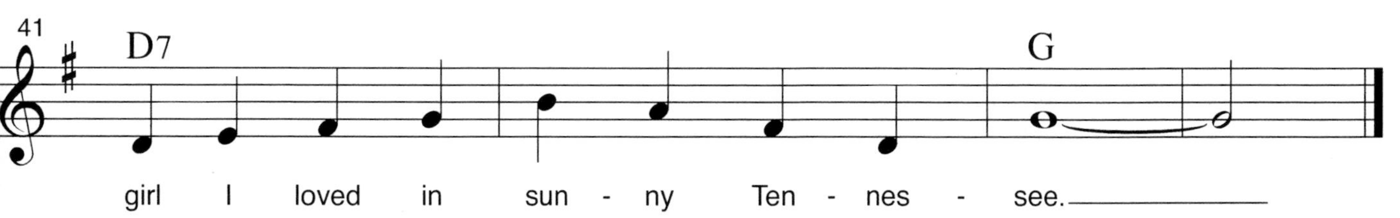
41
D7
G
girl I loved in sun - ny Ten - nes - see.

Give Me Oil in My Lamp

***M:** G; **F:** C or D*
CD 1-Track 57, medley pt. 2

Traditional

G
C
Give me oil in my lamp, keep me burn - ing, Give me

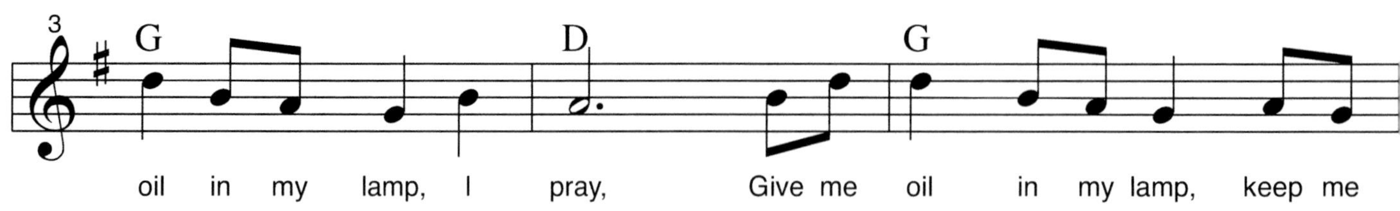
3
G
D
G
oil in my lamp, I pray, Give me oil in my lamp, keep me

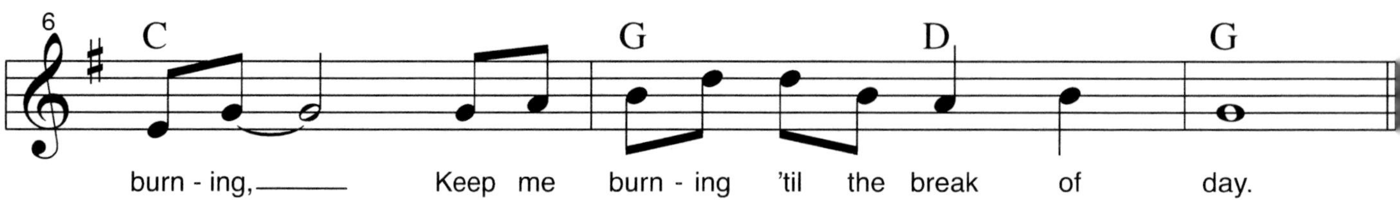
6
C
G
D
G
burn - ing, Keep me burn - ing 'til the break of day.

9
G
C
D
G
Cho: Sing ho - san - nas, Sing ho - san - nas, Sing ho - san - nas to the King.

13
C
D
G
Sing ho - san - nas, Sing ho - san - nas, Sing ho - san - nas to the King.

Give Me the Roses While I Live

M: G; F: C or D
CD 1-Track 58
Cornelius & Rowe
G D G D G C G A7 D G D G
1. Won - der - ful things of folks are said, When they have passed a - way, Ros - es a - dorn the nar - row bed, O - ver the sleep - ing clay.
2. Prais - es are heard not by the dead, Ros - es they can - not see; Let us not wait 'til souls have fled, Gen - er - ous friends to be.
3. Faults are for - giv - en when folks lie, Cold in the nar - row bed. Let us for - give them 'ere they die, Now should the words be said.
Cho: Give me the ros - es while I live, Try - ing to cheer me on. Use - less the flow - ers that you give, Af - ter the soul is gone.

Going Down This Road Feeling Bad

M: G; F: C or D
CD 1-Track 59, medley pt. 1

Traditional

G
G7
Cho: Go - ing down this road feel - ing bad, I'm
Two dol - lar shoes hurt my feet, These

5
C
G G7 C
go - ing down this road feel - ing bad, I'm go - ing down this
two dol - lar shoes hurt my feet, These two dol - lar

10
G
D
road feel - ing bad, Lord, Lord, And I ain't gon - na be
shoes hurt my feet, Lord, Lord, And I ain't gon - na be

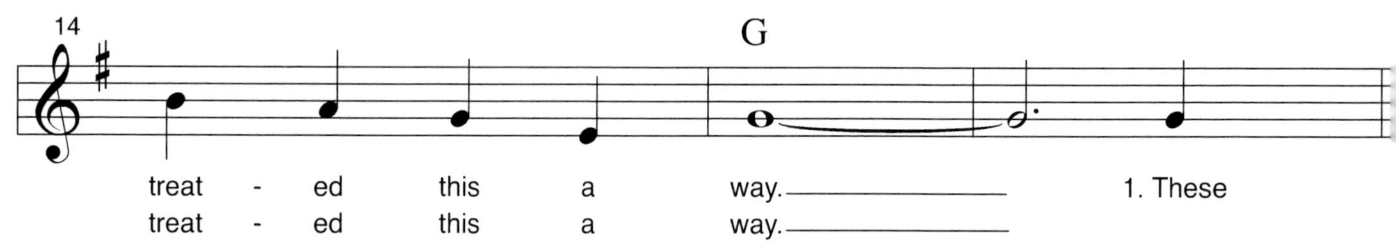
14
G
treat - ed this a way. 1. These
treat - ed this a way.

G G7
2. They feed me on corn bread and beans,
C G G7
They feed me on corn bread and beans,
C G
They feed me on corn bread and beans, Lord, Lord,
D G
And I ain't gonna be treated this a way.

3. I'm going where the chilly winds don't blow, (etc.)
4. I'm going where the water tastes like wine, (etc.)
5. I'm going where the weather suits my clothes, (etc.)

Flatt & Scruggs, B. Monroe, R. Stanley, D. Watson, W. Guthrie
Ken. Colonels, Fiddlin' John Carson, A. Munde, J. Hurst

Photo courtesy of Jim Chancellor

Eck Robertson, the first musician to record a fiddle tune.

Photo courtesy of Joe Carr

Bob Wills, the King of Western Swing at Ft. Worth, TX, television studio KFJZ, 1960s.

Grandfather's Clock

M: G; F: C or D, capo 5 or 7
CD 1-Track 59, medley pt. 2

Henry Clay Work, 187

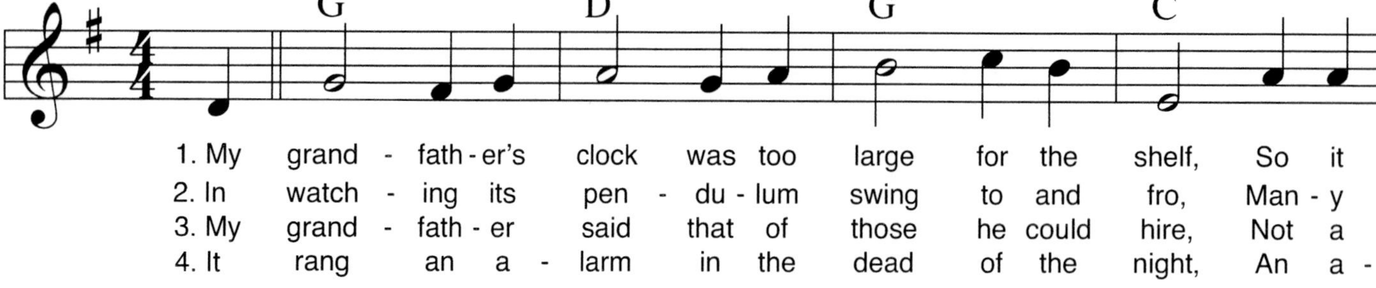
G D G C
1. My grand - fath - er's clock was too large for the shelf, So it
2. In watch - ing its pen - du - lum swing to and fro, Man - y
3. My grand - fath - er said that of those he could hire, Not a
4. It rang an a - larm in the dead of the night, An a -

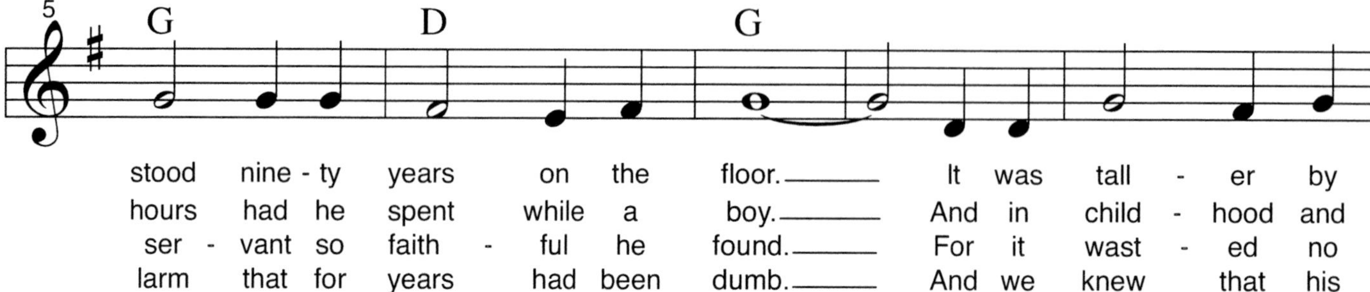
5
G D G
stood nine - ty years on the floor. It was tall - er by
hours had he spent while a boy. And in child - hood and
ser - vant so faith - ful he found. For it wast - ed no
larm that for years had been dumb. And we knew that his

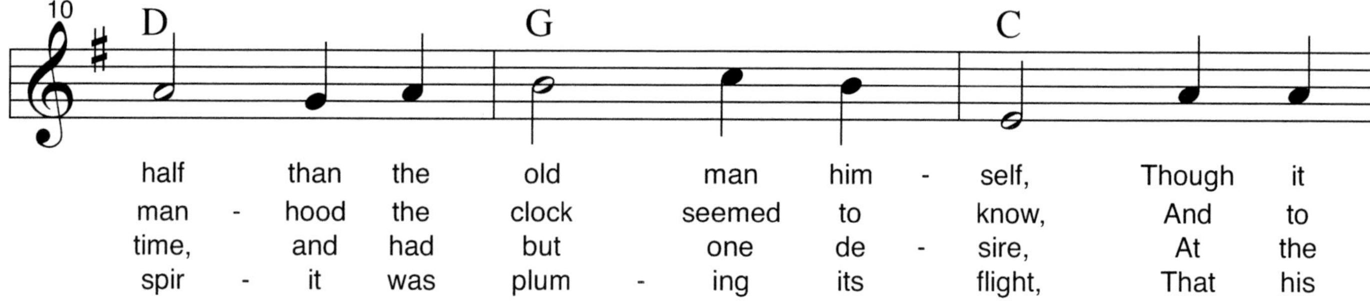
10
D G C
half than the old man him - self, Though it
man - hood the clock seemed to know, And to
time, and had but one de - sire, At the
spir - it was plum - ing its flight, That his

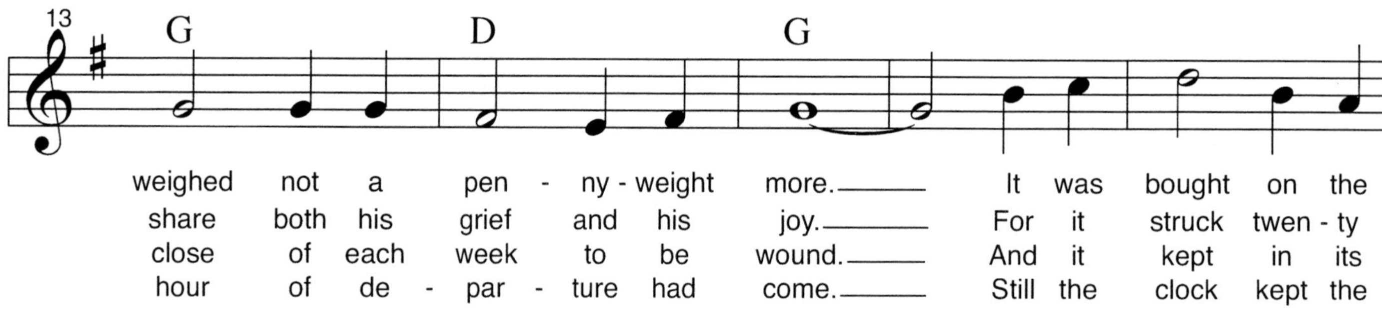
13
G D G
weighed not a pen - ny - weight more. It was bought on the
share both his grief and his joy. For it struck twen - ty
close of each week to be wound. And it kept in its
hour of de - par - ture had come. Still the clock kept the

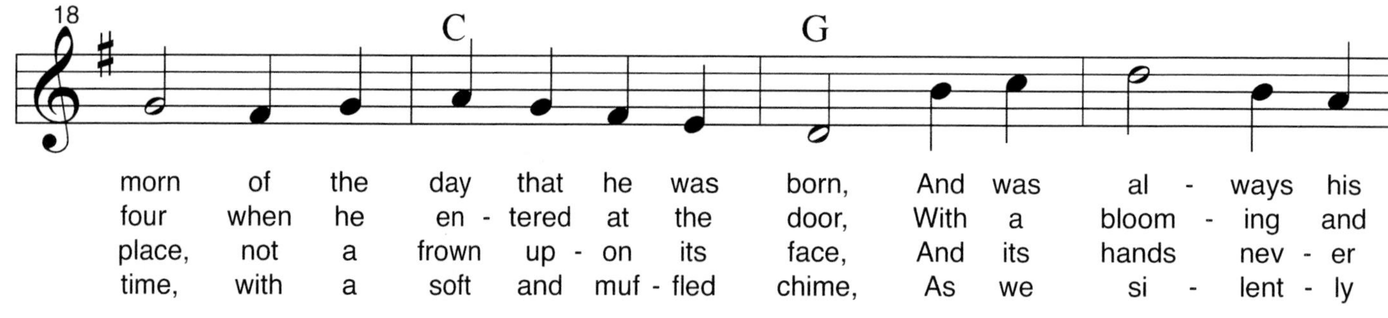
18
C G
morn of the day that he was born, And was al - ways his
four when he en - tered at the door, With a bloom - ing and
place, not a frown up - on its face, And its hands nev - er
time, with a soft and muf - fled chime, As we si - lent - ly

Country Gentlemen, Seldom Scene, A. Munde

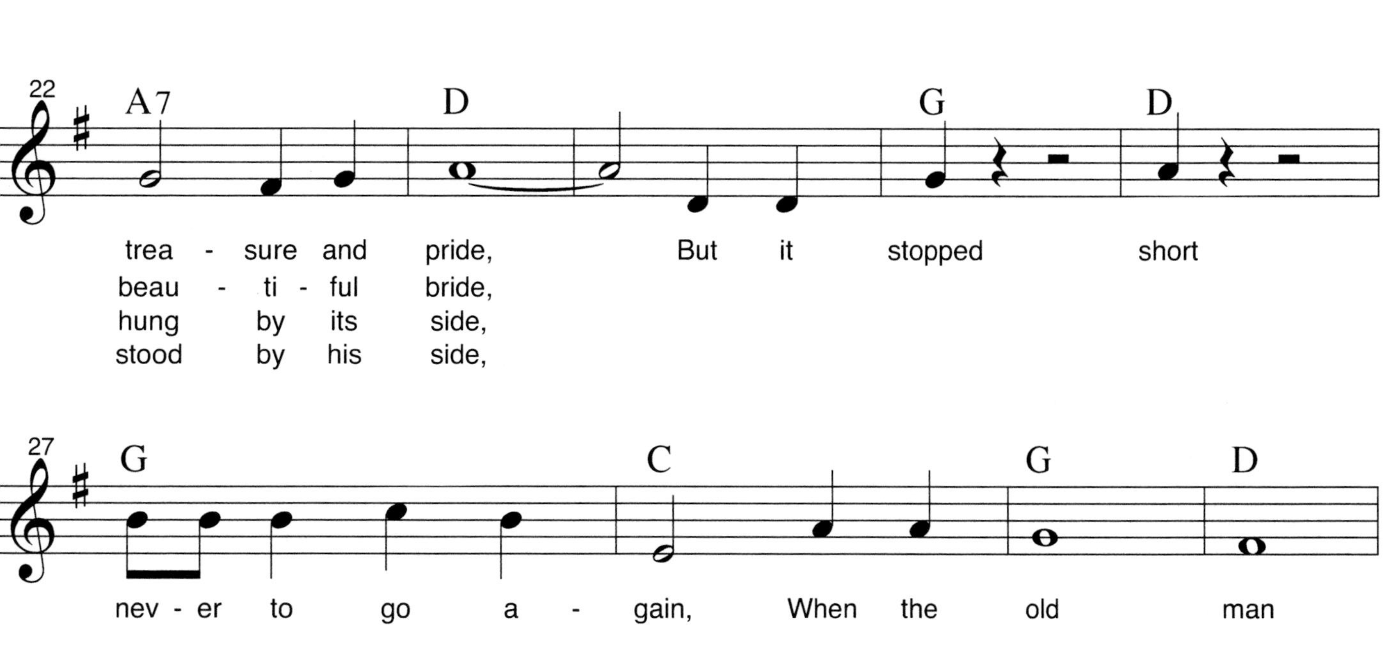
22
A7 D G D
trea - sure and pride, But it stopped short
beau - ti - ful bride,
hung by its side,
stood by his side,
27
G C G D
nev - er to go a - gain, When the old man

31
G G C G
died. Cho: Nine - ty years with - out slum - ber - ing, Tick tock,

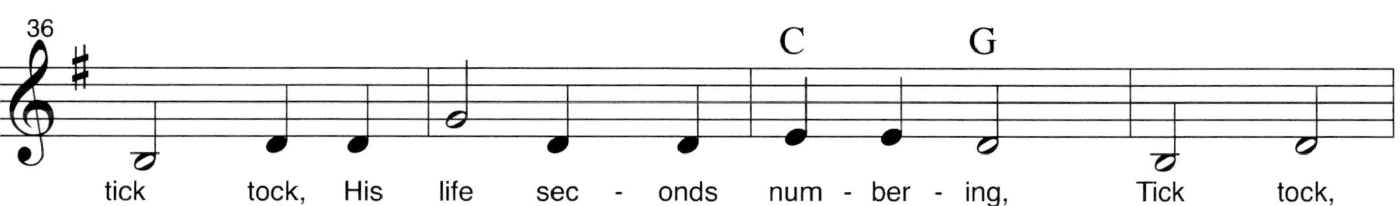
36
C G
tick tock, His life sec - onds num - ber - ing, Tick tock,

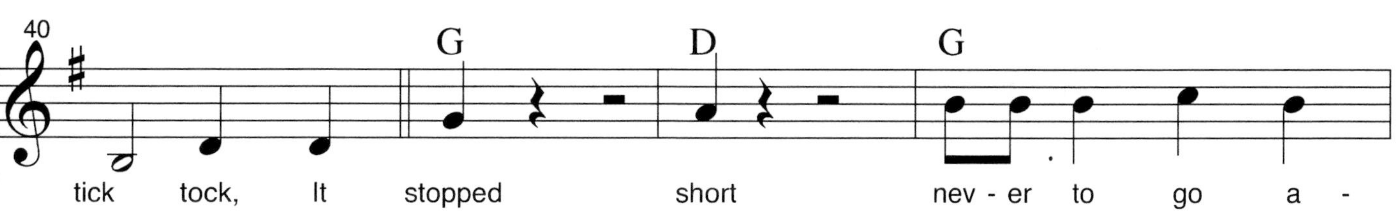
40
G D G
tick tock, It stopped short nev - er to go a -

44
C G D G
gain, When the old man died.

Great Speckled Bird

M: G; F: C or D
CD 1-Track 60

Traditional

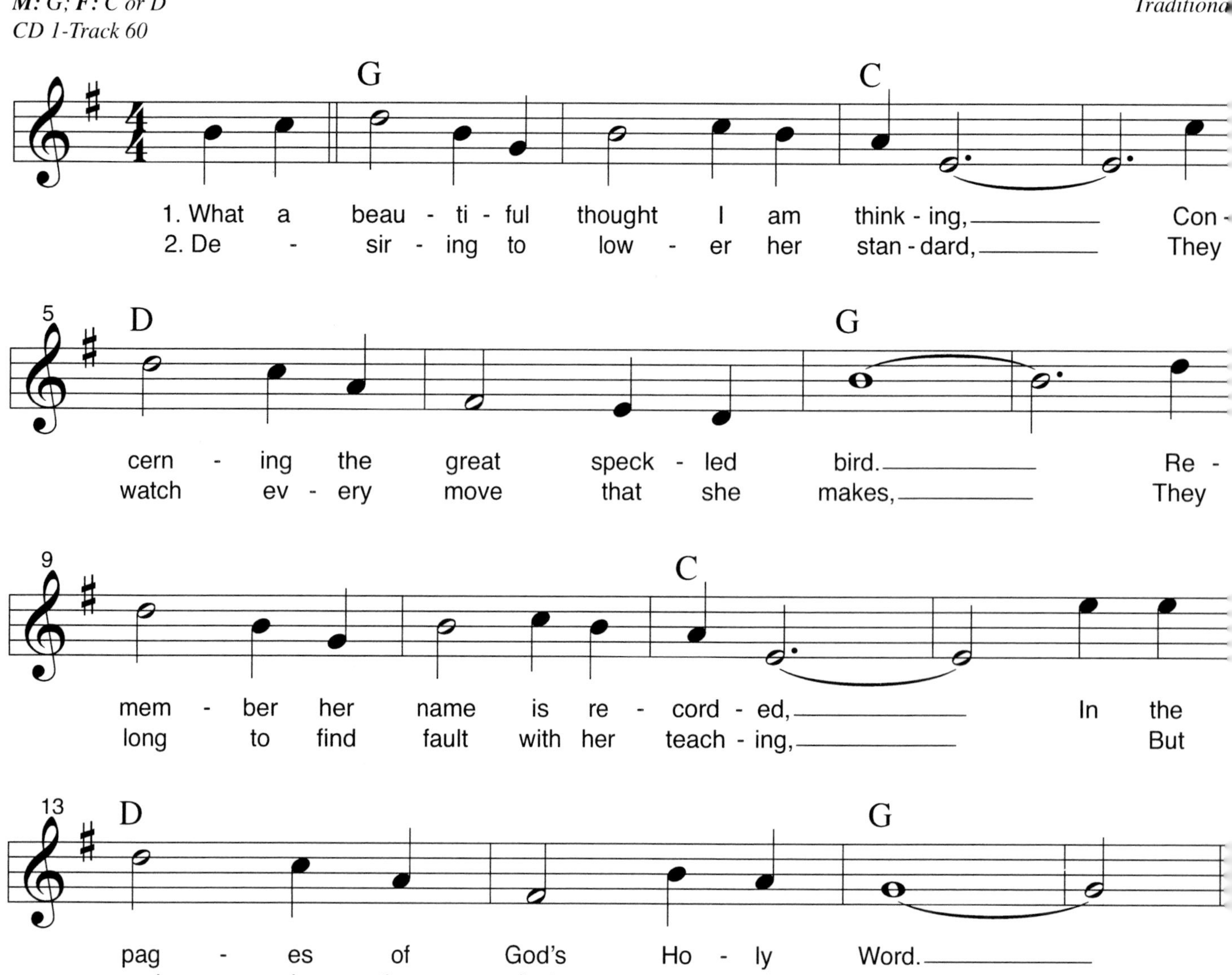
G
C
1. What a beau - ti - ful thought I am think - ing, Con -
2. De - sir - ing to low - er her stan - dard, They
5
D
G
cern - ing the great speck - led bird. Re -
watch ev - ery move that she makes, They
9
C
mem - ber her name is re - cord - ed, In the
long to find fault with her teach - ing, But
13
D
G
pag - es of God's Ho - ly Word.
real - ly they find no mis - take.

G C
3. I am glad to have learned of her meekness,
D G
I'm proud that my name is in her book,
G C
For I want to be one never fearing,
D G
The face of my Saviour's to look.

4. All the other birds flocking 'round her
And she is despised by the squad,
But the great speckled bird in the Bible,
Is one with the great church of God.

5. In the presence of all her despisers,
With a song never uttered before,
She will rise and be gone in a moment,
'Til the great tribulation is o'er.

6. When He cometh descending from heaven,
On the clouds as He writes in His word,
I'll be joyfully carried to meet Him,
On the wings of the great speckled bird.

7. She is spreading her wings for a journey.
She's going to leave by and by,
When the trumpet shall sound in the morning,
She'll rise and go up in the sky.

R. Acuff, M. Wiseman

Green Pastures

: A; ***F:*** *D or E*
D 1-Track 61

Traditional

A E A D
1. Trou - bles and tri - als of - ten be - tray those,
Cho: Go - ing up home to live in green pas - tures,
2. Those who have strayed were sought by the mas - ter,
3. We will not heed the voice of the stran - ger,

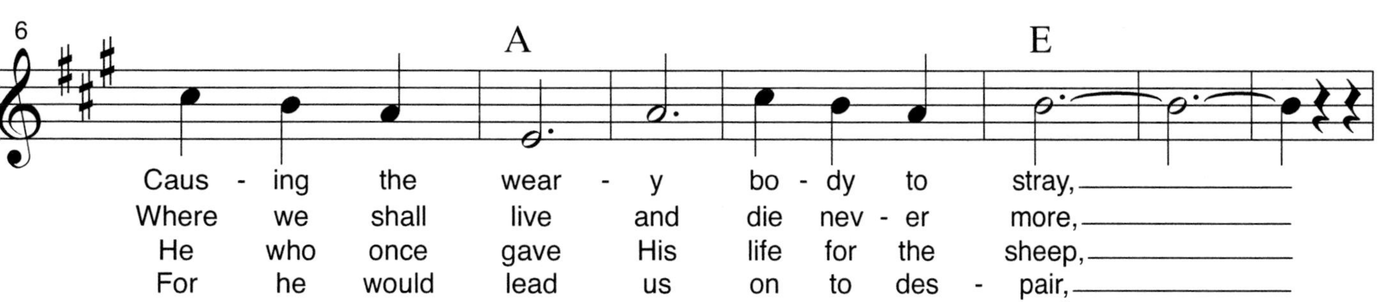
6
A E
Caus - ing the wear - y bo - dy to stray,
Where we shall live and die nev - er more,
He who once gave His life for the sheep,
For he would lead us on to des - pair,

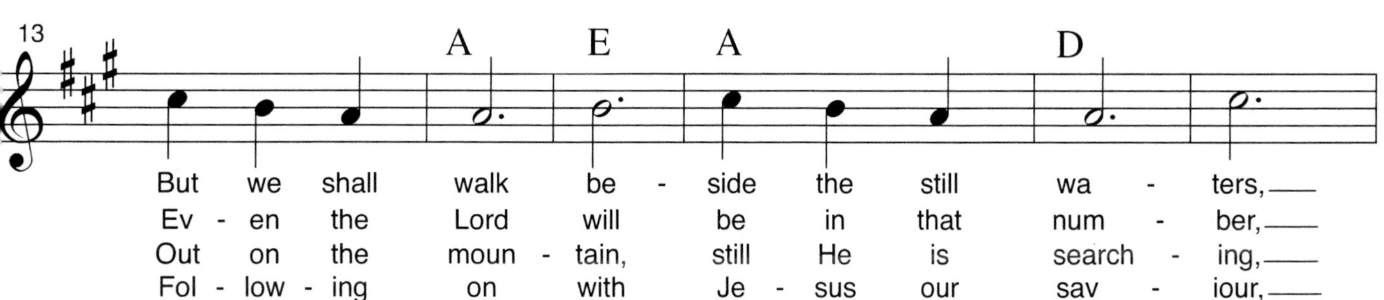
13
A E A D
But we shall walk be - side the still wa - ters,
Ev - en the Lord will be in that num - ber,
Out on the moun - tain, still He is search - ing,
Fol - low - ing on with Je - sus our sav - iour,

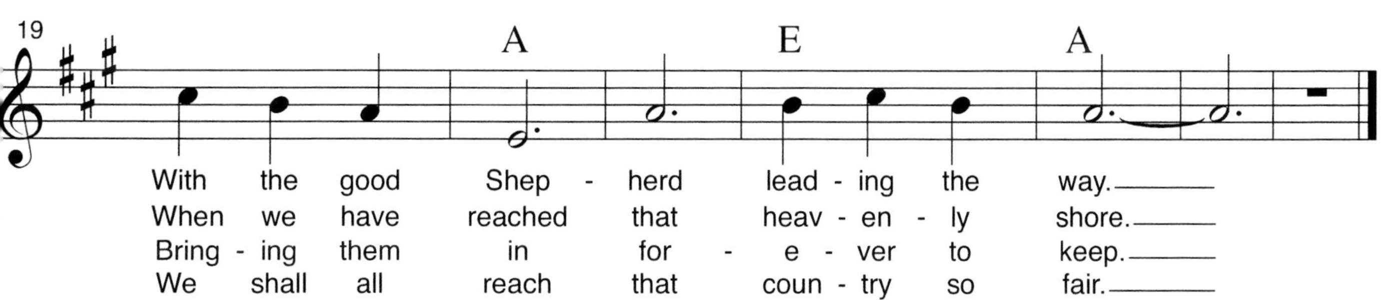
19
A E A
With the good Shep - herd lead - ing the way.
When we have reached that heav - en - ly shore.
Bring - ing them in for - e - ver to keep.
We shall all reach that coun - try so fair.

anley Bros., R. Stanley, E.L. Harris, L. Sparks, Dry Branch Fire Squad

Groundhog

M: *A;* ***F:*** *D or E*
CD 1-Track 62

Traditional

A G A
1. Here comes Sal with a snick - er and a grin,
2. Run here Sal with a ten foot pole,
3. Meat's in the cupboard and the but - ter's in the churn,
4. Watch me boys, I'm a - bout to fall,

3
G A
Here comes Sal with a snick - er and a grin,
Run here Sal with a ten foot pole,
Meat's in the cupboard and the but - ter's in the churn, If
Watch me boys, I'm a - bout to fall,

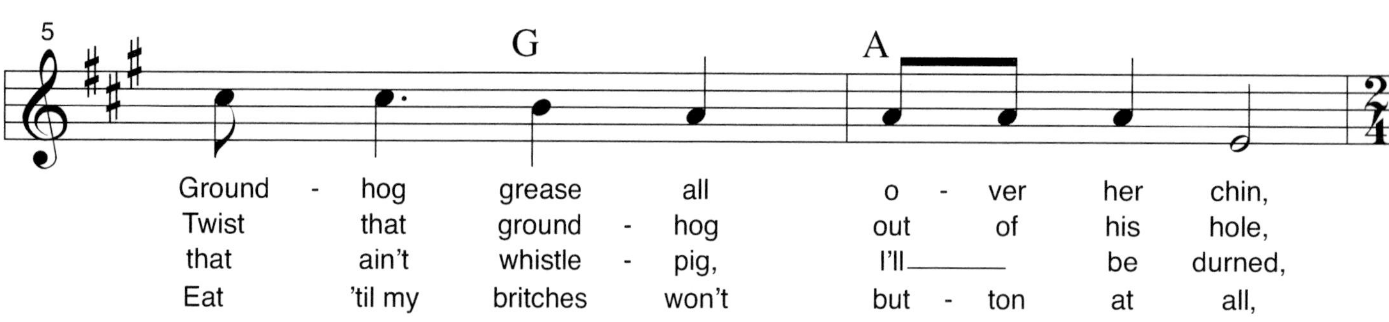
5
G A
Ground - hog grease all o - ver her chin,
Twist that ground - hog out of his hole,
that ain't whistle - pig, I'll be durned,
Eat 'til my britches won't but - ton at all,

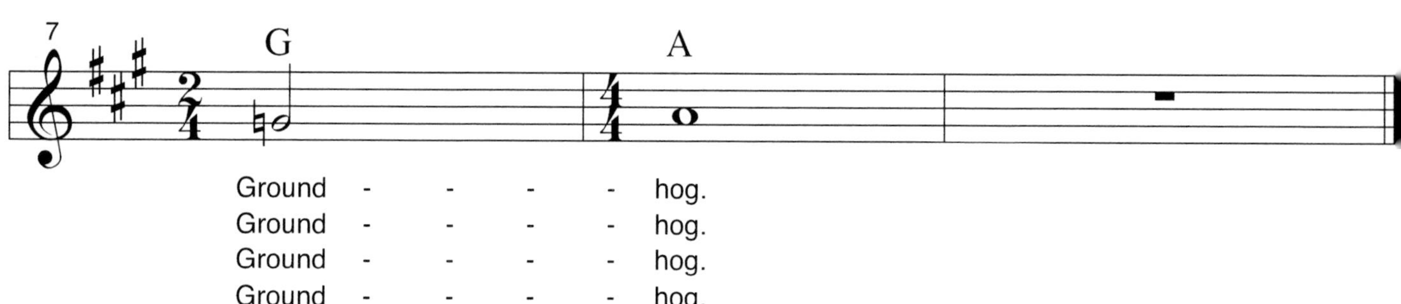
7
G A
Ground - - - - hog.
Ground - - - - hog.
Ground - - - - hog.
Ground - - - - hog.

Stanley Bros., D. Watson, NLCR, Dillards

Hallelujah! I'm Ready

1: C; F: F or G
D 1-Track 63

Traditional

C F C
1. In the dark - ness of night, not a star was in sight, On the
2. Sin - ners don't wait un - til it's too late, He's a
G C
high - way that leads down be - low, But Je - sus came
won - der - ful Sav - ior, you know, Well I fell on my
F C G
in to save us all from sin, Hal - le - lu - jah, I'm read - y to
knees, and he an - swered my pleas, Hal - le - lu - jah, I'm read - y to
C F C
go. Cho: Hal - le - lu - jah, I'm read - y, I can
go.
(I'm read - y), (Hal - le - lu - jah),
G
hear the voic - es sing - ing soft and low, Hal - le -
F C
lu - jah, I'm read - y, Hal - le -
(I'm read - y), Hal - le - lu - jah),
G C
lu - jah, I'm read - y to go.

. Monroe, R. Skaggs, D. Lawson

Hand Me Down My Walking Cane

***M:** G; **F:** C or D*
CD 1-Track 64, medley pt. 1

Traditiona

G
1. Hand me down my walk - ing cane, Hand me
2. Hand me down my bottle of corn, Hand me

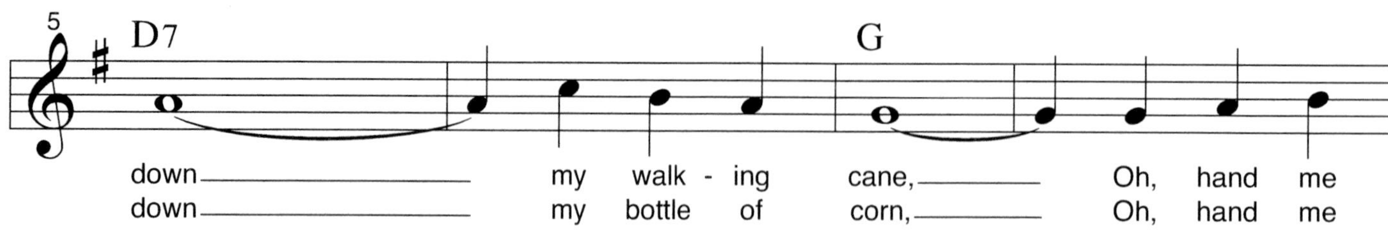
5
D7
G
down my walk - ing cane, Oh, hand me
down my bottle of corn, Oh, hand me

9
C
G
down my walk - ing cane, I'm gon - na catch that mid - night train, For
down my bottle of corn, I'll get drunk as sure's you're born, For

13
D7
G
all my sins are tak - en a - way.
all my sins are tak - en a - way.

3. Oh, I got drunk and I landed in jail, (G)
Oh, I got drunk and I landed in jail, (D7 … G)
Oh, I got drunk and I landed in jail, (C)
With no one to go my bail, (G)
For all my sins are taken away. (D7 … G)

4. The meat is tough, and the beans are bad, (3X)
Oh, my God, I can't eat that,
For all my sins are taken away.

5. The devil chased me 'round a stump, (3X)
I thought he'd catch me at every jump,
For all my sins are taken away.

Goose Island Ramblers, Osborne Bros., Skillet Lickers, N. Blake

Handsome Molly

1: G; F: C or D
CD 1-Track 64, medley pt. 2

Traditional

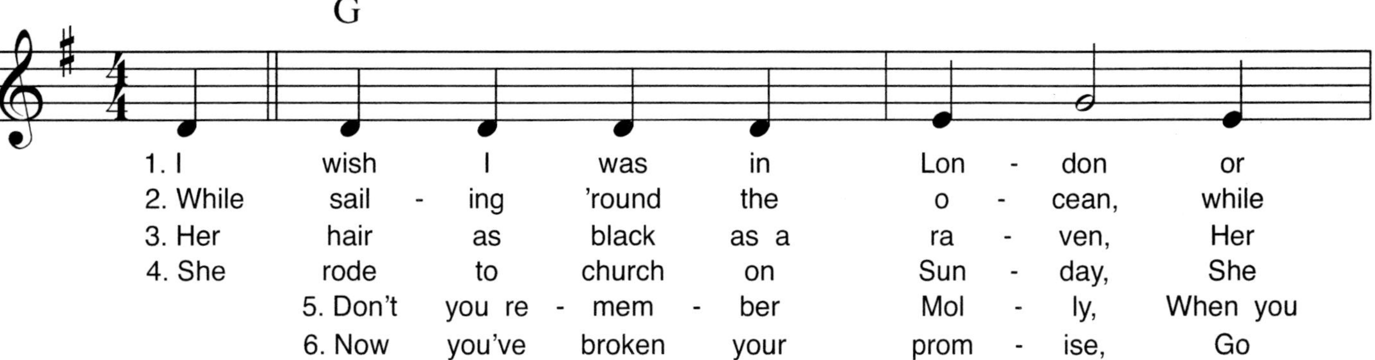

G
1. I wish I was in Lon - don or
2. While sail - ing 'round the o - cean, while
3. Her hair as black as a ra - ven, Her
4. She rode to church on Sun - day, She
5. Don't you re - mem - ber Mol - ly, When you
6. Now you've broken your prom - ise, Go

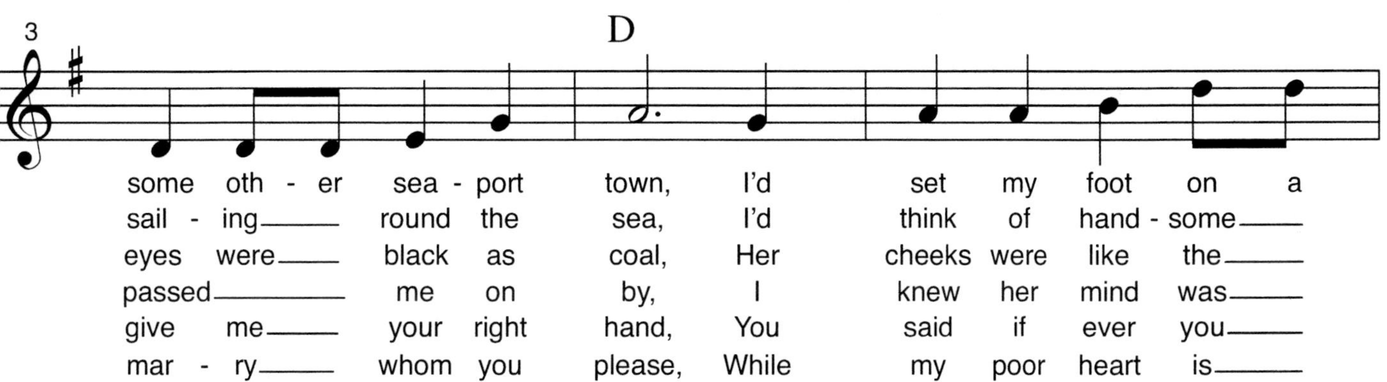

3
D
some oth - er sea - port town, I'd set my foot on a
sail - ing round the sea, I'd think of hand - some
eyes were black as coal, Her cheeks were like the
passed me on by, I knew her mind was
give me your right hand, You said if ever you
mar - ry whom you please, While my poor heart is

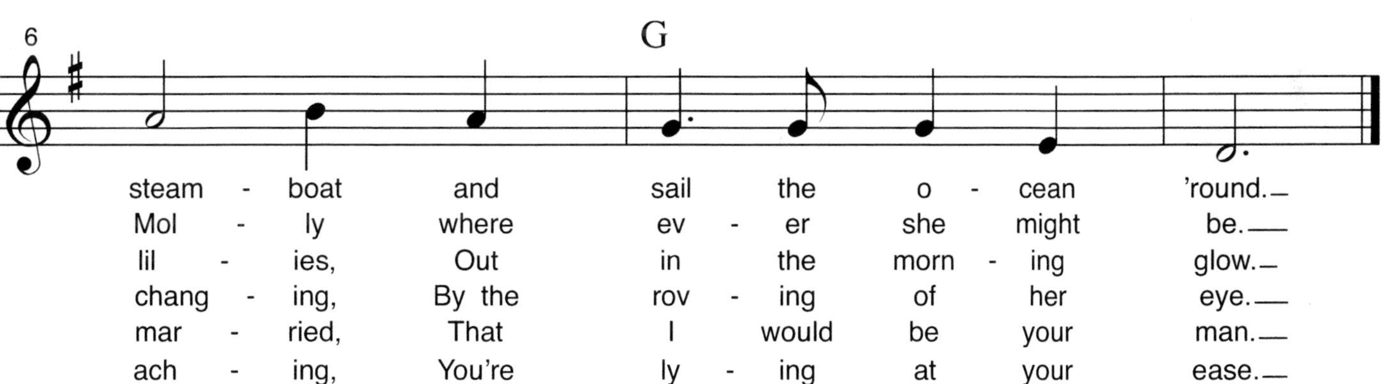

6
G
steam - boat and sail the o - cean 'round.
Mol - ly where ev - er she might be.
lil - ies, Out in the morn - ing glow.
chang - ing, By the rov - ing of her eye.
mar - ried, That I would be your man.
ach - ing, You're ly - ing at your ease.

Flatt & Scruggs, Stanley Bros., R. Stanley, D. Watson, N. Blake, Grayson & Whitter, Country Gentlemen

Hard Times, Come Again No More

***M:** D; **F:** G or A*
CD 1-Track 65, medley pt. 1

Stephen Foster

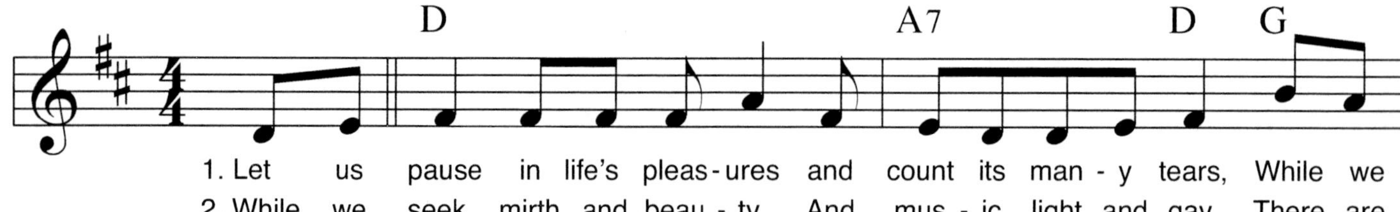
D
A7
D G
1. Let us pause in life's pleas-ures and count its man - y tears, While we
2. While we seek mirth and beau - ty, And mus - ic light and gay, There are
3. There's a pale droop - ing maid - en, Who toils her life a - way, With a
4. 'Tis a sigh that is waft - ed, A - cross the troub - led wave, 'Tis a

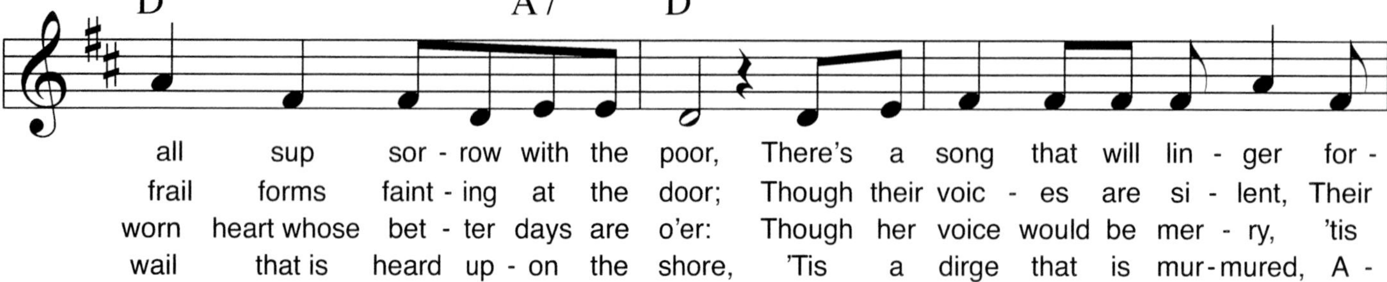
D
A7
D
all sup sor - row with the poor, There's a song that will lin - ger for -
frail forms faint - ing at the door; Though their voic - es are si - lent, Their
worn heart whose bet - ter days are o'er: Though her voice would be mer - ry, 'tis
wail that is heard up - on the shore, 'Tis a dirge that is mur-mured, A -

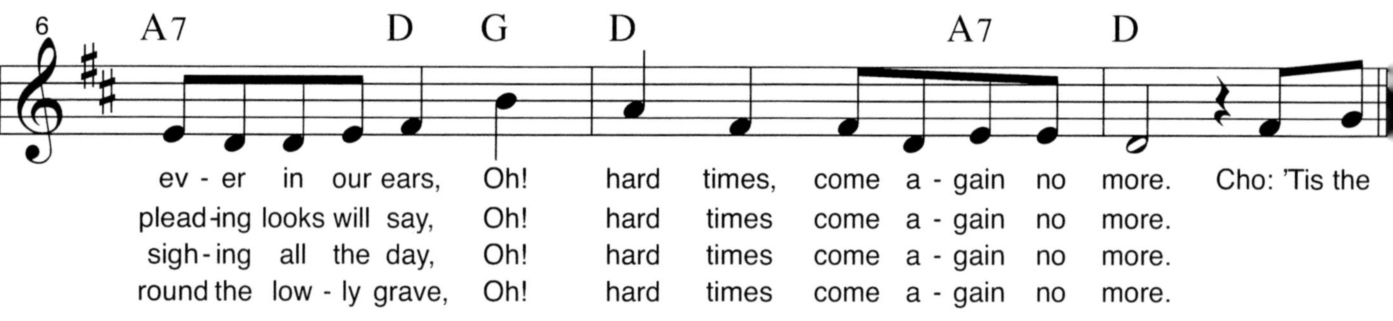
6
A7
D G
D
A7
D
ev - er in our ears, Oh! hard times, come a - gain no more. Cho: 'Tis the
plead-ing looks will say, Oh! hard times come a - gain no more.
sigh-ing all the day, Oh! hard times come a - gain no more.
round the low - ly grave, Oh! hard times come a - gain no more.

9
D
G D
G D
A7
song, the sigh of the wear - y, hard times, hard times, come a-gain no more, Man-y

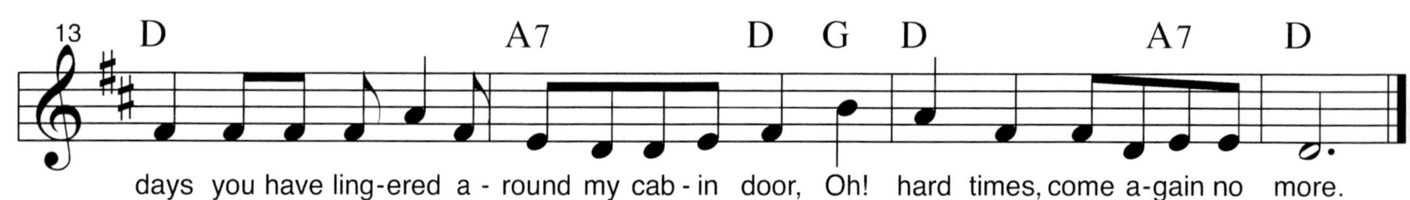
13
D
A7
D G
D
A7
D
days you have ling-ered a - round my cab - in door, Oh! hard times, come a-gain no more.

Dry Branch Fire Squad, J. Stecher & K. Brislin

Have Thine Own Way, Lord

M: D; F: G or A
CD 1-Track 65, medley pt. 2

Pollard & Stebbins, 1907

D G D A
1. Have Thine own way, Lord! Have Thine own way!
2. Have Thine own way, Lord! Have Thine own way!
3. Have Thine own way, Lord! Have Thine own way!
4. Have Thine own way, Lord! Have Thine own way!

7
D
Thou art the Pot - ter, I am the clay,
Search me and try me, Mas - ter to - day,
Wound - ed and wea - ry, Help me I pray,
Hold o'er my be - ing ab - so - lute sway!

13
G D G
Mold me and make me, Af - ter Thy will,
Whit - er than snow, Lord, Wash me just now,
Pow - er, all pow - er, Sure - ly is thine,
Fill with Thy Spir - it, 'Til all shall see

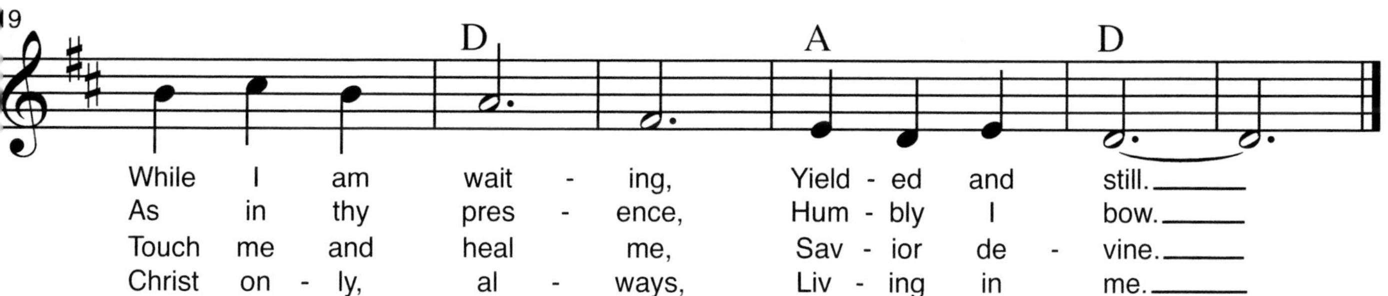
19
D A D
While I am wait - ing, Yield - ed and still.
As in thy pres - ence, Hum - bly I bow.
Touch me and heal me, Sav - ior de - vine.
Christ on - ly, al - ways, Liv - ing in me.

He Was a Friend of Mine

***M:* G; *F:* C or D**

CD 1-Track 66

Tradition[al]

G D G D
1. He was a friend of mine He
2. He died out on the road, He
3. He nev - er done no wrong, He
4. I stole a - way and cried, I
5. He was a friend of mine, He
6
G
was a friend of mine.
died out on the road,
nev - er done no wrong,
stole a - way and cried,
was a friend of mine,
9
Em C
He nev - er had no mon - ey, for to pay his
He nev - er had no mon - ey to pay for his
He was just a poor boy, a long way from
My tears fell like rain - drops the night my old friend
When I hear his name, I just can't keep from
12
D G D G
fine, He was a friend of mine.
board, He was a friend of mine.
home, He was a friend of mine.
died, He was a friend of mine.
crying, He was a friend of mine.

Country Gentlemen, Grateful Dea[d]

Left: Jim Chancellor ("Texas Shorty") on stage 1965.

Right: A teen-aged "Texas Shorty" at home with his mother and father, ca. 1960.

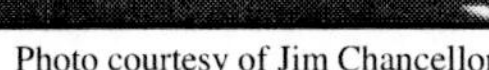

Photo courtesy of Jim Chancellor

Left: "Texas Shorty" with John Hartford, ca. 1998.

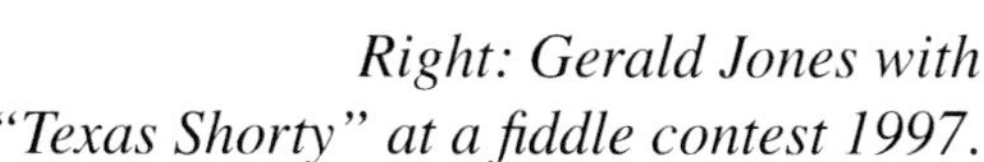

Right: Gerald Jones with "Texas Shorty" at a fiddle contest 1997.

Photo by Leigh Taylor

He Will Set Your Fields on Fire

M: A; *F:* D or E
CD 1-Track 67

Ballew & Bracket

A
D
A
B7
E7
A
D
A
D
A
B7
E7
A
A
1. There's a call that rings, from the throne it springs, to those now gone a - stray. Say - ing "Come ye men with your load of sin, There at the al - tar lay." You don't seem to heed, from the chain of greed, Your con - science nev - er tires. Be as - sured my friend, if you still of - fend, He will set your fields on fire.
2. You have heard His voice, seen the soul re - joice, That trust - ed in His grace. You have blushed with sin, as He knocked with - in, But still you hide your face. From the bless - ed Lord and His own true word, But still you say re - tire. Leave the down - ward path, kin - dle not his wrath, Or He'll set your fields on fire.
3. Won't you take ad - vice, make the sac - ri - fice, Com - plete - ly turn from sin. Tak - ing up the cross, count - ing earth as dross, Let Je - sus live with - in. When temp - ta - tions come, keep on fac - ing home, Your heart will ne - ver tire. But re - joice and pray on the last great day, When He sets this world on fire.
Cho: If you don't from sin re -

Monroe Bros., B. Monroe, Flatt & Scruggs
C. White, Country Gentlemen, Reno & Smiley

18
E7
tire, He will set your fields on fire, You have
21
heard Je - sus call, And in death your soul must
24
A
fall, But my friend if you de - sire, You may
27
D
join the heav - en - ly choir, And re - joice with Him, free from
30
A
B7
E7
A
ev - ery sin, When He sets this world on fire.

High on a Mountain

M: D; F: G or A
CD 1-Track 68
Ola Belle Reed
D A D
1. As I looked at the val-leys down be - low, They were
2. Oh, I wonder if you ev - er think of me, Or if
A D
green just as far as I could see, As my mem - o - ry re -
time has blotted out your mem - o - ry, As I lis - ten to the
C D G D
turned, oh, how my heart did yearn, For you and the
breeze, whis - per gen - tly through the trees, I'll always cher - ish
A D D C
days that used to be. Cho: High on a moun-tain the
what you meant to me.
D G D A D
wind blow - ing free, Think - ing a - bout the days that used to be,
C D G
High on a moun - tain, oh, stand - ing all a - lone,
D A D
Won - der - ing where the years of my life have flown.

Highway of Sorrow

1: C; F: F or G
D 1-Track 69
Bill Monroe
C
Cho: Down a high - way of sor - row, I'm
1. I once had a dar - ling wife,
2. I went back to my dar - ling, I
3
F
C
travel - ing a - lone, I've lost all my true friends, I've
kind, true and sweet, Life seemed so bright and gay,
got down on my knees, I begged her with tear filled eyes to
7
G
C
lost a hap - py home, I'm head - ing for de -
ev - ery - thing com - plete, I fell for an -
give my poor heart ease, But she was hurt so
10
F
C
struc - tion, I'm on the wrong track, Down a
oth - er, who's led my life a - stray, So
deep - ly, she could not for - give, So
13
G7
C
high - way of sor - row there's no turn - ing back.
I'll live in sor - row 'til my dy - ing day.
I'll live in sor - row, as long as I live.

Monroe, D. Grisman, Del McCoury, D. Watson, Johnson Mtn. Boys

Hills of Roane County

M: G; F: C or D
CD 1-Track 70
Traditional
G C G D G C G D G
1. In the beau - ti - ful hills, way back in Roane Coun - ty, There's where I roamed for man - y long years, There's where my heart's been tend - ing most ev - er, That's where the first step of mis - for - tune I made.
2. I was just thir - ty years when I court - ed and mar - ried, A - man - da Gil - braith, I then called my wife, Her broth - er stabbed me for some un - known rea - son, Just three months lat - er I'd tak - en Tom's life.

B. Monroe, Stanley Bros., Blue Sky Boys, Mac Wiseman, T. Rice

G C G
. For twenty five years this whole world I rambled,
D
went to old England to France and to Spain,
G C G
ut I thought of my home way back in Roane County,
D G
boarded a steamer and came back again.

. I was captured and tried in the village of Kingston,
ot a man in the county would speak one kind word,
/hen the jury came in with the verdict next morning,
\ lifetime in prison" was the words that I heard.

. When the train pulled out, poor Mother stood weeping,
nd sister she sat, alone with a sigh,
nd the last words I heard was, "Willie God bless you,"
/as, "Willie God bless you, God bless you, good bye."

. Sweet Martha was grave but Corey was better,
here's better and worse, although you can see,
oys when you write home from the prison in Nashville,
lace one of my songs in your letter for me.

. In the scorching hot sand of the foundry I'm working,
oiling and working my poor life away.
hey'll measure my grave on the banks of old Cumberland,
ust as soon as I've finished the rest of my days.

. No matter what happens to me in Roane County,
o matter how long my sentence may be,
I love my home way back in Roane County,
's a' way back down in East Tennessee.

His Eye is on the Sparrow

M: C; F: F or G
CD 1-Track 71
Martin & Gabriel, 190
C G C F
1. Why should I feel dis - cour - aged, Why should the shad - ows
2. "Let not your heart be troubl - ed," His ten - der word I
3. When - ev - er I am tempt - ed, When - ev - er clouds a -
4 C A7 Dm G7
come, Why should my heart be lone - ly, And long for Heaven and
hear. And rest - ing on His good - ness, I lose my doubts and
rise, When songs give place to sigh - ing, When hope with - in me
8 C G7 C
home, When Je - sus is my por - tion? My con - stant Friend is
fears; Though by the path He lead - eth But one step I may
dies, I draw the clos - er to Him, From care He sets me
12 F G7 C A7 D7 G7
He: His eye is on the spar - row And I know He watch - es
see: His eye is on the spar - row, And I know He watch - es
free; His eye is on the spar - row, And I know He watch - es
16 C F C G7
me; His eye is on the spar - row, And I know He watch - es
me; His eye is on the spar - row, And I know He watch - es
me; His eye is on the spar - row, And I know He cares for
20 C G7 C G7 C
me. Cho: I sing because I'm hap - py, I sing because I'm free, For His
me.
me.
25 F Fm C G7 C
eye is on the spar - row, And I know He watch - es me.

Hold Fast to the Right

1: G; F: C or D
D 1-Track 72
Traditional
G C G
1. Kneel down by the side of your moth - er, my boy, You have
2. You leave us to seek your em - ploy - ment, my boy, By the
3. I gave you to God in your cra - dle, my boy, And I've
4. You will find in your satch - el, a Bi - ble, my boy, It's the
D7 G C
on - ly a mo - ment I know. But stay till I give you this
world you have yet to be tried. But in the temp - ta - tions and
taught you the best that I knew. And as long as His mer - cies per -
book of all oth - ers the best. It will help you to live and pre -
G D7 G
part - ing ad - vice, It is all that I have to be - stow. Cho: Hold
tri - als you meet, May your heart to the Sav - ior con - fide.
mit me to live, I shall nev - er cease pray - ing for you.
pare you to die, And will lead to the gates of the blessed.
G C G D7
fast to the right, hold___ fast to the right, Wher - ev - er your foot - steps may
G C G
roam, And for - sake not the way of sal - va - tion my boy, That you
D7 G
learned from your moth - er at home.

Hold to God's Unchanging Hand

M: F; F: Bb or C
CD 1-Track 73

Wilson & Eiland

F
1. Time is filled with swift tran - sit - ion,
2. Trust in Him who will not leave you,
3. Cov - et not this world's vain rich - es,
4. When your jour - ney is com - plet - ed,
3
C
F
Naught of Earth un - moved can stand, Build your hopes on things e -
What so ev - er years may bring, If by earth - ly friends for -
That so rap - id - ly de - cay, Seek to gain the heaven - ly
When the val - ley you pass thru, Fair and bright the home in
6
C
F
ter - nal, Hold to God's un - chang - ing hand.
sak - en, Still, more close - ly to Him cling.
treas - ures, They will nev - er pass a - way.
glo - ry, Your en - rap - tured soul will view.
9
F
Hold to his hand
Hold to his hand
C
Cho: Hold to God's un - chang - ing hand. Hold to God's un-chang - ing hand.
14
F
C
F
Build your hopes on things e - ter - nal, Hold to God's un-chang - ing hand.

Stanley Bros., Jimmy Martin, D. Grisman

Home Sweet Home

M: D; F: G or A
CD 1-Track 74

Payne & Bishop

D G D A7 D
1. Mid- pleas - ures and pal - a - ces, Al - though— we may roam, Be it
2. I— gaze on the moon— as I tread— the dear wild, And—
3. An— ex - ile from home,— splen - dor daz - zles in vain, Oh,—
5
G D A7 D
e - ver so hum - ble, There's no— place like home. A
feel that my moth - er now thinks— of her child, As she
give me my low - ly thatched cot - tage a - gain! The
9
A D A7 D
charm from the skies— seems to hal - low us there, Which
looks on that moon— from our own— cot - tage door, Through the
birds sing - ing gai - ly that came— at my call, Give me
13
A D A7 D
seek through the world,— Is ne'er met— with else - where.
wood - bine whose fra - grance will cheer— me no more.
them and that peace— of mind dear - er than all.
17
D A7 D G
Cho: Home! home! Sweet, sweet home! There's no— place like
20
D A7 D
home, There's no— place like home!

Flatt & Scruggs, B. Kincaid, J.D. Crowe, Reno & Smiley, D. Bruce & J. Nunally, BG Album Band

Honey in the Rock

M: G; F: C or D
CD 1-Track 75

Traditional

G
1. I've got a home in that rock don't you see?
Cho: Oh, there's honey in the rock for me,

4
D
I've got a home in that rock don't you see?
Oh, there's honey in the rock for me,

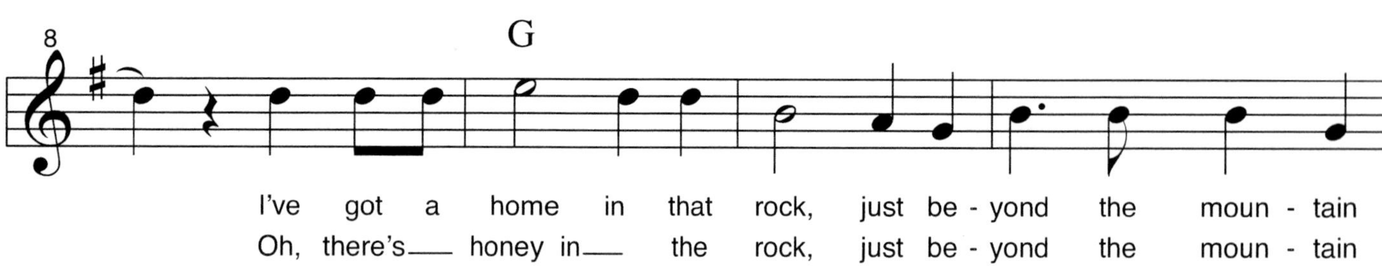
8
G
I've got a home in that rock, just be - yond the moun - tain
Oh, there's honey in the rock, just be - yond the moun - tain

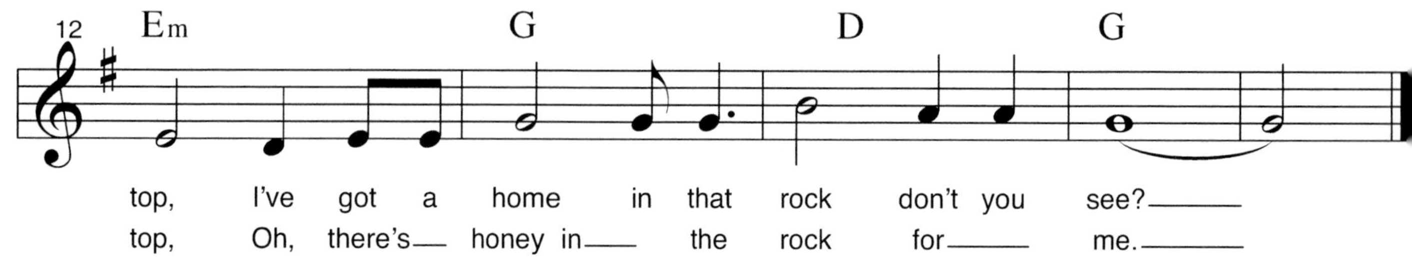
12
Em
G
D
G
top, I've got a home in that rock don't you see?
top, Oh, there's honey in the rock for me.

```
            G
2. God gave Noah the rainbow sign don't you see?
                                                D
God gave Noah the rainbow sign don't you see?
         G
God gave Noah the rainbow sign,
                                   Em
No more water but the fire next time,
         G                D          G
God gave Noah the rainbow sign don't you see?
```

3. Oh, I'm climbing up the King's highway, (2X)
Got old Satan on my track,
Never think of looking back,
Oh, I'm climbing up the King's highway.

Carter Fam., R. Stanley, Lewis Family

Hop High Ladies

*1: D; **F:** G or A* *Traditional*
'D 1-Track 76

D

1. Did you ev - er go to meet - ing Un - cle Joe, Un - cle Joe? Did you
2. Will your horse___ car - ry dou - ble, Un - cle Joe, Un - cle Joe? Will your

A

ev - er go to meet - ing Un - cle Joe, Un - cle Joe? Did you
horse___ car - ry dou - ble, Un - cle Joe, Un - cle Joe? Will your

D

ev - er go to meet - ing Un - cle Joe, Un - cle Joe? I
horse___ car - ry dou - ble, Un - cle Joe, Un - cle Joe? I

G A

don't mind the wea - ther so the wind don't blow.___
don't mind the wea - ther so the wind don't blow.___

D

Cho: Hop high lad - ies 'fore the cake's all dough, Hop high lad - ies 'fore the

A D

cake's all dough, Hop high lad - ies 'fore the cake's all dough, I

G A

don't mind the wea - ther so the wind don't blow.

Hot Corn, Cold Corn

***M:** C; **F:** F or G*
CD 1-Track 77

Tradition

C
G
Cho: Hot corn, cold corn, bring a - long a de - mi - john, Hot corn, cold corn,
1. Up - stairs, down - stairs, out in the kit-chen, Up - stairs, down - stairs,
2. Old Aunt Pol - ly, won't you fill 'er up a - gain? Old Aunt Pol - ly,
3. Preacher's all a' coming and the child - ren are a' cry - ing, Preacher's all a' coming and the

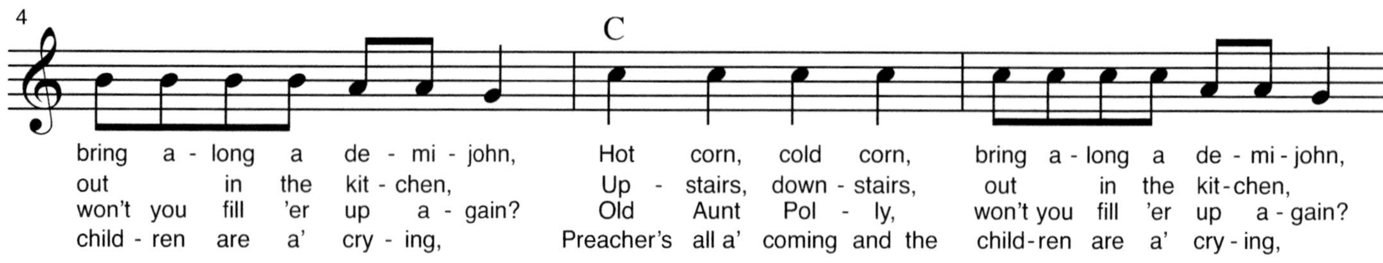
4
C
bring a - long a de - mi - john, Hot corn, cold corn, bring a - long a de - mi - john,
out in the kit - chen, Up - stairs, down - stairs, out in the kit-chen,
won't you fill 'er up a - gain? Old Aunt Pol - ly, won't you fill 'er up a - gain?
child - ren are a' cry - ing, Preacher's all a' coming and the child-ren are a' cry - ing,

7
G
C
Fare thee well Un - cle Bill see you in the morn - ing, yes___ sir!
Old Un - cle Bill just a ra - ring and a pitch - ing, yes___ sir!
Ain't had a drink since I don't know when,___ yes___ sir!
Chick - en necks a' wring - ing and toe - nails a' fly - ing, yes___ sir!

Flatt & Scruggs, Holy Modal Rounders, Here Today
Grisman, Garcia, Rice, NLCR, Dry Branch Fire Squad, D. Bruc

How Can You Treat Me So?

*: E; **F:** A or B*
D 1-Track 78

Dix Bruce

E
1. I been loved and I been hated, To a lone - some life I have been fated, But how can you tre - at me so?
in and out of trouble, I've been so alone and so full of love, But how can you tre - at me
lied and I been cheated, I can't count the ways I been mis - treated, But how can you tre - at me so?
B7
E
1
2. I been
2
so?
E
E7
A
Cho 1: Love has a way of passing - ing me by, I can't hold on ev - en when I try,
B7
A
E
Then here you come to save my life, The cards are stacked and you won't look twice. 3. I been
D.C. al 2nd ending

E
4. I been broke and I been busted, I been robbed by people I trusted,
B7 E
But how can you treat me so?
E
I might win and I might lose, I might be in love, I might have the blues,
B7 E
But how can you treat me so?

Cho 2: All I ever wanted was you,
I've done my part, baby I been true,
When the whole wide world turned me away,
You opened your arms and you would let me stay.

5. In sickness and in health,
Life can be heaven or it can be hell,
But how can you treat me so?

I Ain't Gonna Work Tomorrow

***M:** C; **F:** F or G*
CD 1-Track 79

Traditiona

C
Cho: Oh, I ain't gon - na work to - mor - row,
1. Oh, I've been all a - round this coun - try,
2. Oh, I love my mama and pa - pa too,
3. I'm leaving you this lone - some song,

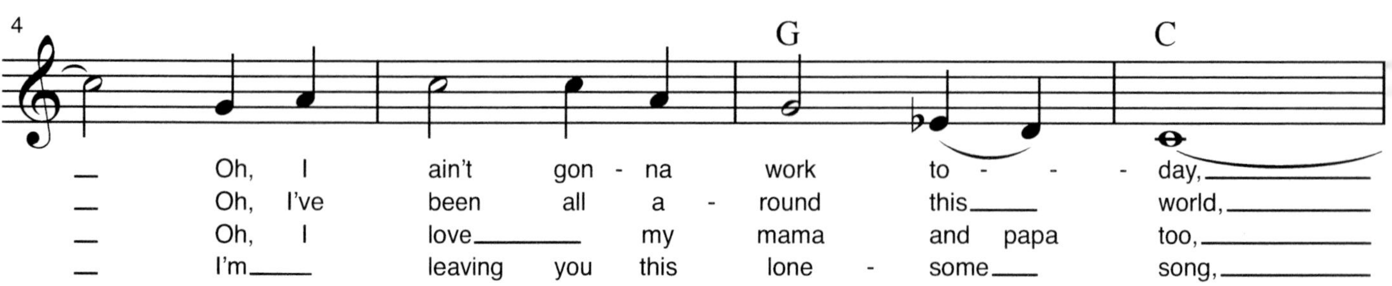
4
G
C
Oh, I ain't gon - na work to - - - day,
Oh, I've been all a - round this world,
Oh, I love my mama and papa too,
I'm leaving you this lone - some song,

8
F
C
I ain't gon - na work to - mor - row,
Oh, I've been all a - round this coun - try,
Oh, I love my mama and pa - pa,
I'm leaving you this lone - some song,

12
G
C
For that is my wed - ding day.
For the sake of one lit - tle girl.
But I'd leave them both to go with you.
'Cause I'm gon - na be gone 'fore long.

Carter Fam., Flatt & Scruggs, Country Gentlemen, Louvin Bros.

I Know You Rider

*1: A mixolydian; **F:** D or E mixolydian*
CD 1-Track 80

A G D A
1. I know you rid - er, Gon - na miss me when I'm gone,
2. Laid down last night, Lord, I could not take my rest,

G D A
I know you rid - er, Gon - na miss me when I'm gone, Gon - na
Laid down last night, Lord, I could not take my rest, My

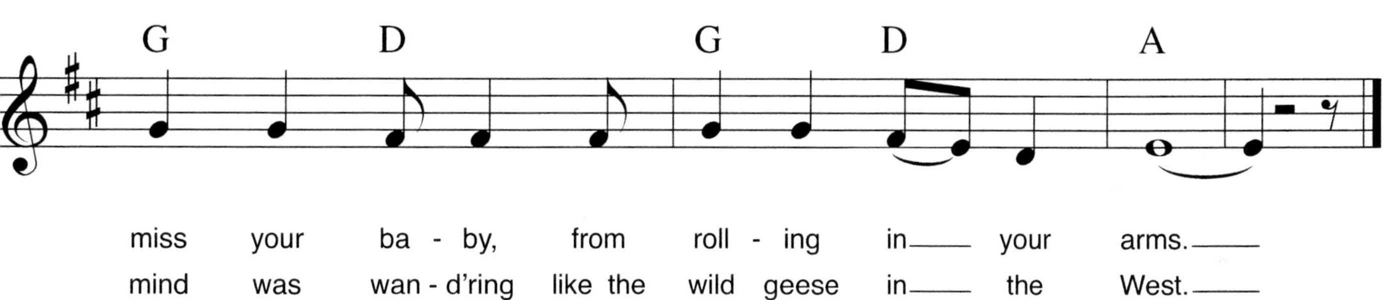

G D G D A
miss your ba - by, from roll - ing in your arms.
mind was wan - d'ring like the wild geese in the West.

A G D A
3. I'm going down to the river, set in my rockin' chair, (2X)
G D G D A
And if the blues don't find me, gonna rock away from here.

4. I know my baby sure is bound to love me some, (2X)
Throws her arms around me like a circle 'round the sun.

5. The sun's gonna shine in my back door some day, (2X)
The wind's gonna rise and blow my blues away.

6. I wish I was a headlight on a northbound train, (2X)
I'd shine my light through the cold Colorado rain.

7. Just as sure as the bird flies in the sky above, (2X)
Life ain't worth living if you ain't with the one you love.

eldom Scene, Grateful Dead

I Never Will Marry

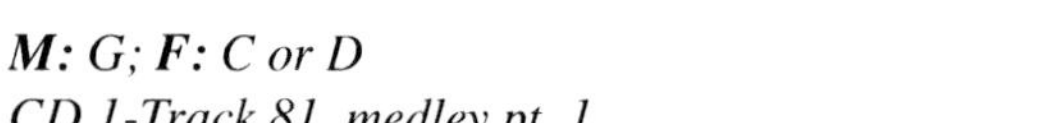
M: G; F: C or D
CD 1-Track 81, medley pt. 1

Traditional

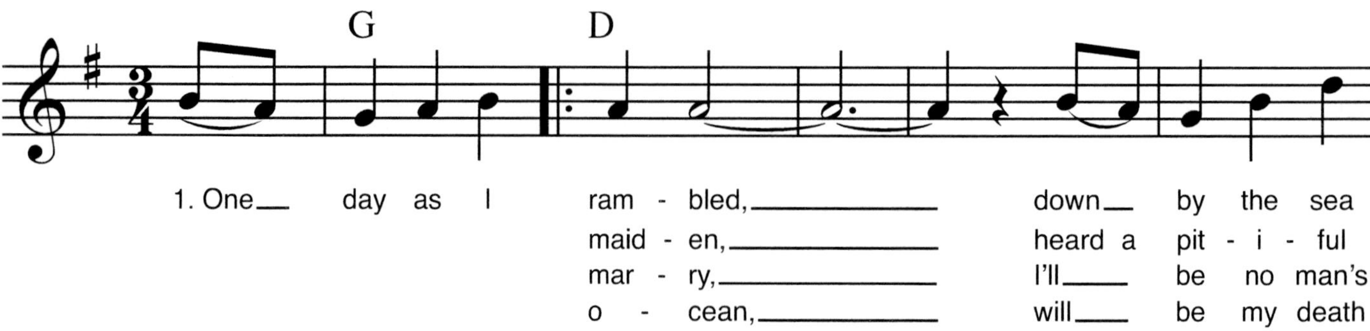
G
D
1. One day as I ram - bled, down by the sea
maid - en, heard a pit - i - ful
mar - ry, I'll be no man's
o - cean, will be my death

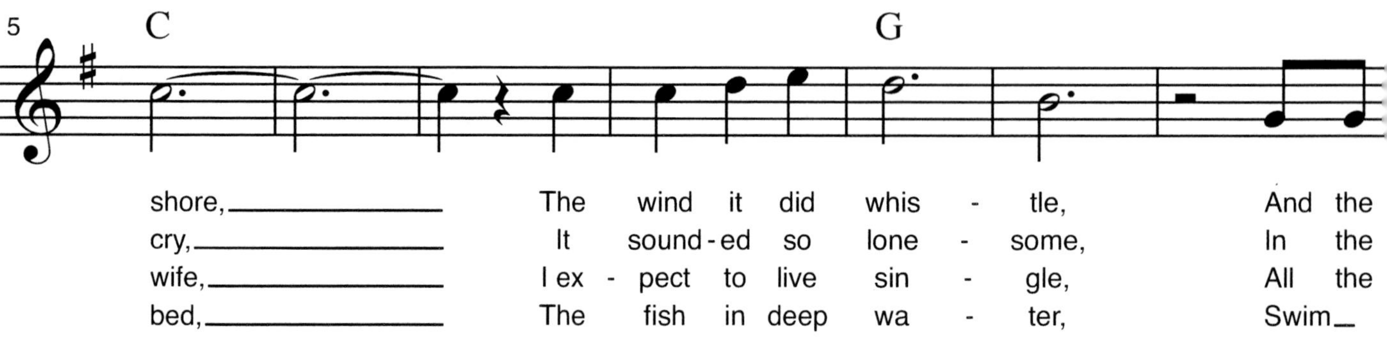
5
C
G
shore, The wind it did whis - tle, And the
cry, It sound - ed so lone - some, In the
wife, I ex - pect to live sin - gle, All the
bed, The fish in deep wa - ter, Swim

12
D
G
Fine
wa - ters did roar.
wa - ters near - by.
days of my life.
o - ver my head.
Last time end after chorus
2. I spied a fair
Cho: I nev - er will
3. The shells in the

G D C
4. My love's gone and left me, he's the one I adore,
G D G
He's gone where I never shall see him no more.

5. She plunged her dear body, in the water's so deep,
She closed her pretty blue eyes, in the water to sleep.

Carter Fam., Country Gentlemen, K. Kallick, J. Val

I Shall Not Be Moved

1: G; F: C or D
'D 1-Track 81, medley pt. 2

Traditional

G
D
1. Glo - ry hal - le - lu - jah, I shall not be moved,
Cho: I shall not be I shall not be moved,

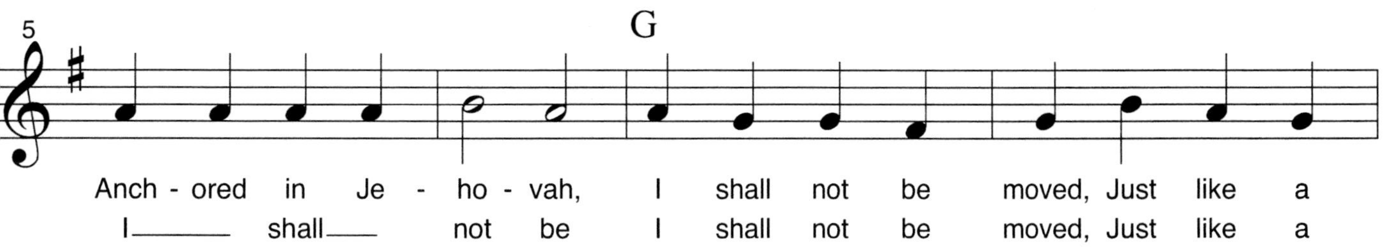
G
Anch - ored in Je - ho - vah, I shall not be moved, Just like a
I shall not be I shall not be moved, Just like a

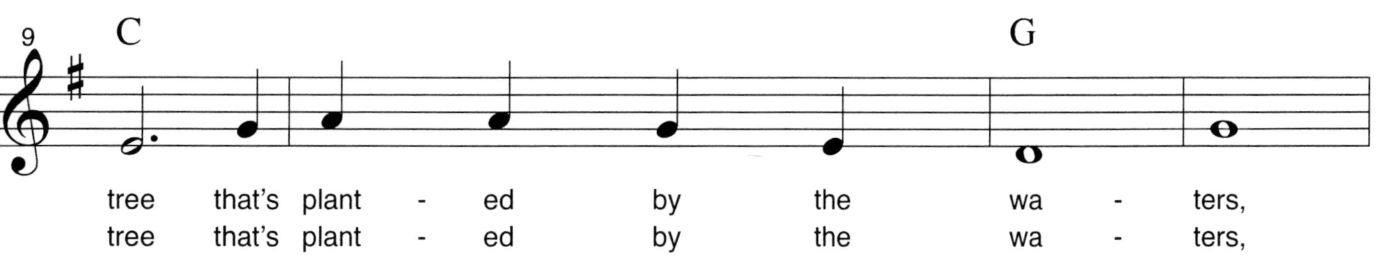
C
G
tree that's plant - ed by the wa - ters,
tree that's plant - ed by the wa - ters,

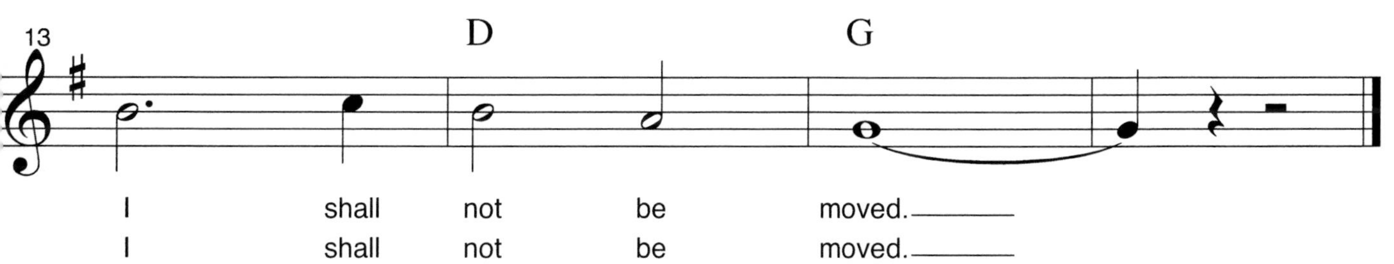
D
G
I shall not be moved.
I shall not be moved.

G D
2. In his love abiding, I shall not be moved,
G
And in Him confiding, I shall not be moved.
C G
Just like a tree that's planted by the waters,
D G
I shall not be moved.

3. Though all Hell assail me, I shall not be moved,
Jesus will not fail me, I shall not be moved. (etc.)

4. Though the tempest rages, I shall not be moved,
On the Rock of Ages, I shall not be moved. (etc.)

reenbriar Boys, Lewis Family, L. Sparks

I Wonder How the Old Folks Are at Home

M: G; F: C or D
CD 1-Track 82
Lambert & Van der Sloot, 190
G C G
1. I won - der how the old folks are at home, I
2. Just a vil - lage and a home - stead on the farm, And a
C
won - der if they miss me while I roam, I
moth - er's love to shield you from all harm, A
G
won - der if they pray for the boy who went a - way, And
moth - er's love so dear and a sweet - heart brave and true, Just a
A D
left his dear old par - ents all a - lone, Cho: I can
vil - lage and a home - stead on the farm.
G C G
hear the cat - tle low - ing in the lane, And I see a - gain the
C G
fields of gol - den grain, I can al - most hear them sigh, as they
A D G
kissed their boy good - bye, I won - der how the old folks are at home.

B. Monroe, R. Stanley, Ken. Colonels, Mac Wiseman, D. Watson
Osborne Bros., Jim & Jesse, Lilly Bros. & D. Stove

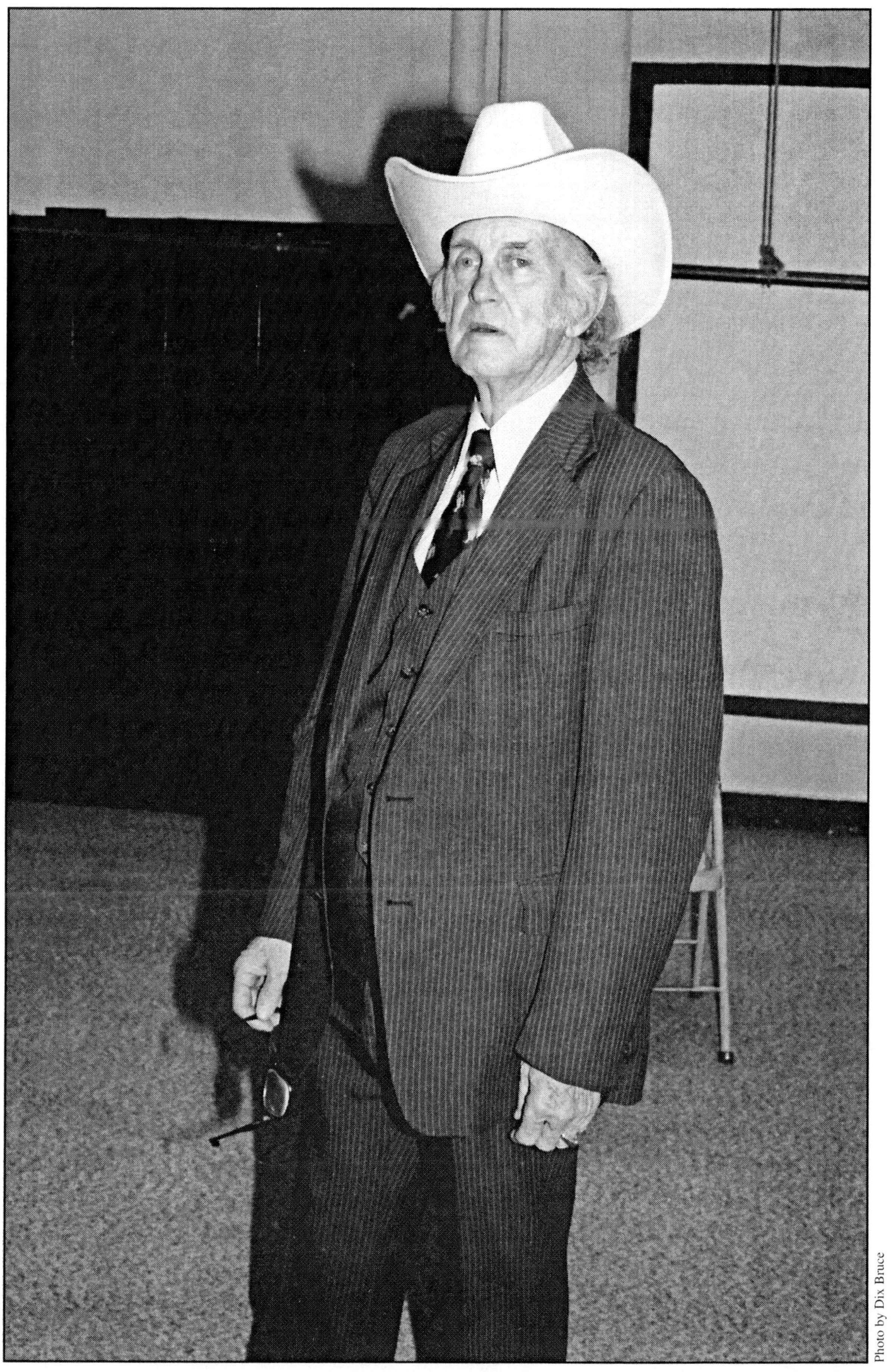

Photo by Dix Bruce

Bill Monroe, the man who invented Bluegrass Music, in 1980.

I'll Be All Smiles Tonight

M: A; F: D or E
CD 1-Track 83

T.B. Ransom, 187

A D A
1. I'll deck my brow with ros - es, My true love may be there.
ev - en those who know me, Will think my heart is light.
8
E A
1.
The gems that oth-ers gave me, Will shine with - in my hair. And
Though my heart may break to - mor - row, I'll be all smiles to - night.
17
2.
A A
be all smiles to - night. Cho: I'll be all smiles to - night, love,
24
D A E7
I'll be all smiles to - night, Though my heart may
30
A
break to - mor - row, I'll be all smiles to - night.

A
2. And when the door he entered,
D A
With a bride upon his arm.
E
I stood and gazed upon him,
A
As though he were some charm.

So, now he smiles on his love,
D A
As once he smiled on me.
E
He meant not to decieve me,
A
There'll be no change in me.

(Chorus after each verse)

3. And when the dance commences,
Oh, how I will rejoice,
I'll sing a song he taught me
Without one faltering voice;
When flatterers come around me
They will think my heart is light,
Though my heart will break tomorrow
I'll be all smiles tonight.

4. And when the dance is over,
And all have gone to rest,
I'll think of him, dear mother,
The one that I love best.
He once did love, believe me,
But he's grown cold and strange,
He sought not to deceive me,
False friends have brought this change.

Carter Fam., B. Clifton, Cox Fam., Louvin Bros., Mac Wisema

I'll Fly Away

K: G; F: C or D
CD 1-Track 84

A.E. Brumlet, 1932

G
1. Some glad morn - ing when this life is o'er,
2. When the shad - ows of this life have gone,
3. Just a few more wear - y days and then,
3
C G
I'll fly a - way, To a home on
I'll fly a - way, Like a bird from these
I'll fly a - way, To a land where
6
D G
God's ce - les - tial shore, I'll fly a - way.
pri - son walls I'll fly, I'll fly a - way.
joys will nev - er end, I'll fly a - way.
9
G
Cho: I'll fly a - way, Oh glo - ry,
11
C G
I'll fly a - way, When I die hal - le -
14
D G
lu - jah by and by, I'll fly a - way.

Stanley Bros., "O Brother" soundtrack, Orborne Bros., Dillards, K. Kallick

I'm Working on a Building

M: D; F: G or A
CD 1-Track 85
Traditional
D
1. If I was a sin - ner, I'll tell you what I would do,
2. If I was a gam - bler, I'll tell you what I would do,
5
A
I'd quit my sin - ning and I'd work on a build - ing
I'd quit my gam - bling and I'd work on a build - ing
8
D
D
too. Cho: I'm work - ing on a build - ing, I'm work - ing on a
too.
11
A
build - ing, I'm work - ing on a build - ing for my Lord,
15
D
for my Lord. It's a Ho - ly Ghost build - ing,
19
it's a Ho - ly Ghost build - ing, It's a Ho - ly Ghost
22
A
D
build - ing for my Lord, for my Lord.

3. If I was a drunkard, I'll tell you what I would do, (etc.)
4. If I was a cheater, I'll tell you what I would do, (etc.)
5. If I was a liar, I'll tell you what I would do, (etc.)
6. If I was a preacher, I'll tell you what I would do,
"I'd keep on preaching and I'd work on a building too."

Carter Fam., B. Monroe, Stanley Bros., R. Stanley,
Ken. Colonels, Hot Rize, Johnson Mtn. Boys, Seldom Scene

In the Garden

: G; F: C or D
D 1-Track 86

C.A. Miles, 1912

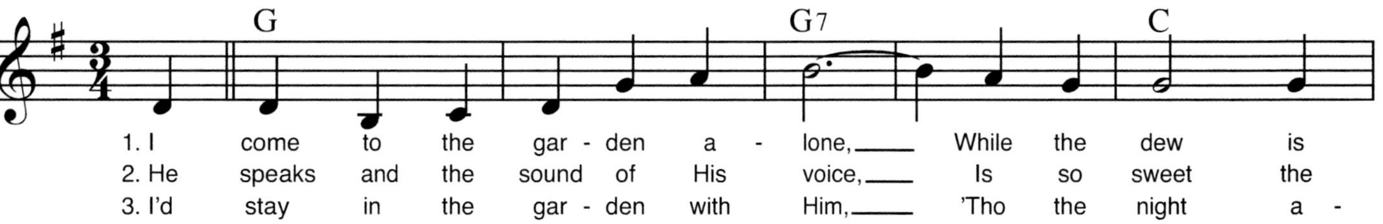
G G7 C
1. I come to the gar - den a - lone, While the dew is
2. He speaks and the sound of His voice, Is so sweet the
3. I'd stay in the gar - den with Him, 'Tho the night a -

G D7
still on the ros - es, And the voice I hear, fall - ing
birds hush their sing - ing, And the mel - o - dy that He
round me be fall - ing, But He bids me go; through the

G E7 A7 D7 A7 D7
on my ear, The Son of God dis - clos - es:
gave to me, With - in my heart is ring - ing:
voice of woe, His voice to me is call - ing:

G D7
Cho: And He walks with me, And He talks with me, And He

C D7 G B7
tells me I am His own. And the joy we share as we

Em Gdim G D7 G
tar - ry there, None oth - er has ev - er known.

In the Pines

***M:** D; **F:** G or A*
CD 1-Track 87

Traditional

D G
1. The long - est train I ev - - er
Cho: In the pines, in the pines, where the sun never
2. I asked my captain for the time of the
3. Lit - tle girl, little girl, what have I
4
D A7 D
saw went down that Geor - gia line.
shines And we shiver when the cold winds blow.
day, He said he'd thrown his watch a - way.
done, That makes you treat me so?
8
G
The en - gine passed at six o'
Woo ooo woo woo ooo
It's a long steel rail, and a short cross
You've caused me to weep, you've caused me to
12
D A7 D
clock, the cab went by at nine.
woo woo ooo woo ooo woo.
tie, I'm on my way back home.
mourn, You've caused me to leave my home.

*B. Monroe, Jimmy Martin, R. Stanley, C. White, Ken. Colonels, Boone Creek
Grateful Dead, Louvin Bros., Mac Wiseman, Osborne Bros., Seldom Scene*

It's Mighty Dark to Travel

M: G; F: C or D
CD 1-Track 88, medley pt. 1

Bill Monroe

G

1. To me she was ___ my lit - tle ___ an - gel, ___
Cho: It's might - y dark ___ for me to ___ trav - el, ___
2. Travel - ing down ___ this lone - some ___ high - way, ___
3. Many a night ___ we strolled to - geth - er, ___

4

C G

___ Sent down to me ___ from God a - bove, ___
___ For my sweet - heart she is gone, ___
___ Think - ing of ___ my love who's gone, ___
___ Talk - ing of ___ our love so fair, ___

8

___ But on that day ___ that I first met her, ___
___ The road is rough ___ and filled with grav - el, ___
___ Know - ing soon ___ we'll be to - geth - er, ___
___ My love for her ___ will nev - er van - ish, ___

12
D G
___ Then I told ___ her of my love. ___
But I must jour - ney on and on. ___
___ She's the on - ly love I've known. ___
___ For I know ___ I'll meet her there. ___

Jesse James

***M:** G; **F:** C or D*
CD 1-Track 88, medley pt. 2

Garshade, ca. 188

G C G
1. Jess - e James was a lad who killed man - y a man, He
2. Jess - e James was a man, a friend to the poor, He'd
5
D G
robbed the Glen - dale train, He took from the
never see a man suffer pain; And with his bro - ther
10
C G
rich and he gave it to the poor, He'd a hand and a
Frank, he robbed the Galla - tin bank, And stopped the
14
D G C
heart and a brain. Cho: Poor Jess - e had a wife to
Glen - dale train.
19
G D
mourn for his life, Three child - ren they were brave,
24
G C
But the dir - ty lit - tle co - ward who shot Mis - ter
28
G D G
How-ard, Has laid poor Jess - e in his grave.

 R. Stanley, Osborne Bros., Fiddlin' John Carson, Country Gentlemen, W. Guthrie

G C G
. It was on a Wednesday night and the moon was shining bright,
D
hey robbed the Glendale train,
G C G
nd the people they did say, for many miles away,
D G
was robbed by Frank and Jesse James.

Repeat chorus after each verse)

. It was with his brother Frank that he robbed the Gallatin bank,
nd carried the money from the town;
was in this very place that they had a little chase,
nd they shot Captain Sheets to the ground.

. They went to the crossing, not very far from there,
nd there they did the same;
Vith the agent on his knees, he delivered up the keys,
o the outlaws, Frank and Jesse James.

. It was Robert Ford, that dirty little coward,
wonder how he does feel,
e ate Jesse's bread and he slept in Jesse's bed,
hen he laid poor Jesse in his grave.

. It was on a Saturday night and Jesse was at home
alking with his family brave,
obert Ford came along like a thief in the night,
nd laid poor Jesse in his grave.

. The people held their breath when they heard of Jesse's death,
nd wondered how he ever came to die.
was one of the gang, called little Robert Ford,
e shot poor Jesse on the sly.

. Jesse went to his rest with his hand on his breast,
he devil will be upon his knee,
e was born one day in the county of Clay,
nd came from a solitary race.

Jimmie Brown, the Newsboy

M: D; F: G or A
CD 1-Track 89

W.S. Hays, 187

D
1. I___ sell the morn - ing pa - per sir my
2. You can hear me yell - ing "Morn - ing Star"___
3. Nev - er mind___ sir how I look, don't
4. I'm___ aw - ful cold___ and hun - gry sir, my
5. My___ fath - er died___ a drunk - ard sir, I've
6. My___ moth - er al - ways tells me sir, I've

3
A7
name is Jim - my Brown,___ Ev - ery bod - y
running a - long the street,___ Got no hat___ up -
look at me and frown,___ I sell the morn - ing
clothes are might - y thin,___ I wander a - bout___ from
heard my moth - er say,___ I am help - ing
nothing in the world to lose,___ I'll get a place___ in

6
D
knows that I'm___ the news - boy of the town.___
on my head,___ no shoes up - on my feet.___
pap - er sir,___ my name is Jim - mie Brown.___
place to place___ my dail - y bread to win.___
moth - er sir,___ as I jour - ney on my way.___
heav - en sir,___ to sell the Gos - pel News.___

Carter Fam., Flatt & Scruggs, B. Monroe, C. White, Mac Wiseman

John Hardy

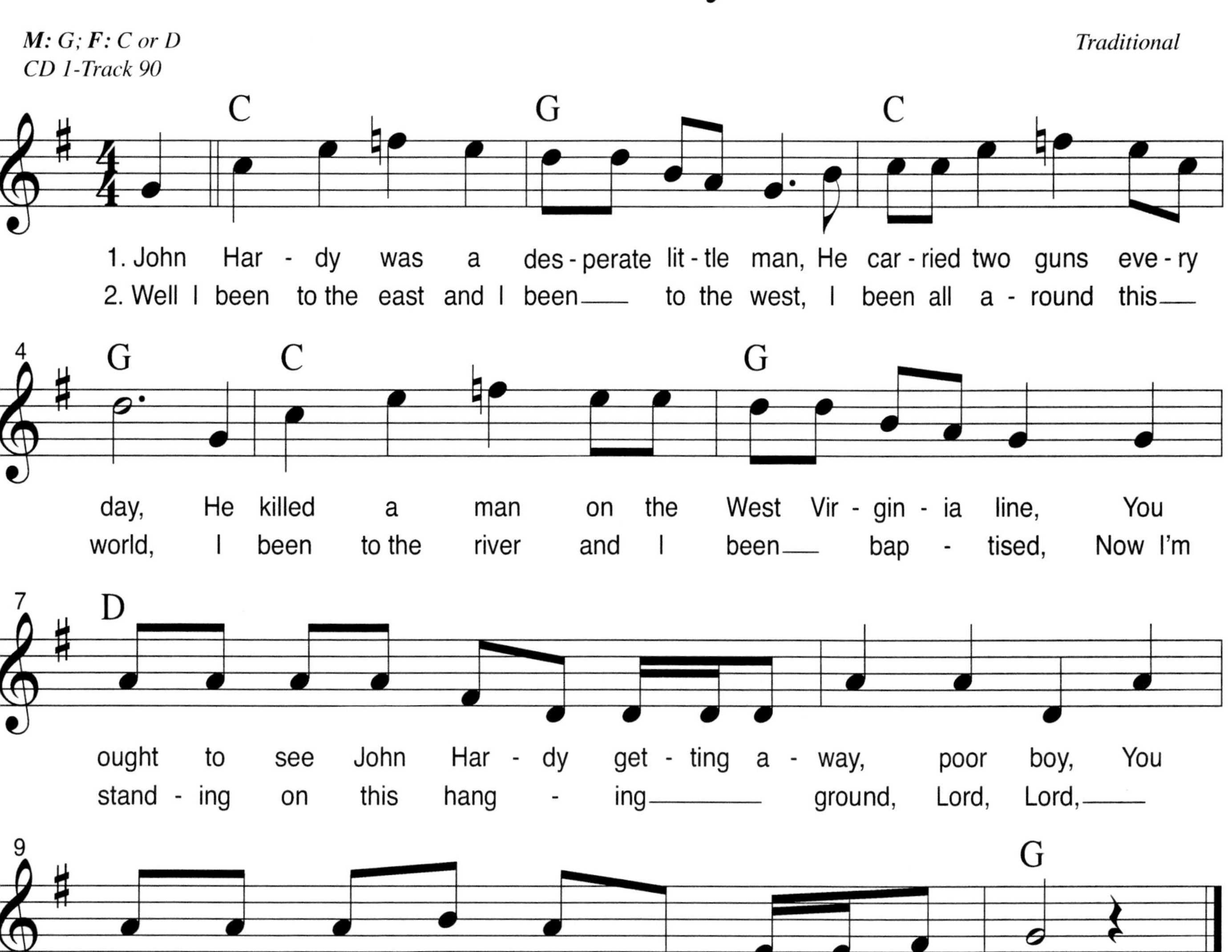

M: G; F: C or D
CD 1-Track 90
Traditional
C G C
1. John Har - dy was a des - perate lit - tle man, He car - ried two guns eve - ry
2. Well I been to the east and I been to the west, I been all a - round this
G C G
day, He killed a man on the West Vir - gin - ia line, You
world, I been to the river and I been bap - tised, Now I'm
D
ought to see John Har - dy get - ting a - way, poor boy, You
stand - ing on this hang - ing ground, Lord, Lord,
G
ought to see John Har - dy get - ting a - way.
Stand - ing on this hang - ing ground.

C G
Hangman, hangman, hold your rope,
G
st a little while,
C G
ıought I heard my father's voice,
D
: travelled ten thousand long miles, Lord, Lord,
G
avelled ten thousand long miles.

Did you bring me any silver or gold,
money to pay my fee?
did you come to see me hung,
on this hanging tree, Lord, Lord,
on this hanging tree?

No, I didn't bring no silver nor gold,
r money to pay your fee,
t I did come to see you hung,
on that hanging tree, Lord, Lord,
on that hanging tree.

6. Hangman, hangman, hold your rope,
Just a little while,
I thought I heard my sweetheart's voice,
She travelled ten thousand long miles, Lord, Lord,
Travelled ten thousand long miles.

7. Oh yes, I brought that silver and gold,
And money to pay your fee,
I have come for to take you home,
And keep you there with me, Lord, Lord,
And keep you there with me.

8. Well, John Hardy run for that old state line,
It was there he thought he'd go free,
But a man walked up and took him by the arm,
Saying "Johnny walk along with me, Lord, Lord,
Johnny walk along with me."

9. Well the first one to visit John Hardy in his cell,
Was a little girl dressed in blue,
She came down to that old jail cell,
Singing "Johnny, I've been true to you, Lord knows,
Johnny I've been true to you."

10. Then the next one to visit John Hardy in his cell,
A little girl dressed in red,
She came down to that old jail cell,
Singing "Johnny, I'd rather see you dead, Lord, Lord,
God knows, Johnny I'd rather see you dead."

11. John Hardy stood in his old jail cell,
The tears running down from his eyes,
He said "I've been the death of many poor boy,
But my six-shooter never told a lie, Lord, Lord,
No my six-shooter never told a lie."

ırter Fam., Flatt & Scruggs, B. Monroe. Ken. Colonels, Poor Richard's Almanac

John Henry

M: C; F: F or G
CD 1-Track 91

Traditional

C
1. When John Hen - ry was a lit - tle ba - by, Just a'
2. John Hen - ry had a lit - tle wo-man, And her
5
G
C
sit - ting on his pap - py's knee, Well he picked up his
name was Pol - ly Anne, John Hen - ry took
10
ham - mer and a lit - tle piece of steel, Said "That
sick and he had to go to bed, Pol - ly
13
ham - mer's gon - na be the death of me, Lord, Lord,
Anne drove steel like a man, Lord, Lord, Polly
17
G
C
Ham - mer's gon - na be the death of me."
Anne drove steel like a man.

B. Monroe, Flatt & Scruggs, Stanley Bros., R. Stanley, Jimmy Martin, Ken. Colonels, D. Watson, W. Guthrie, Skillet Lickers, Fiddlin' John Carson, Dry Branch Fire Squad

C
. Captain said to John Henry,
G
Gonna bring me a steam drill 'round,
C
ionna take that steam drill out on the job,
ionna drive that steel on down, Lawd, Lawd,
G C
ionna drive that steel on down."

. John Henry told his captain,
aid, "A man ain't nothin' but a man,
nd before I'd let that steam drill beat me down,
l die with this hammer in my hand, Lawd, Lawd,
l die with the hammer in my hand."

. Now the captain told John Henry,
believe this mountain's caving in,"
ohn Henry said to his captain, "Oh my,
's my hammer just a'sucking wind, Lawd, Lawd,
's my hammer just a' sucking wind."

. John Henry told his captain,
ooky yonder what I see,
our drill's done broke and your hole's done choke,
nd you can't drive steel like me, Lawd, Lawd,
nd you can't drive steel like me."

. John Henry was hammering on the mountain,
nd his hammer was striking fire,
e drove so hard 'til he broke his poor heart,
nd he laid down his hammer and he died, Lawd, Lawd,
aid down his hammer and he died.

. They took John Henry to the graveyard,
nd they buried him in the sand,
nd every locomotive come roaring by,
ays, "Yonder lies a steel driving man, Lawd, Lawd,
onder lies a steel driving man."

Jordan

M: G; F: C or D
CD 1-Track 92
Traditional
G
1. Oh sin - ner as you tread life's jour - ney, Take Je - sus as your dai - ly
2. That aw - ful day of judge - ment, Is com - ing in the by and
4
guide, Though you may feel pure and saint - ly, With -
by, We'll see our Lord des - cend - ing, In
7
A
D
out him walk - ing by your side, But
glor - y from on high, Oh,
10
G
when you come to make the cross - ing, At the
let us keep in touch with Jes - us, And
12
end - ing of your pil - grim way, If you e - ver will meet our
in his grace the love of God, We may be ev - er called
15
D
G
Sav - iour, You'll sure - ly meet him on that day
rea - dy, When he calls us o - ver Jor - dan's tide.
18
D
Cho 1: Now look at that cold Jor - dan, Look at those deep

Stanley Bros., E. L. Harris, Ken. Colonels

22
G C D G
wat - ers, Look at that wide riv - er, Oh, hear the migh - ty bil - lows
26
D
roll. You bet - ter take Je - sus with you, He's a true com -
30
G C
pan - ion, For I'm sure with - out him, That you
33
D G
nev - er will make it o'er.
Tag: Oh
37
G D
what, oh what you gon - na do? Oh what, oh what you gon - na
40
G C
say? Oh how, oh how you gon - na feel? When you
43
G D G
come to the end of the way?

Just a Closer Walk with Thee

M: A; F: D or E
CD 1-Track 93

Traditional

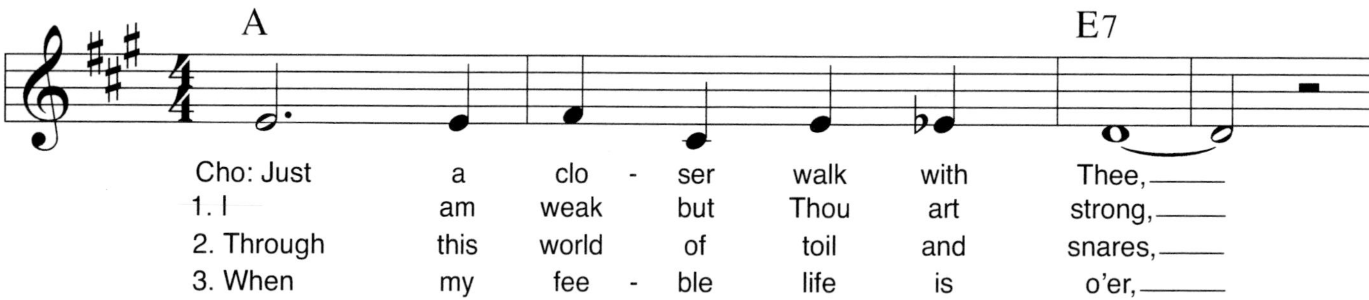

A
E7
Cho: Just a clo - ser walk with Thee,
1. I am weak but Thou art strong,
2. Through this world of toil and snares,
3. When my fee - ble life is o'er,

5
A
Grant it Je - sus, is my plea,
Je - sus keep me from all wrong,
If I fal - ter, Lord, who cares?
Time for me will be no more,

9
A7
D
Dai - ly walk - ing close to Thee, Let it
I'll be sat - is - fied as long,
Who but Thee my bur - den shares? None but
Guide me gent - ly, safe - ly o'er To thy

13
A
E7
A
be, dear Lord let it be.
As I walk close to Thee.
Thee, oh Lord, none but Thee.
shore, dear Lord, to thy shore.

Just as I Am

: C; ***F:*** *F or G*
D 1-Track 94

Elliott & Bradbury

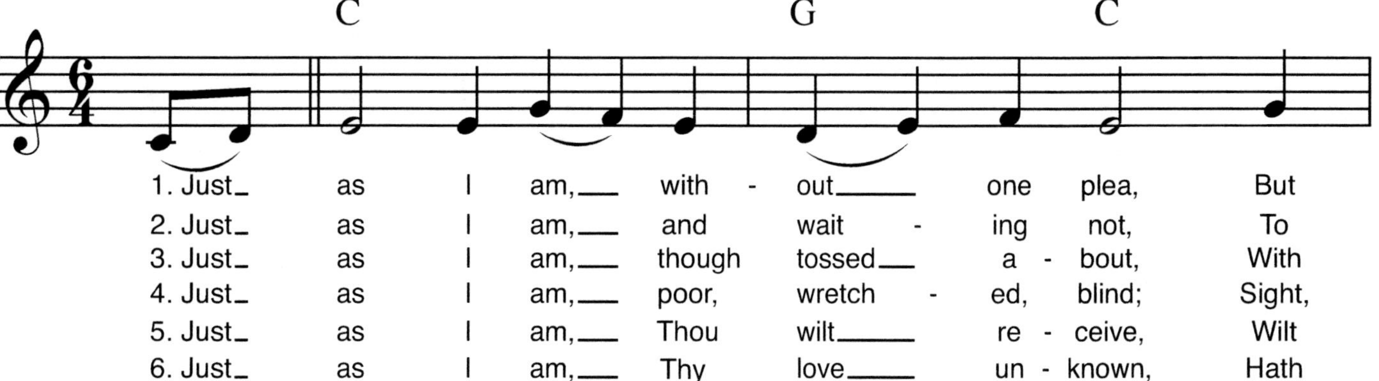

C G C
1. Just_ as I am,__ with - out____ one plea, But
2. Just_ as I am,__ and wait - ing not, To
3. Just_ as I am,__ though tossed__ a - bout, With
4. Just_ as I am,__ poor, wretch - ed, blind; Sight,
5. Just_ as I am,__ Thou wilt____ re - ceive, Wilt
6. Just_ as I am,__ Thy love____ un - known, Hath

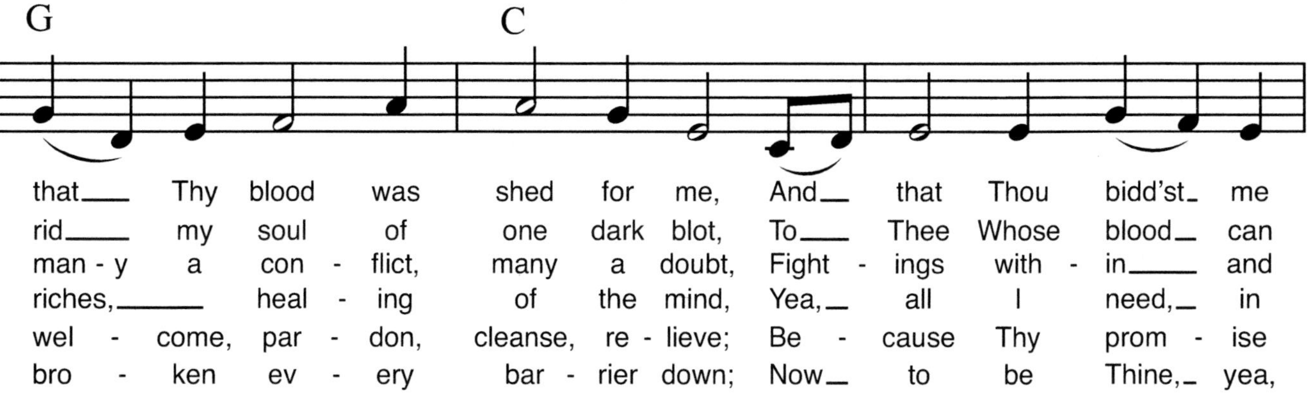

3
G C
that__ Thy blood was shed for me, And_ that Thou bidd'st_ me
rid__ my soul of one dark blot, To__ Thee Whose blood_ can
man - y a con - flict, many a doubt, Fight - ings with - in____ and
riches,_____ heal - ing of the mind, Yea,_ all I need,_ in
wel - come, par - don, cleanse, re - lieve; Be - cause Thy prom - ise
bro - ken ev - ery bar - rier down; Now_ to be Thine,_ yea,

6
F C G C
come to Thee,__ O Lamb of God,_ I come! I come!___
cleanse each spot,__ O Lamb of God,_ I come! I come!___
fears with - out,___ O Lamb of God,_ I come! I come!___
Thee to find___ O Lamb of God,_ I come! I come!___
I be - lieve___ O Lamb of God,_ I come! I come!___
Thine a - lone,___ O Lamb of God,_ I come! I come!___

Just Over in the Gloryland

***M:** A; **F:** D or E*
CD 1-Track 95, medley pt. 1

Acuff & Dean, 1906

A D A
1. I've a home pre - pared, where the saints a - bide, Just
2. I am on my way to those man - sions fair, Just
3. What a joy - ful thought that my Lord, I'll see, Just
4. With the blood washed throng, I will shout and sing, Just
3
E A
o - ver in the Glor - y - land! And I long to be by my
o - ver in the Glor - y - land! There to sing God's praise and His
o - ver in the Glor - y - land! And with kind - red saved, there for -
o - ver in the Glor - y - land! Glad ho - sannas to Christ, the
6
D A E A
Sav - ior's side, Just o - ver in the Glor - y - land! Cho: Just
glor - y share, Just o - ver in the Glor - y - land!
ev - er be, Just o - ver in the Glor - y - land!
Lord and King, Just o - ver in the Glor - y - land!
9
A D A
o - ver in the Glor - y - land, I'll join the hap - py an - gel band, Just
13
E A
o - ver in the Glor - y - land! Just o - ver in the Glor - y - land, There
17
D A E A
with the might - y host I'll stand, Just o - ver in the Glor - y - land!

B. Monroe, Stanley Bros., R. Stanley, Jim & Jesse, Ken. Colonels, J.E. Mainer

Katy Cline

*: A; **F:** D or E*
D 1-Track 95, medley pt. 2

A
Cho: Tell me that you love me, Ka - ty Cline,
1. Who is it knows Ka - ty Cline,
2. If I was a lit - tle bee, A -
3. If I was a lit - tle bird, I'd

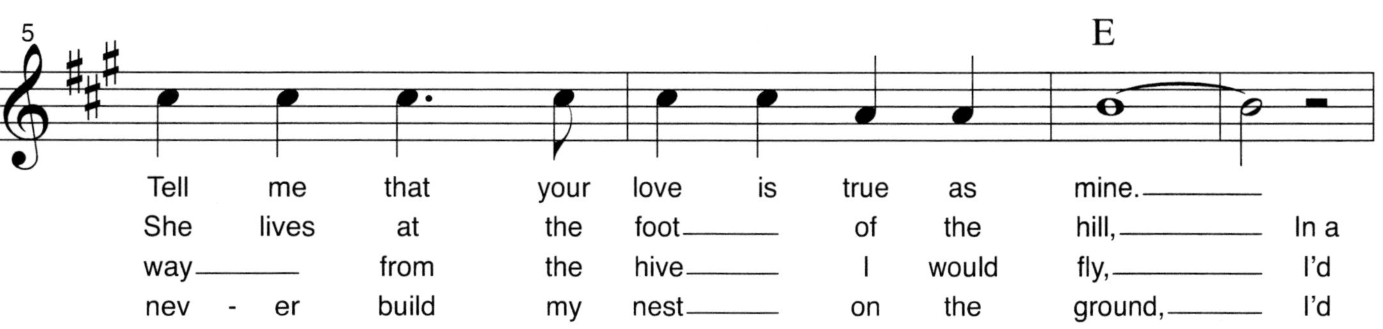
5
E
Tell me that your love is true as mine.
She lives at the foot of the hill, In a
way from the hive I would fly, I'd
nev - er build my nest on the ground, I'd

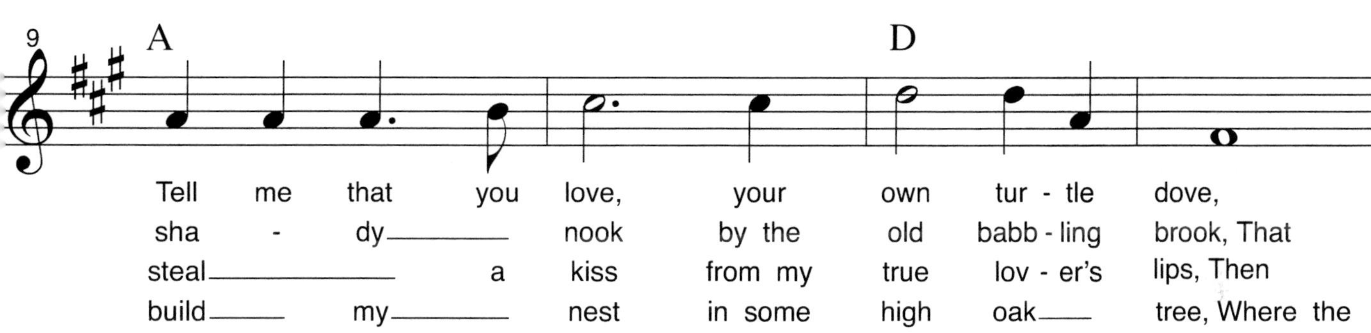
9
A
D
Tell me that you love, your own tur - tle dove,
sha - dy nook by the old babb - ling brook, That
steal a kiss from my true lov - er's lips, Then
build my nest in some high oak tree, Where the

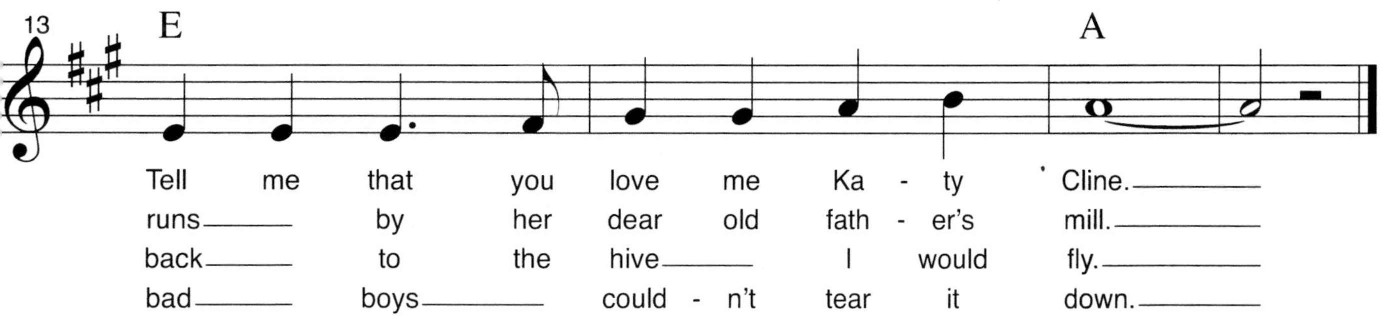
13
E
A
Tell me that you love me Ka - ty Cline.
runs by her dear old fath - er's mill.
back to the hive I would fly.
bad boys could - n't tear it down.

Katy Daley

M: C; F: F or G
CD 1-Track 96

Tradition

C

1. With her old man, she came from Tip - per - ar - y,
Cho: Oh, come on down the moun - tain, Ka - ty Dal - ey,
2. The judge said "Pay at - ten - tion, Ka - ty Dal - ey,
3. So, to the jail, they took poor Ka - ty Dal - ey,
4. Be - fore the pear - ly gates there stood poor Ka - ty,

4 G

In the pi - o - neer days of for - ty - two.
Come on down the moun - tain, Ka - ty do,
I'm sor - ry, that I have to sen - tence you,
Ver - y soon the gates were o - pen wide.
St. Pe - ter said "Good brew - ers they are few,

8

Her old man was shot in Tomb - stone Cit - y, For the
Can't you hear us call - ing Ka - ty Dal - ey? We
All the boys in court have drunk your whis - key, And, to
An an - gel came and took poor Ka - ty Da - ley,
Step in - side the gates dear Ka - ty Da - ley, And

13
C
mak - ing of his good old moun - tain dew.
want to drink your good old moun - tain dew.
tell the truth, I've drunk a lit - tle too.
Took her far a - cross the Great Di - vide.
start to make your good old moun - tain dew."

R. Stanley, Mac Wiseman, Lonesome River Ban

Katy Dear

I: D; F: G or A
CD 1-Track 97

Traditional

G
1. Oh, Ka - ty dear,___ go ask your
2. Oh Will - ie dear,___ I can - not

D G
moth - er,___ If you can be a
ask___ her,___ She's in her room, a'

D A
bride of mine.___ If she says
taking a rest.___ And by her

G D
yes,___ come back and tell___ me,___ If she says
side___ is a sil - ver dag - ger,___ To slay the

A D
no___ we'll run a - way.___
man___ that I love best.___

     G   D
3. Oh, Katy dear, go ask your father,
        G D   A
If you can be a bride of mine.
       G   D
If he says yes, come back and tell me,
       A   D
If he says no, we'll run a-way.

4. Oh, Willie dear, I cannot ask him,
He's in his room a' taking a rest,
And by his side, that silver dagger,
To slay the one, that I love best.

5. Then he picked up that silver dagger,
And stove it through his weary heart.
Saying, "Goodbye Katy, goodbye darling,
At last the time has come to part."

6. Then she picked up that bloody dagger,
And stove it through her lilly white breast,
Saying, "Goodbye Willie, goodbye mother,
I'll die with the one that I love best."

ue Sky Boys, Country Gentlemen, J. Reischman

Keep on the Sunnyside

***M:** G; **F:** C or D*
CD 1-Track 98, medley pt. 1

Blenkhorn & Entwis

G C G
1. There's a dark and a trou - bled side of life, There's a
2. Though the storm in its fu - ry broke to - day, Crush - ing
3. Let us greet with a song of hope each day, Though the
3
D7
bright and a sun - ny - side, too, Though we meet with the dark - ness and
hopes that we cher - ished so dear, Storm and clouds will in time pass a -
mo - ments be cloud - y or fair, Let us trust in our Sav - iour al -
6
G D G
strife, The sun - ny - side we al - so may view.
way, The sun a - gain will shine bright and clear.
ways, Who keep - eth eve - ry - one in His care.
9
G C G
Cho: Keep on the sun - ny - side, Al - ways on the sun - ny - side,
11
D G
Keep on the sun - ny - side of life, It will help us ev - ery day, It will
14
C G C G D G
bright - en all the way, If we keep on the sun - ny - side of life.

Carter Fam., Reno & Harrell, Bluegrass Band, D. Watson
Osborne Bros., Flatt & Scruggs, Mac Wiseman, Nitty Gritty Dirt Band

Henry C. Gilliland, left, holding the decorated fiddle "Texas Shorty" later acquired. See below.

TEXAS SHORTY

Photos courtesy Jim Chancellor

Knoxville Girl

M: G; F: C or D
CD 1-Track 98, medley pt. 2
Traditional
G C
1. I met a lit - tle girl in___ Knox - ville, A town you
2. She fell___ down on her_ bended knees, For mer - cy
6 G
all know well,____ And ev - ery Sun - day eve -
she did cry,_____ "Oh, Wil - lie dear, don't kill me
12 A D G
ning, Out in her home I'd dwell,____ We went to
here, I'm un - pre - pared to die,"_____ She nev - er
18 C G
take an__ eve - ning walk, A - bout a mile from town,____
spoke an - oth - er word, I on - ly beat her more,____
24
I picked a stick up off the ground, And
Un - til the ground a - round__ me, With -
29 D G
knocked that fair girl down.____
in her blood did flow._____

Louvin Bros., Stanley Bros., Blue Sky Boys
Mac Wiseman, Jimmy Martin, Osborne Bros

G
I took her by her golden curls,
C G
drug her 'round and 'round,
threw her into the river,
A D
hat flows through Knoxville town,
G
o down, go down, you Knoxville girl,
C G
ith dark and rolling eyes,
o down, go down, you Knoxville girl,
D G
ou'll never be my bride.

Starting back to Knoxville,
ot there about midnight,
y mother she was worried,
nd woke up in a fright,
aying, "Son, oh son, what have you done,
bloody your clothes so?"
old my anxious mother,
een bleeding at my nose.

I called for me a candle,
light myself to bed,
called for me a handkerchief,
bind my aching head,
olled and tumbled the whole night through,
s troubles were for me,
ke flames of Hell around my bed,
nd in my eyes could see.

They carried me down to Knoxville,
ey put me in a cell,
y friends all tried to get me out,
ut none could go my bail,
n here to waste my life away,
own in this dirty old jail,
ecause I murdered that Knoxville girl,
e girl I loved so well.

Late Last Night

M: C; F: F or G
CD 2-Track 1

Traditional

F C
1. It was late last night when Wil - lie came home, I
Cho: Way down town just a' fool - ing a - round, They

3
G C F
heard him a' rap-ping on the door. He was slip - ping and a' slid - ing with his
took me to the jail, It's oh me, and it's

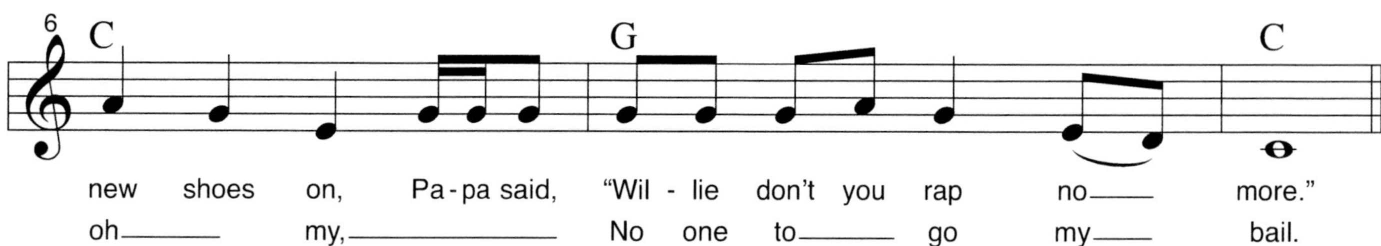
6
C G C
new shoes on, Pa-pa said, "Wil - lie don't you rap no more."
oh my, No one to go my bail.

F C
2. Wish I was over at my sweet Sally's house,
G C
Sitting in that big armed chair,
F C
One arm around this old guitar,
G C
Other one around my dear.

3. This one old shirt is about all I got,
And a dollar is all I crave,
I brought nothing with me into this old world,
Ain't gonna take nothing to my grave.

4. I like the hills of West Virginia,
I like the hills of Tennessee,
North, south, east or west,
It's home, sweet home to me.

D. Watson, Stanley Bros., R. Stanley, T. Rice
Dry Branch Fire Squad, Nitty Gritty Dirt Band

Leave it There

*: D; **F:** G or A*
D 2-Track 2

C.A. Tindley, 1916

D G
1. If the world from you with-hold of its sil - ver and its gold, And you
2. If your bod - y suf - fers pain and your health you can't re - gain, And your
D A D
have to get a - long with mea - ger fare, Just re - mem - ber, in His Word, how He
soul is al - most sink - ing in des - pair, Jes - us knows the pain you feel, He can
G D A D
feeds the lit - tle bird; Take your bur - den to the Lord and leave it there. Cho: Leave it
save and He can heal; Take your bur - den to the Lord and leave it there.
D G
there, leave it there, Take your bur - den to the Lord and leave it
D G
there. If you trust and nev - er doubt, He will sure - ly bring you out. Take your
D A D
bur - den to the Lord and leave it there.

D G
When your enemies assail and your heart begins to fail,
D A
n't forget that God in heaven answers prayer;
D G
will make a way for you and will lead you safely through,
D A D
ke your burden to the Lord and leave it there.

4. When your youthful days are gone and old age is stealing on,
And your body bends beneath the weight of care;
He will never leave you then, He'll go with you to the end,
Take your burden to the Lord and leave it there.

5. If your mother leaves you here, grief and sorrow you must bear,
And you feel the only friend you have is gone,
But whenever you feel alone, He will take you in his arms,
Take your burden to the Lord and leave it there.

Let Me Rest at the End of My Journey

M: G; F: C or D
CD 2-Track 3

Traditiona

G C G
1. Let me rest at the end of my jour - ney, I'm
cow - boy's life on the old cat - tle trail, Herding
5 D G
wear - y, tir - ed, and old. Let me
dog - gies is all that he knows. A cow - boy's
10 C G
rest at the end of my jour - ney, Heav-en is my
life on the old cat - tle trail, From Tex - as to
14 D G C
home and my goal. Cho: Old paint is tired and his
old Mex - i - co.
19 G D
feet are all sore, We'll ride the range no more.
24 G C G
Let me rest at the end of my jour - ney,
29 D G Fine
Heav - en is my home and my goal. 2. A

B. Monroe, R. Stanle

The Letter Edged in Black

': D; F: G or A
D 2-Track 4
Hattie Nevada, 1897
D
A
1. I was stand - ing by my win - dow yes - ter - day morn -
2. He rang the bell and whist - led as he wait -
4
ing, With - out a thought of wor - ry or of
ed, He said "Good morn - ing, to you
7
D
care. When I saw the post - man com - ing up the
Jack," But he lit - tle knew the sor - row that he
11
G
A
D
path - way, With such a hap - py face and jol - ly air.
brought me, When he hand - ed me that let - ter edged in black.


```
D                                          A
3. With trembling hands, I took that letter from him,
                                         D
I broke the seal and this is what it said:
                                                   G
"Come home my boy, your dear old father wants you,
         A                                          D
Come home my boy, your dear old mother's dead."
```

4. "Those angry words I wished I'd never spoken,
You know I didn't mean them don't you Jack?
I bow my head in sadness and in sorrow,
While I'm writing you this letter edged in black."

5. "The last words that your mother ever uttered,
Were 'Tell my boy, I want him to come back,'
May the angels bear me witness I am asking,
Your forgiveness in this letter edged in black."

(Repeat verse 2)

Kincaid, Goose Island Ramblers, Fiddlin' John Carson, Mac Wiseman

Life's Railway to Heaven

M: D; F: G or A
CD 2-Track 5

Traditional

D
1. Life is like a moun - tain rail - road, With an
2. You will roll up grades of trial, You will
3. You will of - ten find ob - struc - tions, look for
4. As you roll a - cross the tres - tle, span - ning
5
G D
en - - - gin - eer that's brave. You must make
cross the bridge of strife. See that Christ
storms of wind and rain. On a fill,
Jor - - dan's swell - ing tide. You be - hold
10
E7
the run suc - cess - ful from the cra - dle to the
is your Con - duct - or on this light - ning train of
or curve, or tres - tle, they will al - most ditch your
the Un - ion De - pot in - to which your train will
15
A7 D
grave. Watch the hills, the curves the tun - nels,
life. Al - ways mind - ful of ob - struc - tion,
train. Put your trust a - lone in Jes - us,
glide. There you'll meet the Super - in - ten - dent,
20
G D D
Nev - er fal - ter, nev - er fail. Keep your hand
do your du - ty, nev - er fail. Keep your hand
nev - er fal - ter, nev - er fail. Keep your hand
God the Fath - er, God the Son. With the heart -

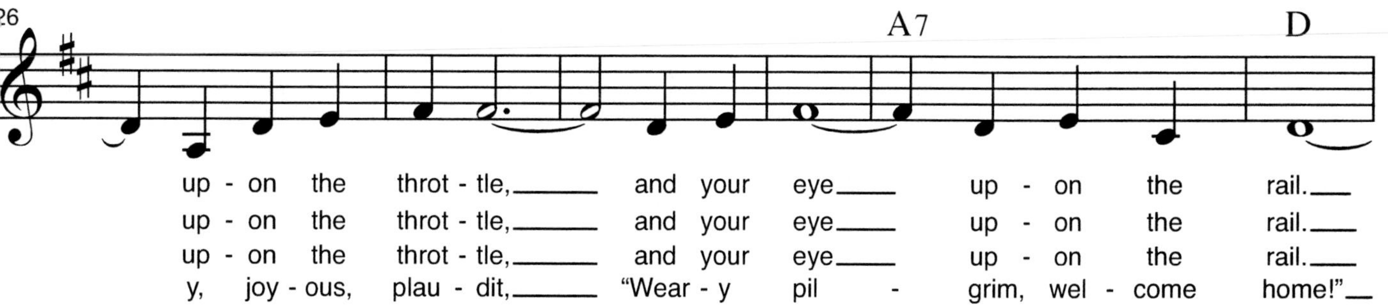
26
A7
D
up - on the throt - tle, and your eye up - on the rail.
up - on the throt - tle, and your eye up - on the rail.
up - on the throt - tle, and your eye up - on the rail.
y, joy - ous, plau - dit, "Wear - y pil - grim, wel - come home!"

32
G
D
Cho: Bless - ed sav - ior thou wilt guide us, 'Till we reach

A7
D
G
that bliss - ful shore, Where the an - gels wait to join us,

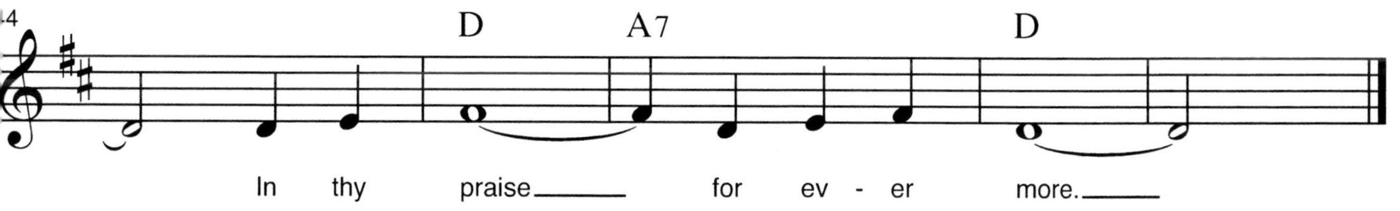
D
A7
D
In thy praise for ev - er more.

Kincaid, B. Monroe, Greenbriar Boys, Blue Sky Boys,
n & Jesse, Nitty Gritty Dirt Band

Li'l Liza Jane

M: C; F: F or G
CD 2-Track 6

Traditiona

C
1. I got a gal and you got none, Li'l Li - za Jane,
2. Li - za Jane done come to me, Li'l Li - za Jane,
3. Come my love and live with me, Li'l Li - za Jane,
4. House and lot in Bal - ti - more, Li'l Li - za Jane,

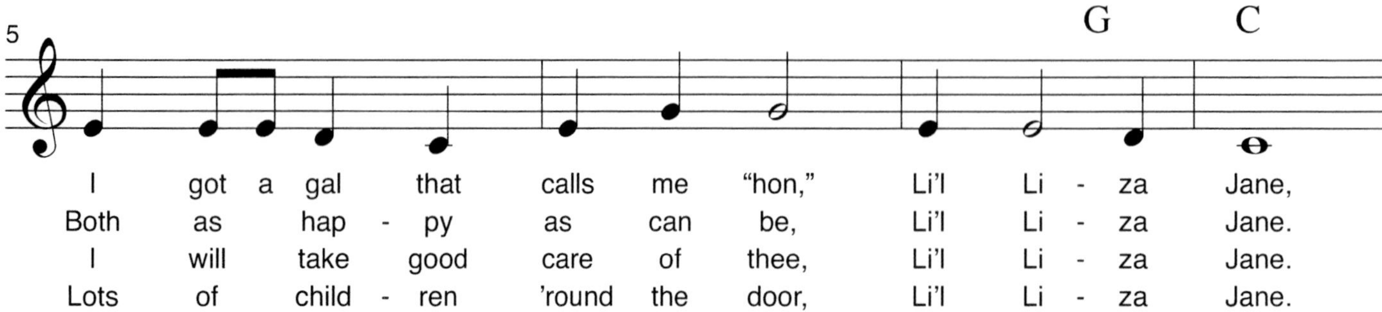
5
G C
I got a gal that calls me "hon," Li'l Li - za Jane,
Both as hap - py as can be, Li'l Li - za Jane.
I will take good care of thee, Li'l Li - za Jane.
Lots of child - ren 'round the door, Li'l Li - za Jane.

9
Cho: Oh, Li'l Li - za, Li'l Li - za Jane,

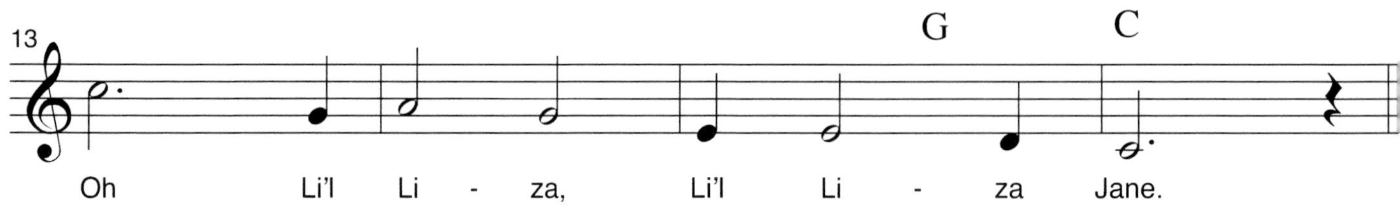
13
G C
Oh Li'l Li - za, Li'l Li - za Jane.

Little Annie

1: C; F: F or G
'D 2-Track 7
Traditional
C F
1. Once more I must leave you lit - tle An - nie, We must
2. When the sun shines down on the moun - tains, And the
3. Now the spring - time has come on the moun - tains, And I'm
C G C
part at the end of the lane, But you prom - ised
wild sheep are wandering all a - lone, And the birds and the
on my way back to the lane, For you prom - ised
F C
me lit - tle An - nie, You'd be wait - ing when the
bees are sing - ing, Then it makes me think that
me lit - tle An - nie, You'd be wait - ing when the
G C G
spring - time comes a - gain. Cho: When the spring - time comes on the
spring - time won't be long.
spring - time comes a - gain.
C G
moun - tain, And the wild flow - ers scat - ter o'er the plains,
C F
I will watch for the leaves to re - turn to the trees, And I'll be
C G C
wait - ing when the spring - time comes a - gain.

Little Bessie

M: *G;* ***F:*** *C or D*
CD 2-Track 8

Crandall & Porter, 1875

G
1. Hug me clos - er, clos - er Moth - er, Put your
2. Some-thing hurts me here dear Moth - er, Like a
3. Just be - fore the lamps were light - ed, Just be -
4. All at once a win - dow o - pened, On a

4
arms a - round me tight, For I'm cold
stone up - on my breast, Oh I won -
fore the child - ren came, While the room
field of lambs and sheep, Some, far out,

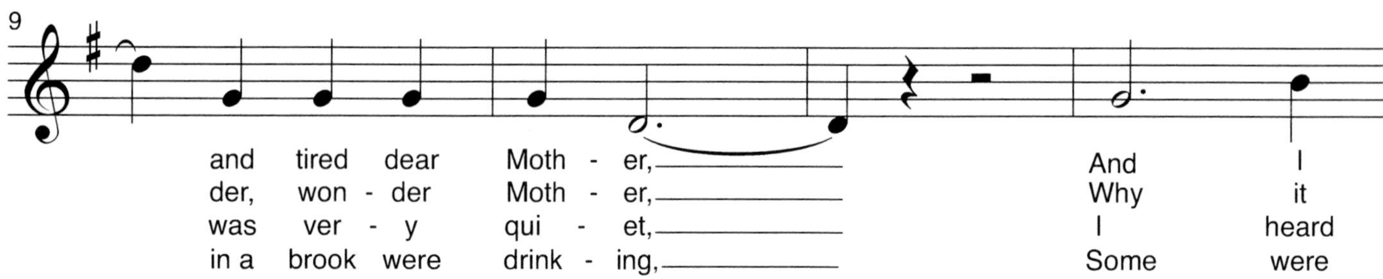
9
and tired dear Moth - er, And I
der, won - der Moth - er, Why it
was ver - y qui - et, I heard
in a brook were drink - ing, Some were

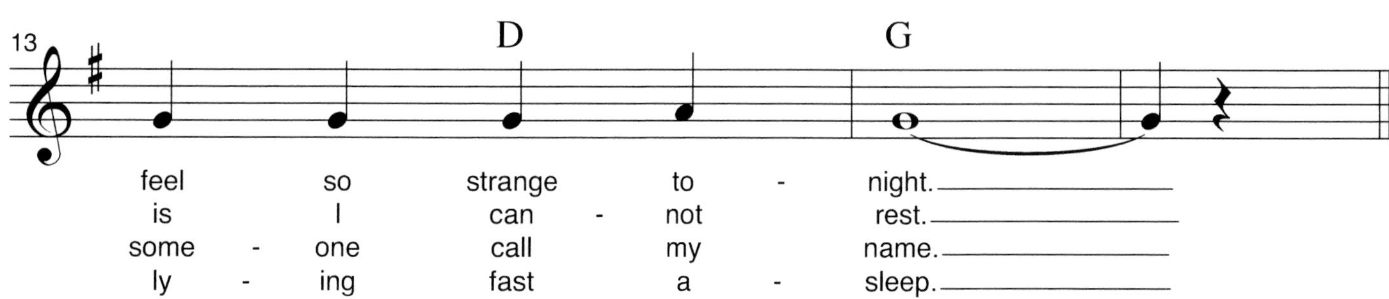
13
D
G
feel so strange to - night.
is I can - not rest.
some - one call my name.
ly - ing fast a - sleep.

Country Gentlemen, Stanley Bros., R. Stanley,
Blue Sky Boys, Dixon Bros., N. Blake, R. Skaggs

G
. In a moment I was looking,
)n a world so bright and fair,
/hich was filled with little children,
D G
nd they seemed so happy there.

. They were singing, oh, so sweetly,
weetest songs I'd ever heard.
hey were singing sweeter, Mother,
han a darling little bird.

. Come up here little Bessie,
ome up here and live with me,
/here little children never suffer,
uffer through eternity.

. Then I thought of all you told me,
f that bright and happy land,
was going when you called me,
/hen you came and kissed my hand.

. I felt so sorry when you called me,
nd from this world I soon must go,
o to sleep and never suffer,
hen dear Mother don't be crying so.

). And the mother pressed her closer,
) her own dear burning breast,
) the heart so near broken,
ay the heart so near its rest.

. At the solemn hour of midnight,
the darkness calm and deep,
ying on her mother's bosom,
ttle Bessie fell asleep.

2. Far up yonder past the portals,
hat are shining very fair,
ttle Bessie now is tended,
y her Savior's loving care.

Little Birdie

M: G; F: C or D
CD 2-Track 9

Traditional

G
D
1. Lit - tle bir - die, lit - tle bir - die,
2. Lit - tle bir - die, lit - tle bir - die,

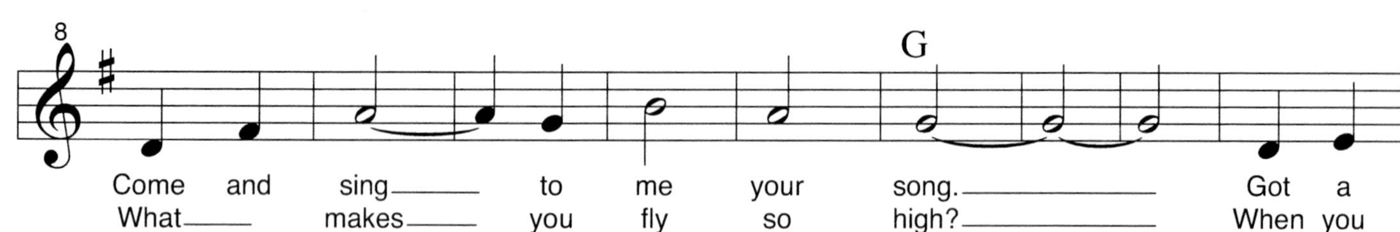

8
G
Come and sing to me your song. Got a
What makes you fly so high? When you

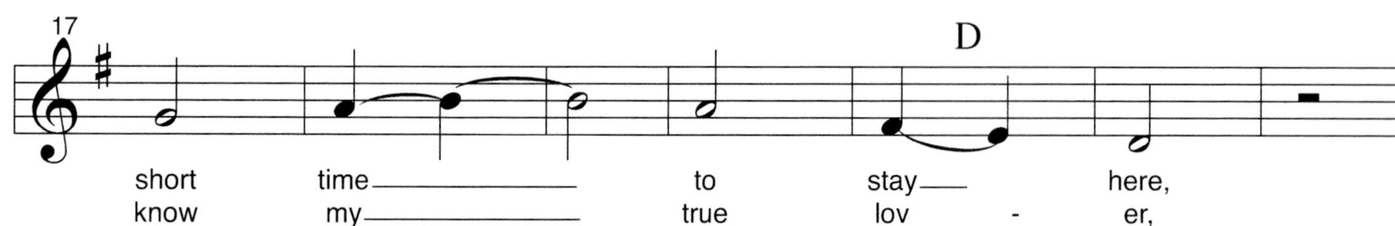

17
D
short time to stay here,
know my true lov - er,

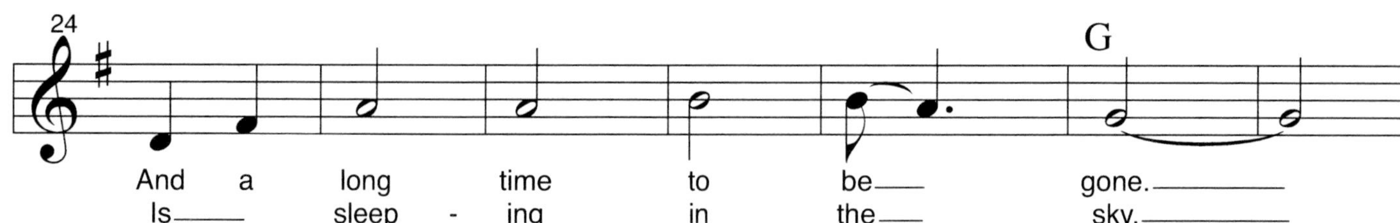

24
G
And a long time to be gone.
Is sleep - ing in the sky.

G D
3. I'm a long way from old Dixie,
G
And my old Kentucky home,
D
Now my parents are both dead and gone,
G
Have no place to call my home.

4. Now I'd rather be a sailor,
'Way out upon the sea,
Then to be at home a married man,
With a baby on my knee.

5. For the married man, he sees trouble,
And the single boy sees none,
I expect to live single,
'Til my days on earth are done.

6. Now I'd rather be in some dark hollow,
Where the sun don't ever shine,
Then to see you love another,
When you promised to be mine.

Flatt & Scruggs, Stanley Bros., R. Stanley, R. Allen & F. Wakefield,
Greenbriar Boys, NLCR, Cox Family, M. Seeger, King Wilkie

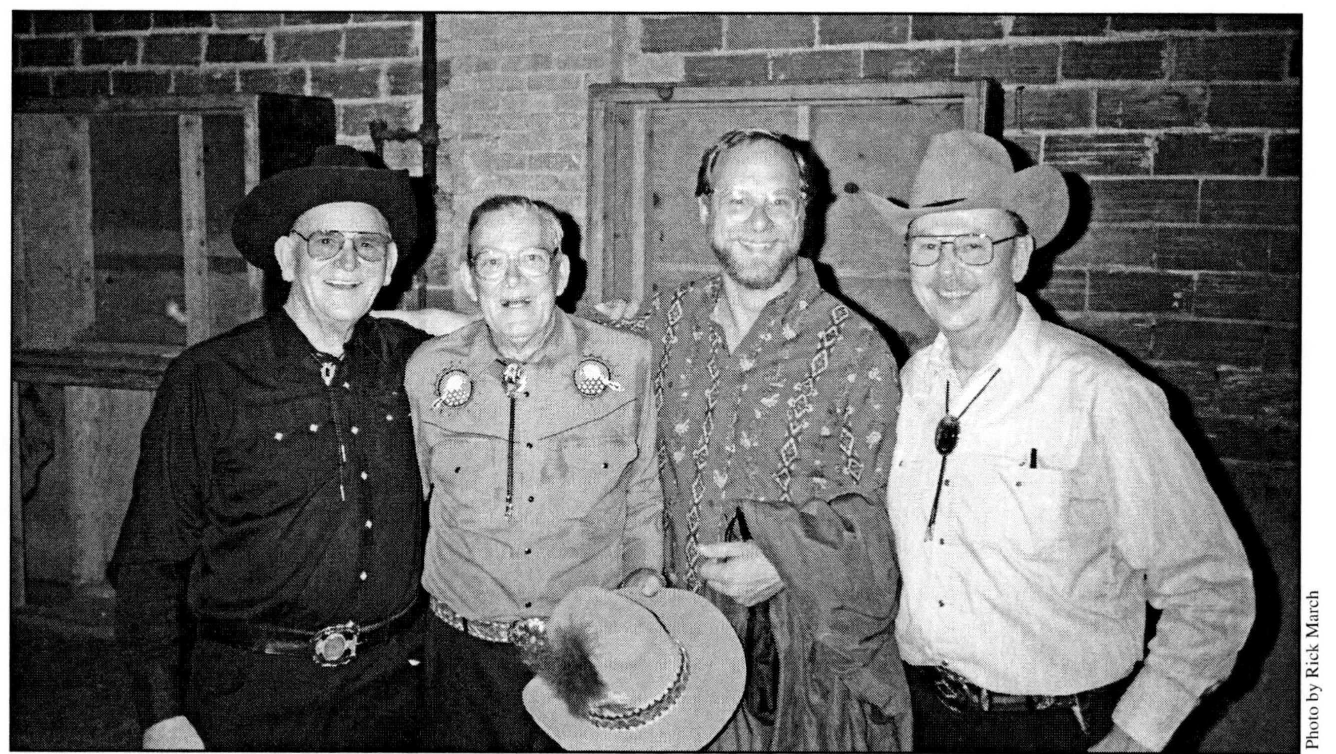

Photo by Rick March

The Goose Island Ramblers with Dix Bruce 1999:
left to right: Wendy Whitford, George Gilbertsen, Dix Bruce, Bruce Bollerud.

Blue
Boys

Photo by Butch Waller

Left to right: Kathy Kallick, Bill Monroe, Julia LaBella, Dix Bruce, San Francisco, late 1970s.

Little Maggie

***M:** G; **F:** C or D*
CD 2-Track 10, medley pt. 1

Traditional

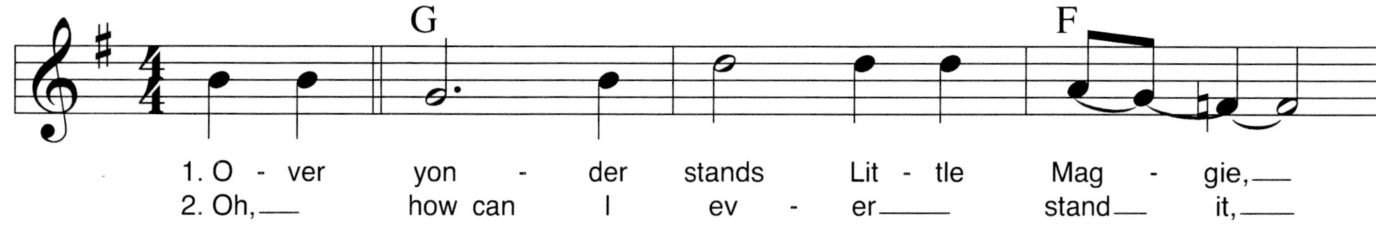
G
F
1. O - ver yon - der stands Lit - tle Mag - gie,
2. Oh, how can I ev - er stand it,

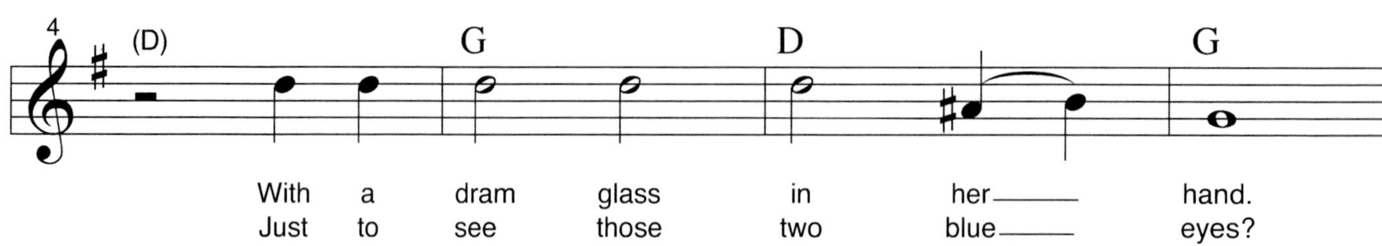
4
(D)
G
D
G
With a dram glass in her hand.
Just to see those two blue eyes?

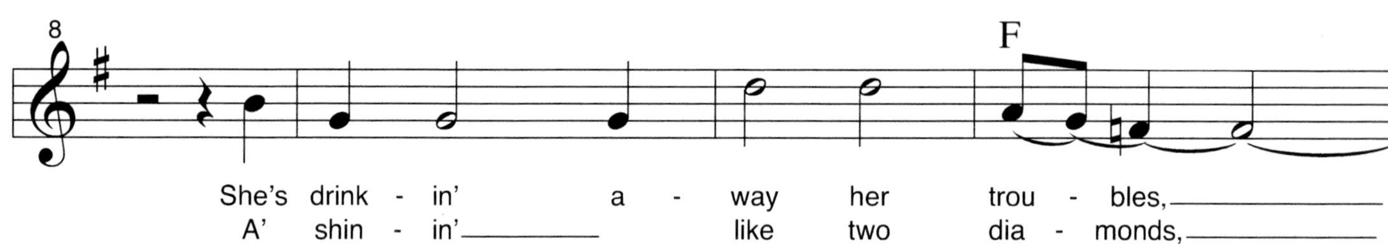
8
F
She's drink - in' a - way her trou - bles,
A' shin - in' like two dia - monds,

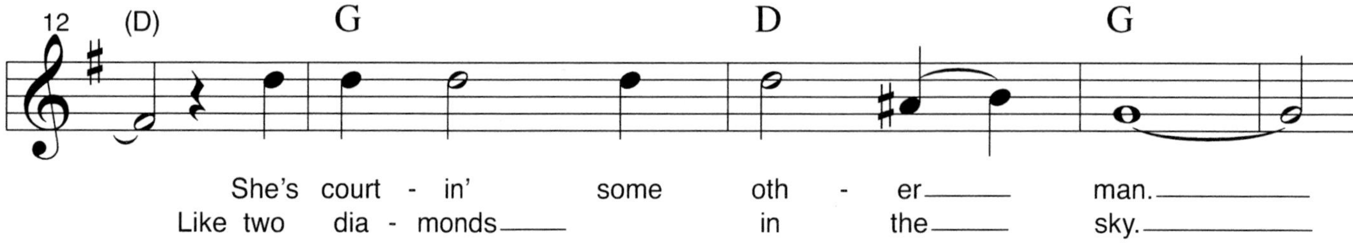
12
(D)
G
D
G
She's court - in' some oth - er man.
Like two dia - monds in the sky.

Stanley Bros., R. Stanley, B. Monroe, Flatt & Scruggs, J. Martin
R. Allen & F. Wakefield, Grayson & Whitter, R. Skaggs, T. Adams

G   F   (D)
. Last time I saw little Maggie,
                G   D   G
he was sitting on the banks of the sea.
                                F   (D)
/ith a forty-four around her,
          G   D   G
nd a banjo on her knee.

. Lay down your last gold dollar,
ay down your gold watch and chain.
ttle Maggie's gonna dance for daddy,
sten to that old banjo ring.

. Pretty flowers were made for blooming,
retty stars were made to shine.
retty girls were made for loving,
ttle Maggie was made for mine.

. March me down to the station,
/ith my suitcase in my hand.
n going away for to leave you,
n going to some far distant land.

I'd rather be in some dark hollow,
'here the sun don't never shine.
hen to know you're another man's darling,
nd no longer a darling of mine.

Sometimes I have a nickel,
nd sometimes I have a dime.
ometimes I have ten dollars,
ıst to pay little Maggie's fine.

Go away, go away little Maggie,
o and do the best that you can.
I get me another woman,
ɔu can get you another man.

Little Old Log Cabin in the Lane

***M:** G; **F:** C or D*
CD 2-Track 10, medley pt. 2

W.S. Hays, 187

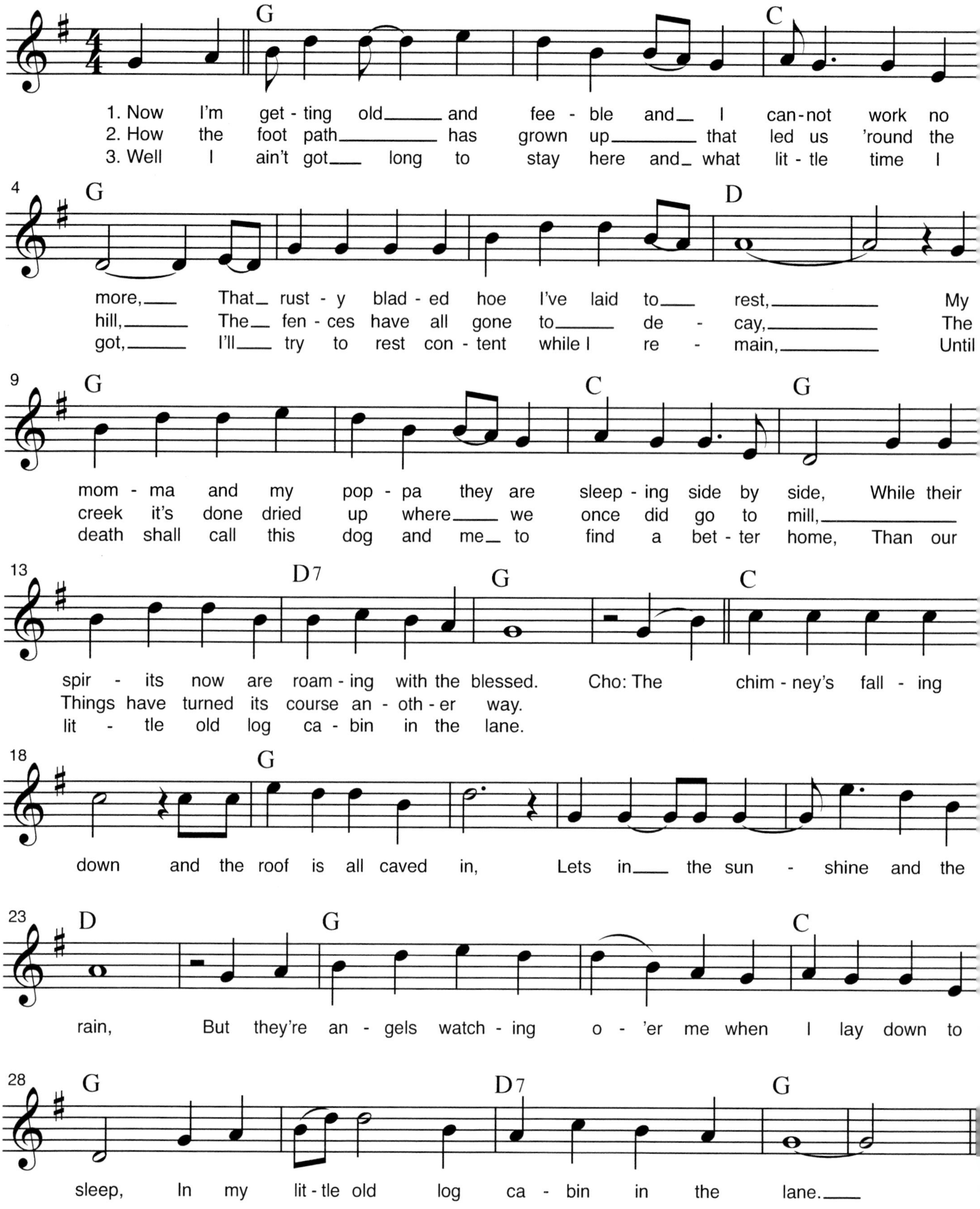

1. Now I'm get - ting old___ and fee - ble and_ I can-not work no
2. How the foot path___ has grown up___ that led us 'round the
3. Well I ain't got___ long to stay here and_ what lit - tle time I

more,___ That_ rust - y blad - ed hoe I've laid to___ rest,___ My
hill,___ The_ fen - ces have all gone to___ de - cay,___ The
got,___ I'll___ try to rest con - tent while I re - main,___ Until

mom - ma and my pop - pa they are sleep - ing side by side, While their
creek it's done dried up where___ we once did go to mill,___
death shall call this dog and me_ to find a bet - ter home, Than our

spir - its now are roam - ing with the blessed. Cho: The chim - ney's fall - ing
Things have turned its course an - oth - er way.
lit - tle old log ca - bin in the lane.

down and the roof is all caved in, Lets in___ the sun - shine and the

rain, But they're an - gels watch - ing o - 'er me when I lay down to

sleep, In my lit - tle old log ca - bin in the lane.___

Little Rosewood Casket

: C; **F:** *F or G*
D 2-Track 11

Goullaud & White, 1870

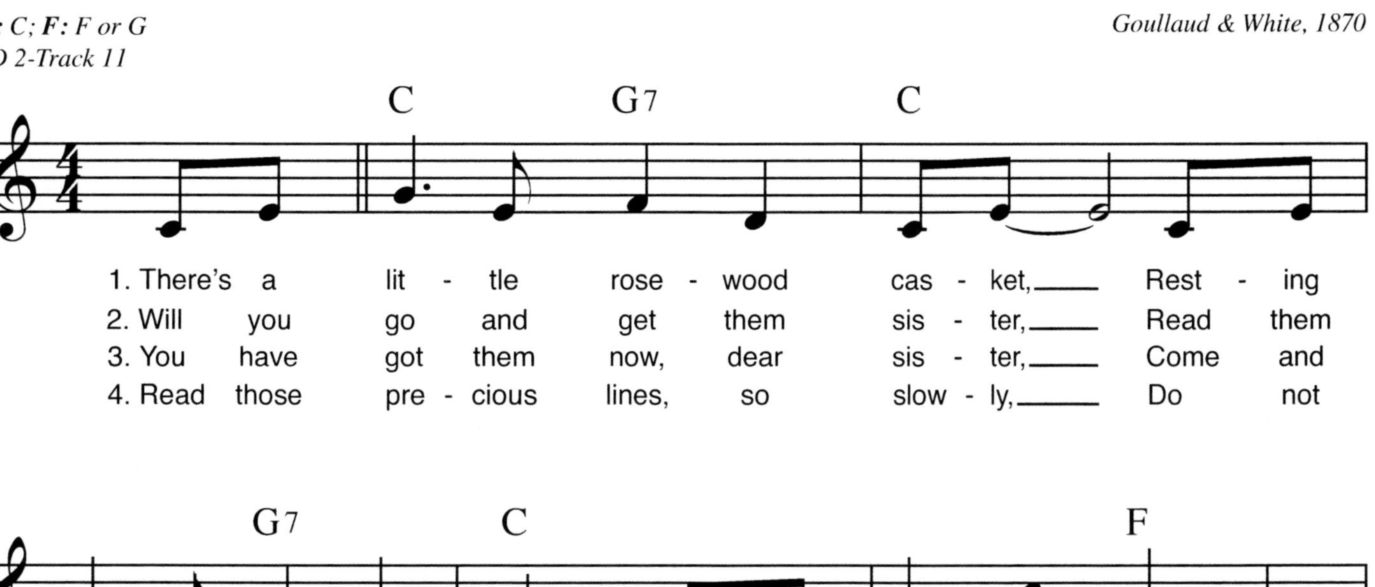
C G7 C
1. There's a lit - tle rose - wood cas - ket, Rest - ing
2. Will you go and get them sis - ter, Read them
3. You have got them now, dear sis - ter, Come and
4. Read those pre - cious lines, so slow - ly, Do not

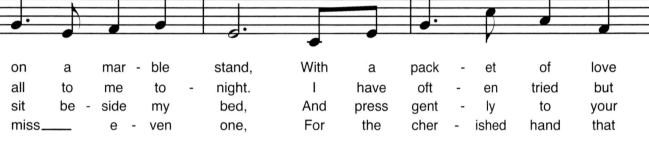

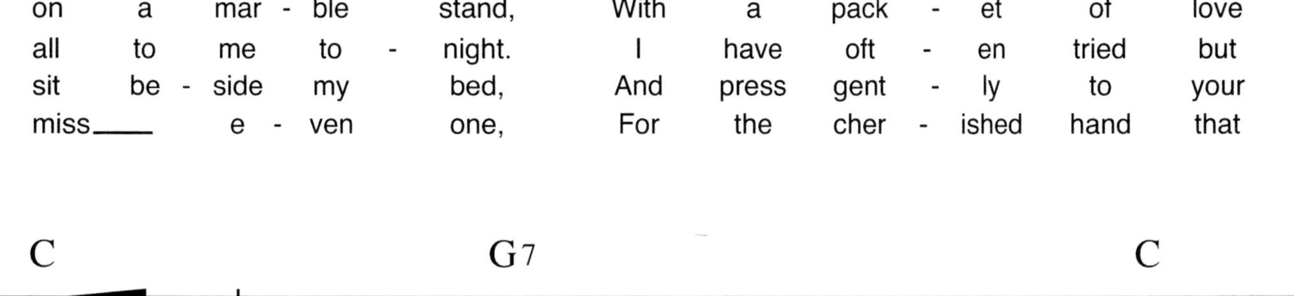
G7 C F
on a mar - ble stand, With a pack - et of love
all to me to - night. I have oft - en tried but
sit be - side my bed, And press gent - ly to your
miss e - ven one, For the cher - ished hand that

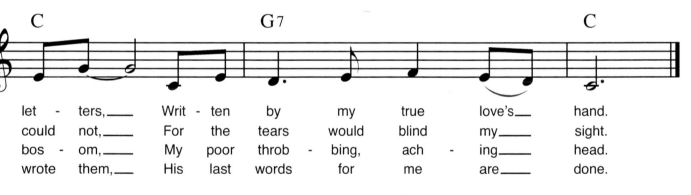

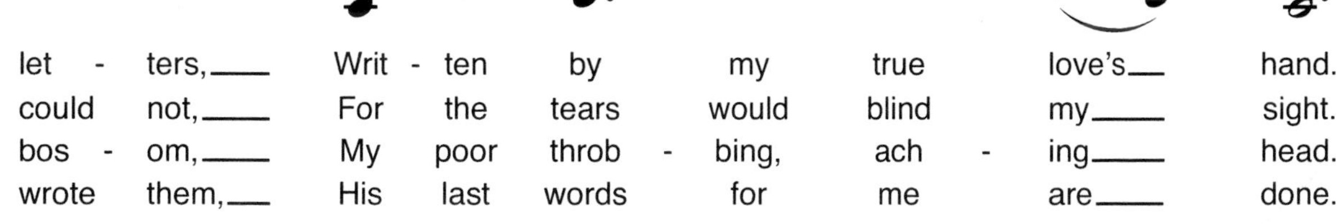
C G7 C
let - ters, Writ - ten by my true love's hand.
could not, For the tears would blind my sight.
bos - om, My poor throb - bing, ach - ing head.
wrote them, His last words for me are done.

Photo by Dix Bruce

Kenny Baker, longtime fiddler with Bill Monroe and the Bluegrass Boys, ca. 1982.

anley Bros., Osborne Bros., Mac Wiseman, K. Kallick

Little Sadie

M: Em; F: Am
CD 2-Track 12

Traditiona

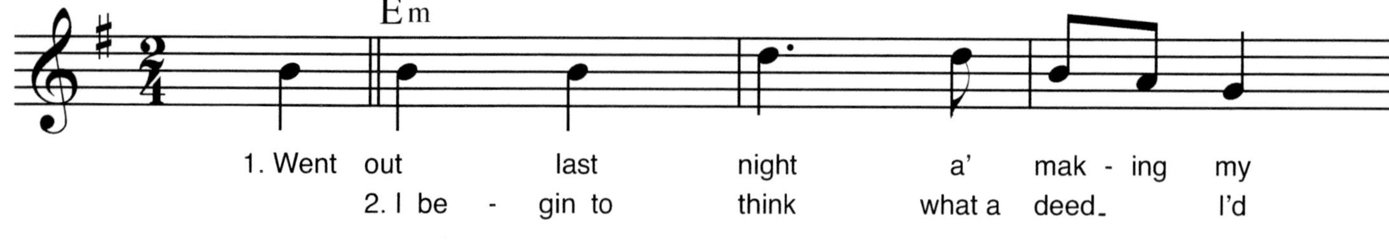
Em
1. Went out last night a' mak - ing my
2. I be - gin to think what a deed I'd

4
D
rounds, I met lit - tle Sad - ie and I blowed her
done, Grabbed my hat and a - way I

8
B7
D
down, Went right home and I went to bed, A
run, Made a good run but I run too slow, They

13
B7
Em
for - ty four smoke - less un - der - my head.
ov - er - took me in Jer - i - cho.

Em
3. Standing on the corner reading a bill,
D B7
Up stepped the sheriff from Thomasville,
D
Says, "Young man is your name Brown?
B7 Em
Remember the night you blowed Sadie down?"

4. Oh, yes sir, my name is Lee,
I murdered little Sadie in the first degree,
First degree and the second degree,
If you got any papers will you read 'em to me?

5. Took me downtown, they dressed me in black,
They put me on the train and they took me back,
Had no one for to go my bail,
Crammed me back in the county jail.

6. Judge and the jury, took their stand,
Judge had his papers in his right hand,
Forty one days, forty one nights,
Forty one years to wear the ball and the stripes.

D. Watson, T. Rice, Grisman, Garcia, Rice, D. Grisman, T. O'Brien

Little Willie

': G; F: C or D
D 2-Track 13

Traditional

G
F
1. When I was in my six - teenth year,
2. We were so far a - way from home,
3. My moth - er was so kind to me,
4. "It's nat - ure, nature, my dear little girl,

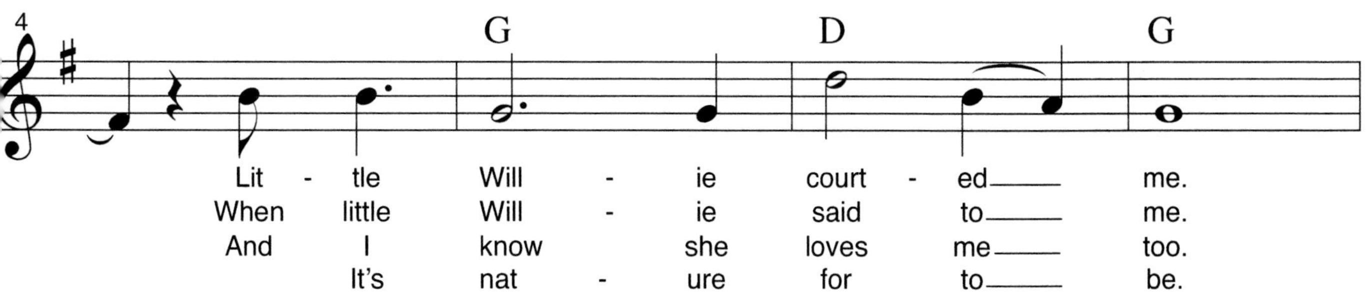
4
G
D
G
Lit - tle Will - ie court - ed me.
When little Will - ie said to me.
And I know she loves me too.
It's nat - ure for to be.

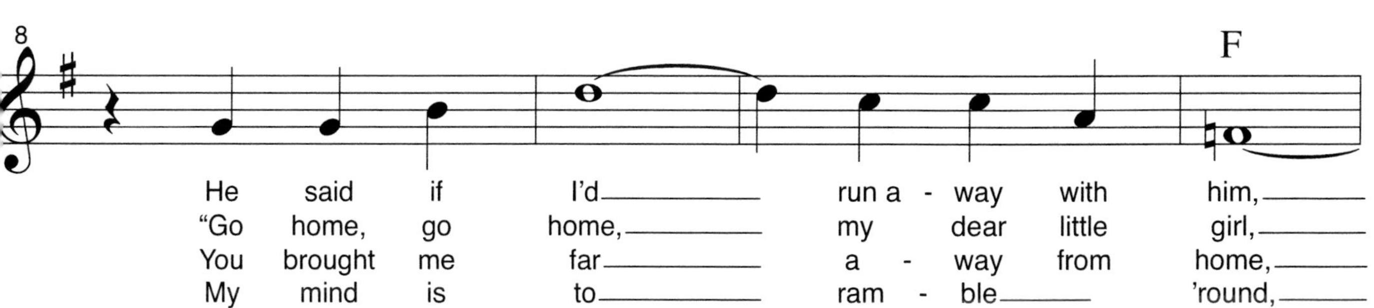
8
F
He said if I'd run a - way with him,
"Go home, go home, my dear little girl,
You brought me far a - way from home,
My mind is to ram - ble 'round,

12
G
D
G
His dar - ling wife I could be.
My wife you can nev - er be."
How can you leave me here?
And I bid this wide world a - dieu."

Lonesome Valley

***M:** G; **F:** C or D*
CD 2-Track 14, medley pt. 1

Traditional

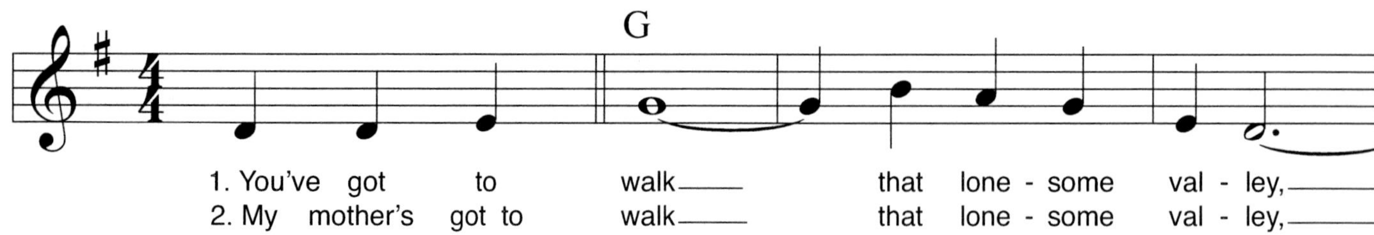
G
1. You've got to walk that lone - some val - ley,
2. My mother's got to walk that lone - some val - ley,

4
D7
G
You've got to walk, it by your - self,
She's got to walk, it by her - self,

8
C
G
Ain't no - bod - y here can walk it for you,
Ain't no - bod - y here can walk it for her,

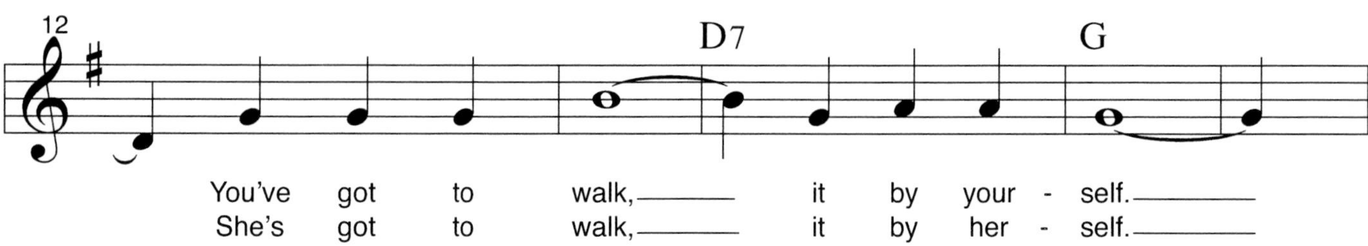
12
D7
G
You've got to walk, it by your - self.
She's got to walk, it by her - self.

My brother's got to walk, etc.
My sister's got to walk, etc.
My father's got to walk, etc.
All sinners got to walk, etc.

Carter Fam., Monroe Bros., B. Monroe

Long Journey Home

I: G; F: C or D
D 2-Track 14, medley pt. 2

Traditional

G

1. Black smoke's a ris - ing and it sure - ly is a train,
2. Lost all my mon - ey but a two___ dol - lar bill,
3. Cloud - y in the West___ and it looks___ like___ rain,
4. Dark and a' rain - ing and I want___ to go home,
5. Home - sick and lone-some and I'm feel - ing kind - ly blue,

C G

Sure - ly is a train boys, sure - ly is a train,
Two___ dol - lar bill boys, two___ dol - lar bill,
Looks___ like___ rain, boys, looks___ like___ rain,
Want___ to go home, boys, want___ to go home,
Feel-ing kind - ly blue, boys, feel - ing kind - ly blue,

Black smoke's a ris - ing and it sure - ly is a train, I'm
Lost all my mon - ey but a two___ dol - lar bill, I'm
Cloud - y in the West___ and it looks___ like___ rain, I'm
Dark and a' rain - ing and I want___ to go home, I'm
Home - sick and lone-some and I'm feel - ing kind - ly blue, I'm

D G

on my long jour - ney home.___
on my long jour - ney home.___
on my long jour - ney home.___
on my long jour - ney home.___
on my long jour - ney home.___

onroe Bros., Stanley Bros., R. Stanley, D. Watson,
Grisman, Ken. Colonels,
CR, Country Gentlemen, Jim & Jesse,
hnson Mtn. Boys, L. Sparks, Lilly Bros.

Lord, I'm Coming Home

M: G; F: C or D
CD 2-Track 15

Wm. J. Kirkpatrick, 189

G C G
1. I've wan - dered far a - way from God, Now I'm
2. I've wast - ed man - y pre - cious years, Now I'm
3. I'm tired of sin and stray - ing, Lord, Now I'm
6
D G C
com - ing home; The paths of sin too long I've
com - ing home; I now re - pent with bit - ter
com - ing home; I'll trust Thy love, be - lieve Thy
12
G D G
trod, Lord, I'm com - ing home.
tears, Lord, I'm com - ing home.
Word, Lord, I'm com - ing home.
17
G C G
Cho: Com - ing home, com - ing home, Nev - er -
22
D G C G
more to roam, O - pen wide Thine arms of love,
29
D G
Lord, I'm com - ing home.

G C G
4. My soul is sick, my heart is sore,
D
Now I'm coming home;
G C G
My strength renew, my hope restore,
D G
Lord, I'm coming home.

5. My only hope, my only plea,
Now I'm coming home;
That Jesus died, and died for me.
Lord, I'm coming home.

6. I need His cleansing blood, I know,
Now I'm coming home;
O wash me whiter than the snow,
Lord, I'm coming home.

Stanley Bros., Country Gentlemen, Jim & Jesse
J. Martin, Louvin Bros., Mac Wiseman

Mama Don't Allow

M: C; F: F or G
CD 2-Track 16

Traditional

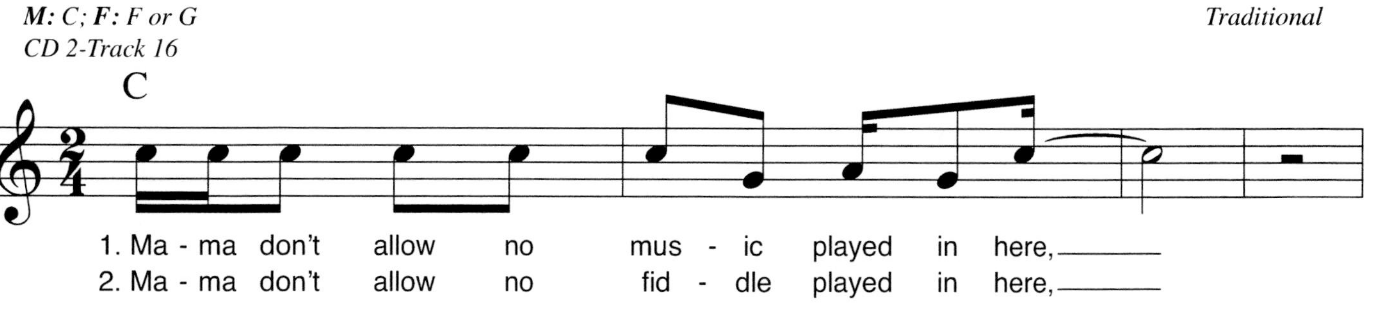

C
1. Ma - ma don't allow no mus - ic played in here,
2. Ma - ma don't allow no fid - dle played in here,

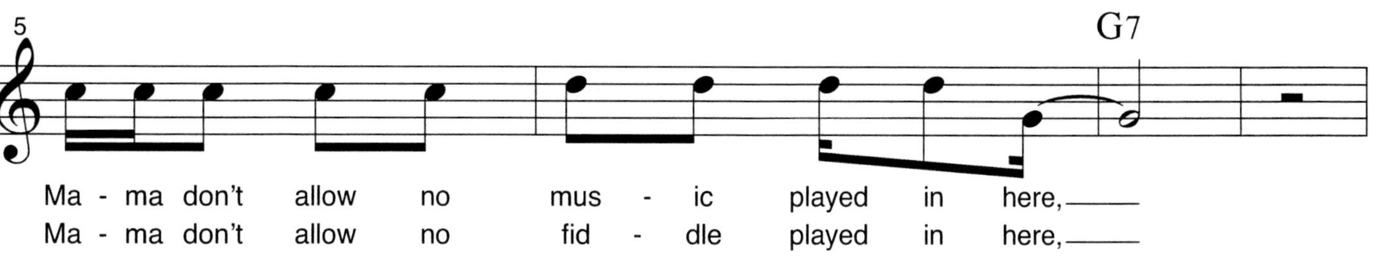

5
G7
Ma - ma don't allow no mus - ic played in here,
Ma - ma don't allow no fid - dle played in here,

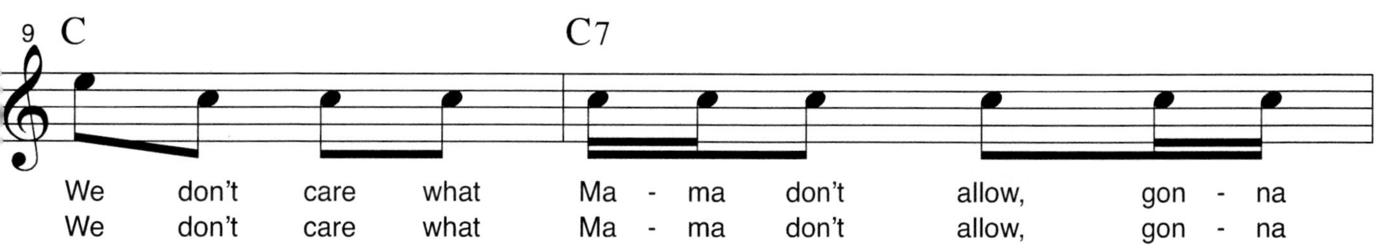

9
C
C7
We don't care what Ma - ma don't allow, gon - na
We don't care what Ma - ma don't allow, gon - na

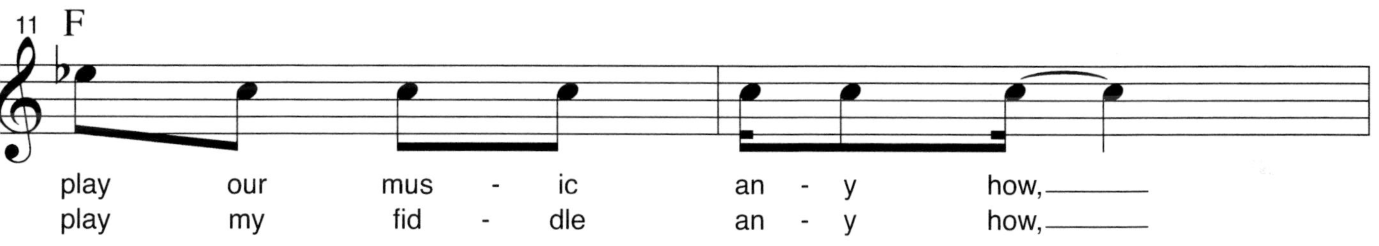

11
F
play our mus - ic an - y how,
play my fid - dle an - y how,

13
C
G7
C
Ma - ma don't allow no mus - ic played in here!
Ma - ma don't allow no fid - dle played in here!

Mama don't allow no banjo playing here, etc.
Guitar, mandolin, Dobro, etc.

att & Scruggs, Stanley Bros., R. Stanley, D. Watson, J.E. Mainer

Man of Constant Sorrow

***M:** D; **F:** G or A*
CD 2-Track 17

Dick Burnett, ca. 191

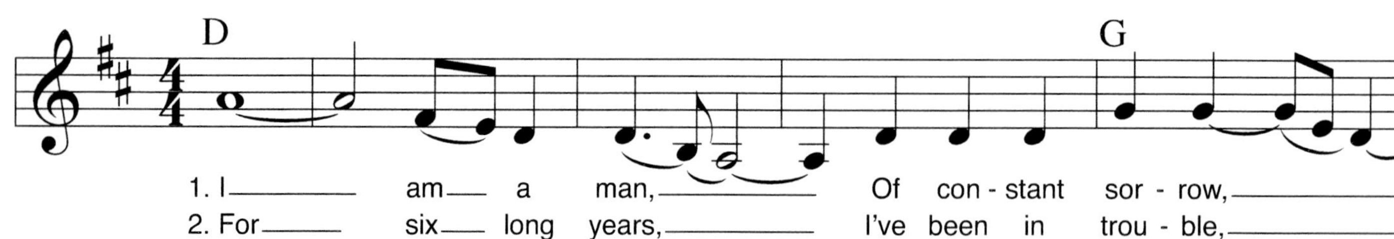
D
G
1. I am a man, Of con - stant sor - row,
2. For six long years, I've been in trou - ble,

6
A
D
I've seen trou - ble all my days. I
No pleas - ure here on earth I find. For

12
G
bid fare - well, To old Ken - tuck - y,
in this world, I'm bound to ram - ble,

16
A
D
The place where I was borned and raised.
I have no friends to help me now.

D G
3. It's fare thee well, my own true lover,
A D
I never expect to see again.
G
For I'm bound to ride, that northern railroad,
A D
Perhaps I'll die upon this train.

4. You can bury me, in some deep valley,
For many years where I may lay.
Then you may learn, to love another,
While I am sleeping in my grave.

5. Maybe your friends think, I'm just a stranger,
My face you never will see no more.
But there is one promise that is given,
I'll meet you on God's golden shore.

Stanley Bros., R. Stanley, "O Brother" soundtrack
Grisman, Garcia, Rice, Blue Highway, Bluegrass Band, Dillards, P. Rowa

The Maple on the Hill

: G; F: C or D
D 2-Track 18

G.L. Davis, 1880

G
1. Near a qui - et coun - try vil - lage grew a
2. We would sing love songs to - geth - er when the
3. Don't for - get me lit - tle dar - ling when they've
4. I will soon be with the an - gels on that

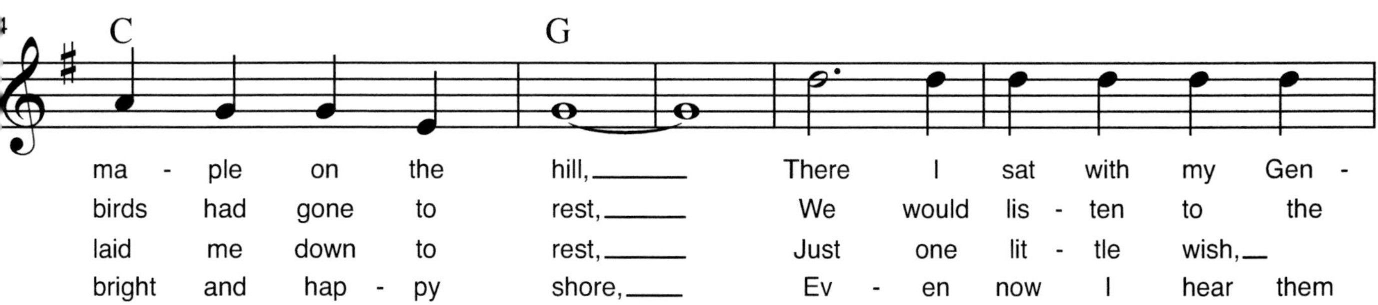
C G
ma - ple on the hill,
birds had gone to rest,
laid me down to rest,
bright and hap - py shore,
There I sat with my Gen -
We would lis - ten to the
Just one lit - tle wish,
Ev - en now I hear them

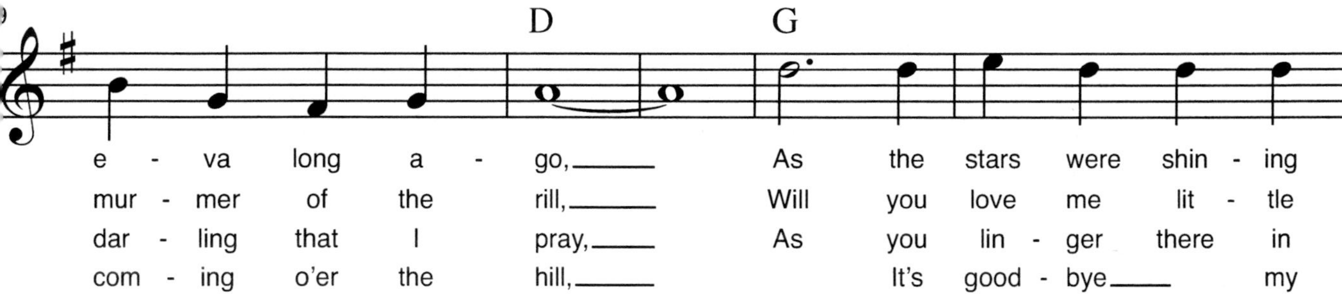
D G
e - va long a - go,
mur - mer of the rill,
dar - ling that I pray,
com - ing o'er the hill,
As the stars were shin - ing
Will you love me lit - tle
As you lin - ger there in
It's good - bye my

C G
bright - ly we could hear the whip - poor - wills, When we
dar - ling as you did those star - ry nights, When we
sad - ness think - ing, dar - ling, of the past, Let your
dar - ling, it is time for us to part, I must

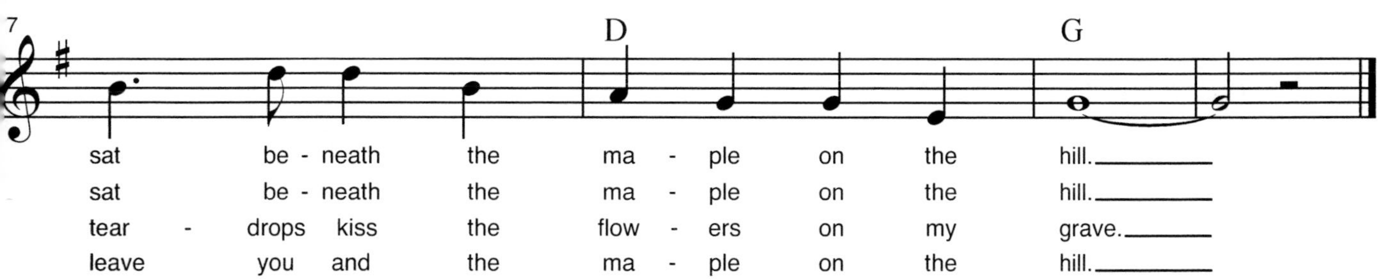
D G
sat be - neath the ma - ple on the hill.
sat be - neath the ma - ple on the hill.
tear - drops kiss the flow - ers on my grave.
leave you and the ma - ple on the hill.

anley Bros., R. Stanley, Dixon Brothers, Mac Wiseman, J.E. Mainer

Methodist Pie

M: D; F: G or A
CD 2-Track 19, medley pt. 1
Traditional
D
1. I was down to camp meet-ing the oth-er af-ter-noon, To
2. They all go there to have a good time, And
3. They catch a hold of hands and they march a-round a ring, Keep a'
3
A7
hear them shout and sing. To tell one an-oth-er how they
eat on the grub so sly. Have apple-sauce but-ter with
sing-ing all the while. You'd think it was a cy-clone com-ing
6
D
loved each oth-er, And to make hal-le-lu-jah ring.
sugar in the gourd, And a great big Method-ist pie. You
through the air, You could hear them shout a half a mile. Now the
9
Old Un-cle Dan'-l, and bro-ther Eb-en-e-zer, And
ought to hear the ring-ing when they all get to sing-ing, That
bells ring loud and a great big crowd, Breaks
11
A7
Ru-fus with his lame girl Sue. Aunt Pol-ly, and Me-lin-da and
good old "Bye and Bye." See Jim-my Mc-Gee in the
ranks and up they fly. While I took a board of the
14
D
old Moth-er Ben-der, I nev-er seen a hap-pi-er crew.
top of the tree, Singing, "How is this for high?"
sugar in the gourd, And I cleaned up the Meth-o-dist pie.

 B. Kincaid, Goose Island Ramblers, B. Clifton, Greenbriar Boys

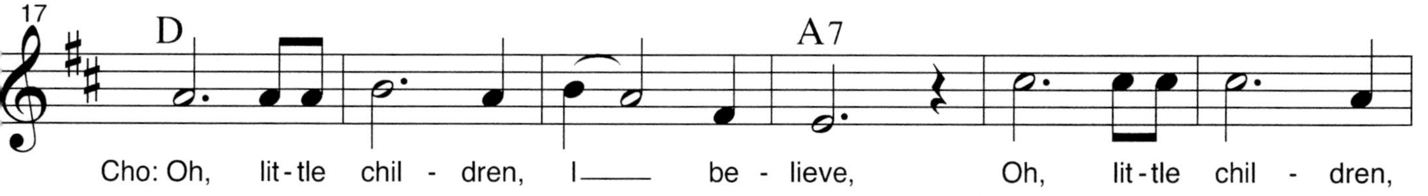
17
D
A7
Cho: Oh, lit-tle chil - dren, I___ be - lieve, Oh, lit-tle chil - dren,
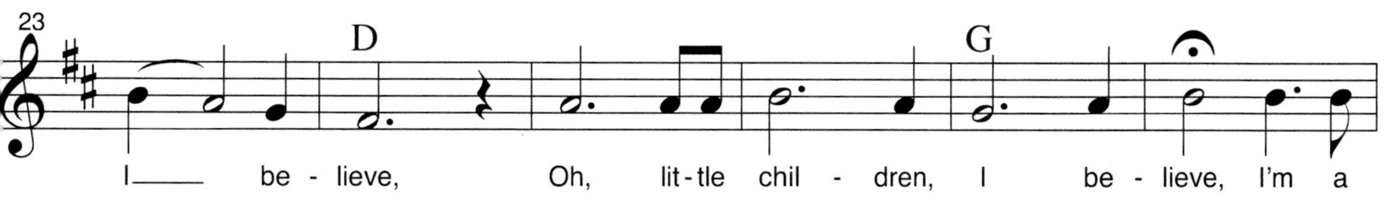
23
D
G
I___ be - lieve, Oh, lit-tle chil - dren, I be - lieve, I'm a

29
A7
D
D
Meth-od - ist 'til I die. I'm a Meth - od - ist, a Meth - od - ist
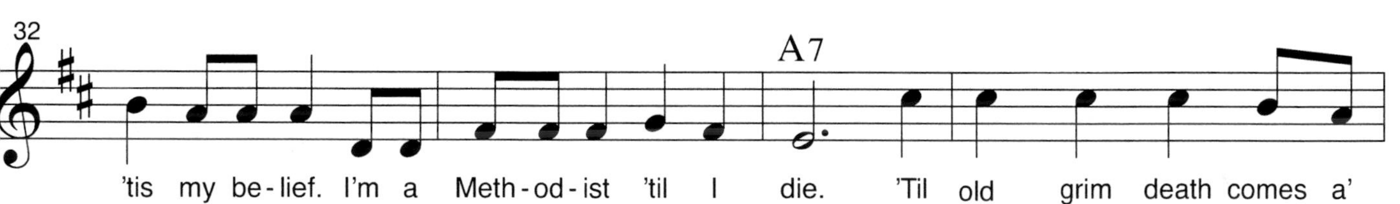
32
A7
'tis my be-lief. I'm a Meth-od-ist 'til I die. 'Til old grim death comes a'
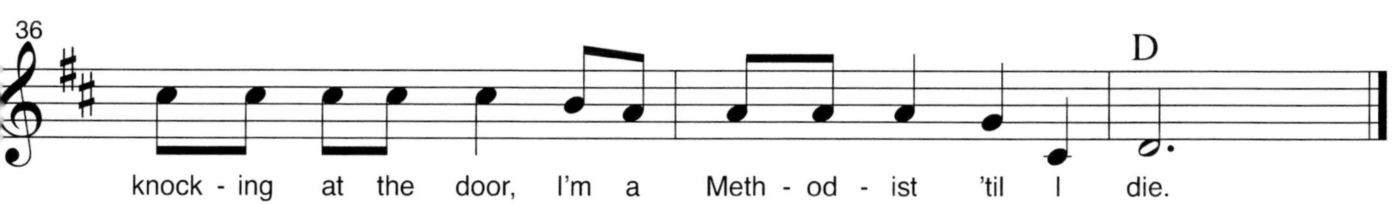
36
D
knock - ing at the door, I'm a Meth - od - ist 'til I die.

Midnight on the Stormy Deep

***M:** D; **F:** G or A*
CD 2-Track 19, medley pt. 2

Tradition

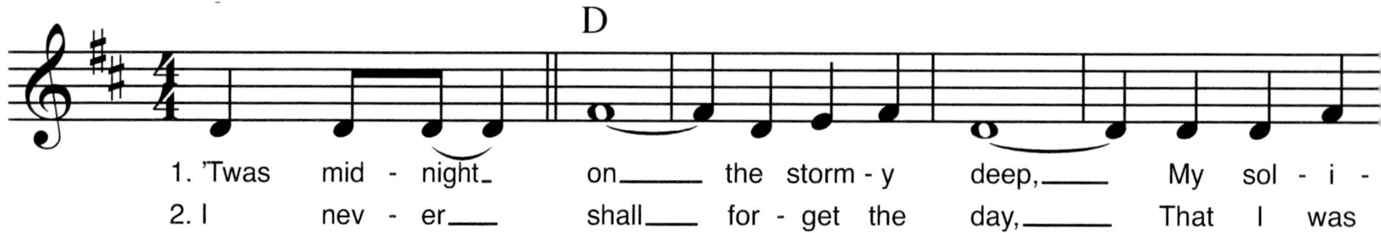
D
1. 'Twas mid - night on the storm - y deep, My sol - i -
2. I nev - er shall for - get the day, That I was

5
tar - - - y watch I keep, And think of
forced to go a - way, In sil - ence

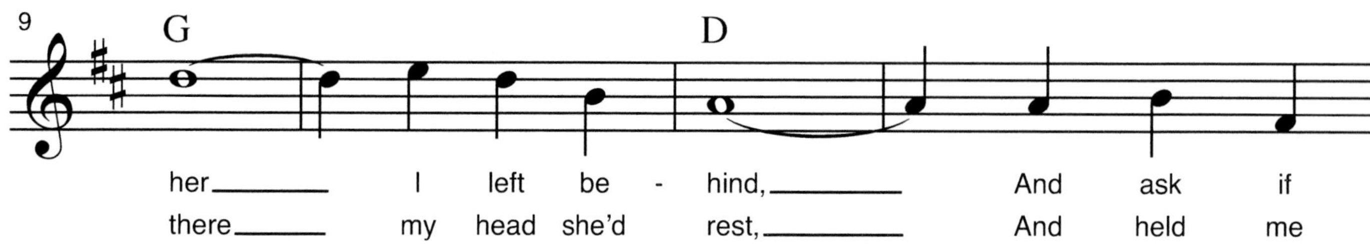
9
G
D
her I left be - hind, And ask if
there my head she'd rest, And held me

13
A
D
she'd be true and kind.
to her lov - ing breast.

D
3. Oh Willy don't go back to sea,
There's other girls as good as me,
G D
But none can love you true as I,
A D
Pray don't go where the bullets fly.

4. The deep, deep sea may us divide,
And I may be some other's bride,
But still my thoughts will oft times stray,
To thee when thou are far away.

5. I never have proved false to thee,
The love I gave is true and kind,
But you have proved untrue to me,
I can no longer call thee mine.

6. Then fare thee well, I'd rather make,
My home upon some icy lake,
Where the southern sun refuses to shine,
Then to trust a love so false as thine.

B. Monroe, D. Watson, Dry Branch Fire Squad, P. Rowan, T. Ric

Milwaukee Blues

': C; F: F or G
D 2-Track 20

Traditional

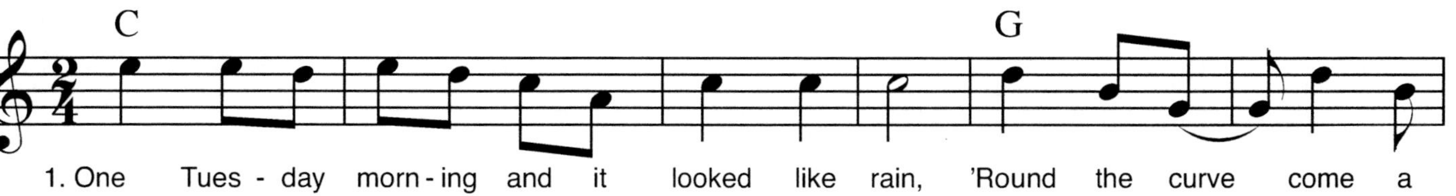
C
G
1. One Tues - day morn - ing and it looked like rain, 'Round the curve come a

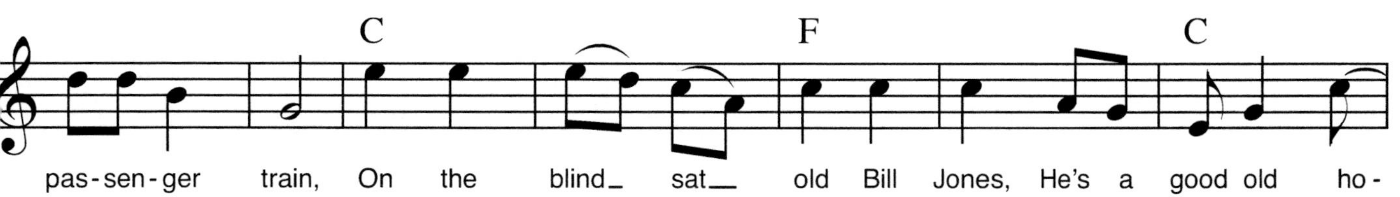
C
F
C
pas - sen - ger train, On the blind_ sat_ old Bill Jones, He's a good old ho -

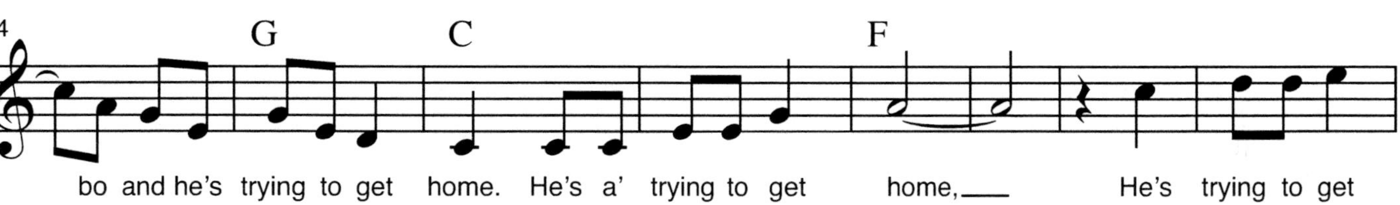
4
G
C
F
bo and he's trying to get home. He's a' trying to get home,___ He's trying to get

2
C
G
C
home,___ He's a good old ho - bo and he's trying to get home.___

C
2. Way down in Georgia on a tramp,
G
The roads are getting muddy and the leaves are getting damp,
C F
Got to catch a freight train, leave this town
C G C
Cause they don't 'low no hoboes a' hanging around.
F C
Hanging around, hanging around,
G C
They don't 'low no hoboes a' hanging around.

3. Left Atlanta one morning 'fore day,
The brakeman said, "You'll have to pay.'
Had no money so I pawned my shoes,
I want to go west, I've got the Milwaukee blues.
Got the Milwaukee blues, got the Milwaukee blues,
I want to go west, I got the Milwaukee blues.

4. Old Bill Jones said before he died,
"Fix the road so the 'boes can ride.
When they ride, they will ride the rods,
Put all their trust in the hands of God.
In the hands of God, in the hands of God,
Put all their trust in the hands of God.

5. Old Bill Jones said before he died,
There's two more roads he'd like to ride.
Fireman said, "What can it be?"
"The Southern Pacific and the Santa Fe.
Santa Fe, yes, the Santa Fe,
The Southern Pacific and the Santa Fe."

Poole, Red Clay Ramblers, J. Carr & A. Munde

Molly and Tenbrooks

M: G; F: C or D
CD 2-Track 21

Traditional

G
1. Run, Mol - ly, run, run, Mol - ly,
2. Tenbrooks was a big bay horse, he wore a shag - gy
4
C
G
run, Ten - brooks gon - na beat you to the
mane, Run all 'round Mem - phis,
7
bright shin - ing sun. To the bright shin - ing
beat the Mem - phis train. Beat the Mem - phis
10
D
G
sun, oh, Lord, To the bright shin - ing sun.
train, oh Lord, Beat the Mem - phis train.


```
G                                                C
3. Tenbrooks said to Molly, "What makes your head so red?"
                    G             D            G
"Running in the hot sun with a fever in my head.
                              D            G
Fever in my head, oh Lord, fever in my head."
```

4. Molly said to Tenbrooks, "You're looking mighty squirrel,"
Tenbrooks said to Molly, "I'm leaving this old world." (etc.)

5. Out in California where Molly done as she pleased,
She come back to old Kentucky, got beat with all ease. (etc.)

6. The women's all a' laughing, the children all a' crying,
Men folks all a' hollering, old Tenbrooks a' flying. (etc.)

7. Kuyper, Kuyper, you're not riding right,
Molly's a beatin' old Tenbrooks clear out of sight. (etc.)

8. Kuyper, Kuyper, Kuyper, my son,
Give Tenbrooks the bridle and let old Tenbrooks run. (etc.)

9. Go and catch old Tenbrooks and hitch him in the shade,
We're gonna bury old Molly in a coffin ready made. (etc.)

B. Monroe, Stanley Bros., J.D. Crowe, Country Gentlemen, E. Taylor Bluegrass Band, Country Gazette, Jimmy Martin, J. Val, Osborne Bros., B. Monroe, Seldom Scene, D. Grisman, Carter Fam., Bluegrass Album Band, D. Watson, K. Kallick

My Home's Across the Blue Ridge Mountains

': D; F: G or A
D 2-Track 22

Traditional

D
1. My home's a - cross the Blue Ridge
2. Rock my ba - by feed him
3. How can I keep from
4. I'm going back to North Car - o -
3
A7
Moun - tains, My home's a - cross the Blue Ridge
can - dy, Rock my ba - by feed him
cry - ing? How can I keep from
lin - a, I'm going back to North Caro -
7
D
Moun - tains, My home's a - cross the Blue Ridge
can - dy, Rock my ba - by feed him
cry - ing? How can I keep from
lin - a, I'm going back to North Car - o -
11
A7
Moun - tains, And I nev - er ex - pect to
can - dy, And I nev - er ex - pect to
cry - ing? When I nev - er ex - pect to
lin - a, And I nev - er ex - pect to
14
D
see you an - y - more.
see you an - y - more.
see you an - y - more?
see you an - y - more.

My Little Georgia Rose

M: G; F: C or D
CD 2-Track 23

Bill Monroe

G C G
1. Now come and lis - ten to my sto - ry, A sto - ry
2. Her moth - er left her with an - oth - er, A care - free
3. We of - ten sang old songs to - geth - er, I watched her
D G C
that I know is true, A lit - tle rose bloomed in
life she had planned, The ba - by now is a
do her lit - tle part, She smiled at me when I would
G D G
Geor - gia, With hair of gold and a heart so true. Cho: Way
la - dy, The one her moth - er could - n't stand.
tell her, That she was my sweet - heart.
C G
down in the Blue Ridge moun - tains, Way down
D G
where the tall pines grow, Lives my sweet - heart of the
C G D G
moun - tains, She's my lit - tle Geor - gia rose.

B. Monroe, Seldom Scene, D. Grisman

New River Train

*: G; **F:** C or D*
D 2-Track 24, medley pt. 1

Traditional

G
Cho: I'm rid - ing on that New Riv - er Train,
1. Dar - ling you can't love one,

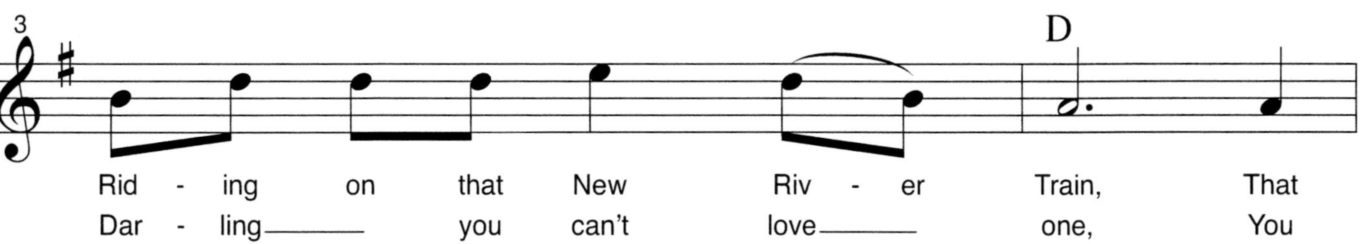

3
D
Rid - ing on that New Riv - er Train, That
Dar - ling you can't love one, You

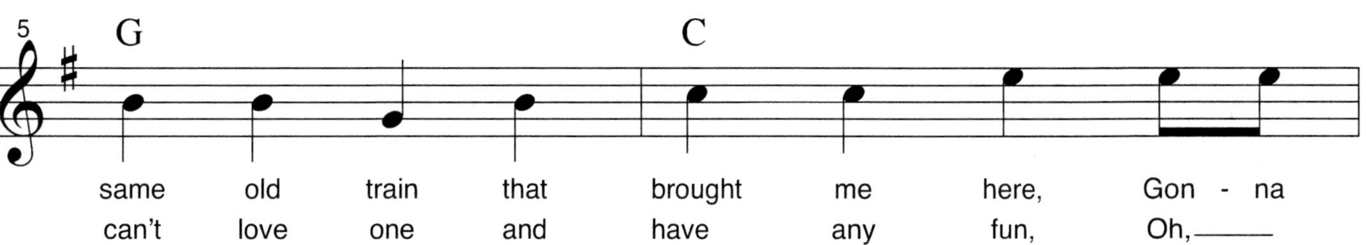

5
G
C
same old train that brought me here, Gon - na
can't love one and have any fun, Oh,

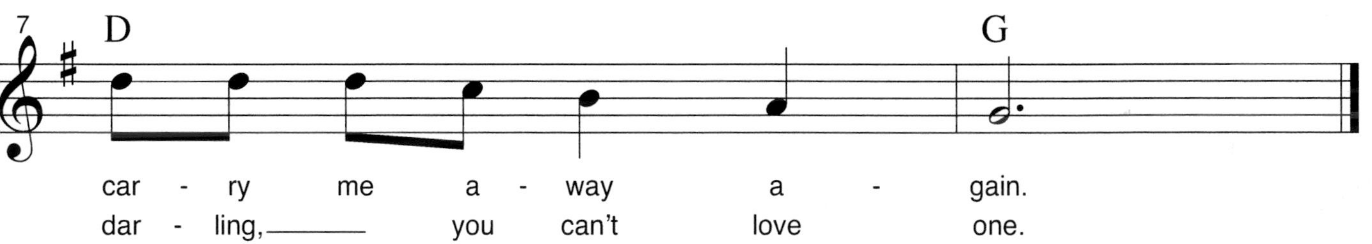

7
D
G
car - ry me a - way a - gain.
dar - ling, you can't love one.

G
2. Darling, you can't love two,
D
Darling, you can't love two,
G C
You can't love two and your little heart be true,
D G
Oh, darling, you can't love two.

3. Darling, you can't love three, (2X)
You can't love three and still love me,
Oh, darling, you can't love three.

4. Darling, you can't love four, (2X)
You can't love four and love me anymore,
Oh, darling, you can't love four.

onroe Bros., B. Monroe, D. Watson, Seldom Scene, Ken. Colonels

Nine Pound Hammer

M: G; F: C or D
CD 2-Track 24, medley pt. 2

Traditional

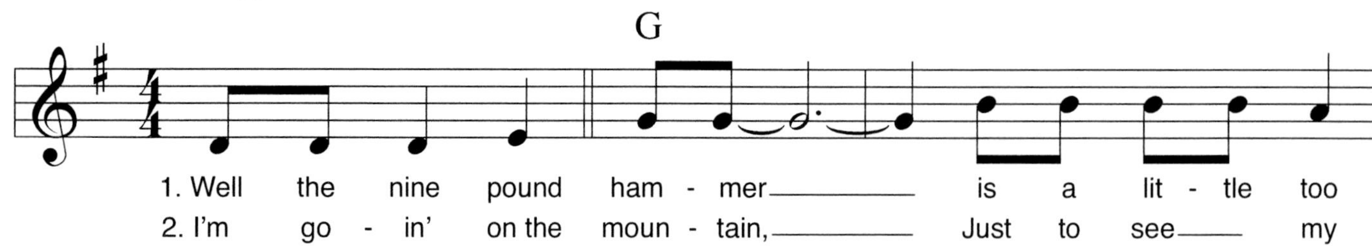
G
1. Well the nine pound ham - mer is a lit - tle too
2. I'm go - in' on the moun - tain, Just to see my

3
C G D G
hea - vy, Bud-dy, for my size, Bud - dy, for my size.
ba - by, And I ain't coming back, Lord I ain't coming back.

8
G C
Cho: So roll on bud - dy, Don't you roll so slow,

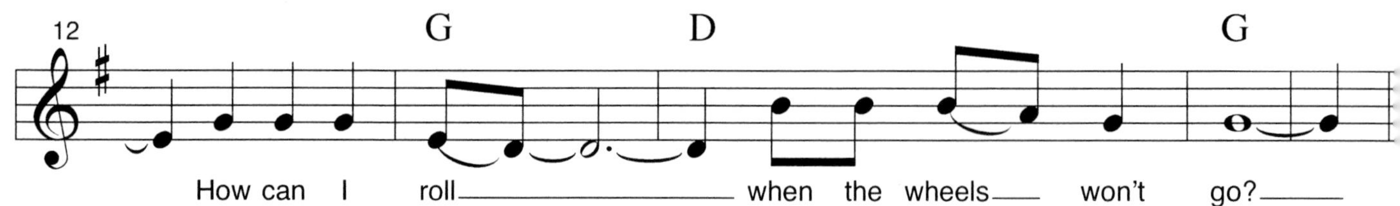
12
G D G
How can I roll when the wheels won't go?

G C
3. There ain't no hammer, in this tunnel,
G D G
That can ring like mine, that can ring like mine.

4. This nine pound hammer, it killed John Henry,
But it won't kill me, no it won't kill me.

5. It's a long way to Harlan, it's a long way to Hazard,
Just to get a little brew, just to get a little brew.

6. I'm working all day, down under ground,
Black as night, it's black as night.

Monroe Bros., B. Monroe, Flatt & Scruggs, Stanley Bros., R. Stanley
Osborne Bros., T. Rice, D. Watson, R. Allen & F. Wakefield, D. Grisman
Ken. Colonels, C. White, Blue Sky Boys, Jim & Jesse

Nobody's Business

[K]: G; F: C or D
[C]D 2-Track 25

Traditional

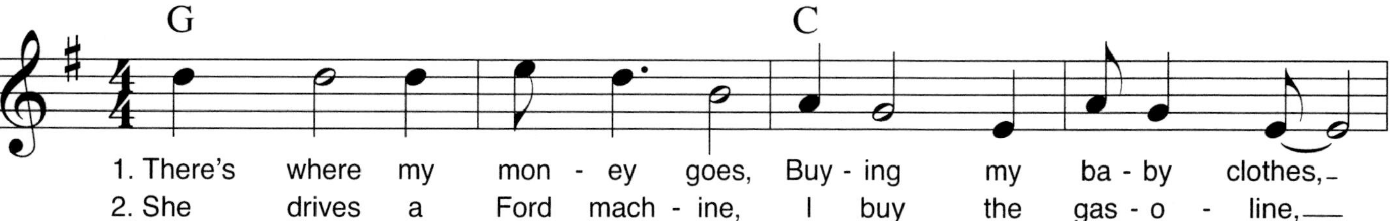

G
C
1. There's where my mon - ey goes, Buy - ing my ba - by clothes,
2. She drives a Ford mach - ine, I buy the gas - o - line,

5
D
G
No - bod - y's bus - iness if I do.
No - bod - y's bus - iness if I do.

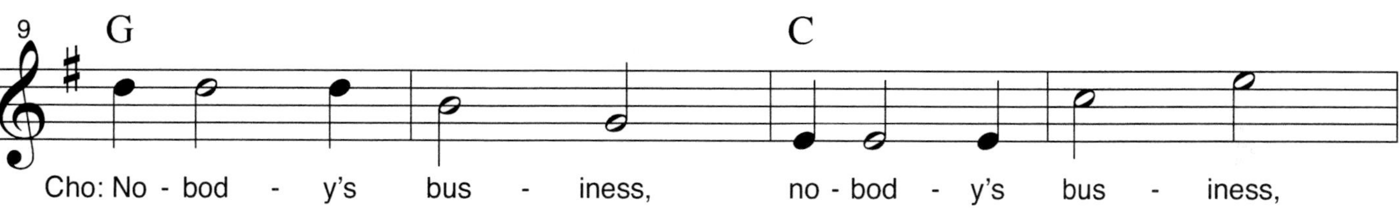

9
G
C
Cho: No - bod - y's bus - iness, no - bod - y's bus - iness,

13
D
G
no - bod - y's bus - iness if I do.

G
3. She's worth her weight in gold,
C
She likes to rock & roll,
D G
Nobody's business if I do,

Chorus:
G C
Nobody's business, Nobody's business,
D G
Nobody's business if I do,

4. My wife's from Alabam,
Way out in no man's land,
Nobody's business if I do, (etc.)

5. Sliced ham and pickled feet,
Ham and eggs and sausage meat,
Nobody's business if I do, (etc.)

6. She rides the limousine,
I crank the old machine,
Nobody's business if I do, (etc.)

[St]anley Bros., N. Blake, Country Gentlemen, L. Sparks, D. Reno

Oh Death

M: Em; F: Am
CD 2-Track 26

Tradition

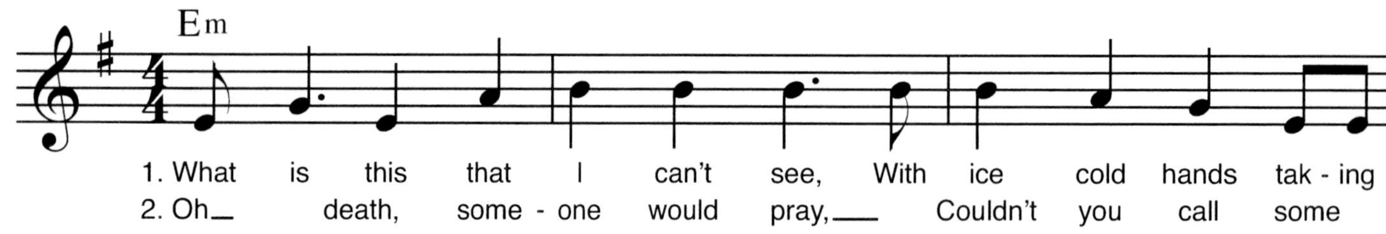
Em
1. What is this that I can't see, With ice cold hands tak - ing
2. Oh death, some - one would pray, Couldn't you call some

4
(B7)
Em
hold of me? I am death, none can ex - cel, I'll
oth - er day? God's child - ren prayed, the preach - ers preached, Th

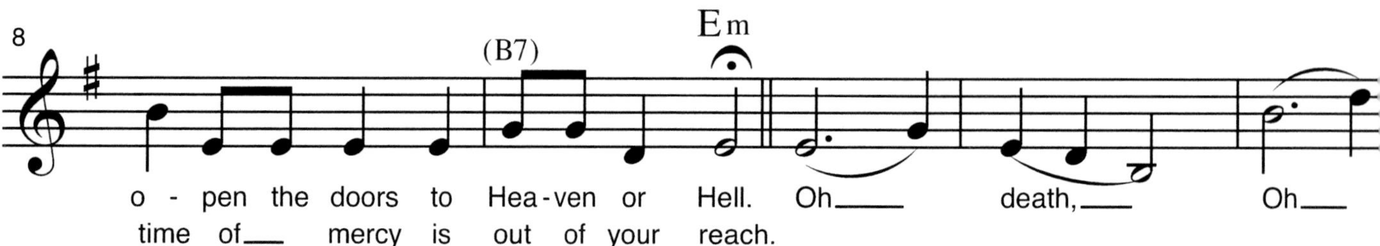
8
(B7)
Em
o - pen the doors to Hea - ven or Hell. Oh death, Oh
time of mercy is out of your reach.

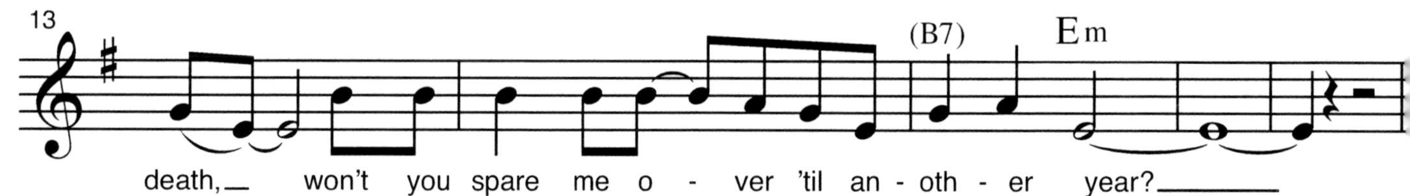
13
(B7)
Em
death, won't you spare me o - ver 'til an - oth - er year?

Em
3. I'll fix your feet so you can't walk,
B7 Em
I'll lock your jaws so you can't talk,
I'll close your eyes so you can't see,
B7 Em
This very hour come go with me.
(Repeat chorus)

4. Death, I come to take the soul,
Leave the body and leave it cold,
To drop the flesh off of the frame,
The earth and worms both have a claim.

5. My mother come to my bed,
Place a cold towel upon my head,
My head is warm, my feet are cold,
Death is moving upon my soul.

6. Oh death, how you treat me,
You close my eyes so I can't see.
You hurt my body, you make me cold,
You've run the life right out of my soul.

7. Oh death, please consider my age,
Please don't take me at this stage,
My wealth is all at your command,
If you will move your icy hand.

8. Old, the young, the rich or poor,
All alike with me, you know,
No wealth, no land, no silver, no gold,
Nothing satisfies me but your soul.

Stanley Bros., R. Stanley, "O Brother" soundtrack, NLCR, Carter Fan

Oh! Didn't He Ramble

*: G; **F:** C or D*
D 2-Track 27, medley pt. 1

Will Handy, 1902

G D G
1. My moth - er raised three grown sons, Bus - ter, Bill and I,
2. He ram - bled in a gam - bling game, he gam - bled on the green, The
C D G
Bus - ter was the black sheep of our lit - tle fam - i - ly,
gam - blers there showed him a trick that he had nev - er seen, He
D G
Moth - er tried to break him of his rough and row - dy ways, Fi - nally had to
lost his roll and jew - el - ry, he like to lost his life, He lost the car that
C D G
get the judge to give him nine - ty days. Cho: And did - n't he
carried him there and some - body stole his wife.
G D G
ram - ble, ram - ble, He ram - bled all a - round, In and out the
D G D G
town, And did-n't he ram - ble, ram - ble, He ram-bled till the butch-ers cut him down.

G D G
He rambled in a swell hotel, his appetite was stout,
D G
ıd when he refused to pay the bill, the landlord kicked him out.
G
e reached a brick to smack him with, and when he went to stop,
D G
ıe landlord kicked him over the fence, right in a barrel of slop.
epeat chorus after each verse)

He rambled through the tunnel once, on board a moving train.
ıother train came rumbling in, and rammed him out again.
rammed him just a block, and then, they caught him on the fly,
ıd with a ton of dynamite, they rammed him to the sky.

5. He rambled to an Irish wake, on one St. Patrick's night.
They asked him what he'd like to drink, they meant to treat him right.
But like the old Kilkenny cats, their backs began to arch.
When he called for orange phosphate, on the seventeenth of March.

6. He rambled to the races, to make a gallery bet.
He backed a horse named Hydrant, and Hydrant's running yet.
He would have had to walk back home, his friends all from him hid.
By luck he met old George Sedam, it's a damn good thing he did.

. Poole, Dixon Bros., Fiddlin' J. Carson

Old Dan Tucker

***M:** G; **F:** C or D* — *Traditional*

CD 2-Track 27, medley pt. 2

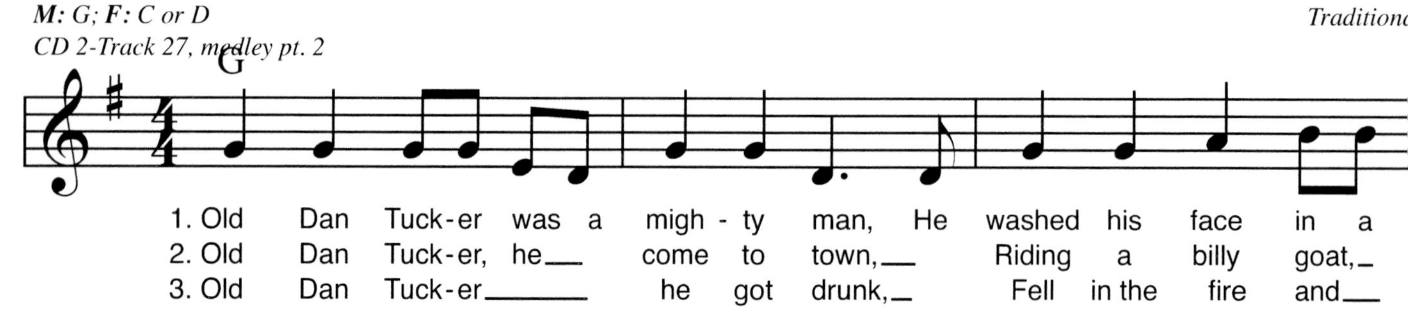
G
1. Old Dan Tuck-er was a migh - ty man, He washed his face in a
2. Old Dan Tuck-er, he__ come to town,__ Riding a billy goat,_
3. Old Dan Tuck-er______ he got drunk,_ Fell in the fire and__

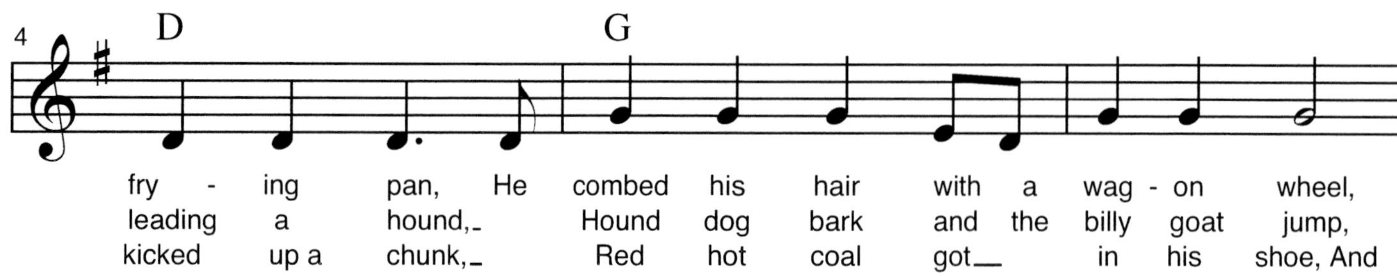
4
D G
fry - ing pan, He combed his hair with a wag - on wheel,
leading a hound,_ Hound dog bark and the billy goat jump,
kicked up a chunk,_ Red hot coal got__ in his shoe, And

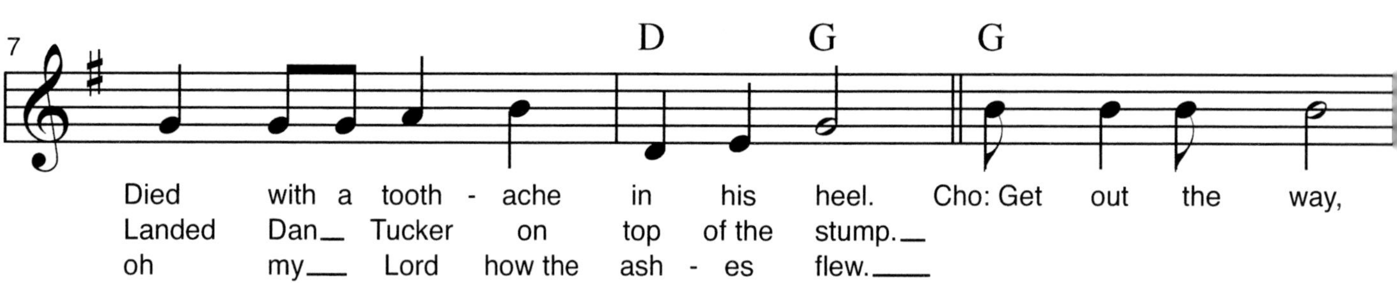
7
D G G
Died with a tooth - ache in his heel. Cho: Get out the way,
Landed Dan__ Tucker on top of the stump.__
oh my__ Lord how the ash - es flew.____

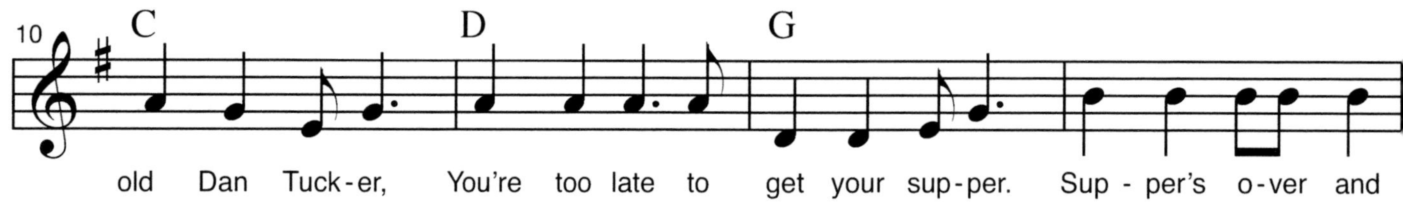
10
C D G
old Dan Tuck-er, You're too late to get your sup-per. Sup - per's o-ver and

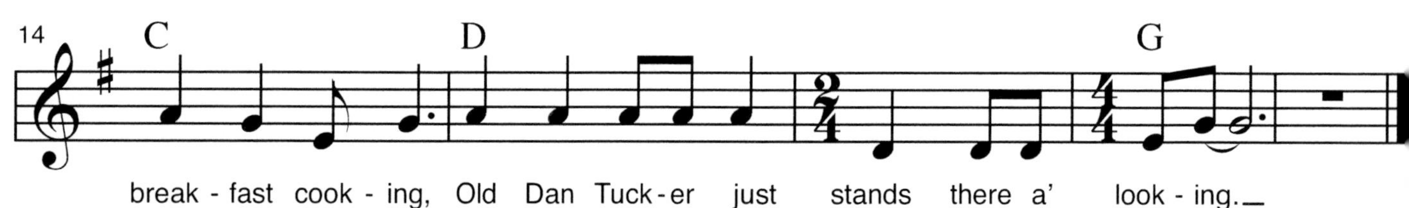
14
C D G
break - fast cook - ing, Old Dan Tuck-er just stands there a' look - ing._

Skillet Lickers, Fiddlin' John Carson, Hot Rize, L. Lewis & T. Rozum

Old Home Place

*: G; **F:** C or D*
D 2-Track 28

Webb & Jayne

G B7 C G
1. It's been ten long years since I left my home, In the
2. I fell in love with a girl from the town,
3. The girl ran off with some - bod - y else, The
4. Now the geese fly south and the cold wind blows, As
5
D G
hol - low where I was born, Where the cool fall
I thought that she'd be true, Then I ran a -
tav - erns took all my pay, And here I
I stand here and hang my head, I've lost my
10
B7 C G
nights make the wood smoke rise, And the fox hun - ter
way to Char - lottes - ville, And worked in a
stand where the old home stood, Be - fore they
love, I've lost my home, And now I
14
D G D
blows his horn. Cho: What have they done to the
saw - mill crew.
took it a - way.
wish that I was dead.
19
G A D7
old home place? Why did they tear it down?
24
G B7 C
And why did I leave my plow in the
28
G D G
field, And look for a job in the town?

llards, J.D. Crowe

Old Joe Clark

M: D; F: G or A
CD 2-Track 29

Tradition

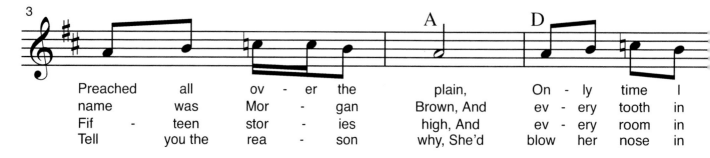

D
1. Old Joe Clark, the preach - er's son,
2. Old Joe Clark, he had a mule, His
3. Old Joe Clark, he had a house,
4. Nev - er mar - ry that old woman,
3
A D
Preached all ov - er the plain, On - ly time I
name was Mor - gan Brown, And ev - ery tooth in
Fif - teen stor - ies high, And ev - ery room in
Tell you the rea - son why, She'd blow her nose in

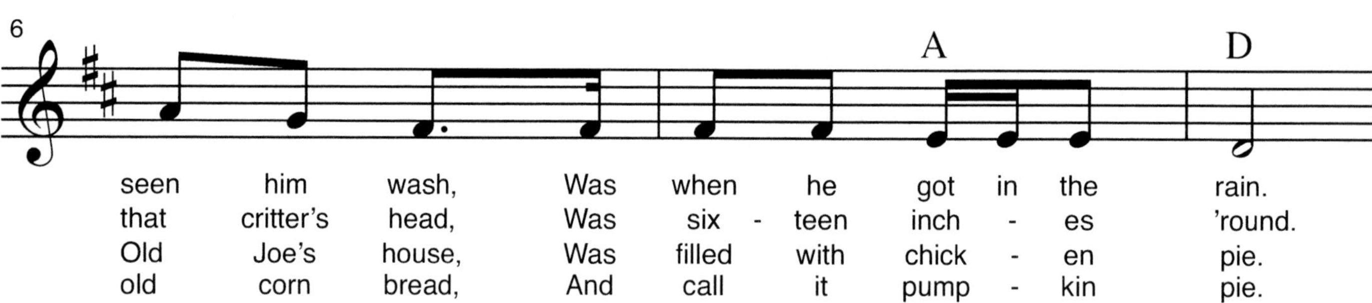
6
A D
seen him wash, Was when he got in the rain.
that critter's head, Was six - teen inch - es 'round.
Old Joe's house, Was filled with chick - en pie.
old corn bread, And call it pump - kin pie.

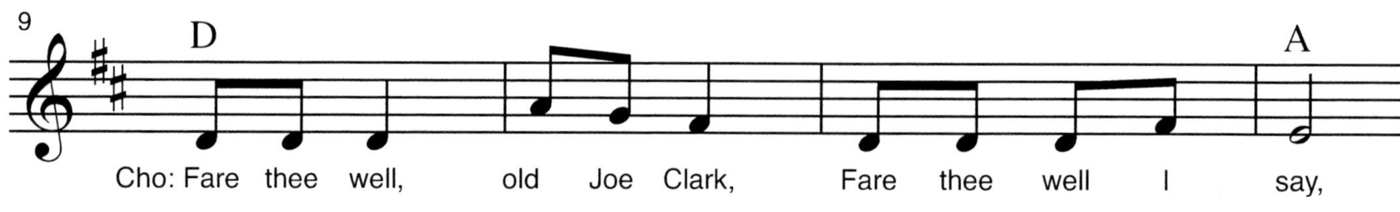
9
D A
Cho: Fare thee well, old Joe Clark, Fare thee well I say,

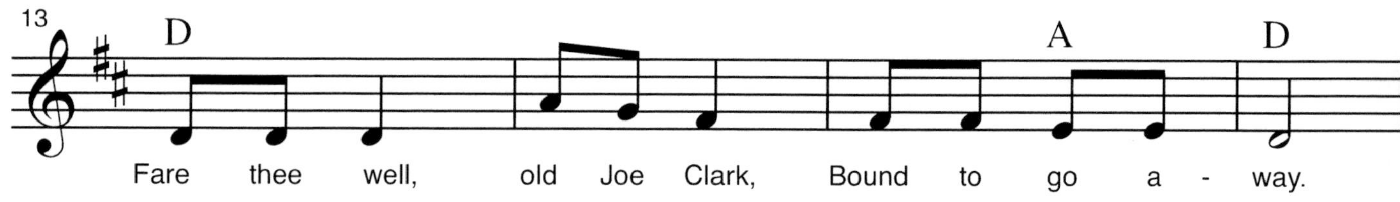
13
D A D
Fare thee well, old Joe Clark, Bound to go a - way.

Texas Shorty, Flatt & Scruggs, B. Monroe, Goose Island Ramblers, Ken. Colonel
C. White, Skillet Lickers, Red Allen, D. Dillard, T. Adams, T. Trischka, A. Munc

Old Man at the Mill

: G; F: C or D
D 2-Track 30

Traditional

G F G
Chorus: Same old man liv - ing at the mill, the
1. Down sat an owl with its head all white, A
2. Then said a raven, as she flew, "If
3. My old man's from Kal - a - ma - zoo,
3
D
mill turns a - round of its own free will, One
lone - some day and a lone - some night,
I was a young one I'd have two,
he don't wear no, yes I do,
5
G
hand in the hop - per and the oth - er in the sack,
Thought I heard a pre - ty girl say, "You
One for the git and the oth - er for to sew, I'll
First to the left and then to the right,
7
D G
Lad - ies step for - ward and the gents fall back.
court all night and sleep all day."
have an - other string for my bow, bow, bow."
This old mill grinds day and night.

illards, D. Watson, NLCR

Old Paint

M: G; F: C or D
CD 2-Track 31
Traditiona
G
1. I ride an old paint, I lead an old Dan, I'm
2. Old Bill Jones had a daugh - ter and a son,
3. When I die, take my sad - dle from the wall,
D G
going to Mon - tan - a to throw a Hool - i -
One went to Den - ver and the oth - er we - nt
Put it on my po - ny and lead him from his
D G
han. They feed 'em in the coul - ees, they wa - ter in the
wrong. His wife she died in a pool room
stall. Tie my bones to his back, turn our fac - es to the
D G
draw, Their tails are all mat - ted, their backs are all
fight, but still he keeps sing - ing from morn - ing 'til
west, And we'll ride the prair - ie that we love the
D G
raw. Cho: Ride a - round lit - tle do - gies, ride arou - nd re - al
night.
best.
D G
slow, for the fier - y and the snuf - fy are rar - ing to go.

Woody Guthrie, Riders in the Sk

The Old Rugged Cross

*: A; **F:** D or E*
D 2-Track 32

Geo. Bennard, 1913

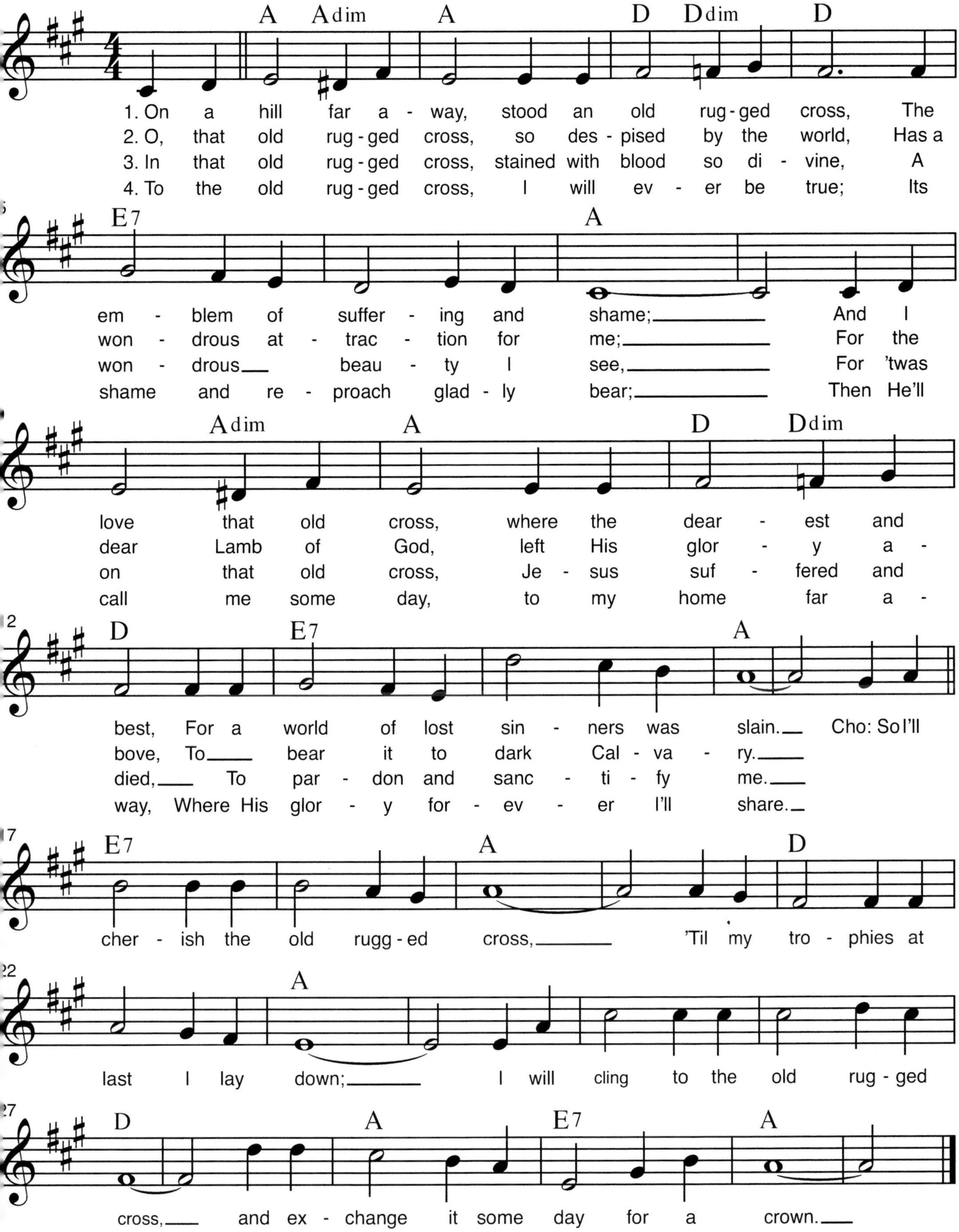

1. On a hill far away, stood an old rugged cross, The emblem of suffering and shame; And I love that old cross, where the dearest and best, For a world of lost sinners was slain. Cho: So I'll
2. O, that old rugged cross, so despised by the world, Has a wondrous attraction for me; For the dear Lamb of God, left His glory above, To bear it to dark Calvary.
3. In that old rugged cross, stained with blood so divine, A wondrous beauty I see, For 'twas on that old cross, Jesus suffered and died, To pardon and sanctify me.
4. To the old rugged cross, I will ever be true; Its shame and reproach gladly bear; Then He'll call me some day, to my home far away, Where His glory forever I'll share.

Cho: So I'll cherish the old rugged cross, 'Til my trophies at last I lay down; I will cling to the old rugged cross, and exchange it some day for a crown.

Old Time Religion

M: *G;* ***F:*** *C or D*
CD 2-Track 33

Traditional

G
Cho: Gim - me that old - time re - li - gion, Gim - me that
1. Makes me love ev - ery - bod - y, Makes me

3
D
G
old - time re - li - gion, Gim - me that old - time re -
love ev - ery - bod - y, Makes me love ev - ery -

6
C
G
D
G
li - gion, And it's good e - nough for me.
bod - y, And it's good e - nough for me.

```
           G
2. It was good for our mothers,
          D          G
It was good for our mothers,
                          C
It was good for our mothers,
           G     D        G
And it's good enough for me.
```

3. It has saved all our fathers, (3X, etc.)
4. It will save all our children, (3X, etc.)
5. It was good for Paul and Silas, (3X, etc.)
6. It was good for the Prophet Daniel, (3X, etc.)
7. It was good for the Hebrew children, (3X, etc.)
8. It was tried in the fiery furnace, (3X, etc.)
9. It will do when I'm a'dying, (3X, etc.)
10. It will take us all to heaven, (3X, etc.)

R. Stanley, Jim & Jesse

On and On

: G; F: C or D
D 2-Track 34
Bill Monroe
G C
1. Trav - eling down this long lone - some
Cho: On and on I'll fol - low my
cried, I've cried for you lit - tle
have to fol - low you my
4
G
high - way, I'm so lone - some I could
dar - ling, And I won - der where she can
dar - ling, It breaks my heart to hear your
dar - ling, I can't sleep when the sun goes
7
D G
cry, Mem - ories of how we
be, On and on I'll
name, My friends they al - so
down, By your side is
11
C G
once loved each oth - er, And
fol - low my dar - ling, And I
love you my dar - ling, And they
my des - tin - a - tion, The road is
13
D G
now you are say - ing good - bye.
wonder if she ever thinks of me. 2. I've
think that I am to blame. 3. I
clear and that's where I'm bound.

Over the Hills to the Poorhouse

M: G; F: C or D
CD 2-Track 35
Traditional
G C D
1. Oh how can it be they have driv - en, Their fath - er so
2. Oh heav - en, I'm sad and I'm wear - y, See the tears, how they
3. Long years since Mar - y was tak - en, My faith - ful, af -
4. Oh me, on the door - step up yon - der, I've set with my
5. I gave them the house they were born in, A deed to the
6
G
help - less and old? Oh God, may their crimes be for -
course down my cheek, This world is so lone - ly and
fec - tion - ate wife, Since then I'm a - lone and for -
babes on my knee, No fath - er so hap - py or
farm and more, I gave them the place that they
11
C D G
giv - en, To per - ish out here in the cold. Cho: I'm
wear - y, My heart for re - lief vain - ly seeks.
sak - en, The light has died out of my life.
fon - der, Than I of my lit - tle ones three.
lived on, And now I am turned from its door.
17
G D
old, I'm help - less and fee - ble, And the days of my
22
G C
youth have gone by, And o - ver the hills to the poor house,
28
D G
I must wan - der a - lone there to die.

Flatt & Scruggs, R. Allen & F. Wakefield, Country Gentlemen

Pass Me Not

*: G; **F:** C or D*
D 2-Track 36

Crosby & Doan, ca.1870

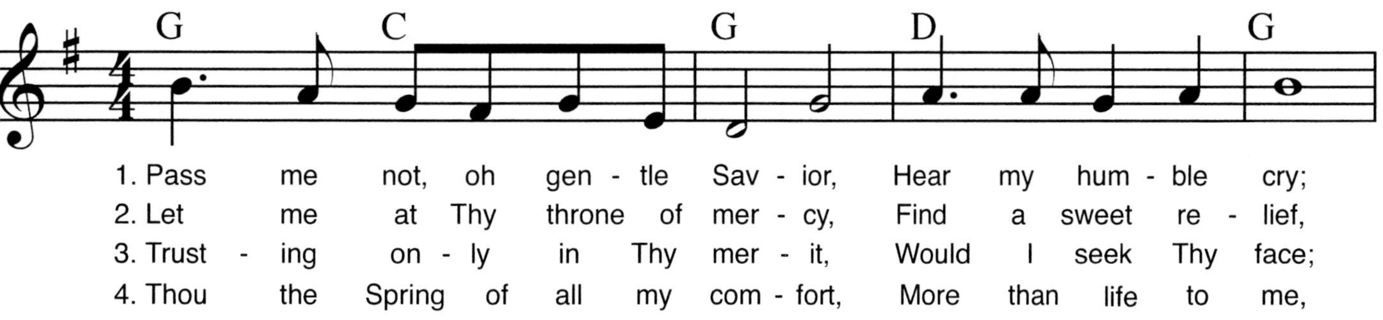
G C G D G
1. Pass me not, oh gen - tle Sav - ior, Hear my hum - ble cry;
2. Let me at Thy throne of mer - cy, Find a sweet re - lief,
3. Trust - ing on - ly in Thy mer - it, Would I seek Thy face;
4. Thou the Spring of all my com - fort, More than life to me,

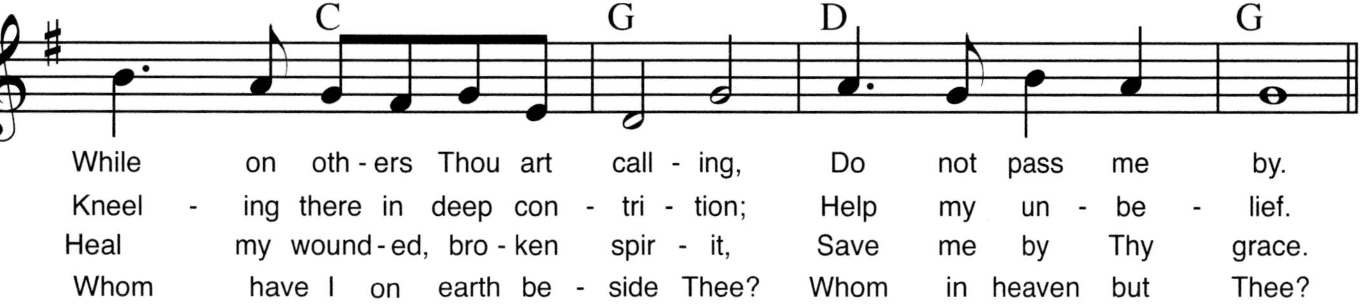
C G D G
While on oth - ers Thou art call - ing, Do not pass me by.
Kneel - ing there in deep con - tri - tion; Help my un - be - lief.
Heal my wound - ed, bro - ken spir - it, Save me by Thy grace.
Whom have I on earth be - side Thee? Whom in heaven but Thee?

G C G D
Cho: Sav - ior, Sav - ior, Hear my hum - ble cry;

3
G C G D G
While on oth - ers Thou art call - ing, Do not pass me by.

Paul and Silas

M: G; F: C or D
CD 2-Track 37
Tradition
G
1. Paul and Si - las bound in jail, all night
2. Paul and Si - las prayed to God, all night
3. That old jail - er locked the door, all night
4. That old jail it reeled and rocked, all night
5. He - brew children in the burn - ing fire, all night
C
G
long, Paul and Si - las bound in jail, all night
long, Paul and Si - las prayed to God, all night
long, That old jail - er locked the door, all night
long, That old jail it reeled and rocked, all night
long, He - brew children in the burn - ing fire, all night
long, Paul and Si - las bound in jail, all night
long, Paul and Si - las prayed to God, all night
long, That old jail - er locked the door, all night
long, That old jail it reeled and rocked, all night
long, He - brew children in the burn - ing fire, all night
D
G
long, Say - ing, "Who shall de - liv - er poor me?"
long, Say - ing, "Who shall de - liv - er poor me?"
long, Say - ing, "Who shall de - liv - er poor me?"
long, Say - ing, "Who shall de - liv - er poor me?"
long, Say - ing, "Who shall de - liv - er poor me?"

Flatt & Scruggs, Stanley Bros., F. Wakefield, Country Gentleme

Pig in a Pen

: G; F: C or D *Traditional*
D 2-Track 38

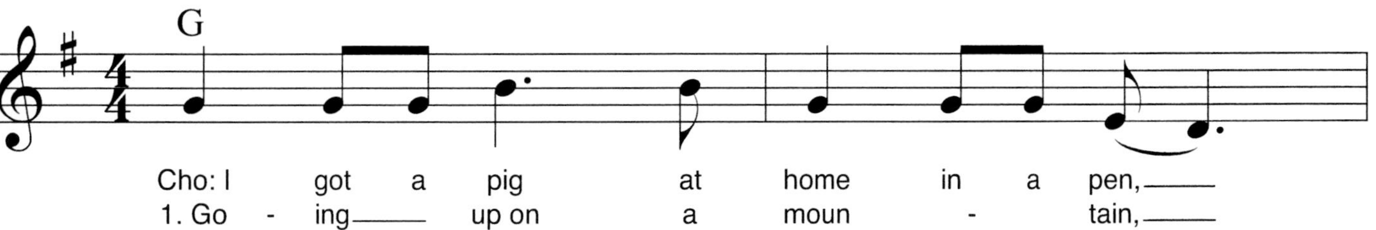
G
Cho: I got a pig at home in a pen,
1. Go - ing up on a moun - tain,

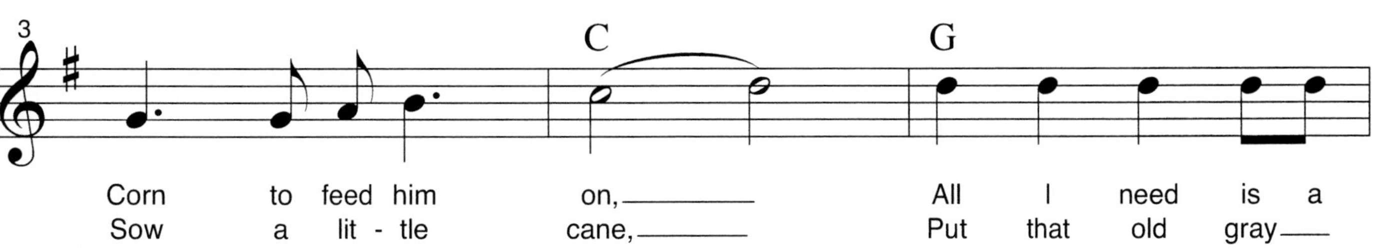
3
C
G
Corn to feed him on,
Sow a lit - tle cane,
All I need is a
Put that old gray

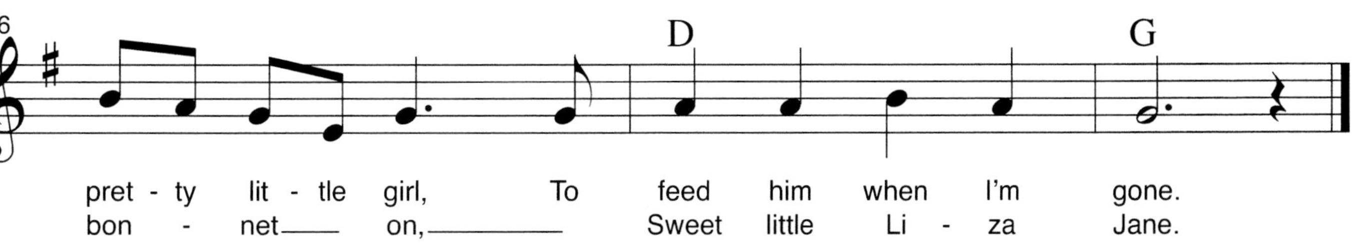
6
D
G
pret - ty lit - tle girl, To feed him when I'm gone.
bon - net on, Sweet little Li - za Jane.

G
2. Going up on a mountain,
C
To sow a little cane,
G
Raise a barrel of sorghum,
D G
Sweet little Liza Jane.

3. Black smoke arising,
Surely is a train,
Put that old gray bonnet on,
Little Liza Jane.

4. Bake them biscuits baby,
Bake 'em good and brown,
When you get them biscuits baked,
I'm Alabama bound.

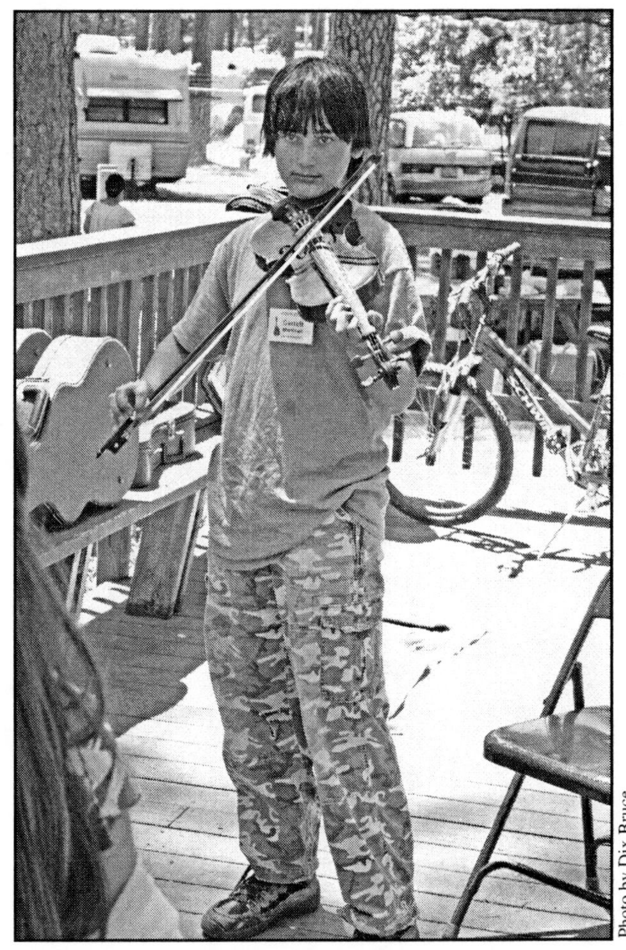

Photo by Dix Bruce

anley Bros., R. Stanley, B. Monroe, V. Williams, R. Skaggs, Old & in the Way

Poor Ellen Smith

M: G; F: C or D
CD 2-Track 39
Traditional
G
1. Poor El - len Smith, how she was
2. They picked up her bod - y and carried it a -
3. I got a let - ter yes - ter - day and I read it to -
4. My days in this pris - on are end - ing at
C G D G
found, Shot through the heart ly - ing cold on the ground. Her
way, Now she's a sleeping in some lone - some old grave. They
day, The flowers on her grave have all fad - ed a - way. I'm
last, I'll nev - er be free from the sins of my past.
clothes were all scat - tered and cov - ered the ground, And
picked up their ri - - fles and hunt - ed me down, They
go - ing back home and I'll stay when I go, On
Poor El - len Smith, how she was found,
C G D G
blood marked the spot where poor El - len was found.
found me a' loaf - ing all a - round the town.
poor El - len's grave, pret - ty flow - ers I'll sow.
Shot through the heart ly - ing cold on the ground.

J. Martin, Stanley Bros., Flatt & Scruggs, NLCR
E. Taylor, Country Gentlemen, Reno & Harrell, J. Val
Mac Wiseman, N. Blake, Bluegrass Intention

Precious Memories

: G; **F:** C or D
D 2-Track 40

J.B.F. Wright

G
C
G
D
1. Pre - cious mem - ories, un - seen an - gels, Sent from some - where to my soul,
2. Pre - cious fa - ther, lov - ing moth - er, Fly a - cross the lone - ly years,

9
G
C
G
D
G
How they lin - ger, ev - er near me, And the sac - red past un - fold.
And old home scenes of my child - hood, In fond mem - o - ry ap - pear.

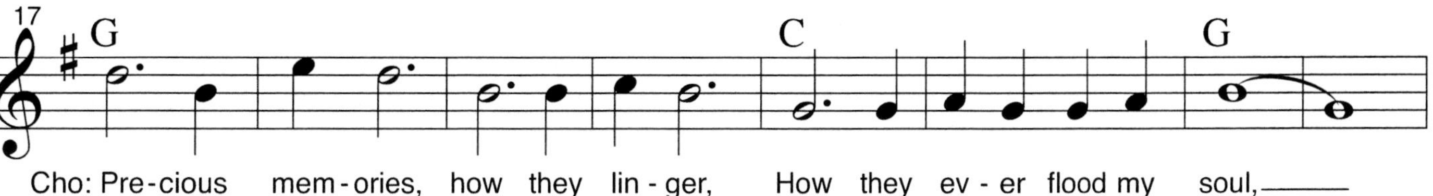

17
G
C
G
Cho: Pre - cious mem - ories, how they lin - ger, How they ev - er flood my soul,

25
C
G
D
G
In the still - ness, of the mid - night, Pre - cious, sa - cred scenes un - fold.


```
G              C      G
3. In the stillness of the midnight,
                          D
Echoes from the past I hear;
G                   C       G
Old time singing, gladness bringing,
           D                 G
From that lovely land somewhere.
```

4. I remember mother praying,
Father, too on bended knee;
Sun is sinking, shadows falling,
But their prayers still follow me.

5. As I travel on life's pathway,
Know not what the years may hold;
As I ponder, hope grows fonder,
Precious memories flood my soul.

anley Bros., B. Monroe

Pretty Polly

M: G; F: C or D
CD 2-Track 41
Traditional
G
1. Oh Pol - ly, pret - ty Pol - ly would you
2. My mind is to mar - ry and
3
take me un - kind?
nev - er to part, My
6
Pol ly, pret - ty Pol - ly would you
mind is to mar - ry and
9
take me un - kind? For me to sit be -
nev - er to part, The first time I
12
D
G
side you and tell you my mind.
saw you it wound - ed my heart.

Stanley Bros., R. Stanley, Dillards, C. White, D. Grisman, NLCR, D. Watson, D. Boggs

G
Oh, Polly, pretty Polly, come and go along with me,
olly, pretty Polly, come and go along with me,
D G
efore we get married some pleasure to see.

He led her over mountains and valleys so deep,
e led her over mountains and valleys so deep,
olly mistrusted and then began to weep.

Saying, "Willie, oh Willie, I'm afraid of your ways,
Villie, oh Willie, I'm afraid of your ways,
ne way you've been rambling, you'll lead me astray."

Well Polly, pretty Polly, your guess is about right,
olly, pretty Polly, your guess is about right,
dug on your grave the best part of last night.

Then he led her a little farther and what did they spy?
ed her a little farther and what did they spy?
new-dug grave with a spade lying by.

She knelt down before him a' pleading for her life,
nelt before him a' pleading for her life,
et me be a single girl if I can't be your wife."

Now Polly, pretty Polly, that never can be,
olly, pretty Polly, that never can be,
our past reputation's been trouble to me.

). He stabbed her in the heart and her blood it did flow,
e stabbed her in the heart and her blood it did flow,
nd into the grave pretty Polly did go.

. Then he went down to the jail house and what did he say?
e went to the jail house and what did he say?
ve killed pretty Polly and tried to get away."

?. Now gentlemen and ladies, I bid you farewell,
entlemen and ladies, I bid you farewell,
or killing pretty Polly my soul must go to hell.

Put My Little Shoes Away

M: G; F: C or D
CD 2-Track 42

Mitchell & Pratt, 18

G C G

1. Come and bathe my fore - head moth - er,
Go and tell my lit - tle play - mates,

5 D G

For I'm grow - ing ver - y weak, Let one
That I nev - er more will play, Give them

10 C G

drop of wa - ter moth - - - er, Fall up -
all my toys, but moth - - - er, Put my

14 D G C

on my burn - ing cheek. Cho: You will
lit - tle shoes a - way.

18 G

do this, won't you moth - er? Please re -

22 D G C

mem - ber what I say, Give them all my toys, but

27

G D G
moth - er, Put my lit - tle shoes a - way.

B. Monroe, Jimmy Marti

G   C   G
. Santa Claus, he brought them to me,
                        D
/ith a lot of other things,
       C   G
nd I think he brought an angel,
         D   G
/ith a pair of golden wings.
      C   G
will be an angel, Mother,
                             D
y perhaps another day,
            C   G
ou will do this for me, Mother,
          D   G
ut my little shoes away.

. Soon the baby will be larger,
nen they'll fit his little feet,
/on't he look so nice and cunning,
/hen he walks upon the street?
n going to leave you, Mother,
o remember what I say,
ou will do this for me, Mother,
ut my little shoes away.

Now I'm growing tired, dear Mother,
oon I'll say to you "Good Day,"
lways remember what I told you,
ut my little shoes away.
m about to leave you, Mother,
o remember what I say,
ou will do this for me, Mother,
ut my little shoes away.

Two fiddle greats: left, Stephane Grappelli with Darol Anger, in the early 1980s.

Photo by Dix Bruce

Railroad Bill

***M:** C; **F:** F or G*
CD 2-Track 43

Traditional

C
G7
C
1. Rail - road Bill, Rail - road Bill,
2. Rail - road Bill he was a mighty mean man,

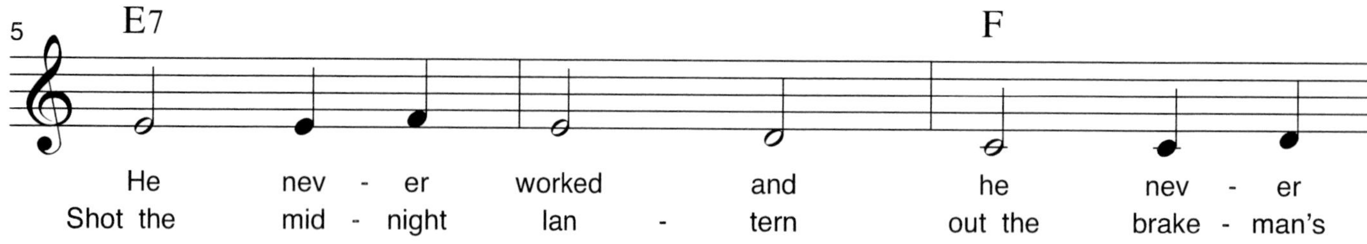
E7
F
He nev - er worked and he nev - er
Shot the mid - night lan - tern out the brake - man's

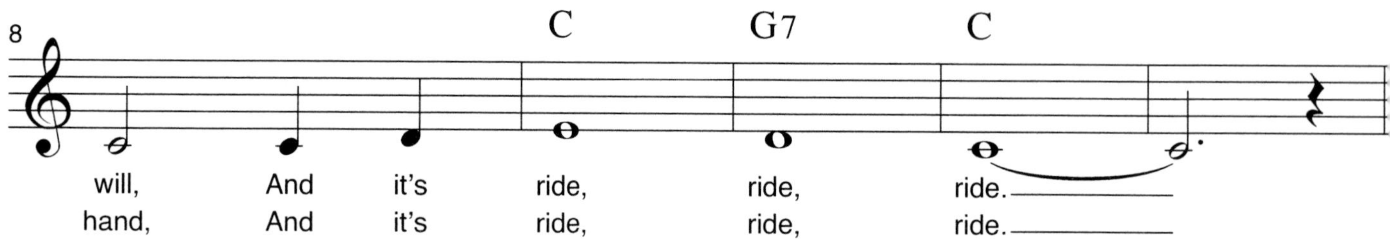
C
G7
C
will, And it's ride, ride, ride.
hand, And it's ride, ride, ride.

C G7 C
3. Railroad Bill took my wife,
E7 F
Said if I didn't like it, he would take my life,
C G7 C
And it's ride, ride, ride.

4. Going on a mountain, going way out west,
Thirty-eight special sticking out of my vest,
And it's ride, ride, ride.

5. Gonna buy me a pistol, long as my arm,
Kill everybody that's ever done me harm,
And it's ride, ride, ride.

6. I've got a thirty-eight special on a forty-five frame,
How can I miss him when I got dead aim,
And it's ride, ride, ride.

7. Honey, babe, do you think that I'm a fool,
Think that I'd quit you with the weather still so cool,
And it's ride, ride, ride.

D. Bruce & J. Nunally, D. Watson, E. Baker, Skillet Licker

Rain and Snow

: Am dorian; F: Dm or Em dorian
D 2-Track 44
Traditional
Am
1. I mar - ried me a wife, she give me
2. She came down the stairs, comb - ing
3. I done all I can do, to try to
4. She came in - to the room, where she
3
D
trou - ble all of my life, She ran me
back her yel - low hair, And her
get a - long with you, And I'm
met her fa - tal doom, And I'm
6
Am
D
out in that cold rain and snow. Rain and
cheeks were as red as a rose. As a
not gonna be treated this a' way, This a'
not gonna be treated this a' way, This a'
10
Am
D
snow, Lord, She ran me
rose, Lord, And her
way, Lord, And I'm
way, Lord, And I'm
15
Am
D
out in that cold rain and snow.
cheeks were as red as a rose.
not gonna be treated this a' way,
not gonna be treated this a' way,

Rank Strangers to Me

M: G; F: C or D
CD 2-Track 45

Albert E. Brumle

1. I wan - dered a - gain, to my home in the moun - tains,
2. I searched eve - ry face, for a sign of a loved one,
3. "They all moved a - way," said the voice of a stran - ger,
Where in youth's ear - ly dawn, I was hap - py and free,
And I asked eve - ry one, where the old folks could be,
"To a beau - ti - ful home, by a bright crys - tal sea,"
I looked for my friends, but I nev - er could find them,
I went down the road, to in - quire of some neigh - bors,
Some beau - ti - ful day, I'll meet them in heav - en,
I found they were all rank stran - gers to me.
But found they were, too, rank stran - gers to me.
Where no one will be a stran - ger to me.
Cho: Eve - ry - bod - y I met, seemed to be a rank stran - ger,
No moth - er or dad, not a friend could I see,
They knew not my name, and I knew not their fac - es,
I found they were all, rank stran - gers to me.

Stanley Bros., R. Stanley, Hot Rize, D. Watson, Osborne Bros., Country Gentleme

Red Rocking Chair

: G; ***F:*** *C or D*
D 2-Track 46

Traditional

G Em
1. Well I ain't got no use for your red rock - ing chair,
2. It's who'll rock the cra - dle, who'll sing the song?

G Em
Ain't got no hon - ey ba - by now, Lord, Lord,
Who'll rock the cra - dle when I'm gone, Lord, Lord?

D G
Ain't got no hon - ey ba - by now.
Who'll rock the cra - dle when I'm gone?


```
G                                Em
3. I'll rock the cradle, I'll sing the song,
G                              Em
I'll rock the cradle when you're gone, Lord, Lord,
D                              G
I'll rock the cradle when you're gone.
```

4. It's all I can do, all I can say,
Ain't gonna be treated this a' way, Lord, Lord,
Ain't gonna be treated this a' way.

5. It's all I can do, all I can say,
Sing it to you mama next pay day, Lord, Lord,
Sing it to you mama next pay day.

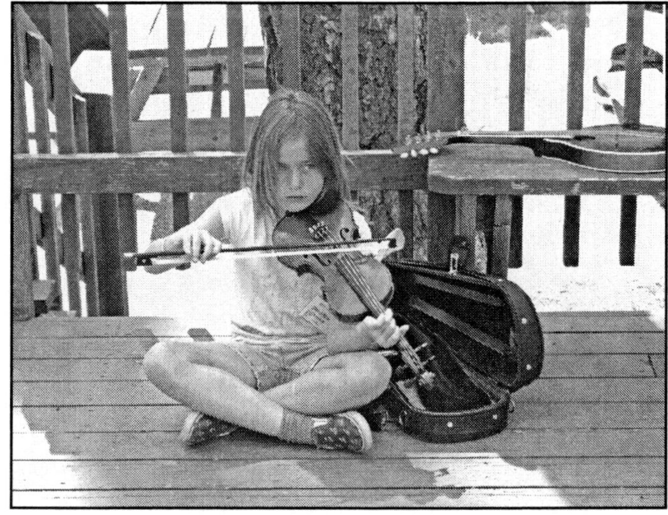

Photo by Dix Bruce

Monroe, Country Gentlemen, D. Watson, Reno & Harrell,
y Branch Fire Squad, J.D. Crowe, Mac Wiseman, Muleskinner, Kruger Bros.

Red Wing

M: C; F: F or G
CD 2-Track 47
Chattaway & Mills, 190
C F C
1.There once lived an In - dian maid, A shy lit - tle prair - ie maid, Who
2. She watched for him day and night, She kept all the camp fires bright, And
G7 C D G
sang a lay, a love song gay, As on the plain she'd while a - way the day; She
un - der the sky, each night she would lie, And dream a - bout his com - ing by and by, But
C F C
loved a war - rior bold, This shy lit - tle maid of old, But
when all the braves re - turned, The heart of Red Wing yearned, For
G7 C D G C
brave and gay, he rode one day, To bat - tle far a - way. Cho: Now, the
far, far a-way, her war - ri - or gay, Fell brave - ly in the fray.
F C G
moon shines to - night on pret - ty Red Wing, The bree - zes sigh - ing,
C F
the night birds cry - ing, For a - far, 'neath his star her brave is
C G7 C
sleep - ing, While Red Wing's weep - ing, her heart a - way.

N. Blake, Osborne Bros., R. Smiley, J. McEuen
A. Munde, L. Flatt & B. Monroe

Reuben's Train

: D; **F:** G *or* A
D 2-Track 48

Traditional

D
1. Reu - ben made a train, and he put it on the track, And he
go - ing to the east, I'm___ go - ing to the west, I'm___

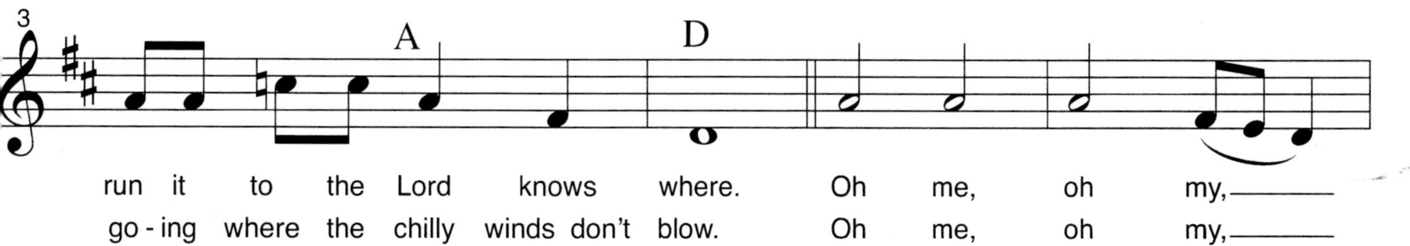

3
A
D
run it to the Lord knows where. Oh me, oh my,___
go - ing where the chilly winds don't blow. Oh me, oh my,___

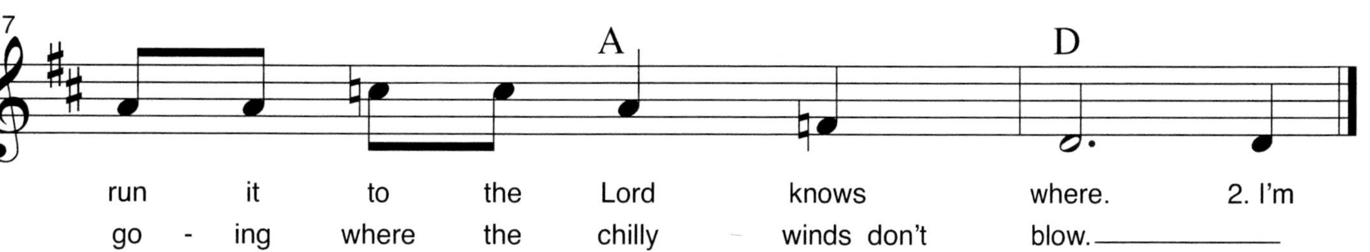

7
A
D
run it to the Lord knows where. 2. I'm
go - ing where the chilly winds don't blow.___


```
              D
3. If that train's running right, see my woman tomorrow night.
                    A              D
I'm nine hundred miles away from home.
                              A              D
Oh me, oh my, nine hundred miles away from home.
```

4. You ought to been uptown, to see that train come down,
You could hear the whistle blow a hundred miles.
Oh me, oh my, hear the whistle blow a hundred miles.

5. Last night I lay in jail, had no money to go my bail,
Lord, how it sleeted and it snowed.
Oh me, oh my, Lord how it sleeted and it snowed.

6. Oh, the train that I ride, is a hundred coaches long,
You can hear the whistle blow a hundred miles.
Oh me, oh my, you can hear the whistle blow a hundred miles.

7. I got myself a blade, laid Reuben in the shade,
I'm starting me a graveyard of my own.
Oh me, oh my, starting me a graveyard of my own.

tt & Scruggs, D. Watson, Holy Modal Rounders,
Rice, D. Bruce and J. Nunally

Rocky Top

M: G; F: C or D
CD 2-Track 49
Beaudleaux & Felice Brya
G C G
1. Wish that I was on old Rock - y Top,
2. Once I had a girl on Rock - y Top,
3. Once two stran - gers climbed old Rock - y Top,
4. Corn won't grow at all on Rock - y Top,
5. I've had years of cramped up ci - ty life,
3 Em D G
Down in the Ten - nes - see hills, Ain't no smog - gy
Half bear the oth - er half cat, Wild as a mink, but
Look - ing for a moon - shine still, Stran - gers ain't come
Dirt's too rock - y by far, That's why all the
Trapped like a duck in a pen, All I know is
6 C G Em D G
smoke on Rock - y Top, Ain't no tel - e - phone bills.
sweet as so - da pop, I still dream a - bout that.
down from Rock - y Top, Reck - on they nev - er will.
folks on Rock - y Top, Get their corn from a jar.
it's a pit - y life, Can't be sim - ple a - gain.
9 Em D F C
Chorus: Rock - y Top, you'll al - ways be, Home sweet home to me,
13 G F G
Good old Rock - y Top, Rock - y Top, Ten - nes - see,
17 F G
Rock - y Top, Ten - nes - see.

Roll in My Sweet Baby's Arms

': A; **F:** D or E
D 2-Track 50

Traditional

A
1. I ain't gon - na work on the rail - road, I ain't gon - na
2. Now where were you last Fri - day night, While I was
E7 A A7
work on the farm, I'll lay a - round the shack 'til the
ly - ing in jail? Out walk - ing the streets with an -
D E7 A
mail train gets back, And I'll roll in my sweet ba - by's arms.
oth - er man, Wouldn't even go my bail.
A
Cho: Roll in my sweet ba - by's arms, Roll in my
E7 A A7
sweet ba - by's arms, Lay a - round the shack 'til the
D E7 A
mail train gets back, And I'll roll in my sweet ba - by's arms.

A
3. I know your parents don't like me,
E7
They drove me away from your door,
A A7 D
If I had my life to live over,
E7 A
I'd never go there any more.

4. Mama's a beauty operator,
Sister can weave and spin,
Pappa's got an interest in an old cotton mill,
My, how the money rolls in!

5. Sometimes there's a change in the weather,
Sometimes there's a change in the sea,
Sometimes there's a change in my own true love,
But there's never a change in me.

onroe Bros., Flatt & Scruggs, B. Monroe, R. Stanley, J.D. Crowe, luegrass Band, D. McCoury, Scruggs/Watson/Skaggs, Lilly Bros.

Roll on Buddy

***M:** G; **F:** C or D*
CD 2-Track 51

Traditiona

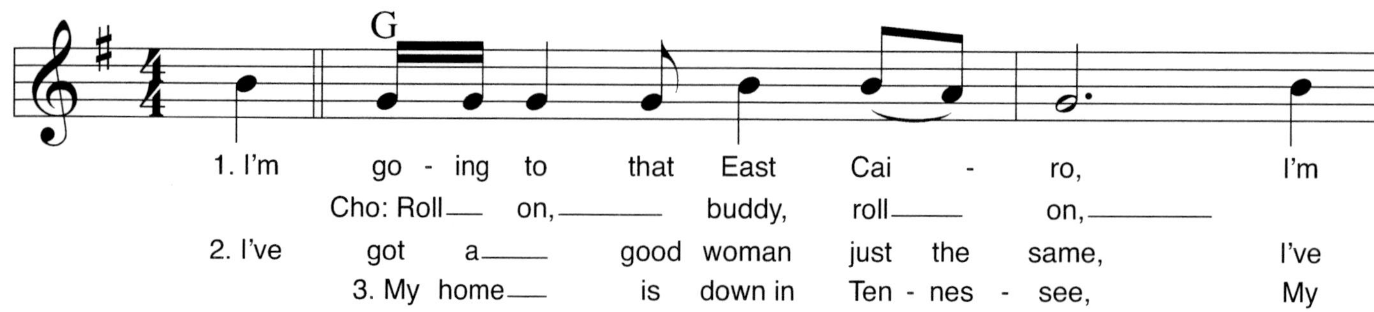
G
1. I'm go - ing to that East Cai - ro, I'm
Cho: Roll on, buddy, roll on,
2. I've got a good woman just the same, I've
3. My home is down in Ten - nes - see, My

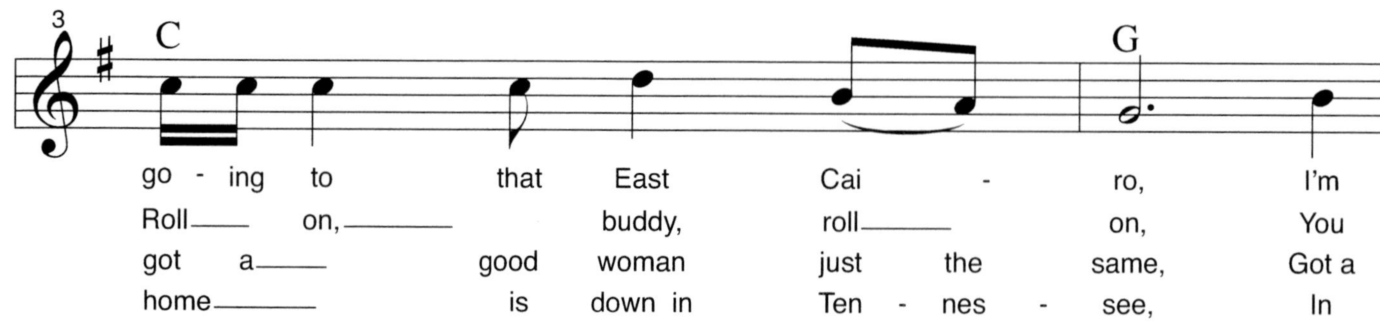
3
C
G
go - ing to that East Cai - ro, I'm
Roll on, buddy, roll on, You
got a good woman just the same, Got a
home is down in Ten - nes - see, In

5
C
G
go - ing to the east, I'm go - ing to the west, I'm
would-n't roll so slow if you knew what I know, So
wo - man just the same, says she's gon - na change her name, I've
Ten - nes - see, that's where I long to be,

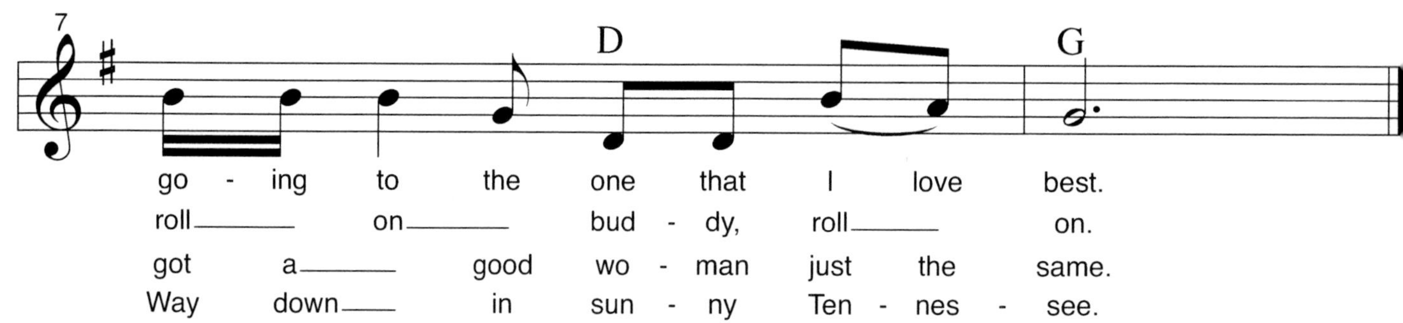
7
D
G
go - ing to the one that I love best.
roll on bud - dy, roll on.
got a good wo - man just the same.
Way down in sun - ny Ten - nes - see.

Monroe Bros., B. Monroe, R. Stanley, Ken. Colonels,
V. Williams, D. Watson, D. McCoury

Roving Gambler

: G; F: C or D
D 2-Track 52

Traditional

G
1. I am a rov - ing gam - bler, I've gam - bled all a - round, When -
2. I had not been in Fris - co___ many more weeks than three,___

C G C G
ev - er I meet with a deck of cards, I lay my mon - ey down.
I___ met up with a pretty little girl, She fell in love with me.

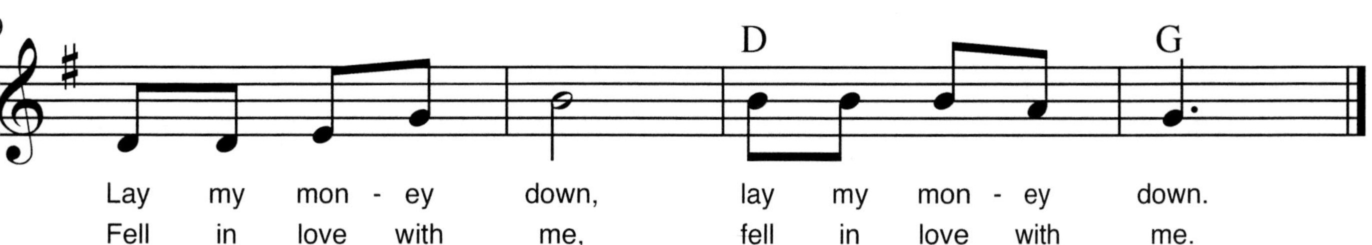
D G
Lay my mon - ey down, lay my mon - ey down.
Fell in love with me, fell in love with me.

G
She took me in her parlor, she cooled me with her fan,
C G
ıe whispered low in her mother's ear,
C G
love this gambling man.
D G
›ve this gambling man, love this gambling man."

Oh daughter, oh dear daughter, how can you treat me so?
›ave your dear old mother,
ıd with a gambler go,
ith a gambler go, with a gambler go?

Oh mother, oh dear mother, you cannot understand,
you ever see me a'coming back,
be with the gambling man,
ith the gambling man, with the gambling man.

6. I left her in Frisco and I ended up in Maine,
I met up with a gambling man,
We got in a poker game,
Got in a poker game, got in a poker game.

7. We put our money in the pot and dealt the cards around,
I saw him deal from the bottom of the deck,
So I shot that gambler down,
Shot the gambler down, shot the gambler down.

8. Now I'm up in prison, got a number for my name,
Jailer said as he locked the door,
"You've gambled your last game,
Gambled your last game, gambled your last game."

ınley Bros., Country Gentlemen, P. Rowan,
Watson, B. Clifton, Mac Wiseman

Sailor on the Deep Blue Sea

M: D; F: G or A
CD 2-Track 53

Traditiona

D G

1. It was on one sum - mer's eve - ning,___ Just a -
2. Oh, he prom - ised to write me a let - ter,___ He___
3. Oh, my moth - er's dead and bur - ied,___ My___
4. Oh___ cap - tain, can you tell me___ Where___
5. Fare - well to friends and re - la - tions,___ It's the

3 D A D

bout the hour of three, When my dar - ling start - ed to
said he'd write to me, But I've not heard from my___
pa's for - sak - en me, And I have no one for to
can my sail - or be, Oh___ yes, my lit - tle___
last you'll see of me, For I'm go - ing to end my

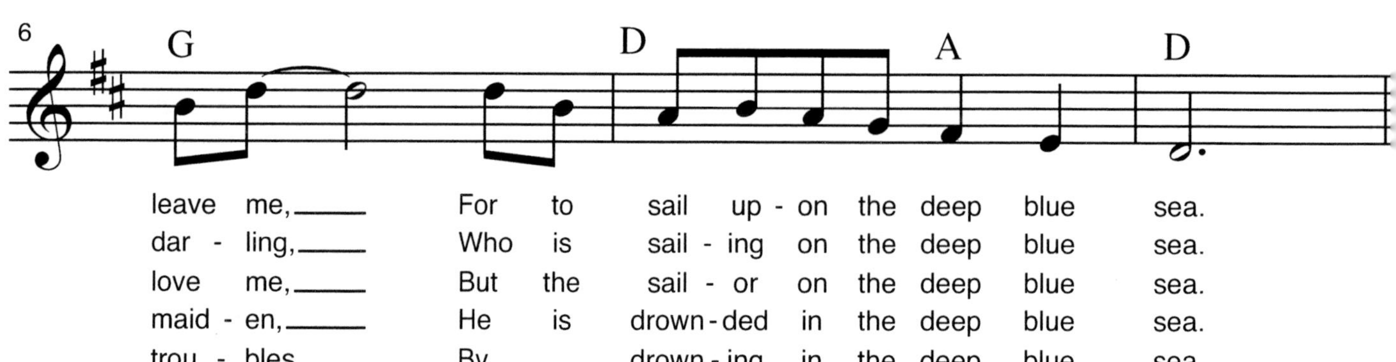
6
G
D
A
D
leave me,___ For to sail up - on the deep blue sea.
dar - ling,___ Who is sail - ing on the deep blue sea.
love me,___ But the sail - or on the deep blue sea.
maid - en,___ He is drown - ded in the deep blue sea.
trou - bles,___ By___ drown - ing in the deep blue sea.

Carter Fam., NLC

Sally Goodin

*1: A; **F:** D or E*
'D 2-Track 54

Traditional

A
1. Had a piece of pie, And I had a bowl of pud - din,'
2. Looked down the road and I see my Sal - ly com - ing,
3. Love a ta - ter pie and I love an ap - ple pud - din', And

E
A
Give it all a - way, Just to see Sal - ly Good - in.
Thought to my soul that I'd kill my - self a - run - ning.
I love a lit - tle gal they call Sal - ly Good - in.

A
E
A

G
4. I dropped the tater pie and I left the apple puddin',
D G
Went across the mountain to see my Sally Goodin.

5. Sally is my dooxy and Sally is my daisy,
When Sally says she hates me I think I'm going crazy.

6. Little dog'll bark and the big dog'll bite you,
Little gal'll court you and a big gal'll fight you.

7. Raining and a' pouring and the creek's
running muddy,
I'm so drunk I can't stand steady.

8. I'm goin up the mountain and marry little Sally,
Raise corn on the hillside and the devil
in the valley.

'att & Scruggs, B. Monroe, R. Stanley, C. White,
ot Rize, NLCR, A. Munde, J. Hickman

Shady Grove

Bluegrass style

***M:** C; **F:** F or G*
CD 2-Track 55

Traditiona

C
Cho: Sha - dy Grove, my lit - tle miss,
1. If you see my lit - tle miss,
2. Eve - ry time I walk this road,
3
Sha - dy Grove, my dar - - ling,
If you see my dar - ling,
Al - ways dark and cloud - - y,
5
Sha - dy Grove, my lit - tle miss,
If you see my lit - tle miss,
Eve - ry time I see that gal,
7
G
C
Go - ing back to Har - lan.
Tell her I'm going to Har - lan.
Al - ways tell her how - dy.

C
4. Fly around, my pretty little dove,
Fly around, my daisy,
Fly around, my pretty little love,
G C
Bound to drive me crazy.

5. Wish I was in Shady Grove,
Sitting in a rocking chair,
And if those blues would bother me,
I'd rock away from there.

6. All I want is a pig in a pen,
Corn to feed him on,
Pretty little girl to stay at home,
Feed him when I'm gone.

7. Wish I had a banjo string,
Made of golden twine,
Every tune I'd play on it,
I wish that girl was mine.

8. Wish I had a needle and thread,
Fine as I could sew,
I'd sew that pretty girl to my side,
And down the road I'd go.

9. Some come here to fiddle and dance,
Some come here to tarry,
Some here to fiddle and dance,
I come here to marry.

B. Monroe, Garcia & Grisman, Ken. Colonels
Hot Rize, D. Watson, Grisman, Garcia, Rice

Shady Grove

Old Time style

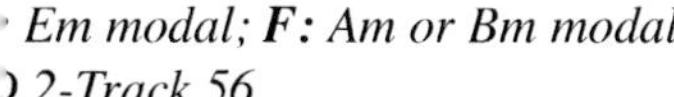
Em modal; **F:** Am or Bm modal
) 2-Track 56

Traditional

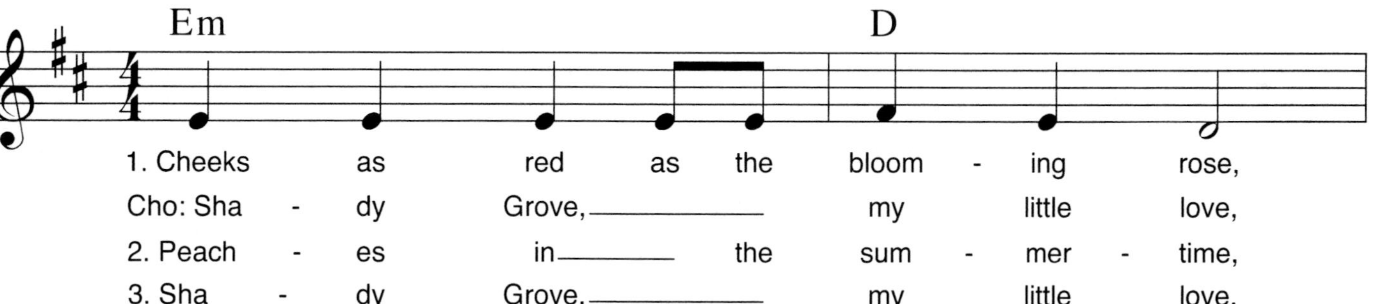
Em
D
1. Cheeks as red as the bloom - ing rose,
Cho: Sha - dy Grove, my little love,
2. Peach - es in the sum - mer - time,
3. Sha - dy Grove, my little love,

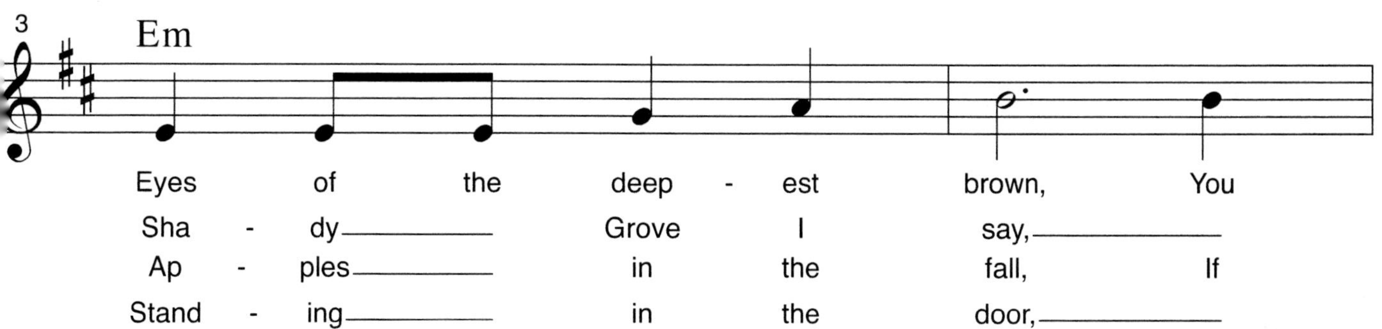
3
Em
Eyes of the deep - est brown, You
Sha - dy Grove I say,
Ap - ples in the fall, If
Stand - ing in the door,

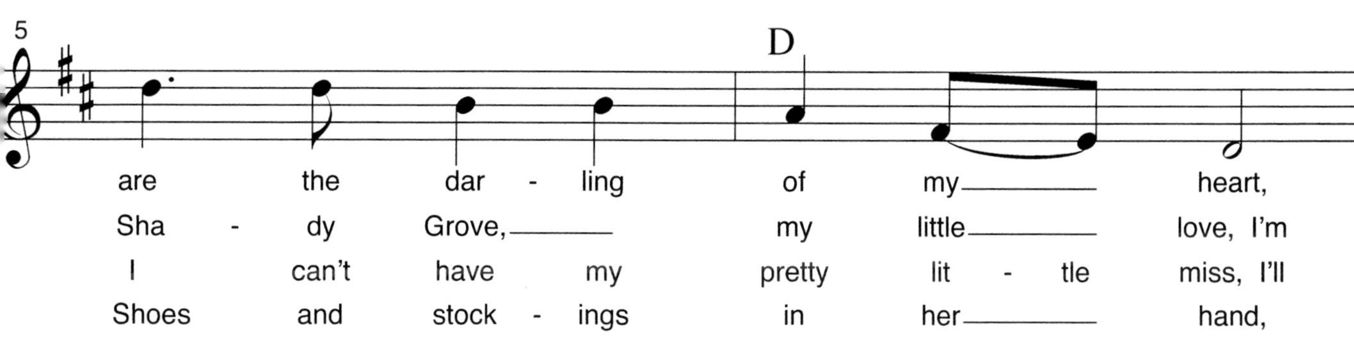
5
D
are the dar - ling of my heart,
Sha - dy Grove, my little love, I'm
I can't have my pretty lit - tle miss, I'll
Shoes and stock - ings in her hand,

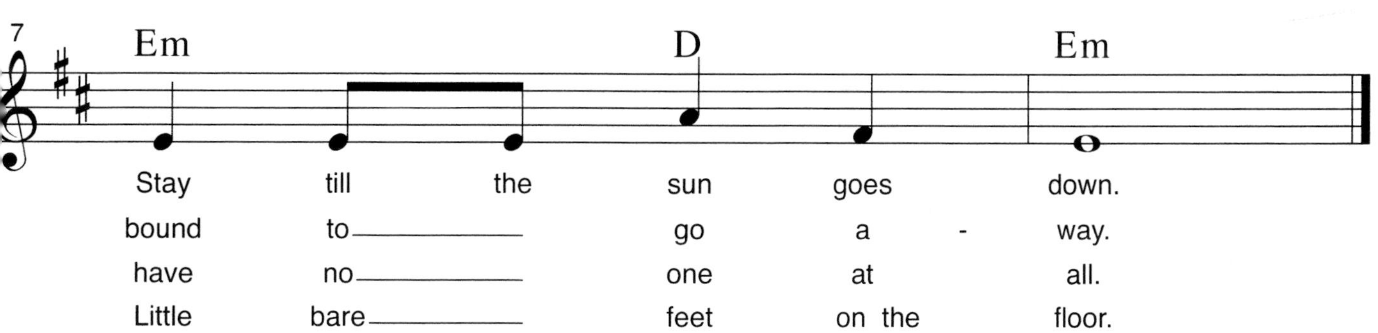
7
Em
D
Em
Stay till the sun goes down.
bound to go a - way.
have no one at all.
Little bare feet on the floor.

Shall We Gather at the River

M: C; F: F or G
CD 2-Track 57

Robert Lowry

C
G7
1. Shall we gath - er at the riv - er, Where bright an - gel feet hav
2. On the bos - om of the riv - er, Wash - ing up its sil - ve

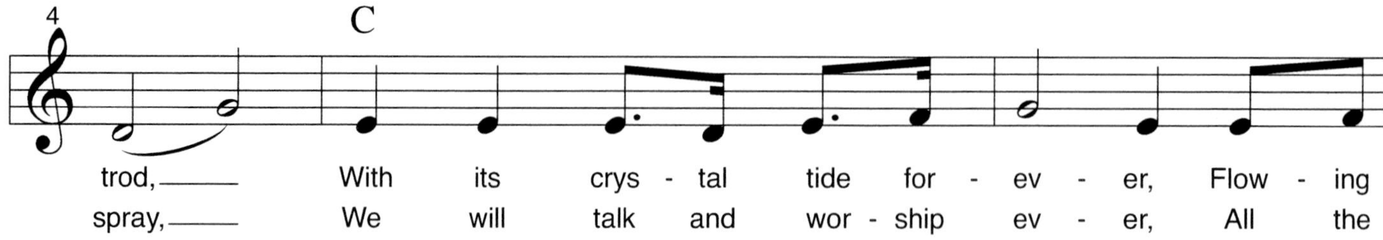
4
C
trod, With its crys - tal tide for - ev - er, Flow - ing
spray, We will talk and wor - ship ev - er, All the

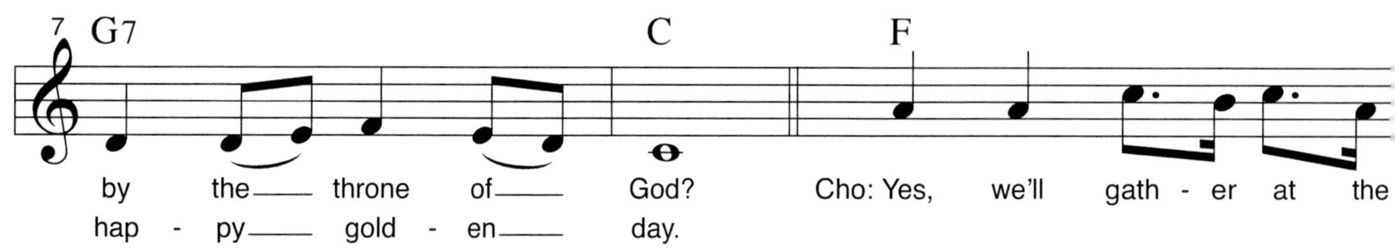
7
G7
C
F
by the throne of God? Cho: Yes, we'll gath - er at the
hap - py gold - en day.

10
C
G7
C
riv - er, The beau - ti - ful, the beau - ti - ful riv - er;

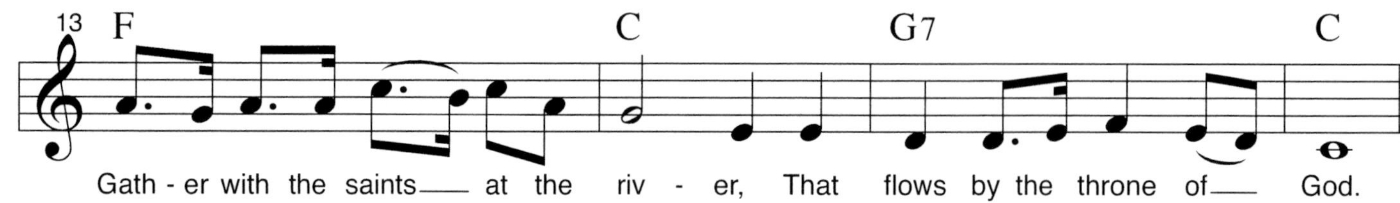
13
F
C
G7
C
Gath - er with the saints at the riv - er, That flows by the throne of God.

C
3. 'Ere we reach the shining river,
G7
Lay we every burden down;
C
Grace our spirits will deliver,
G7 C
And provide a robe and crown.

4. At the smiling of the river,
Mirror of the Savior's face,
Saints, whom death will never sever,
Lift their songs of saving grace.

5. Soon we'll reach the shining river,
Soon our pilgrimage will cease;
Soon our happy hearts will quiver,
With the melody of peace.

Mac Wiseman, Uncle Dave Maco

A Short Life of Trouble

': C; ***F:*** *F or G*
D 2-Track 58

Traditional

C
Cho: A short life of trou - ble, A
1. You know what you prom - ised, It's
2. I hear that train a'com - ing, She's
5
F
C
F
few more words to part, A short
been some time a - go, You prom -
going by the sta - tion door, I'd rather be
10
C
life of troub - le, dear girl, Poor
ised you'd mar - ry me, Standing
dead and in my grave, Than
13
G
C
boy with an ach - ing heart.
in your ma - ma's door
see my dar - ling go.

C
3. Now you've broken your promise,
F C
Go marry whom you may,
F C
For this old world's so big and so wide,
G C
I'll ramble back some day.

4. Now you've gone and left me,
I don't know what I'll do,
I'd give the world and half of my life,
Just to be married to you.

5. I see my coffin coming,
My shroud and all is on,
To take me to some lonesome graveyard,
And let the grave be my home.

6. And when my days have ended,
Will you come sow some flowers,
To show to the people 'round you,
The heart you've broken lies there.

Watson, R. Stanley, Grayson & Whitter, Burnett & Rutherford,
ue Sky Boys, E. Taylor, Mac Wiseman

Shortenin' Bread

***M:** D; **F:** G or A*
CD 2-Track 59

Tradition

D
1. Three lit - tle child - ren, lay - ing in bed,
2. When those chil - dren sick in bed,
3
A D
Two were sick and the oth - er 'most dead.
Heard that talk a - bout short - nin' bread.
5
Sent for the doc - tor, doc - tor said,
They got up well and dance and sing,
7
A D
"Feed these child - ren some short - nin' bread."
Skip - ping 'round they cut the Pig - eon Wing.
9
D
Cho: Ma - ma's lit - tle ba - by loves short - nin,' short - nin,'
11
A D
Ma - ma's lit - tle ba - by loves short - nin' bread.

Silver Threads Among the Gold

': G; F: C or D
D 2-Track 60

Rexford & Danks, 1901

G D7 G D7 G
1. Dar - ling, I am grow - ing old,— Sil - ver threads a - mong the gold,
2. When your hair is sil - ver white, And your cheeks no lon - ger bright,
5
D7 G D7 G
Shine up - on my brow to - day,— Life is fad - ing fast a - way.
With the ros - es of the May,— I will kiss your lips and say:
9
D7 G D A7 D7
But, my dar - ling, you will be, will be, Al - ways young and fair to me,
"Oh! my dar - ling, mine a - lone, a - lone, You have nev - er old - er grown,
13
G D7 G D7 G
Yes, my dar - ling, you will be,— Al - ways young and fair to me.
Yes, my dar - ling, mine a - lone,— You have ne - ver old - er grown."

```
G           D7                G
3. Love can never more grow old.
D7                                G
Locks may lose their brown and gold,
G           D7               G
Cheeks may fade and hollow grow,
D7                              G
But the hearts that love will know.
D7                       G
Never, never, winter's frost and chill,
D        A7              D7
Summer warmth is in them still;
G        D7              G
Never winter's frost and chill,
D7                              G
Summer warmth is in them still.
```

4. Love is always young and fair.
What to us is silver hair?
Faded cheeks or steps grown slow,
To the heart that beats below?
Since I kissed you, mine alone, alone,
You have never older grown;
Since I kissed you, mine alone,
You have never older grown.

no & Smiley, Fiddlin' John Carson, Blue Sky Boys, K. Baker

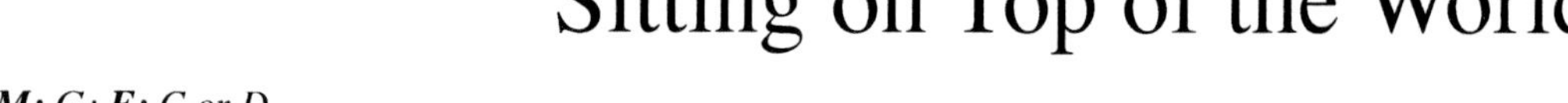

Sitting on Top of the World

M: G; F: C or D
CD 2-Track 61

Traditiona

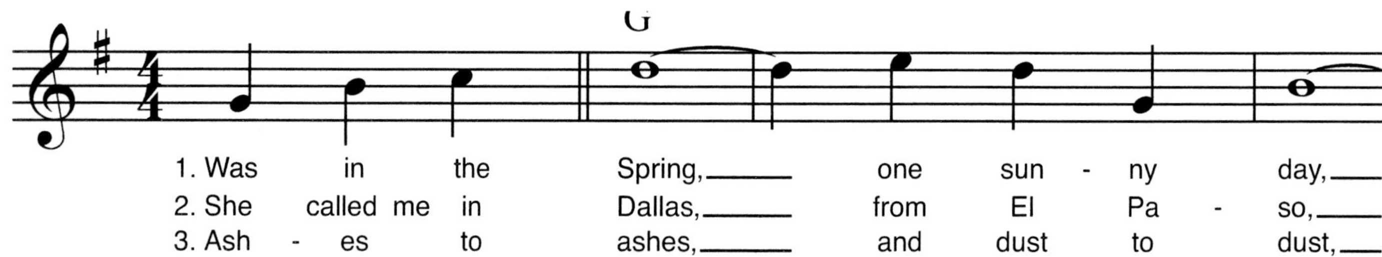
G
1. Was in the Spring, one sun - ny day,
2. She called me in Dallas, from El Pa - so,
3. Ash - es to ashes, and dust to dust,

4
C
G
My good gal left me, she went a - way.
Said, "Come back Dad - dy, Lord I need you so."
Show me a wom - an, any man can trust.

8
Cho: And now she's gone, and I don't wor - ry, Lord, I'm

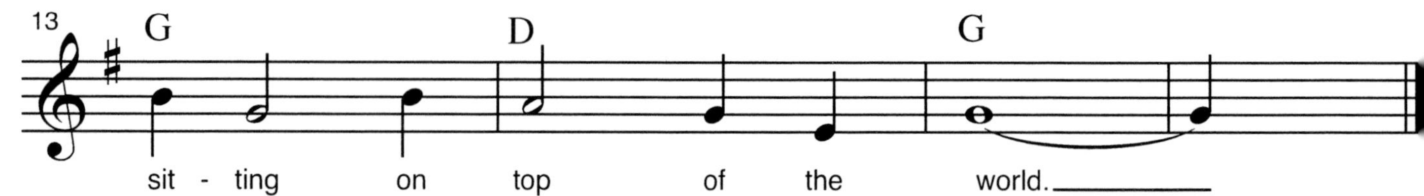
13
G
D
G
sit - ting on top of the world.

G
4. Mississippi River, long, deep and wide,
C G
The woman I'm loving's, on the other side.
Chorus: But now she's gone, and I don't worry,
D G
Lord, I'm sitting on top of the world.

5. You don't like my peaches, don't you shake my tree,
Get out of my orchard, let my peaches be. (Chorus)

6. Don't you come here running, poking out your hand,
I'll get me a woman, like you got your man. (Chorus)

B. Monroe, R. Stanley, D. Watson, F. Wakefiel
D. Bruce & J. Nunally, Nitty Gritty Dirt Ban

Softly and Tenderly

*: G; **F:** C or D*
D 2-Track 62

W.L. Thompson

G C G
1. Soft - ly and ten - der - ly Je - sus is call - ing,
2. Why should we tar - ry when Je - sus is plead - ing,
3. Time is now fleet - ing, the mo - ments are pass - ing,
4. O, for the won - der - ful love He has prom - ised,
Em A7 D7
Call - ing for you and for me.
Plead - ing for you and for me?
Pass - ing from you and from me;
Prom - ised for you and for me!
G C G
See, on the por - tals He's wait - ing and watch - ing,
Why should we lin - ger and heed not His mer - cies,
Sha - dows are gath - er - ing, death - beds are com - ing,
Though we have sinned, He has mer - cy and par - don,
Em C G D7 G
Watch - ing for you and for me. Cho: Come
Mer - cies for you and for me?
Com - ing for you and for me.
Par - don for you and for me.
D7 G D7 G D7 E7 A7 D7 A7 D7
home, Come home, You who are wear - y come home
G C G Em C G D7 G
Ear - nest-ly, ten - der - ly Je-sus is call ing, Call ing "O sin-ner come home!"

Somebody Touched Me

M: G; F: C or D
CD 2-Track 63
Traditional
G
1. While I was pray - ing, Some - bod - y touched me,
Cho: Glory, glo - ry, glo - ry, Some - bod - y touched me,
C
G
While I was pray - ing, Some - bod - y touched me,
Glory, glo - ry, glo - ry, Some - bod - y touched me,
While I was pray - ing, Some - bod - y
Glory, glo - ry, glo - ry, Some - bod - y
touched me, It must have been the
touched me, It must have been the
D
G
hand of our Lord.
hand of our Lord.

G
2. While I was preaching, somebody touched me,
C G
While I was preaching, somebody touched me,
While I was preaching, somebody touched me,
D G
It must have been the hand of our Lord.

3. While I was singing, somebody touched me, etc.

B. Monroe, Stanley Bros., R. Stanley, Dillards, D. Watson

Standing in the Need of Prayer

: G; F: C or D
D 2-Track 64
Traditional
G
1. Not my broth - er, not my sis - ter, but it's me, oh Lord,
2. Not the proph - et, not the preach - er, but it's me, oh Lord,
Stand - ing in the need of prayer, Not my broth - er, not my sis - ter, but it's
Stand - ing in the need of prayer, Not the dea - con, not the tea - cher, but it's
D
G
me, oh Lord, Stand - ing in the need of prayer. Cho: It's
me, oh Lord, Stand - ing in the need of prayer.
G
me, it's me, it's me, oh Lord, Stand-ing in the need of prayer, It's
D
G
me, it's me, it's me, oh Lord, Stand-ing in the need of prayer.

untry Gentlemen, Hot Rize, Johnson Mtn. Boys

Sugar Hill

M: G; F: C or D
CD 2-Track 65
Tradition
G C D G G C D G C D G
1. Grab your fidd - le off the wall, Get your ban - jo, Bill.
2. Pos - sum on the rail fence, Look - ing at the sun.
3. Pos - sum in the 'sim - mon tree, Rac - coon on the ground.
4. Asked my girl to mar - ry me, She bet - ter say, "I will."
Hitch the hors - es to the shay, We're going to Sug - ar Hill.
Hound dog com - ing down the road, Ol' pos - sum bet - ter run.
Rac - coon said, "You orn - ery cuss, Shake them 'sim - mons down."
Or I'll pack up all my duds, And go to Sug - ar Hill.
Cho: Gon - na get your eye knocked out, Gon - na get your fill,
Gon - na get your eye knocked out, To go to Sug - ar Hill, hill,
hill, Hill, hill, hill, Gon - na get your
eye knocked out, To go to Sug - ar Hill.

Sweet By and By

: G; **F:** C or D
D 2-Track 66

Bennett & Webster

G C G
1. There's a land that is fair - er than day, And by
2. We shall sing on that beau - ti - ful shore, The mel -
3. To our boun - ti - ful Fath - er a - bove, We will
D G C
faith we can see it a - far; For the Fath - er waits o - ver the
o - di - ous songs of the blest, And our spir - its shall sor - row no
of - fer the tri - bute of praise, For the glor - i - ous gift of His
G D G
way, To pre - pare us a dwell - ing place there. Cho: In the
more, Not a sigh for the bless - ing of rest.
love, And the bless - ings that hal - low our days.
G D7 G
sweet by and by, We shall meet on that beau - ti - ful shore; In the
3
C G D G
sweet by and by, We shall meet on that beau - ti - ful shore.

Douglas, Mac Wiseman, D. Parton

Sweet Sunny South

M: G; F: C or D
CD 2-Track 67

W.L. Bloomfield, 185

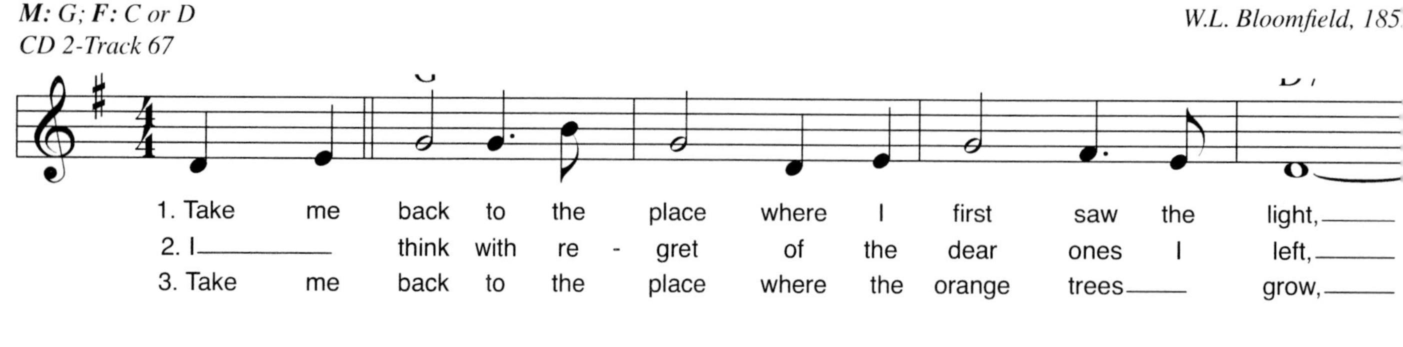

G
D7
1. Take me back to the place where I first saw the light,
2. I think with re - gret of the dear ones I left,
3. Take me back to the place where the orange trees grow,

5
G
C
To the sweet sun - ny south take me home, Where the
Of the warm hearts that shel - tered me then, Of
To my cot in the ev - er - green shade, Where the

10
G
C
G
D7
mock - ing - birds sung me to sleep ev - ery night,
wife and of dear ones of whom I'm be - reft,
flowers from the riv - er's green mar - gins may blow,

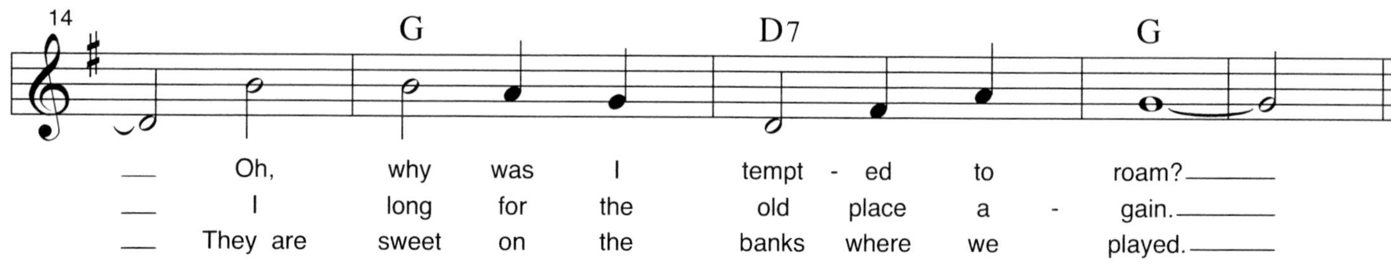

14
G
D7
G
Oh, why was I tempt - ed to roam?
I long for the old place a - gain.
They are sweet on the banks where we played.

G D7
4. The path to our cottage they say has grown green,
G C
And the place is quite lonely around,
G C G D7
I know that the smiles and the forms I have seen,
G D7 G
Now lie deep in the soft mossy ground.

5. Take me back, let me see what is left that I know,
Could it be that the old house is gone?
The dear friends of my childhood indeed must be few,
And I must lament all alone.

6. But yet I'll return to the place of my birth,
Where my children have played 'round the door,
Where they pulled the white blossoms that garnished the earth
Which will echo their footsteps no more.

7. Take me back to the place where my little ones sleep,
Where poor massa lies buried close by,
O'er the graves of my loved ones, I long to weep,
And among them to rest when I die.

C. Poole, Grisman, Garcia, Rice, K. Hall, Bluegrass Album Band, T. O'Brien

Swing Low, Sweet Chariot

I: G; F: C or D
D 2-Track 68
Traditional
G C G
Cho: Swing low, Sweet char - i - ot.___ Com - in' for to car - ry me
4 D7 G C G D7
home. Swing low, Sweet char - i - ot.___ Com - in' for to car - ry me
8 G G C G
home. 1. Well, I looked o - ver Jor - dan and what did I see,___
2. If___ you get to heav - en be - fore___ I do,___
3. I'm___ some - times___ up and I'm some - times down,
11 D G
Com - in' for to car - ry me home, A band of an - gels a'
Com - in' for to car - ry me home, Tell all my friends___ I'm
Com - in' for to car - ry me home, But still I know I'm___
14 C G D G
com - in' af - ter me,___ Com - in' for to car - ry me home.
com - in' there___ too,___ Com - in' for to car - ry me home.
heav - en - ly___ bound,___ Com - in' for to car - ry me home.

Monroe, Stanley Bros., R. Allen & F. Wakefield, Louvin Bros.

Take This Hammer

M: G; F: C or D
CD 2-Track 69
Tradition
G
Cho: Take this ham - mer, car - ry it to the
1. If he asks you, was I
2. If he asks you, was I
3. I don't want your cold iron
4. I don't want your green - back
3
D
cap - tain, Take this ham - mer, car - ry it to the
run - ning, If he asks you, was I
laugh - ing, If he asks you, was I
shack - les, I don't want your cold iron
dol - lar, I don't want your green - back
7
G
cap - - tain, Take this ham - mer,
run - - ning, If he asks you,
laugh - ing, If he asks you,
shack - les, I don't want your
dol - - - lar, I don't want your
10
C
car - ry it to the cap - tain, Tell him I'm
was I run - ning, Tell him I's
was I laugh - ing, Tell him I's
cold iron shack - les, They hurt my
green - back dol - lar, It hurts my
13
G
D
G
gone boys, tell him I'm gone.
fly - ing, tell him I's flying.
cry - ing, tell him I's crying.
leg, hurt my leg.
pride, it hurts my pride.

Flatt & Scruggs, C. White, J.D. Crowe, Country Gentlemen, Osborne Bro.

Talk About Sufferin'

: Em; F: Am or Bm
D 2-Track 70
Traditional
Em
1. Talk a- bout suf-fer-in' here be - low___ and let's keep a' fol-low-in' Je - sus,
2. Talk a - bout suf-fer-in' here be - low___ and let's keep a' lov - in'___ Je - sus.
Talk a-bout suf-fer - in' here be - low___ and let's keep a' fol-low-in' Je - sus,
Talk a-bout suf-fer - in' here be - low___ and let's keep a' fol-low-in' Je - sus.
Em G A
The___ Gos - pel train is com - ing, Now
Oh,___ can't you hear it, fath - ers, And
Em G
don't you want to go? And___ leave this world of
don't you want to go? And___ leave this world of
A Em
sor - row and trou - bles here___ be - low?
tri - als and trou - bles here___ be - low?

Oh, can't you hear it Mother, Sister, etc.

There's More Pretty Girls Than One

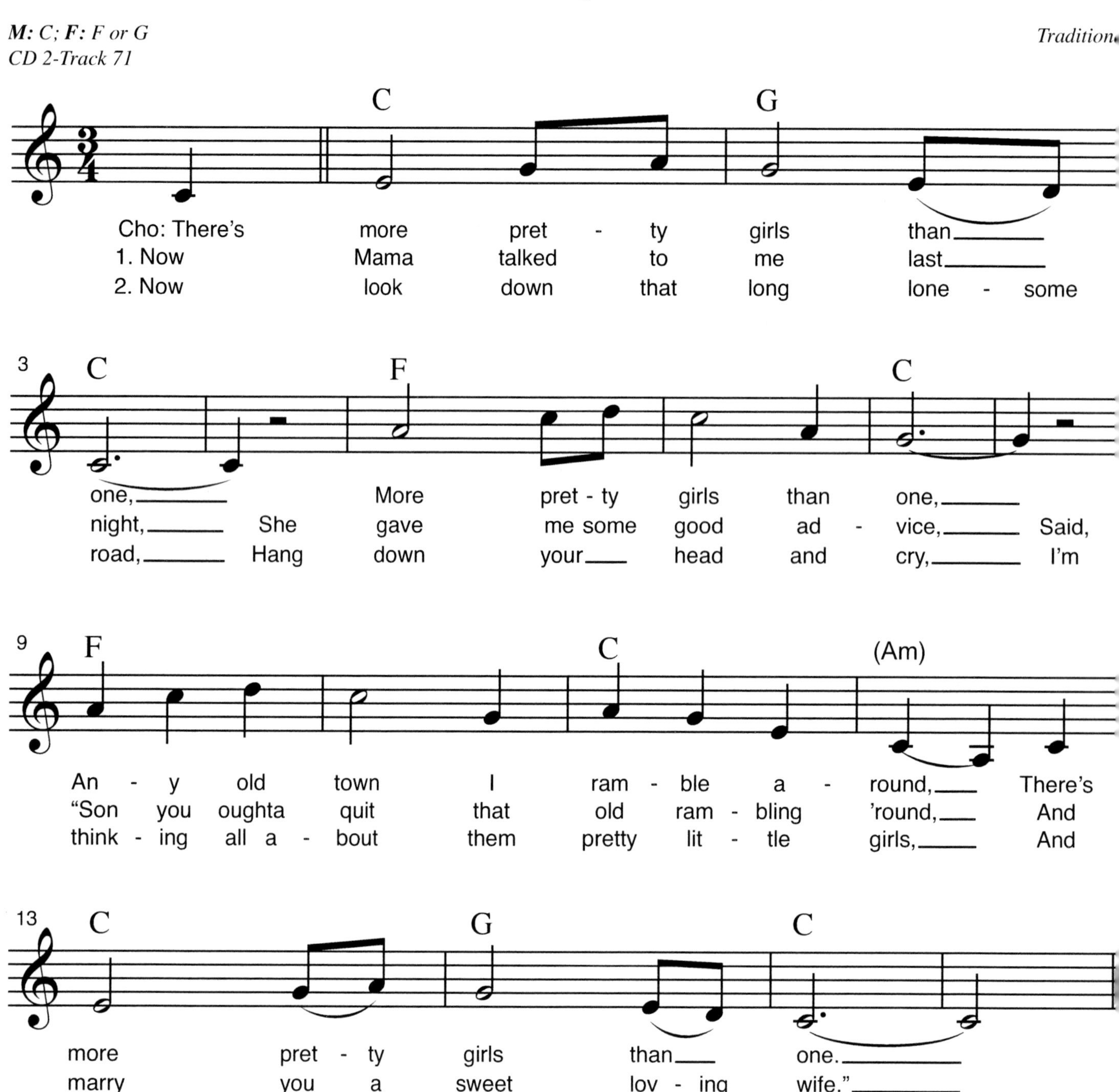

M: C; F: F or G
CD 2-Track 71
Traditional
C G
Cho: There's more pret - ty girls than
1. Now Mama talked to me last
2. Now look down that long lone - some
3
C F C
one, More pret - ty girls than one,
night, She gave me some good ad - vice, Said,
road, Hang down your head and cry, I'm
9
F C (Am)
An - y old town I ram - ble a - round, There's
"Son you oughta quit that old ram - bling 'round, And
think - ing all a - bout them pretty lit - tle girls, And
13
C G C
more pret - ty girls than one.
marry you a sweet lov - ing wife."
hoping that I'll nev - er die.

They Gotta Quit Kickin' My Dawg Aroun'

: G; F: C or D
) 2-Track 72
Oungst & Perkins, 1912
G C D G C D G C G D G C D G
1. Once me and Lem Briggs and old Bill Brown,
we___ passed by Sam John - son's store, A
Took a load of corn to town. Old Jim Dawg, that
passel of yapes came out the door. Lem's dog stopped to
orn - ery cuss, He just nat - ur' - ly foll - owed us. As
smell a box, They threw at him___ a bunch of rocks.___
Cho: Ev - ery time I go to town, The boys keep kick - in' my
dawg a - roun'. Makes no differ - ence if he is a hound, You
got - ta quit kick - in' my dawg a - roun'.___

G C
2. They tied a tin can to his tail,
D G
Drove him past the county jail.
C
That plum natur'ly made me sore,
D G
Lem, he cussed and Bill he swore.
G C
Me and Lem Briggs and old Bill Brown,
D G
Lost no time in jumping down.
C
We whipped those guys upon the ground,
D G
For kickin' that old hound dog aroun'.

3. Well, they say that a dog can't hold no grudge,
Once when I got too much budge,
Those town ducks tried to do me up,
But, they didn't count on old Lem's pup.
He saw his duty there and then,
He lit into those gentlemen,
He sure messed up the courthouse square,
With rags and meat and hunks of hair.

This Little Light of Mine

***M:** C; **F:** F or G*
CD 2-Track 73

Tradition

C
1. This lit - tle light of mine, I'm gon - na let it shine,
2. Hide it under a bushel, no! I'm gon - na let it shine,
3. Won't let Sa-tan blow it out, I'm gon - na let it shine,
4. Let it shine 'til Je - sus comes, I'm gon - na let it shine,
5
F
C
This lit - tle light of mine, I'm gon - na let it shine,
Hide it under a bushel, no! I'm gon - na let it shine,
Won't let Sa - tan blow it out, I'm gon - na let it shine,
Let it shine 'til Je - sus comes, I'm gon - na let it shine,

9
E7
Am
This lit - tle light of mine, I'm gon-na let it shine, Let it
Hide it under a bushel, no! I'm gon-na let it shine, Let it
Won't let Sa - tan blow it out, I'm gon-na let it shine, Let it
Let it shine 'til Je - sus comes, I'm gon-na let it shine, Let it

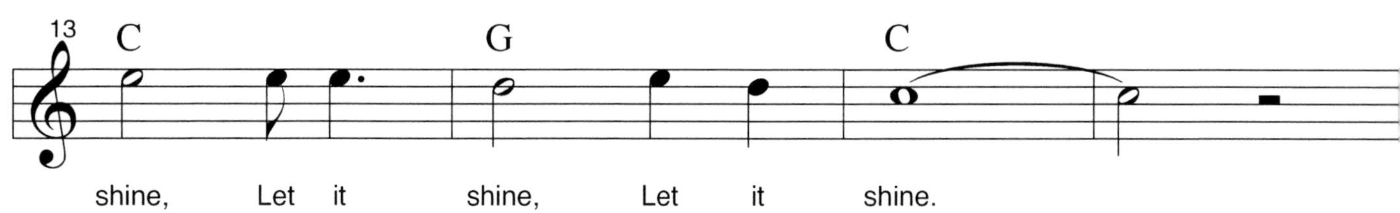
13
C
G
C
shine, Let it shine, Let it shine.

This Train

: G; **F:** C or D
) 2-Track 74

Traditional

G
1. This train is bound for glo - ry, this train,
2. This train don't carry no gam - blers, this train,
3. This train don't carry no li - ars, this train,
4. This train don't carry no rus - tlers, this train,
5
D7
This train is bound for glo - ry, this train,
This train don't carry no gam - blers, this train.
This train don't carry no li - ars, this train,
This train don't carry no rus - tlers, this train,
9
G
This train is bound for glo - ry,
This train don't carry no gam - blers,
This train don't carry no li - ars,
This train don't carry no rus - tlers,
11
C7
don't car - ry noth - ing but the right - eous and the ho - ly
no hyp - o - crites, no mid - night ram - blers,
no hyp - o - crites and no high fly - ers,
no street walk - ers, no two - bit hus - tlers,
13
G
D7
G
This train is bound for glo - ry, this train.
This train is bound for glo - ry, this train.
This train is bound for glo - ry, this train.
This train is bound for glo - ry, this train.

This World is Not My Home

M: G; F: C or D
CD 2-Track 75
Traditiona
G C G
1. This world is not my home, I'm just a' pass - ing through, My
2. I have a pre - cious mother who's up in glor - y - land, I
3. Just over in glor - y - land, there'll be no dy - ing there, The
4. They're all ex - pect - ing me and that's one thing I know, I'll
5
A7 D
trea - sures are laid up some - where be-yond the blue, The
don't ex - pect to stop un - til I shake her hand, She's
saints are shout - ing "victory" and sing - ing ev - ery - where, I
trust His sav - ing grace while travel - ing here be - low,
9
G C G
an - gels beck - on me, from heav - en's o - pen door, And I
wait - ing now for me in heav - en's o - pen door, And I
hear the voice of them that's gone on be - fore, And I
He will take me through, though I am weak and poor, And I
13
D G
can't feel at home in this world an - y - more.
can't feel at home in this world an - y - more.
can't feel at home in this world an - y - more.
can't feel at home in this world an - y - more.
18
G C G
Cho: Oh, Lord, you know, I have no friend like you, If hea - ven's not my home then
24
A7 D G C
Lord what will I do? The an - gels beck - on me from heav - en's o - pen
29
G D G
door, And I can't feel at home in this world an - y more.

Monroe Bros., B. Monroe, Stanley Bros., Jimmy Martin, Blue Highway, NLC

Train, Train, Train

*: G; **F:** C or D*
D 2-Track 76

by Dix Bruce

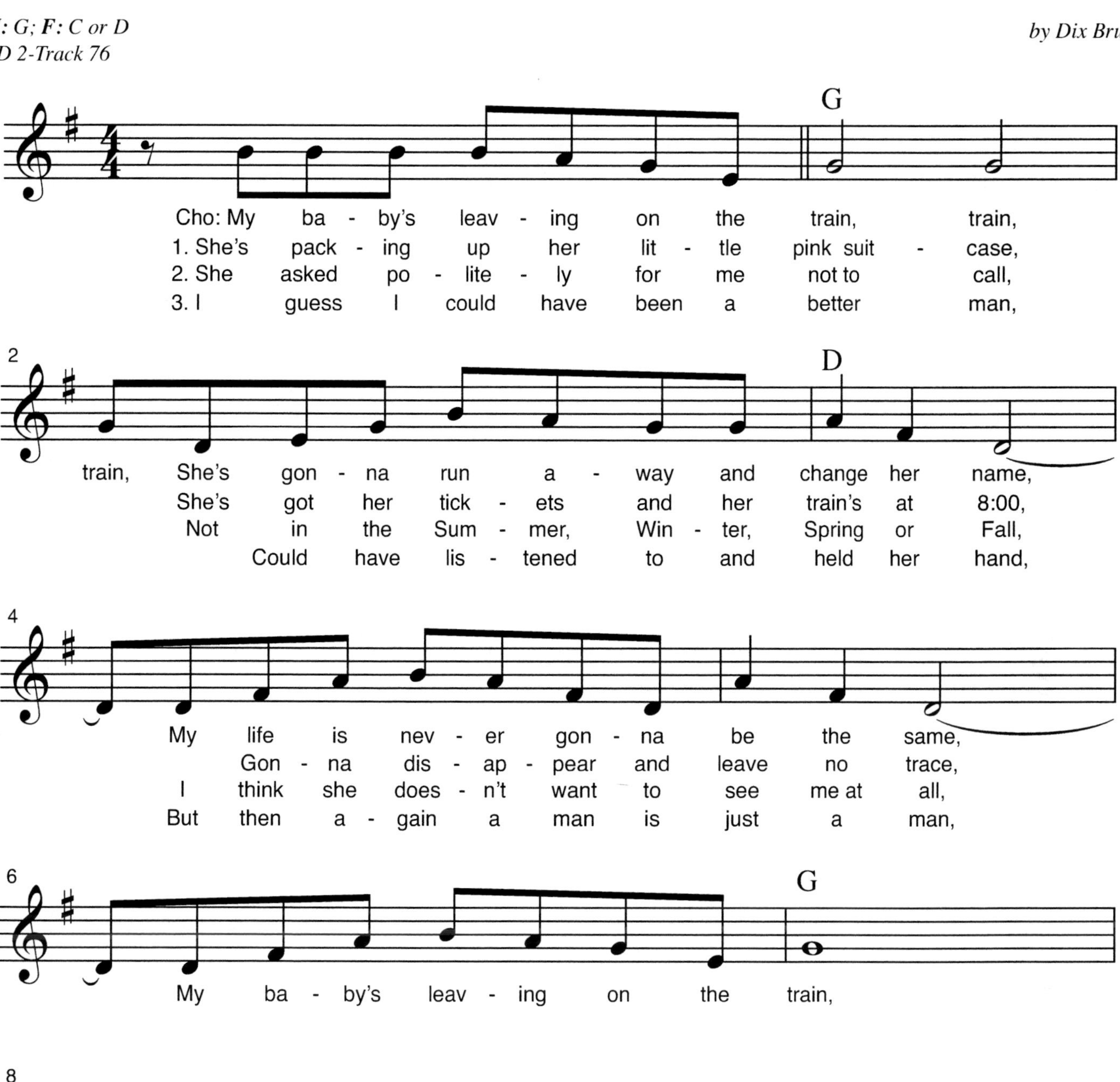
G
Cho: My ba - by's leav - ing on the train, train,
1. She's pack - ing up her lit - tle pink suit - case,
2. She asked po - lite - ly for me not to call,
3. I guess I could have been a better man,
D
train, She's gon - na run a - way and change her name,
She's got her tick - ets and her train's at 8:00,
Not in the Sum - mer, Win - ter, Spring or Fall,
Could have lis - tened to and held her hand,
My life is nev - er gon - na be the same,
Gon - na dis - ap - pear and leave no trace,
I think she does - n't want to see me at all,
But then a - gain a man is just a man,
G
My ba - by's leav - ing on the train,
train, She said she's leav - ing on the train.

The Train That Carried My Girl From Town

***M:** D; **F:** G or A*
CD 2-Track 77

Traditiona

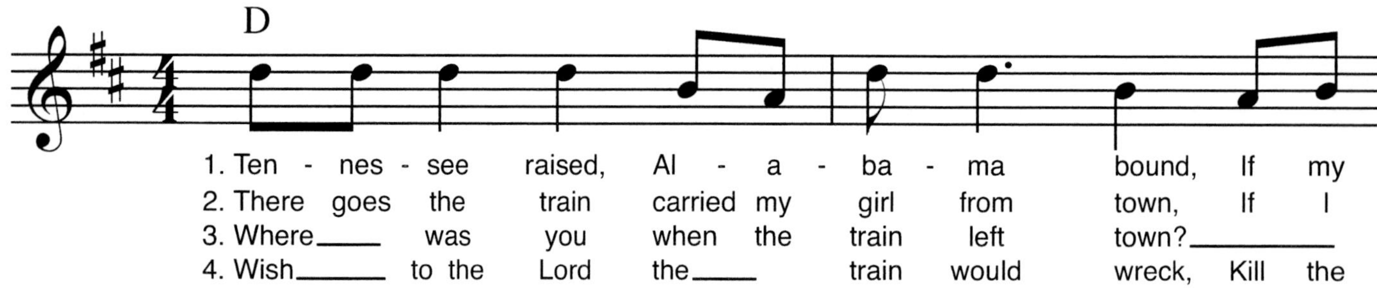

D
1. Ten - nes - see raised, Al - a - ba - ma bound, If my
2. There goes the train carried my girl from town, If I
3. Where___ was you when the train left town?___
4. Wish___ to the Lord the___ train would wreck, Kill the

3
A D
girl leaves me, I'm gon - na move from town.
knowed her num - ber, Lord, I'd flag her down,
Standing on the cor - ner head a' hang - ing down.
en - gi - neer,___ break the fire - man's neck.

5
D A D
Cho: Hate that train that car-ried my girl from town, Hate, hate, hate.___

D
5. Hello central, give me 6-0-9,
A D
Just wanna talk to that brown of mine.
Cho: Hate that train that carried my girl from town,
A D
Hate, hate, hate. (Repeat chorus after each verse)

6. Rations on the table, coffee's getting cold,
Some old rounder stole my jelly roll.

7. If I had a gun I'd let the hammer down,
Lord, I'd shoot that rounder took my girl from town.

8. There goes my girl, somebody call her back,
She put her hands in my money sack.

9. Ashes to ashes and dust to dust,
Show me a woman a man can trust.

Flatt & Scruggs, D. Watson, Longview

The Unclouded Day

G; F: C or D
2-Track 78
J.K. Alwood, 1890
G C G
1. Oh they tell me of a home far be - yond the skies, Oh they
2. Oh they tell me of a home where my friends have gone, Oh they
3. Oh they tell me of a King in His beau - ty there, And they
4. Oh they tell me that He smiles on His chil - dren there, And His
D
tell me of a home far a - way, Oh they
tell me of that land far a - way, Where the
tell me that mine eyes shall be - hold, Where He
smile drives their sorrows all a - way; And they
G C G
tell me of a home where no storm clouds rise,
tree of life in e - ter - nal bloom,
sits on the throne that is whit - er than snow,
tell me that no tears ev - er come a - gain,
D G
Oh, they tell me of an un - cloud - ed day.
Sheds its fra - grance through the un - cloud - ed day.
In the ci - ty that is made of gold.
In that love - ly land of un - cloud - ed day.
G
Cho: Oh, the land of cloud - less day, Oh, the land of an
D G
un - cloud - ed sky, Oh, they tell me of a home where no
C G D G
storm clouds rise, Oh, they tell me of an un - cloud - ed day.

Martin, Osborne Bros.

Wabash Cannonball

***M:** G; **F:** C or D*
CD 2-Track 79

Woode & Fulmer, 18

G
1. From the great At - lan - tic O - cean to the wide Pa - cif - ic
Cho: List - en to the jin - gle, the rum - ble and the
2. She came down from Bir - ming - ham one cold De - cem - ber
4
C D
shore, From the queen of flow - ing moun - tains to the south - land by the
roar, As she glides a - long the wood - land through the hills and by the
day, As she pulled in - to the sta - tion you could hear all the peo - ple
8
G
shore, She's might - y tall and hand - some, known quite well by
shore, Hear the might - y rush of the en - gine, hear the lone - some ho - bo's
say, There's a girl from Ten - nes - see, she's long and she's
12
C D G
all, She's the reg - u - lar com - bin - a - tion of the Wa - bash Can - non - ball.
squall, You're trav - el - ing through the jun - gle on the Wa - bash Can - non - ball.
tall, She came down from Bir - ming - ham on the Wa - bash Can - non - ball.

G C
3. Our eastern states are dandy, so the people always say,
D G
From New York to St. Louis, and Chicago by the way,
C
From the hills of Minnesota, where the rippling waters fall,
D G
No changes can be taken, on the Wabash Cannonball.

4. Here's to Daddy Claxton, may his name forever stand,
And always be remembered in the courts thoughout the land
His earthly race is over and the curtains 'round him fall,
We'll carry him home to victory on the Wabash Cannonball.

5. I have rode the I.C. Limited, also the Royal Blue,
Across the eastern countries on mail car number two,
I have rode those highball trains from coast to coast that's all
But I have found no equal to the Wabash Cannonball.

Carter Fam., R. Acuff, Flatt & Scruggs, B. Monroe, Mac Wisemar
Louvin Bros., Osborne Bros., Claire Lynch, Nitty Gritty Dirt Ban

Walk in Jerusalem Just Like John

*: F; **F:** Bb or C*
) 2-Track 80

Traditional

F
1. Oh John, oh John, now what did you say?
2. Oh, some come crippled and some come lame,
3. Oh, John said the city was just four square,
3
C F
Walk in Je - ru - sa - lem just like John, That I'll be there at the
Walk in Je - ru - sa - lem just like John, Gonna meet you walking in
Walk in Je - ru - sa - lem just like John, And he de - clared he'd
6
C F
crown - ing day, Walk in Je - ru - sa - lem just like John.
Je - sus' name, Walk in Je - ru - sa - lem just like John.
meet me there, Walk in Je - ru - sa - lem just like John.
9
B♭ F
Cho: I want to be read - y, I want to be read - y, I want to be
14
Dm F C F
read - y, Lord To walk in Je - ru - sa - lem just like John.

F
4. When Peter was preaching at the Pentacost,
C F
Walk in Jerusalem just like John,
He was endowed with the Holy Ghost,
C F
Walk in Jerusalem just like John.

F Bb F
Cho: I want to be ready, I want to be ready,
Dm
I want to be ready, Lord
F C F
To walk in Jerusalem just like John.

5. If you get there before I do,
Walk in Jerusalem just like John,
Tell all my friends I'm a'coming too,
Walk in Jerusalem just like John. (Chorus)

Monroe, D. Watson, Newgrass Revival, Country Gentlemen

Walking in My Sleep

M: C; F: F or G
CD 2-Track 81

Traditional

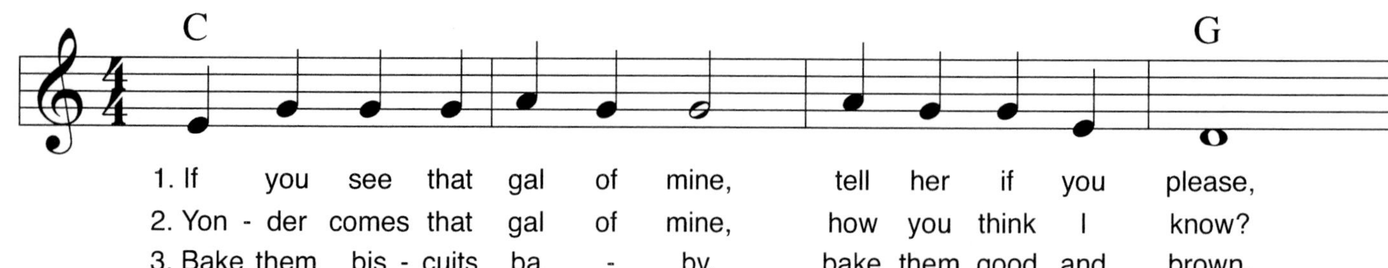
C
G
1. If you see that gal of mine, tell her if you please,
2. Yon - der comes that gal of mine, how you think I know?
3. Bake them bis - cuits ba - by, bake them good and brown,

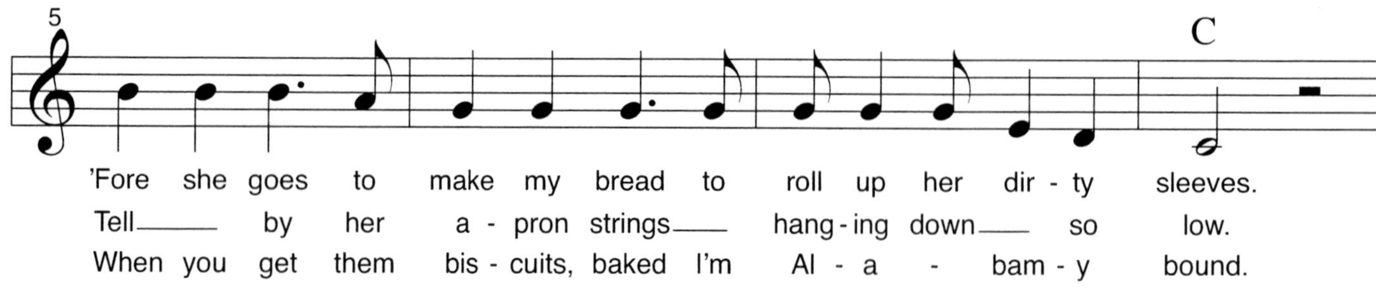
5
C
'Fore she goes to make my bread to roll up her dir - ty sleeves.
Tell by her a - pron strings hang - ing down so low.
When you get them bis - cuits, baked I'm Al - a - bam - y bound.

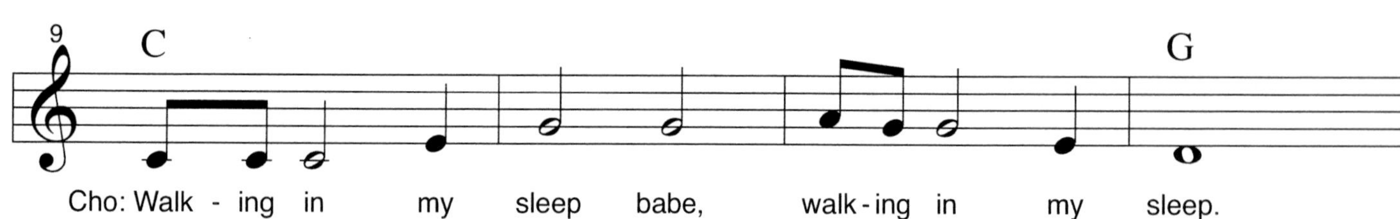
9
C
G
Cho: Walk - ing in my sleep babe, walk - ing in my sleep.

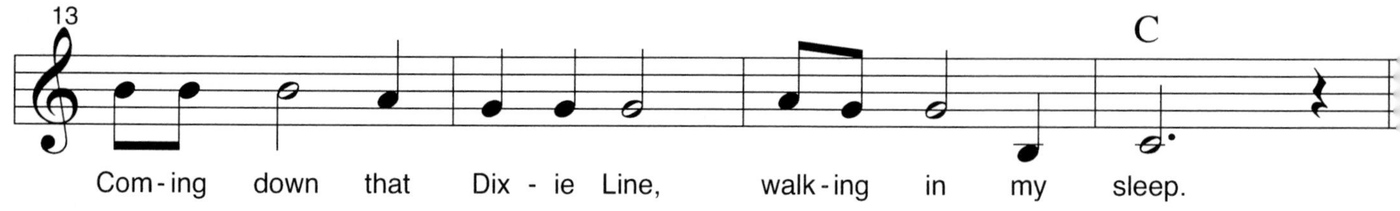
13
C
Com - ing down that Dix - ie Line, walk - ing in my sleep.

The Wayfaring Stranger

*: Dm; **F:** Gm or Am*
) 2-Track 82

Traditional

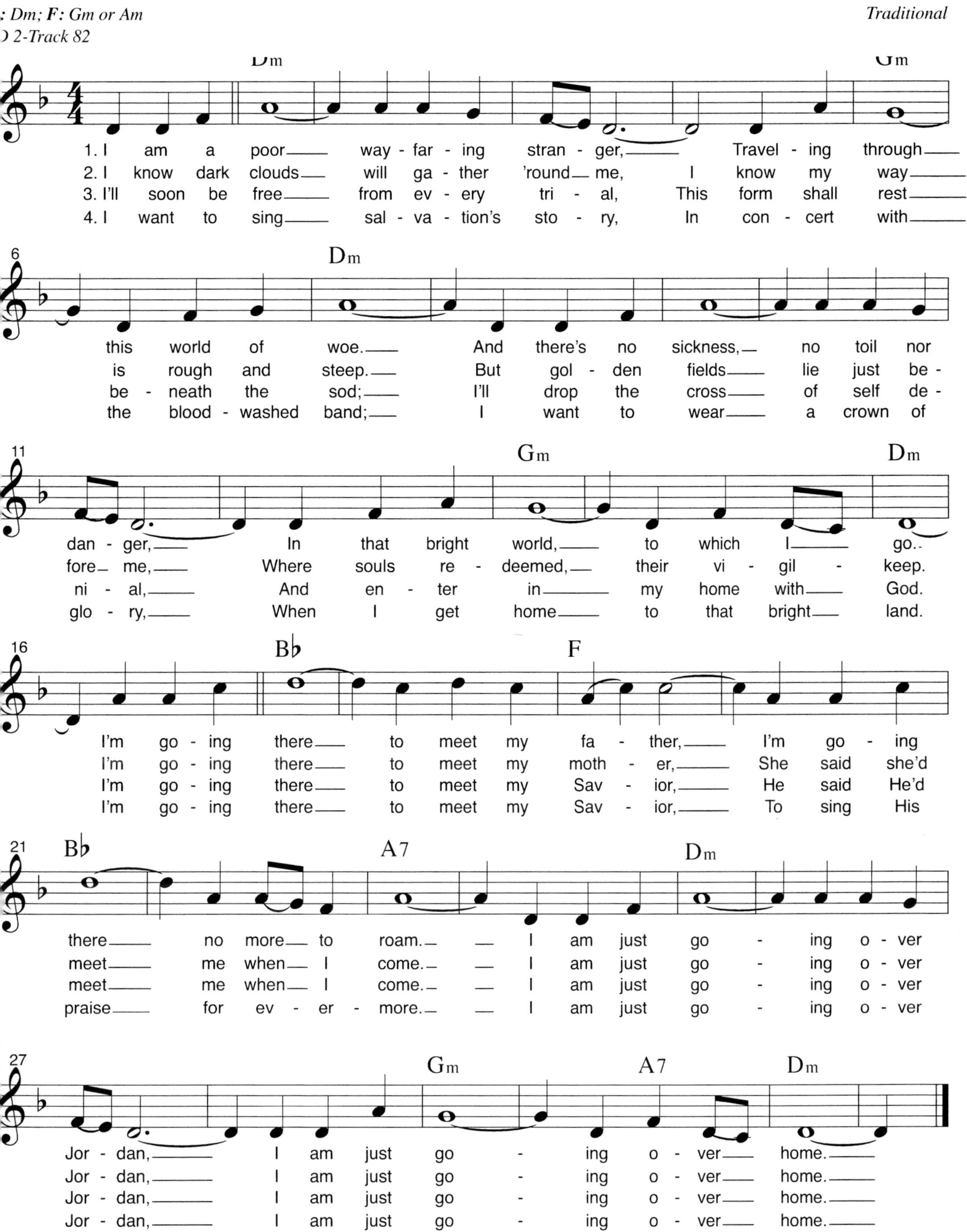

Dm
Gm
1. I am a poor way - far - ing stran - ger, Travel - ing through
2. I know dark clouds will ga - ther 'round me, I know my way
3. I'll soon be free from ev - ery tri - al, This form shall rest
4. I want to sing sal - va - tion's sto - ry, In con - cert with
6
Dm
this world of woe. And there's no sickness, no toil nor
is rough and steep. But gol - den fields lie just be -
be - neath the sod; I'll drop the cross of self de -
the blood - washed band; I want to wear a crown of
11
Gm
Dm
dan - ger, In that bright world, to which I go..
fore me, Where souls re - deemed, their vi - gil - keep.
ni - al, And en - ter in my home with God.
glo - ry, When I get home to that bright land.
16
B♭
F
I'm go - ing there to meet my fa - ther, I'm go - ing
I'm go - ing there to meet my moth - er, She said she'd
I'm go - ing there to meet my Sav - ior, He said He'd
I'm go - ing there to meet my Sav - ior, To sing His
21
B♭
A7
Dm
there no more to roam. I am just go - ing o - ver
meet me when I come. I am just go - ing o - ver
meet me when I come. I am just go - ing o - ver
praise for ev - er - more. I am just go - ing o - ver
27
Gm
A7
Dm
Jor - dan, I am just go - ing o - ver home.
Jor - dan, I am just go - ing o - ver home.
Jor - dan, I am just go - ing o - ver home.
Jor - dan, I am just go - ing o - ver home.

Monroe, D. Watson, T. Rice, E.L. Harris, Bluegrass Alliance, D. Parton, R. Ickes

Were You There When They Crucified My Lord?

***M:** G; **F:** C or D*
CD 2-Track 83, medley pt. 1

Traditional

G D G

1. Were you there when they cruc - i - fied my Lord?
2. Were you there when they nailed Him to the cross?
3. Were you there when they pierced Him in His side?
4. Were you there when the sun re - fused to shine?
5. Were you there when they laid Him in the tomb?

4 D

Were you there when they cruc - i - fied my Lord? Oh,
Were you there when they nailed Him to the cross? Oh,
Were you there when they pierced Him in His side? Oh,
Were you there when the sun re - fused to shine? Oh,
Were you there when they laid Him in the tomb? Oh,

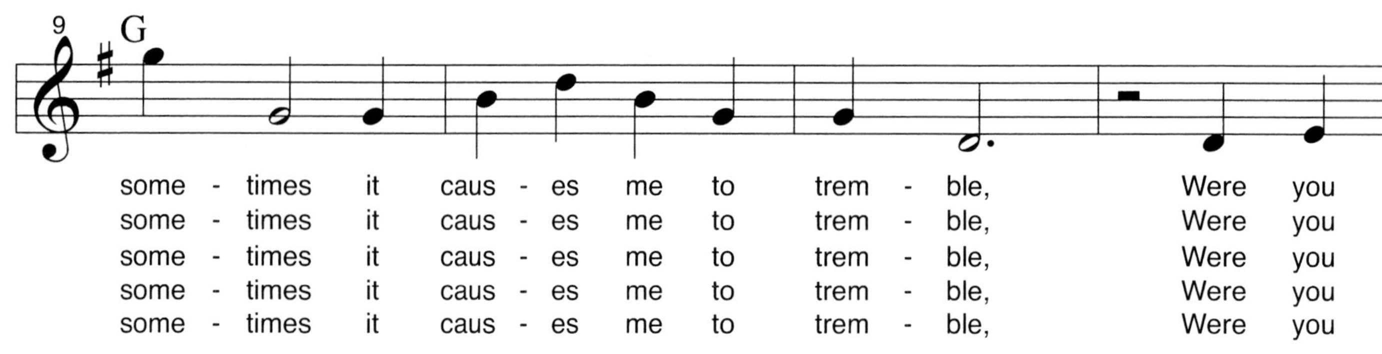
9
G
some - times it caus - es me to trem - ble, Were you
some - times it caus - es me to trem - ble, Were you
some - times it caus - es me to trem - ble, Were you
some - times it caus - es me to trem - ble, Were you
some - times it caus - es me to trem - ble, Were you

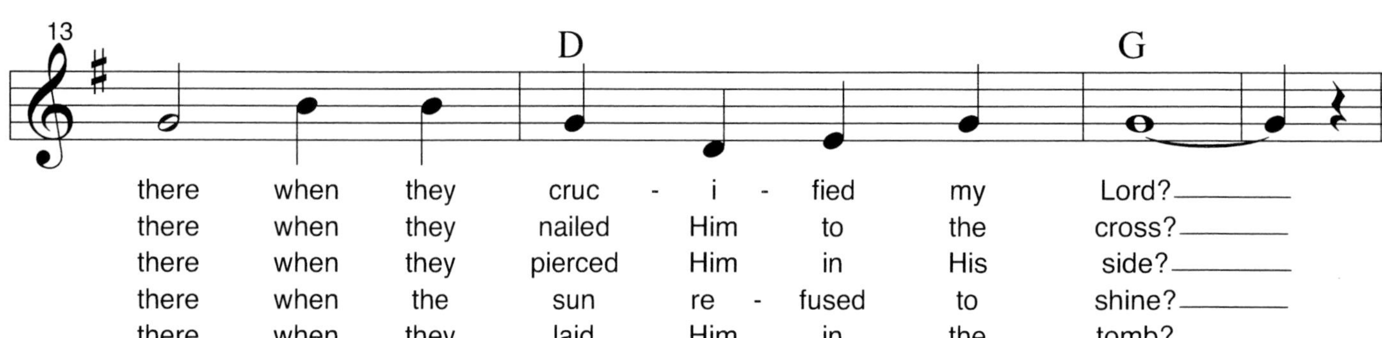
13
D
G
there when they cruc - i - fied my Lord?
there when they nailed Him to the cross?
there when they pierced Him in His side?
there when the sun re - fused to shine?
there when they laid Him in the tomb?

B. Monroe, Blue Sky Boys, Dry Branch Fire Squad, Seldom Scene, R. Skaggs

What a Friend We Have in Jesus

*: G; **F:** C or D*
Ɔ 2-Track 83, medley pt. 2

Converse & Scriven, ca. 1868

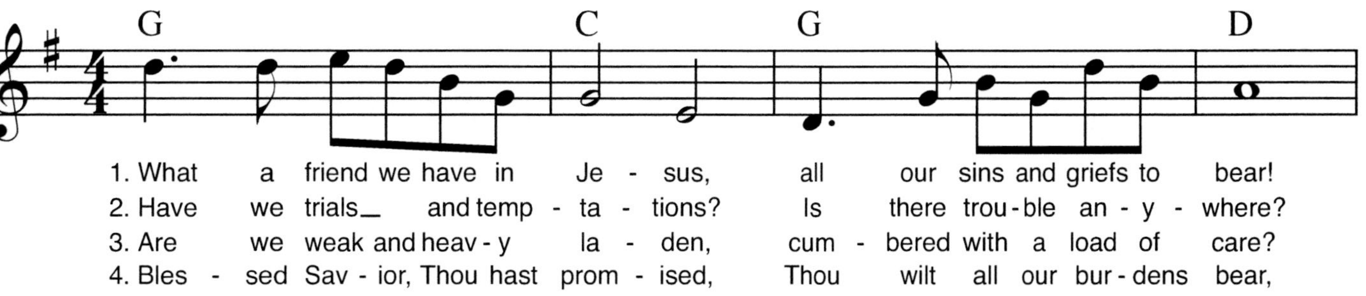
G C G D
1. What a friend we have in Je - sus, all our sins and griefs to bear!
2. Have we trials_ and temp - ta - tions? Is there trou-ble an - y - where?
3. Are we weak and heav - y la - den, cum - bered with a load of care?
4. Bles - sed Sav - ior, Thou hast prom - ised, Thou wilt all our bur - dens bear,

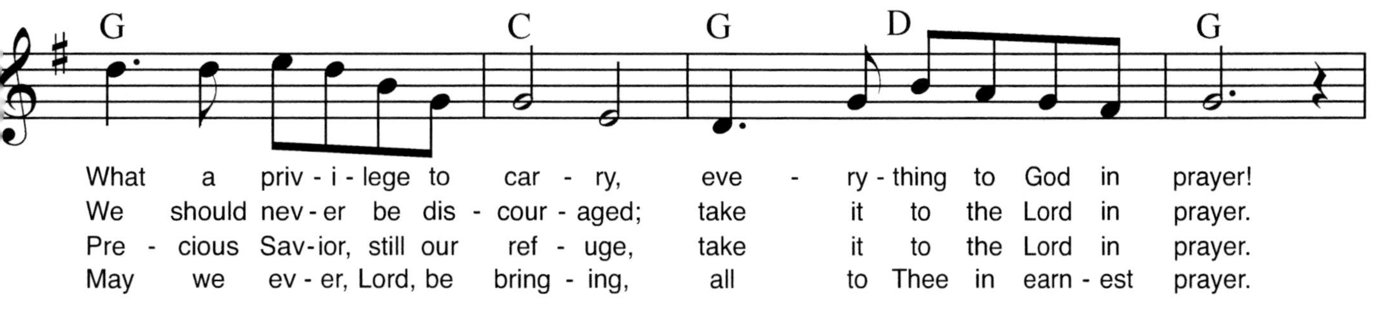
G C G D G
What a priv - i - lege to car - ry, eve - ry - thing to God in prayer!
We should nev - er be dis - cour - aged; take it to the Lord in prayer.
Pre - cious Sav-ior, still our ref - uge, take it to the Lord in prayer.
May we ev - er, Lord, be bring - ing, all to Thee in earn - est prayer.

D G C G D
O, what peace we of - ten for - feit, O, what need-less pain we bear,
Can we find a friend so faith - ful, who will all our bur-dens share?
Do your friends de - spise, for - sake you? Take it to the Lord in prayer!
Soon in glo - ry bright un - cloud - ed, there will be no need for prayer,

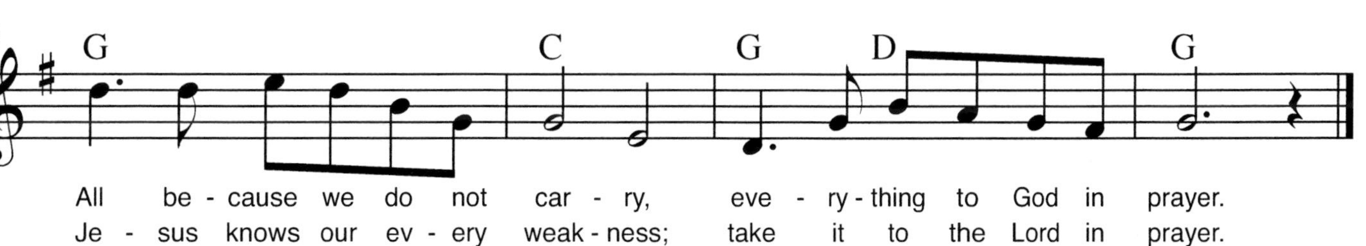
G C G D G
All be - cause we do not car - ry, eve - ry - thing to God in prayer.
Je - sus knows our ev - ery weak - ness; take it to the Lord in prayer.
In His arms He'll take and shield you; you will find a sol - ace there.
Rap - ture, praise and end - less wor - ship, will be our sweet por - tion there.

anley Bros., Osborne Bros., D. Bruce, D. Parton, M. Wiseman

When I Die

M: G; F: C or D
CD 2-Track 84

Dix Bru

G
C
G
1. Will I float with the clouds up a - bove when I die? With the
2. Will my soul be set free to walk the shallow streams? Of the

6
D7
C
G
stars in the hea - vens will I fly? Will I shine with the
sweet thoughts and dreams in my mind? Will my heart beat as

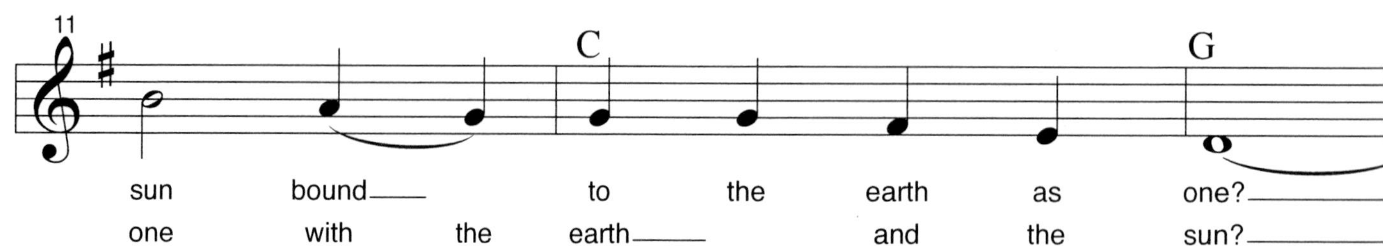

11
C
G
sun bound to the earth as one?
one with the earth and the sun?

14
D7
G
When I die, When I die.
When I die, When I die.


```
          G                                    C
3. Will I roam through the fields down the mountains,
                       G
       cross the land?
                                          D
Wade the rivers down to the ocean sand?
C     G                            C            G
Will I touch trusted friends in a whisper of the wind?
              D      G
When I die, when I die.
```

4. Can I be with my family, can I visit with my friends?
As they spend the short time they were lent?
Will they quietly know that I really did not go?
When I die, when I die.

5. Will the ones that I love someday join me up above
Will we laugh, will we sing, will we cry?
Together will we be through all eternity?
When I die, when I die.

6. Will I grow in the hearts of those I have known?
Will they think of me fondly now and then?
Will I live on and on when my life on earth is done?
When I die, when I die.

When I Lay My Burden Down

: G; ***F:*** *C or D*
) 2-Track 85

Traditional

G
Cho: Glo - ry glo - ry, Hal - le - lu - jah,
1. I'm going home to live with Jes - us,
2. All my trou - bles will be o - ver,
3. Going to meet my lov - ing moth - er,
4. All my sick - ness will be o - ver,
C G
When I lay my bur - den down,
When I lay my bur - den down,
When I lay my bur - den down,
When I lay my bur - den down,
When I lay my bur - den down,
Glo - ry glo - ry, Hal - le - lu - jah,
I'm going home to live with Jes - us,
All my trou - bles will be o - ver,
Going to meet my lov - ing moth - er,
All my sick - ness will be o - ver,
2
D7 G
When I lay my bur - den down.
When I lay my bur - den down.
When I lay my bur - den down.
When I lay my bur - den down.
When I lay my bur - den down.

When My Race is Run

M: G; F: C or D
CD 2-Track 86
Dix Bruc
G C
1. When my race is run, when I'm ly - ing still,
2. When my sun sinks down, be - low shad - owed hills,
G D A
Don't you come a - round, when they read my will.
When the world grows dark and the trees grow still.
D G C
Don't send me flowers and keep from my grave,
Then say a prayer, no one will hear,
G D7 G
It would break your heart to see me this way.
To one who's gone, who loves you dear.
C
Cho: I've known the pain that some - day you'll
G
feel, That emp - ti - ness in - side and tears so
D A D G
real. Then think of me, a life un - ful -
C G D7 G
filled, A - cross the years, I'll love you still.

When the Roll is Called Up Yonder

*· G; **F:** C or D*
) 2-Track 87, medley pt. 1

J.M. Black, 1893

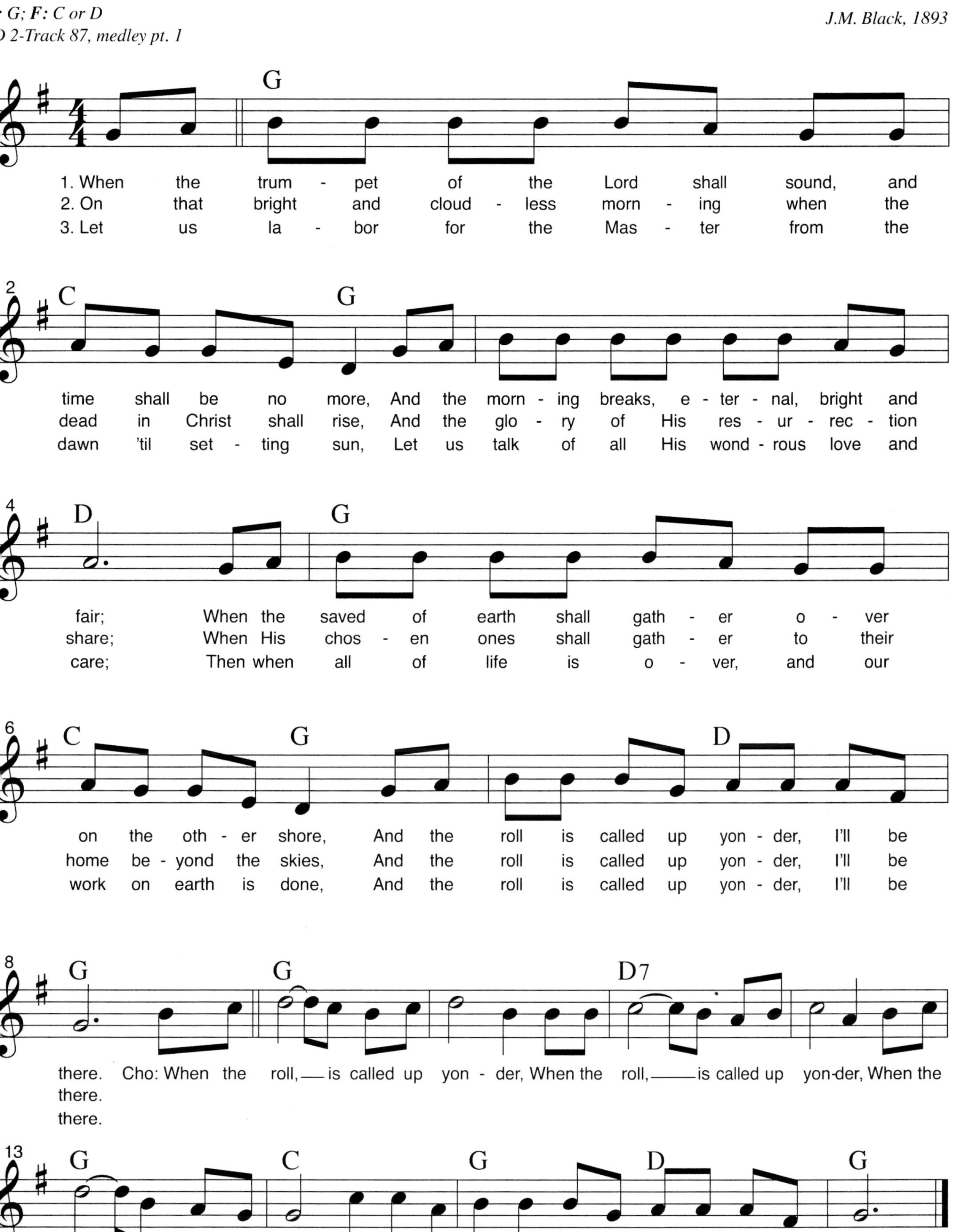
G C G D G C G D G G D7 G C G D G
1. When the trum - pet of the Lord shall sound, and time shall be no more, And the morn - ing breaks, e - ter - nal, bright and fair; When the saved of earth shall gath - er o - ver on the oth - er shore, And the roll is called up yon - der, I'll be there.
2. On that bright and cloud - less morn - ing when the dead in Christ shall rise, And the glo - ry of His res - ur - rec - tion share; When His chos - en ones shall gath - er to their home be - yond the skies, And the roll is called up yon - der, I'll be there.
3. Let us la - bor for the Mas - ter from the dawn 'til set - ting sun, Let us talk of all His wond - rous love and care; Then when all of life is o - ver, and our work on earth is done, And the roll is called up yon - der, I'll be there.
Cho: When the roll, — is called up yon - der, When the roll, — is called up yon-der, When the roll, — is called up yon - der, When the roll is called up yon - der I'll be there.

When the Saints Go Marching In

M: G; F: C or D
CD 2-Track 87, medley pt. 2

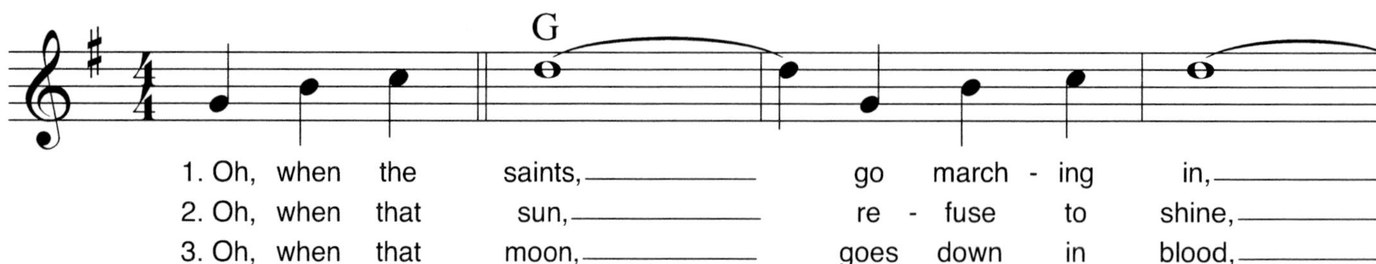
G
1. Oh, when the saints, go march - ing in,
2. Oh, when that sun, re - fuse to shine,
3. Oh, when that moon, goes down in blood,

4
D
Oh, when the saints go march - ing in,
Oh, when that sun re - fuse to shine,
Oh, when that moon goes down in blood,

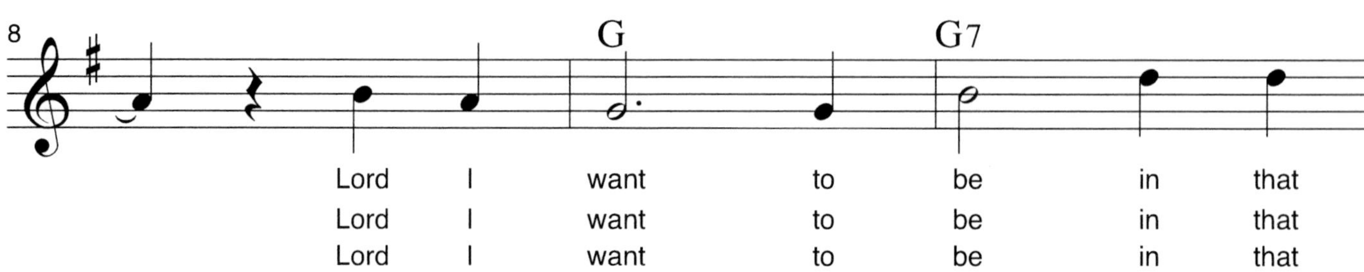
8
G
G7
Lord I want to be in that
Lord I want to be in that
Lord I want to be in that

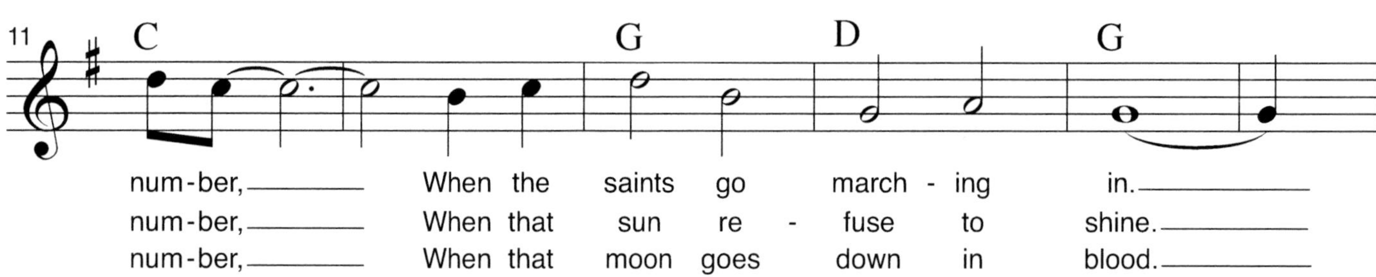
11
C
G
D
G
num-ber, When the saints go march - ing in.
num-ber, When that sun re - fuse to shine.
num-ber, When that moon goes down in blood.

```
                  G
4. Oh, when they crown Him King of kings,
                                D
Oh, when they crown Him King of kings,
        G      G7        C
Lord I want to be in that number,
              G          D     G
When they crown Him King of kings.
```

5. Oh, when they gather 'round the throne, (etc.)
6. Oh, while the happy ages roll, (etc.)
7. Oh, on that hallelujah day, (etc.)

 Monroe Bros., B. Monroe, Flatt and Scruggs, Lilly Bros., Fiddlin' J. Carso

When the Work's All Done this Fall

*: C; **F:** F or G*
D 2-Track 88

Traditional

C
F
1. A group of jol - ly cow - boys dis - cuss - ing plans at ease, Says
2. "When I left my hap - py home, boys, Moth - er for me cried, She
G
C
one, "I'll tell you some - thing, boys, if you will lis - ten please, I
begged me not to leave her, for me she would have died,
F
am an old cow punch - er al - though I'm dressed in rags, I
Moth - er's heart is bro - ken for a wand - ering boy, that's all,
G
C
used to be a tough one and go on great big jags."
With God's help I'll see her when the work's all done this fall."

C F
Well, after the roundup's over, and the shipping's done,
G C
ı going right home boys, before my money's gone,
F
ave changed my ways, boys, no more will the temptors call,
G C
ant to see my mother, when the work's all done this fall."

That very night the cowboy, went out to stand his guard,
e night was dark and cloudy, and storming very hard,
e cattle all got freightened, and rushed in wild stampede,
e cowboy tried to head them, while riding at full speed.

While riding in the darkness, so wildly did he shout,
tried his best to turn them, and head the herd about,
s saddle pony stumbled, and on the boy did fall,
won't see his mother, when the work's all done this fall.

6. His body was so mangled, the boys all thought him dead,
They picked him up so gently, and laid him on the bed,
He opened wide his blue eyes, and looking all around
He motioned for his comrades, to sit near him on the ground.

7. "Well, send my mother my wages, the wages that I've earned,
I won't live to see her, the last steer I have turned,
I'm going to a new range, I've heard the Master's call,
And I won't see my mother, when the work's all done this fall."

8. "Hey George, you take my pistol, Jack you take my bed,
Jim you take my saddle, after I am dead,
Boys, speak of me kindly, when you look upon them all,
For I won't see my mother, when the work's all done this fall."

9. Well, Charlie was buried at daybreak, no tombstone at his head,
Nothing but a little board, and this is what it said,
"Charlie died at daybreak, and he died from the fall,
He won't see his mother, when the work's all done this fall."

Watson, Goose Island Ramblers, B. Clifton, N. Blake, M. Wiseman

When You And I Were Young Maggie

M: F; F: Bb or C
CD 2-Track 89
Johnson
Butterfield, ca. 186
F
Bb
F
C
F
Bb
F
C
F
Bb
F
G7
C
F
Bb
F
C
F
6
12
17
22
27
1. I wan - dered to - day to the hill, Mag - gie, To watch the
2. A ci - ty so si - lent and lone, Mag - gie, Where the young and th
3. They say I am fee - ble with age, Mag - gie, My steps are less
scene be - low, The creek and the old rust - y mill,
gay and the best, In pol - ished white man - sions of stone,
sprite - ly than then; My face is a well writ - ten page,
Mag - gie, Where we sat in the long, long a - go. The
Mag - gie, Have each found a place to rest, Is
Mag - gie, And time a - lone was the pen. And
green grove is gone from the hill, Mag - gie, Where once the
built where the birds used to play, Mag - gie, And join in the
now we are aged and gray, Mag - gie, And the trials of
dais - ies sprung. The old rust - y mill is
songs that were sung; For we sang as gay as
life near - ly done; But to me you're as fair as you
still, Mag - gie, since you and I were young.
they, Mag - gie, when you and I were young.
were, Mag - gie, when you and I were young.

Stanley Bros., Reno & Smiley, Fiddlin' John Carso
Mac Wiseman, D. Grisman, B. Wall

Where the Soul Never Dies

: E; F: A or B
) 2-Track 90
Wm. Golden
tenor
lead
E
A
E
B7
1. To Ca-naan's land I'm on my way, Where the soul of man nev-er dies, My
1. To Ca-naan's land I'm on my way, Where the soul nev-er dies, My
2. A rose is blooming there for me, Where the soul nev-er dies, And
3. A love light beams a - cross the foam, Where the soul nev-er dies, It
4. My life will end in death-less sleep, Where the soul nev-er dies, And
5. I'm on my way to that fair land, Where the soul nev-er dies, Where
5
Chorus:
dark-est night will turn to day, Where the soul of man nev-er dies. Dear
dark-est night will turn to day, Where the soul nev-er dies. No
I will spend e - ter - ni - ty, Where the soul nev-er dies.
shines to light the shores of home, Where the soul nev-er dies.
ev - er - last - ing joys I'll reap, Where the soul nev-er dies.
there will be no part - ing hand, Where the soul nev-er dies.
9
friend there'll be no sad fare - wells, there'-ll be no tear - dimmed eyes, where
sad fare wells, No tear - dimmed eyes, where
13
all is peace and joy and love and the soul of man nev-er dies.
all is love, And the soul nev-er dies

Whitehouse Blues

M: G; F: C or D
CD 2-Track 91, medley pt. 1

G
1. Mc - Kin - ley holl - ered, Mc - Kin - ley squalled,
2. Look here you ras - cal,___ see what you done,
3. Doc come a - run - ning, took off his specs,
C
Doc said, "Mc - Kin - ley, I can't find the
You shot my hus - band and I got your
Said, "Mr. Mc - Kin - ley, better cash in your
G D G
cause, You're bound to die,___ you're bound to die."___
gun,___ Carry you back___ to Wash - ing - ton.___
checks, You're bound to die,___ you're bound to die."___

G
4. Roosevelt's in the White House, doing his best,
C G
McKinley's in the graveyard taking his rest,
D G
He's long gone, long gone.

5. Roosevelt's in the White House, drinking out
of a silver cup,
McKinley's in the graveyard, he's never gonna wake up,
He's long gone, long gone.

6. Hush up little children, now don't you fret,
You're bound to draw a pension from your papa's death
He's long gone, long gone.

7. Jumped on a horse, he threw down his reins,
He said to the horse, "You gotta outrun the train,
From Buffalo to Washington."

8. Nixon's in the Whitehouse, making a mess,
Johnson's in the graveyard, taking his rest,
He's long gone, long gone.

B. Monroe, D. Watson, Greenbriar Boys, Muleskinn
D. McCoury, Dillards, Reno & Harr

Who Broke the Lock?

: G; ***F:*** *C or D, capo 5 or 7*
D 2-Track 91, medley pt. 2

Traditional

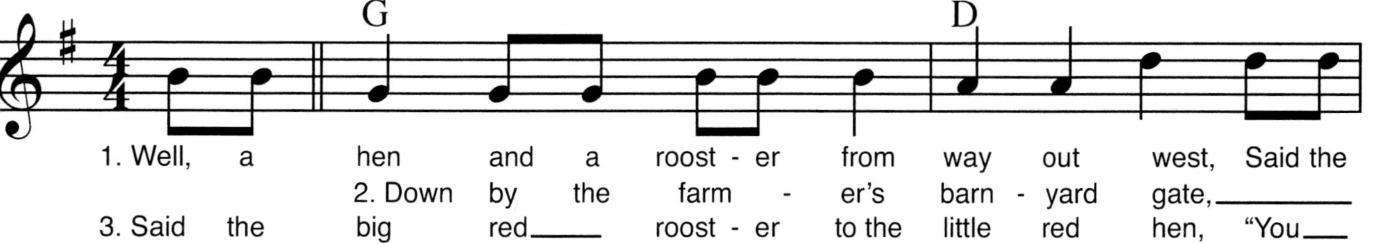

G D
1. Well, a hen and a roost - er from way out west, Said the
2. Down by the farm - er's barn - yard gate,
3. Said the big red roost - er to the little red hen, "You

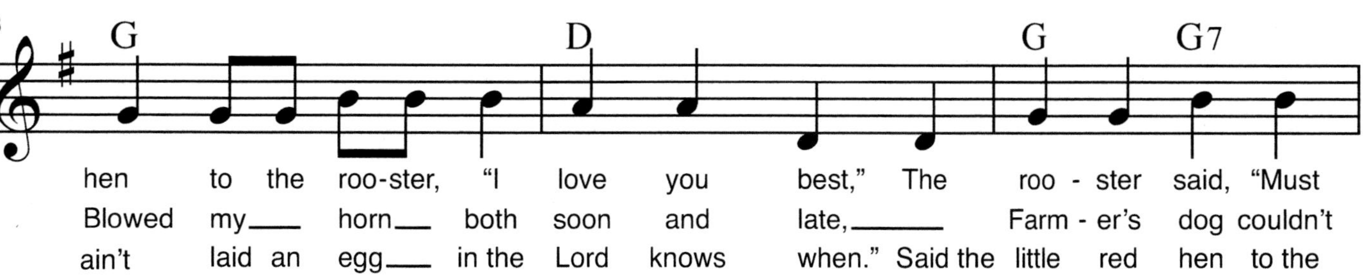

G D G G7
hen to the roo-ster, "I love you best," The roo - ster said, "Must
Blowed my horn both soon and late, Farm - er's dog couldn't
ain't laid an egg in the Lord knows when." Said the little red hen to the

C D G
be a lie, I seen you flirt - ing with the big Shang - hai."
bark nor bite, But the son of a gun, he could read and write.
big red rooster, "You ain't been a - round quite as often as you used to."

G C G A7 D7
Cho: Who broke the lock? I don't know, Who broke the lock? On the hen house door, Well

G G7 C D7
I'll find out be - fore I go, Who broke the lock on the hen house door?

Who Will Sing for Me?

M: A; F: D or E
CD 2-Track 92
Tradition
A
1. Oft I sing for my friends, When death's cold hand I see, But when I am called, Who will sing one song for me?
2. So I'll sing, 'til the end, And help - ful try to be, As - sured that some friends, Will sing one song for me.
3. When crowds shall gath - er round, And look down on me, Will they turn and walk a - way, Or will they sing one song for me?
D
A
B7
E7
A
Cho: I won - der who, Will they sing for me, When I'm called to cross that si - lent sea, Who will sing for me?
E7
A
E7
A
D
A
E7
A

Flatt & Scruggs, Stanley Bros., R. Stanle
Scruggs/Watson/Skaggs, Jimmy Martin, E.L. Harri

Wild Bill Jones

*: G; **F:** C or D*
) 2-Track 93

G
1. As I went out for to take a lit - tle
2. He said, "My age is twen - ty
3. He reeled and he stag - gered and he fell to the
4. So pass a - round that long - necked
D
walk, I walked up - on that wild Bill
one, Too old to be con -
ground, And he gave one dy - ing
bottle, And we'll all go on a
G
Jones. He was walk-ing and a' talk - ing by my
trolled." So I drew my re - volv - er
groan. I threw my arms a - round my
spree. For to - day was the last of that
1
true lov - er's side, And I
from my side, And de -
dar - ling's neck, Say - ing,
wild Bill Jones, And to -
3
D G
bid him to leave her a - lone.
stroyed that poor boy's soul.
"Darling, you'll be left a lone."
mor - row's the last of me.

nley Bros., R. Stanley, Ken. Colonels, Hot Rize,
Boggs, J.E. Mainer, J. Stecher, Alison Krauss

Wildwood Flower

M: C; F: F or G
CD 2-Track 94

Tradition[al]

1. I will twine 'mid the ringlets of my raven black hair,
The lilies so pale and the roses so fair,
The myrtle so bright with an emerald hue,
And the pale aronatus with eyes of bright blue.

2. I will sing and I'll dance, my laugh shall be gay,
I will cease this wild weeping, drive sorrow away,
Though my heart is now breaking, he never shall know,
That his name made me tremble and my pale cheek to glow.

3. I will think of him never, I'll be wildly gay,
I will charm every heart, and the crowd I will sway,
I'll live yet to see him regret the dark hour,
When he won, then neglected, the frail wildwood flower.

4. He told me he loved me, and promised to love,
Through ill and misfortune, all others above,
Another has won him, ah, miser-y to tell,
He left me in silence, no word of farewell.

5. He taught me to love him, he called me his flower,
That blossomed for him all the brighter each hour,
But I woke from my dreaming, my idol was clay,
My visions of love have all faded away.

Carter Fam., Stanley Bros., Flatt & Scruggs, D. Grisman, C. Whi[te]
Ken. Colonels, Lilly Bros., D. Bruce & J. Nunal[ly]

Will the Circle Be Unbroken?

*: G; **F:** C or D*
) 2-Track 95, medley pt. 1

Traditional

G
1. I was stand - ing by my win - dow,
Cho: Will the cir - cle be un - brok - en,
2. Well I told the un - der - tak - er,
3. Oh, I fol - lowed close be - hind her,
4. Went back home, Lord, my home was lone - some,
C
G
On a cold and cloud - y day, When I
Bye and bye Lord bye and bye, There's a
"Un - der - tak - er please drive slow, For that
Tried to hold up and be brave, But I
Since my moth - er, she was gone, All my
saw the hearse come roll - ing, For to
bet - ter home a' wait - ing, In the
bo - dy you are car - rying, Lord, I
could not hide my sor - row, When they
broth - ers, sis - ters cry - ing, What a
D
G
car - ry my moth - er a - way.
sky Lord in the sky.
hate to see her go."
laid her in her grave.
home so sad and lone.

Will There Be Any Stars in My Crown?

M: G; F: C or D
CD 2-Track 95, medley pt. 2

Sweney & Hewitt, ca 189

G
Am
1. I am think - ing to - day of that beau - ti - ful land, I shall
2. In the strength of the Lord let me la - bor and pray, Let me
3. Oh what joy it will be when His face I be - hold, Liv - ing

3
D7
G
reach when the sun go - eth down; When through won - der - ful grace by my
watch as a win - ner of souls, That bright stars may be mine in the
gems at his feet to lay down! It would sweet - en my bliss in the

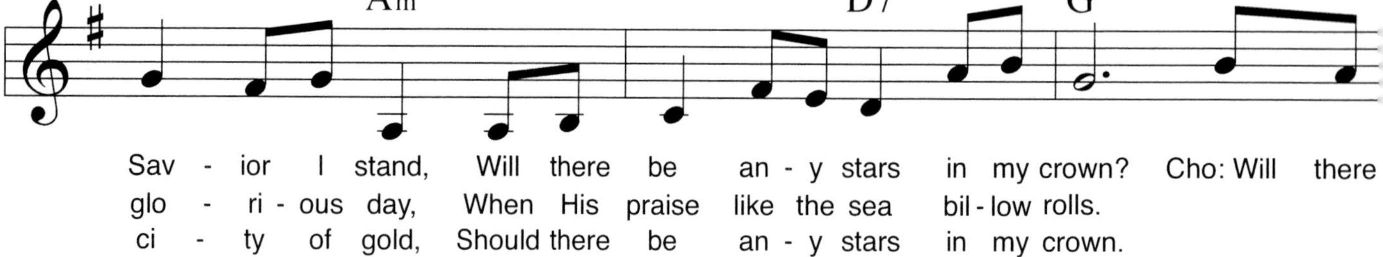
6
Am
D7
G
Sav - ior I stand, Will there be an - y stars in my crown? Cho: Will there
glo - ri - ous day, When His praise like the sea bil - low rolls.
ci - ty of gold, Should there be an - y stars in my crown.

9
G
D7
be an - y stars, an - y stars in my crown, When at eve - ning the sun go - eth down? When I

13
G
C
G
D7
G
wake with the blest in God's man - sions of rest, Will there be an - y stars in my crown?

Seldom Scene, B. Clifton, Cox Fa

Willie My Darling

M: G; F: C or D
CD 2-Track 96

G
C
D
1. They tell me it's sin - ful to flirt,
They say that my
Cho: Wil - lie my dar - ling come back,
I will ev - er be
2. I re - mem - ber the night when he said,
That he loved me far

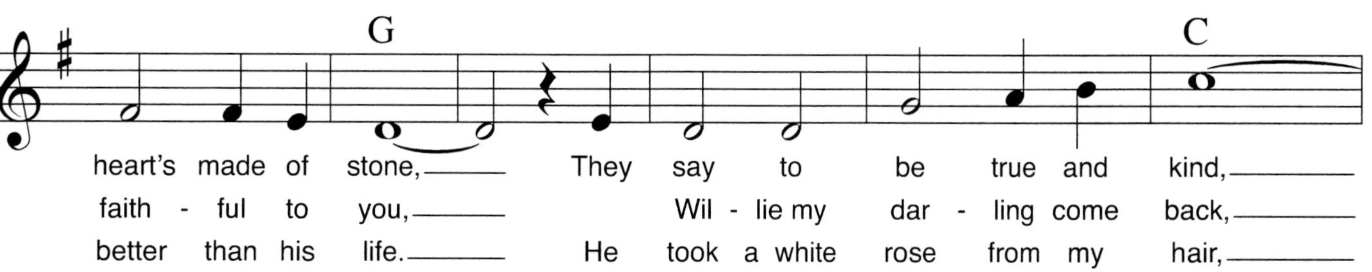
G
C
heart's made of stone,
They say to be true and kind,
faith - ful to you,
Wil - lie my dar - ling come back,
better than his life.
He took a white rose from my hair,

D
G
Or else leave the poor boy a - lone.
I will ev - er be faith - ful to you.
And asked me to be his dear wife.

G C
3. "Well, Willie," I said with a smile,
D G
"I'm afraid that I'll have to say no,
C
'Cause Papa and Mama aren't willing,"
D G
Then he said, "Goodbye, I must go."

4. Next morning poor Willie was found,
He was drowned in the pond by the mill.
In the cold, icy waters so deep,
That flowed from the brink of the hill.

5. His blue eyes forever were closed,
And damp were his curls so fair.
And close to his pale lips he held,
The white rose that he took from my hair.

Worried Man Blues

M: C; F: F or G
CD 2-Track 97, medley pt. 1

Tradition

C
Cho: It takes a wor-ried man to sing a wor - ried song, It
1. I went a-cross the river, And I lay down to sleep, I

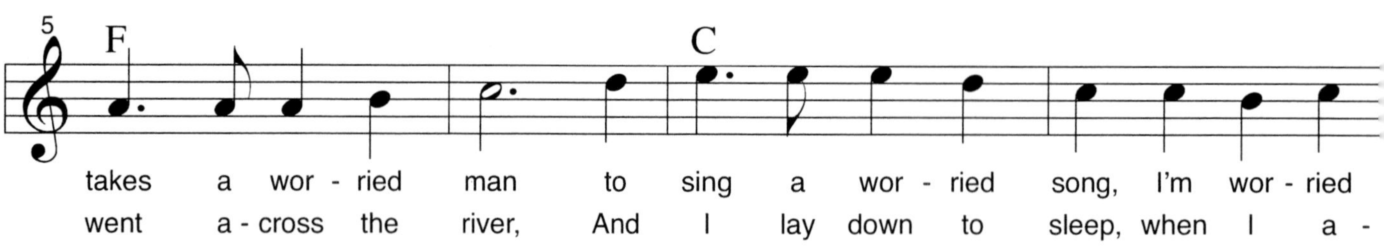

5
F
C
takes a wor - ried man to sing a wor - ried song, I'm wor - ried
went a - cross the river, And I lay down to sleep, when I a -

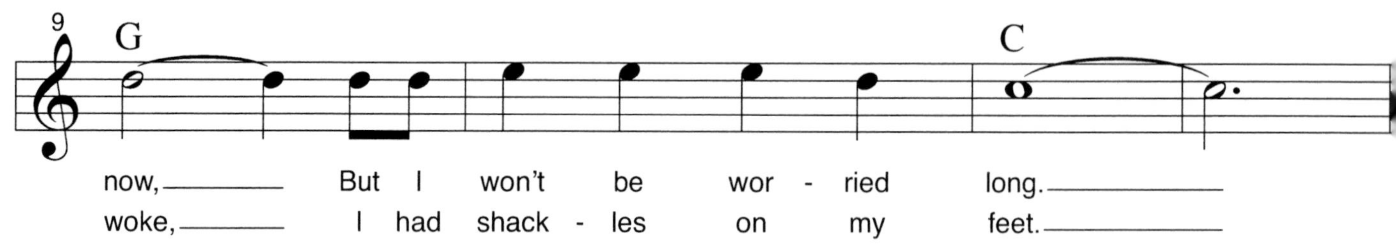

9
G
C
now, But I won't be wor - ried long.
woke, I had shack - les on my feet.

C
2. Twenty nine links of chain around my leg,
F C
Twenty nine links of chain around my leg,
G C
And on each link an initial of my name.

3. I asked the judge, what might be my fine,
I asked the judge, what might be my fine,
Twenty one years on the R.C. Mountain Line.

4. If anyone should ask you, who composed this son
If anyone should ask you, who composed this song,
Tell them 'twas I, and I sing it all day long.

5. I looked down the track, as far as I could see,
I looked down the track, as far as I could see,
A little hand was waving after me.

Carter Fam., Flatt & Scruggs, Stanley Bros., NLCR, Blue Sky Boy
Reno & Harrell, Jim & Jesse, Osborne Bros., W. Guthr

The Wreck of the Old 97

*': C; **F:** F or G*
D 2-Track 97, medley pt. 2

C
F
1. Oh, they gave him his or - ders down at Mon - roe, Vir -
2. He___ turned 'round and said___ to his black filth - y

C
G
gin - ia, Say - ing, "Steve, you're way be - hind time,___ This is
fire - man,___ "Hey, shovel on a lit - tle more coal,___ And___

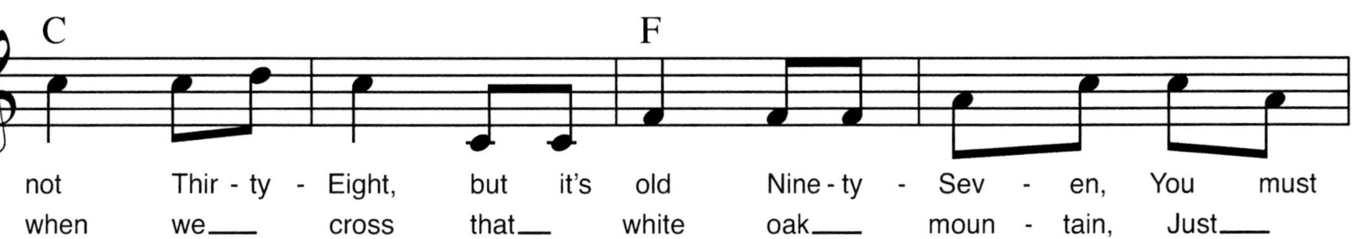
C
F
not Thir - ty - Eight, but it's old Nine - ty - Sev - en, You must
when we___ cross that___ white oak___ moun - tain, Just___

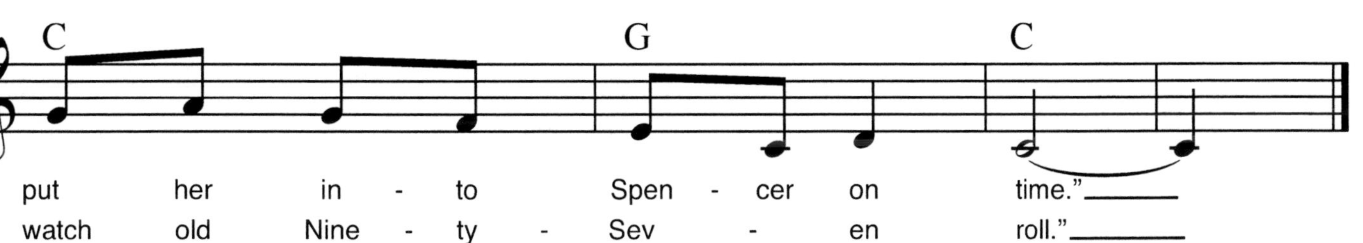
C
G
C
put her in - to Spen - cer on time."___
watch old Nine - ty - Sev - en roll."___

C F
3. It's a mighty rough road from Lynchburg to Danville,
C G
And lying on a three mile grade,
C F
It was on that grade that he lost his average,
C G C
You see what a jump he made.

4. He was going down the grade making ninety miles an hour,
When his whistle broke into a scream,
He was found in the wreck with his hand on the throttle,
And scalded to death by the steam.

5. Well, a telegram came to Washington City,
And this is how it read:
"The brave engineer that run old Ninety-Seven,
Is lying in old Danville dead."

6. Now all you ladies, heed, take warning,
From this time on and learn,
Never speak harsh words to your true loving husband,
He may leave you and never return.

:illet Lickers, Flatt & Scruggs, Bluegrass Band,
'ac Wiseman, NLCR, N. Blake, W. Guthrie

You're a Flower Blooming in the Wildwood

***M:** G; **F:** C or D*
CD 2-Track 98

Traditional

G C
1. On an even - ing long a - go, when the sun was sink - ing
2. Well, the let - ter came to me, from a cap - tain on the
3. He's gone for - ev - er more, he can - not come back to
4
D G
low, My dar - ling went to sail a - cross the sea. It was
sea, That told me my dar - ling was dead. Oh the
shore, He's drown - ded down be - low, you see. When it's
9
C
in the month of June, when the ros - es were in bloom, He
shock and great sur - prise, put the tear - drops in my eyes, When I
in the month of June, and the ros - es are in bloom, It
13
D G
took me in his arms and said to me: Cho: "You're a
thought a - bout the last words that he said:
seems to me I hear my dar - ling say:
17
G
flow - er bloom - ing in the wild - wood, You're a flow - er bloom - ing there for
23
D G C
me, Sweet - er than the morn - ing dew, and I'll soon re - turn to
28
D G
you, You're a flow - er bloom - ing there for me."

D. McCoury, Goose Island Ramblers

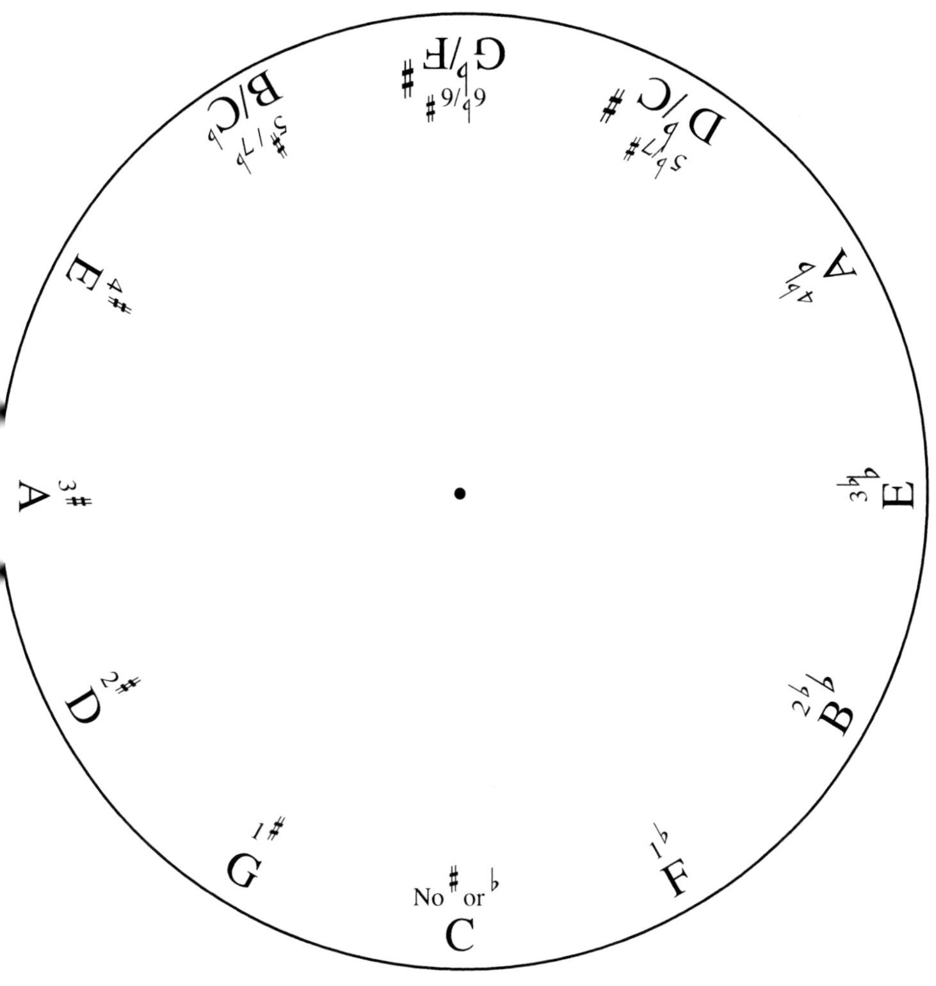
G♭/F#
6♭/6#
D♭/C#
5♭/7#
A♭
4♭
E♭
3♭
B♭
2♭
F
1♭
No # or ♭
C
G
1#
D
2#
A
3#
E
4#
B/C♭
5#/7♭

Musix Transposer Wheel

rint this page on card stock. Carefully ut out both wheels. Punch a small hole t the dot in the middle of each. Attach e smaller wheel to the larger wheel ith a paper fastener making sure both heels can spin independently. To anspose, follow directions on inner heel.

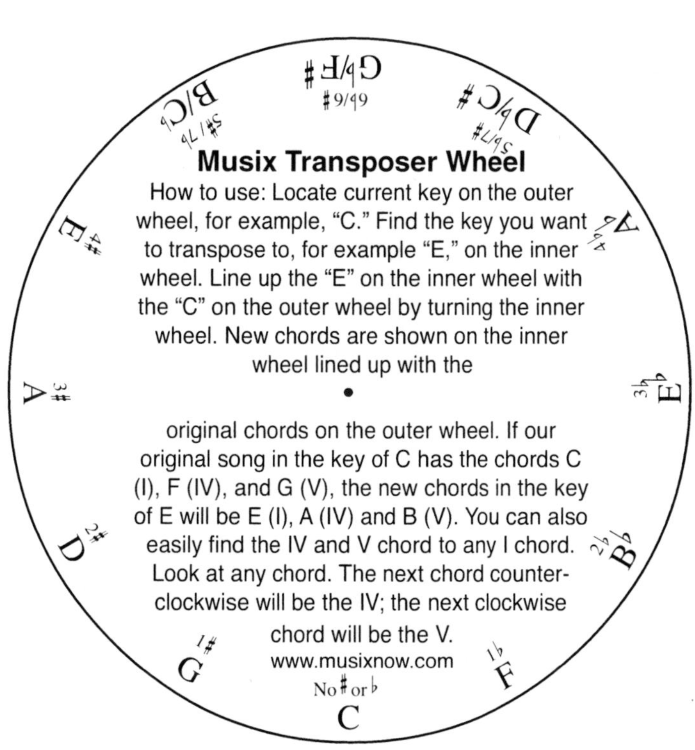
Musix Transposer Wheel
How to use: Locate current key on the outer wheel, for example, "C." Find the key you want to transpose to, for example "E," on the inner wheel. Line up the "E" on the inner wheel with the "C" on the outer wheel by turning the inner wheel. New chords are shown on the inner wheel lined up with the
original chords on the outer wheel. If our original song in the key of C has the chords C (I), F (IV), and G (V), the new chords in the key of E will be E (I), A (IV) and B (V). You can also easily find the IV and V chord to any I chord. Look at any chord. The next chord counter-clockwise will be the IV; the next clockwise chord will be the V.
www.musixnow.com
No # or ♭
C
G
1#
F
1♭
D
2#
B♭
2♭
A
3#
E♭
3♭
E
4#
A♭
4♭
B/C♭
D♭/C#
G♭/F#

Fiddlers to Check Out

In no particular order.

Alexander "Eck" Robertson. A great Old-Time fiddler from Texas. Eck is credited with being the first country musician to be recorded in 1922. One of the first songs waxed at that session was "Sally Goodin."

Benny Edward Martin. Bluegrass fiddler from Sparta, Tennessee, who played with Flatt and Scruggs and invented the 8-string fiddle.

Paul Warren. From Hickman County, Teneessee, he played on Kitty Wells recordings such as "It Wasn't God Who Made Honky-Tonk Angels" and "Release Me." In 1954 he joined Flatt & Scruggs.

Johnny Gimble. An award-winning fiddle player and considered one of the most important fiddlers in the genre's history. Played 5-string fiddle with Bob Wills, Merle Haggard, and many others.

Benny Thomasson. Influential Texas fiddle style great who taught Texas Shorty, Mark O'Connor, and others. Benny won too many contests to count.

Kenny Baker. Former coal miner and fiddle player best known for his 25 year tenure with Bill Monroe and The Bluegrass Boys. Baker is considered to be one of the most influential fiddlers in bluegrass music. Known for his smooth "long-bow" style.

Byron Berline. He is considered to be a modern fiddle masters and is one of the most significant figures in contemporary bluegrass music. He has recorded with The Rolling Stones, Bob Dylan, Elton John, The Byrds, Earl Scruggs, Dillard & Clark, Willie Nelson, Bill Monroe, Doc Watson, John Denver, Rod Stewart, The Eagles, The Band, Vince Gill, Emmylou Harris, Tammy Wynette, Alabama, Mary Chapin Carpenter, The Dillards, Mason Williams, Bill Wyman, Manhattan Transfer, Joe Diffee, The Doobie Brothers, Lucinda Williams, Mickey Gilley, and many others.

Alison Krauss. Probably the most famous and celebrated bluegrass fiddler and singer ever. She began her performing in her early teens and has since sold over 10 million records and been awarded 26 Grammy Awards. She has been a strong influence, both with her fiddling and singing, on younger generations of contemporary bluegrass musicians.

Curly Ray Cline. A bluegrass and old time fiddler from West Virginia known for his work with the Lonesome Pine Fiddlers and Ralph Stanley. Curly Ray did studio work for many musicians such as Jimmy Martin, Bobby Osborne, Rex and Eleanor Parker and Hobo Jack Adkins.

Bobby Hicks. A Grammy Award winning bluegrass fiddler and a professional musician for more than fifty years. Played and recorded with Jim Eanes, Bill Monroe, Porter Wagoner, Ricky Skaggs, Jesse McReynolds and the Virginia Boys, among others.

Stuart Duncan. An award-winning bluegrass musician who played with the Nashville Bluegrass Band and has worked with such stars as George Strait, Dolly Parton, Reba McEntire, and Barbara Streisand, to name a few.

Ramona Jones. A fine old-time fiddle and mandolin player best known for playing with her husband, Grandpa Jones. The former Ramona Riggins met Grandpa Jones, while both were working at WLW Cincinnati on the Boone County Jamboree. Through the years she has continued to perform and record.

obert Russell "Chubby" Wise. A bluegrass fiddler who began playing with Bill Monroe's Blue Grass Boys 1942. He then played with Clyde Moody, the York Brothers, Flatt & Scruggs, and Hank Snow's Rainbow anch Boys. He worked as a session musician with Mac Wiseman and Red Allen.

mes Robert (Bob) Wills. Western swing musician, songwriter, and bandleader of the Texas Playboys, consid-ed by many music authorities one of the fathers of Western Swing. He brought us "Faded Love," "San Anto-o Rose," and many other great western swing standards.

uddy Spicher. Spicher started in the late 1950s as part of the backing band for Audrey Williams, the widow of ank Williams. He later played with Hank Snow and the Charles River Valley Boys. Spicher became a Nash-lle-based session musician, backing the likes of Bob Dylan. He was also one of the band members of Area ode 615 with other Nashville sessions musicians and the Western Swing band Asleep at the Wheel.

m "Texas Shorty" Chancellor. Influential World Champion Texas fiddler who learned from Eck Robertson d Benny Thomasson. Probably the only fiddler to appear on the old television show **What's My Line**.

na Jae. Described as "The First Lady of Country Fiddle." In 1974 Jana Jae became the first female mem-r of Buck Owens' Buckaroos. She was part of the regular team of performers on the popular "Hee Haw" levision show and has appeared with such country music greats as Chet Atkins, Roy Clark, Ray Stevens, the akridge Boys, Mel Tillis, Ricky Skaggs and the Nitty Gritty Dirt Band.

otty Stoneman. Scotty Stoneman has been called the Jimi Hendrix of the violin by Peter Rowan. Born into e old time Stoneman Family, he was a great, influential and powerful fiddler probably best know for his work ith The Kentucky Colonels.

ack MaGaha. Nashville's "dancing fiddle man" who performed with Dolly Parton, Porter Wagoner and the uegrass band Smiley & Reno, who was a mainstay at the Opryland theme park during the 70's and 80's, and ho was known for his spastic and hyper performances.

ter Tate. Spent his early years in bands such as those led by Jimmy Martin and Carl Story, whose tour-g group was the Rambling Mountaineers. He played with Bill Monroe's Bluegrass Boys for many years, ith his own Bluegrass Cut-Ups, and various groups under artists such as Billy Edwards, John Palmer, Herschel zemore, Jim Eanes, Cliff Waldron, Wesley Golding, Gene Burrows, Bobby Hicks, and Tom McKinney. He rformed and recorded with Lester Flatt & The Nashville Grass, and was the last fiddler ever employed by att.

urie Lewis. Laurie spent the early days of her music career in the San Francisco Bay Area playing fiddle and ss in a variety of regional bands. She was a popular contest fiddler in the 1970s. She now tours internationally d her music covers a range of styles from traditional and old time to modern country.

Notes on Selected Songs by Dix Bruce

For a complete alphabetical listing of all the songs in this book, see the Table of Contents on page 2.

A

All the Good Times, p. 12: An eloquent description of the despair lost love can bring.

Amazing Grace, p. 13: Probably the greatest hit of spiritual music, it appeals to people with a wide variety of beliefs.

Angel Band, p. 14: I love the comforting message of "Angel Band." Quite a different point of view from "He Will Set Your Fields on Fire (p. 94)

Angeline, the Baker, p. 15: Probably the source for the instrumental "Angelina Baker." This vocal version is quite happy and peppy considering that the story is about a slave who's sweetheart has "gone away," no doubt sold to another owner. Like many songs of the pre-Civil War period, this one idealized slave and plantation life. "Darling Nellie Gray" (p. 56) has a very similar story but is much more somber in tone.

Angels Rock Me To Sleep, p. 16: Another comforting image of death.

Are You From Dixie?, p. 18: One of a vast repertoire of songs that idealize the sunny south including "Sweet Sunny South," (p. 216) "Bl Ridge Mountain Blues," (p. 30) "The Girl I Loved in Sunny Tennessee." (p. 76) These types of songs, some from the mid-1800s, so as recent as the latest pop country hit, have resonated across the US and throughout the world. Of course we're not all from the south but we all have a mother, maybe a sweetheart, or a warm concept of home. That might explain the enduring popularity of these types songs.

Are You Washed in the Blood of the Lamb?, p. 20: This one, along with many other great old time gospel songs, comes from my worn Baptist hymnal "Tabernacle Hymns." You can still find these for a dollar or two or three in used books stores.

Arkansas Traveller, p. 21: You probably sang this as "Bringing Home a Baby Bumble Bee" as a kid. My dream is to play "Arkansas Traveller" for Bill Clinton. It's probably been done.

As I Went Down in the Valley to Pray, p. 66: See "Down in the Valley to Pray." (p. 66)

Aunt Dinah's Quilting Party, p. 22: Sometimes titled "Seeing Nellie Home."

Away in a Manger, p. 23*:* One of my favorites since childhood. Peaceful and reassuring. Makes a good bluegrass Christmas song.

B

Banks of the Ohio, p. 24: I love the melody to this grisly but popular murder ballad. There must be hundreds of versions of it with a variety of different lyrics. On some the chorus is, "Only say that you'll be mine/And in no other's arms entwine." In the version in this book t third verse makes little sense. Suddenly we're talking about the sea instead of the Ohio River. No matter, it's still a powerful song and good example of the "folk process" where lyrics are repeated, misheard, changed, repeated, etc.

Beautiful Life, A, p. 25: Who could argue with the sentiments expressed in this song? It's usually performed in an intricate vocal quartet arrangement. Like several other similar songs, I've simplified the arrangement in this book for clarity and the sake of space. Listen to one of the original recordings to hear the vocal arrangement.

Beautiful Star of Bethlehem, p. 26: One of the prettiest Christmas songs and one often performed by bluegrass bands.

Bile Them Cabbage Down, p. 28: There are several songs with similar verses about one mammal in a tree, the other on the ground imploring him to "shake some 'simmins (persimmons) down." Wendy Whitford of the Goose Island Ramblers always sang "Shake them *cinnamons* down."

Black Eyed Susie, p. 29: Compare this song with "Blue Eyed Verdie" and some of the verses in "Pig in a Pen," among other songs with similar lyrics.

Blue Ridge Mountain Blues, p. 30: This song is unusual in that subsequent choruses have alternate lyrics. Some singers also fit in lyrics th include "Want to see my old dog Trey."

Bluebirds are Singing for Me, The, p. 31: Usually performed with a "call-and-response" chorus with repeated or echoed lines: "There's a bluebird singing" / *"There's a bluebird singing"* / "In the Blue Ridge Mountains" / *"In the Blue Ridge Mountains,"* etc.

Boil That Cabbage Down, Boil The Cabbage Down, Boil Them Cabbage Down, p. 28: See "Bile Them Cabbage Down."

Bound to Ride, p. 32: When I hear this song, I imagine a young bachelor riding the train, far away from home and sweetheart, eating saltin crackers because they're so cheap. I remember in my own youth when Kraft Macaroni and Cheese could be had for $.25 a package. Tough to prepare and eat in a moving vehicle though.

ight Morning Stars, p. 33: Often performed a capella. This arrangement is shown with accompanying chords.

ing Back to Me My Wandering Boy, p. 34: Bill Monroe's version of this song is called "Out in the Cold World."

ffalo Gals, p. 35: Another one we sang as kids. Of course that was during "The Enlightenment" when most public schools had art and music classes.

lly of the Town, The, p. 36: A great song then and now! We've still got bullies coming out of the woodwork and heroes ready to take 'em on. A G diminished chord can be substituted for the Gb chord.

ry Me Beneath the Willow, p. 38: One of the first folk or old time songs players learn. A "must know."

H-I-C-K-E-N, p. 39: Originally a pop song from 1902.

n't You Hear Me Callin'?, p. 40: Also the title of a comprehensive biography of Monroe, *Can't You Hear Me Callin': The Life of Bill Monroe, Father of Bluegrass* by Richard D. Smith (Warner Books). The chorus is often sung as "I loved you best," but "Bess" was Monroe's long time companion and bass player Bessie Lee Mauldin. You decide how to sing it.

reless Love, p. 41: A standard in the folk, bluegrass, and jazz repertoires. I first heard the "in the family way" lyrics when I discovered them while doing research for this book. The song makes much more sense in this light.

ildren Go Where I Send Thee, p. 42: Reminiscent of "The Twelve Days of Christmas" with the numbers and repetitions of characters. Listen to the CD to hear how the chorus grows upon repetition. Great bluegrass Christmas song.

urch in the Wildwood, The, p. 43: I remember my grandmother Nellie Bruce singing this to us grandkids. The chorus is often performed with multiple parts. My grandmother would crack us up singing the bass part, which was a chant below the melody on the chorus: "Oh come, come, come, come…"

ndy, p. 44: Another I learned in grade school music class. I was pleasantly surprised to discover it in the bluegrass repertoire.

ld Jordan, p. 126: See "Jordan." (p. 126)

lumbus Stockade Blues, p. 45: This one makes a great hard country or rockabilly song.

me All Ye Fair and Tender Ladies, p. 71: See "Fair and Tender Ladies." (p. 71)

o Coo, The, p. 51: See "Cuckoo, The" (p. 51)

tton-Eyed Joe, p. 46: A standard for fiddlers in all types of country and old time music.

awdad Song, The, p. 48: Makes a wonderful kids' bluegrass song.

ipple Creek, p. 49: Most often played as an instrumental but when it is sung, the lyrics are usually only sung on part one. Also known as "Shootin' Creek."

ckoo, The, p. 51: I love the verses, melancholy mood, and varied verses of "The Cuckoo," alternately titled "The Coo Coo."

niel Prayed, p. 52: I'd heard "Daniel Prayed" for years but really got into it when I transcribed a Doc Watson recording with three vocal parts, lead, tenor, and bass, for my Doc Watson and Clarence Ashley book (MB97056) published by Mel Bay. It's a wonderful old time gospel trio arrangement. Check it out. The version in this book is simplified and written with just the lead voice. The book is packed with songs that have become "greatest hits" of old time and bluegrass.

nny Boy, p. 54: Often played as an instrumental, this song's lyrics are haunting and beautiful. War takes its toll on all those involved in it but surely mothers bear the greatest burden.

rling Corey, p. 55: Notice the close similarity in lyrics between "Darling Corey" and "Little Maggie." (p. 150) Many of the songs in **The Parking Lot Picker's Songbook,** and indeed in the greater traditional American music repertoire, share lines, whole verses, or themes with other songs. Credit the "folk process" of hearing songs, adding verses, swapping lyrics or melodies, mixing the whole thing up and serving it new as each individual singer adapts a song.

rling Nellie Gray, p. 56: One of the most powerful songs I've ever heard. When Jim Nunally and Dix perform it, an older listener invariably comes up to tell us they'd learned the song in grade school, but had never heard verse four. "Darling Nellie Gray" has been a popular song for generations, for obvious reasons, published again and again, but that particular verse, the one that gave the lyric its power and the song its meaning, was censored. Many people mistakenly assume this is a Stephen Foster composition when in fact it was composed by B.R. Hanby. I hear a similarity in the movement and tone of the melody between this and Bob Wills' classic "Faded Love."

Darling Will You Ever Think of Me?, p. 58: I wanted to include a few of my compositions in **The Parking Lot Picker's Songbook.** Here's one that I hope you'll enjoy.

Deep Elem Blues, p. 59: I first learned this when I played in Frank Wakefield's band in the late 1970s. It's a comical look at the bad part of town.

Diamonds in the Rough, p. 60: Worth learning for the metaphor alone. Performed in both 4/4 (as written) and 6/8 (on CD).

Didn't He Ramble, p. 173: See "Oh! Didn't he Ramble." (p. 173)

Do Lord, p. 61: The C♯7 and F♯m chords in measure eleven are enclosed in parenthesis noting that they are optional. In the process of collecting the songs for this book, I consulted several hymnals. To my surprise I found that the harmonies in my old Baptist hymnal often included these somewhat "modern" sounding chords, the three dominant and the six minor.

Don't Let Your Deal Go Down, p. 62: This arrangement combines elements from different old time and more modern bluegrass sources. Compare these lyrics with "Storms are on the Ocean."

Don't You Hear Jerusalem Moan?, p. 64: A fun and funny song that's slightly "crooked" with an extra vocal phrase. And, could we ever have enough songs that make fun of preachers and authority in general? Here's another set of lyrics:

1) Well I went to church last Sunday morning/Don't you hear Jerusalem moan?/ Heard all them sinners just a moaning and a groaning/Don't you hear Jerusalem moan?

2) I'm gonna get down on my knees today,

Don't you (etc.)

Let Jesus wash my sins away, (etc.)

3) There's many souls lost here in sin,

Don't you go and talk to them, (etc.)

Down Among the Budded Roses, p. 65: One I learned from Wendy Whitford and the Goose Island Ramblers and a "true" song with a perfect image that says it all: "Down among the budded roses/I am nothing but a stem." As the others are coming into the bloom of life the singer's own life seems overdue to a lost love. Compare with "Wildwood Flower" (p. 246) and "Little Rosewood Casket." (p. 153)

Down in the Valley to Pray, p. 66: This song is performed as "Down to the River to Pray" in the film "O Brother Where Art Thou?"

Down in the Willow Garden, p. 67: I'm not sure what "burglar's wine" is, unless it's a mickey. Some people sing "burgundy wine."

Down the Road, p. 68: The Greenbriar Boys and Country Gazette performed this with an added chorus: "Down the road, down the road, Got a little pretty girl down the road." Flatt & Scruggs left the chorus out. You can fill in your own name in the lyric "Old man (or woman) ____ (insert your name here)."

Down to the River to Pray, p. 66: See "Down in the Valley to Pray." (p. 66)

E

East Virginia Blues, p. 70: This is a truly epic story and there are several versions of it that are sung in old time and bluegrass circles. Compare it with "Katy Dear." (p. 133) The lyrics to "East Virginia Blues" vary according to version. For example, in verse two, some versions have white lilies on her breast and in verse #4, the second and third lines are also sung "Where she lies on her bed of rest, For in her hand she holds a dagger." The order and number of verses varies widely.

End of My Journey, p. 140: See "Let Me Rest at the End of My Journey." (p. 140)

F

Fair and Tender Ladies, p. 71: Lots of great songs came to bluegrass from the folk revival of the 1960s. These types of songs were often performed by the more "modern" bluegrass groups like the Osborne Brothers and the Country Gentlemen.

Fathers Have a Home Sweet Home, p. 72: Often performed with lead, tenor, and bass vocal parts.

Feast Here Tonight, p. 73: Sometimes called "Rabbit in a Log," this song is a classic. The definitive version was recorded by the Monroe Brothers.

Footprints in the Snow, p. 75: Bill Monroe's version sets the bluegrass standard for this song.

G

Girl I Left in Sunny Tennessee, The, p. 76: (see "Girl I Loved in Sunny Tennessee, The") (p. 76)

Girl I Loved in Sunny Tennessee, The, p. 76: The original source of this song is a sentimental pop song from 1899. It's often called "The Girl I *Left* in Sunny Tennessee."

Give Me Oil in My Lamp, p. 78: From the Baptist canon.

Give Me the Roses While I Live, p. 79: A popular theme in several different traditional and old time songs. It's as true today as it was a hundred or more years ago. Don't let someone slip away without them knowing of your love or admiration. It can happen in the blink of an eye.

Going Down This Road Feeling Bad, p. 80: Also known as "Lonesome Road Blues" and the basis of Earl Scruggs' instrumental of the same name. It's sometimes performed with an Em chord in measure twelve over the lyrics "Lord/And I."

Going Up Cripple Creek, p. 49: See "Cripple Creek." (p. 49)

Going Up Home to Live in Green Pastures, p. 85: See "Green Pastures." (p. 85)

Grandfather's Clock, p. 82: Long a hit with banjo pickers and guitar fingerpickers, this one also makes a wonderful vocal with its eerie story.

Green Pastures, p. 85: Another Stanley standard with a beautiful, peaceful view of the great beyond.

Groundhog, p. 86: Red Allen repeats the word "groundhog" twice more as a kind of chorus.

H

Hallelujah! I'm Ready, p. 87: A few of the songs in **The Parking Lot Picker's Songbook** are written with basic two part vocal arrangements. You can hear the arrangement on the accompanying CD.

Hand Me Down My Walking Cane, p. 88: Long a favorite among folkies, Norman Blake does a great old time version of this song.

Handsome Molly, p. 89: Every generation updates traditional music. My favorite update of "Handsome Molly" is a kind of Latin-Reggae romp by the Extended Playboys. Try to find that on your iTunes! In one of Doc Watson's earlier versions of "Handsome Molly" he sings "I wish I was in London/or some other *depot* town."

Hard Times, Come Again No More, p. 90: This is still a very popular song among folk singers, especially at group sings.

He Was a Friend of Mine, p. 92: I first heard a version of this on a Byrds' LP where it was rewritten about John F. Kennedy's assassination. Since that time in the mid-1960s, I've heard it performed in several folk contexts including bluegrass and traditional blues.

Ie Will Set Your Fields on Fire, p. 94: Talk about your fire and brimstone! This one is usually performed with an intricate, multi-voice arrangement.

Iigh on a Mountain, p. 96: One incredible song by Ola Belle Reed. The image, melody, modal chord movement, story, and tone of it all make it a classic and a "must-know" song.

Iighway of Sorrow, p. 97: Bill Monroe had a reputation as a gruff, tough and stubborn curmudgeon. When I interviewed him in the early 1980s, he found this to not be the case, exactly. While reserved and private, he also showed a great sense of humor and a playful streak. He was expansive on many subjects from his own legacy to his thoughts about rock and jazz as well as his views on life. It's amazing to me that he revealed himself as much as he did in compositions like "Highway of Sorrow," "It's Mighty Dark to Travel," (p. 119) and "Can't You Hear Me Calling." (p. 40) He was truly a great artist.

ls of Roane County, p. 98: For me, a cryptic verse like: "Sweet Martha was grave but Corey was better/There's better and worse, although you can see," kicks this song into greatness. It's mysterious, beautiful, unknowable.

is Eye is on the Sparrow, p. 100: From "Tabernacle Hymns." Singer and actress Ethel Waters sang "His Eye is on the Sparrow" beautifully and soulfully as part of the Billy Graham Crusades in the 1950s and 1960s.

old Fast to the Right, p. 101: In this case I believe "right" refers to the "correct way" as opposed to any node in the political spectrum.

old to God's Unchanging Hand, p. 102: Soothing words for modern life.

ome Sweet Home, p. 103: This song has been a hit for well over a hundred years. Jim Nunally and I play it quite often and audiences still love it.

p High Ladies, p. 105: Often played as an instrumental, this song is also known as "Uncle Joe" and "Mrs. McCleod's Reel," among other titles.

t Corn, Cold Corn, p. 106: Wonderful goofy song that seems to have something to do with John Barleycorn.

How Can You Treat Me So?, p. 107: I had Bill Monroe's voice in mind as I wrote this one.

I

I am a Man of Constant Sorrow, p. 160: See "Man of Constant Sorrow." (p. 160)

I Know You Rider, p. 109: Originally a blues, this one has been adapted by rock groups and "modern" bluegrass bands, most notably, The Seldom Scene.

I Ride an Old Paint, p. 178: See "Old Paint." (p, 178). From the cowboy repertoire.

I Shall Not Be Moved, p. 111: From the gospel repertoire and popular in old time gospel, jazz, bluegrass, and folk circles. It was an important and symbolic marching song during the civil rights movement of the 1950s and 1960s.

I Wonder How the Old Folks Are at Home, p. 112: Good old pop song from 1909. Popularized in bluegrass by Mac Wiseman.

I'll Be All Smiles Tonight, p. 114: I first heard this from Wendy Whitford of the Goose Island Ramblers. It's a wonderful take on the woman's point of view of a breakup. It's sung by both men and women. See also "Little Rosewood Casket" (p. 153) and "Wildwood Flower." (p. 246)

I'll Fly Away, p. 115: Everybody's favorite gospel/bluegrass song.

I'm Ready, p. 87: See "Hallelujah! I'm Ready." (p. 87)

I'm Sitting on Top of the World, p. 210: See "Sitting on Top of the World." (p. 210)

I'm Standing in the Need of Prayer, p. 213: See "Standing in the Need of Prayer." (p. 213)

In the Garden, p. 117: From "Tabernacle Hymns."

In the Pines, p. 118: Another great bluesy standard of bluegrass and old time music.

It's Mighty Dark to Travel, p. 119: Bill Monroe overheard the phrase "it's mighty dark to travel" in a barber shop as someone mentioned that they had a long way to travel in the dark of night. Monroe turned the phrase into a bluegrass standard.

J

Jesse James, p. 120: If you're gonna be an outlaw, you'd better have somebody write a sympathetic folk song about you. This song is all about primitive attempts at "spin." Woody Guthrie wrote a similar but politically charged song about "Pretty Boy Floyd."

Jimmie Brown, the Newsboy, p. 122: A sentimental parlor tune from the late 1800s. Like much of their repertoire, the Carter Family adapted it to fit their style in the late 1920s. Flatt & Scruggs version from the early 1950s brought this great song into the bluegrass repertoire.

John Hardy, p. 123: See "Jesse James" (p. 120) above. Hardy didn't get quite the treatment in song that Jesse did. I say, pay the extra few bucks, get a good songwriter.

John Henry, p. 124: There must be over a hundred different versions of "John Henry." It's been so popular over the years because it so dramatically tells the story of automation and human against machine.

Jordan, p. 126: The chorus to "Jordan" is often performed with the bass voice taking the lead on the first clause of each phrase of the chorus. Bass solo: "Now look at that," ensemble joins in "cold Jordan," etc.

Just a Closer Walk with Thee, p. 128: This one is popular in many musical genres from gospel and blues to dixieland and bluegrass.

Just as I Am, p. 129: You mature youngsters may remember this theme from the televised Billy Graham crusades of the 1950s and beyond. Willie Nelson recorded a beautiful instrumental version for his *Red Headed Stranger* LP.

Just Over in the Gloryland, p. 130: Another song whose popularity spans many musical genres from gospel and blues to dixieland and bluegrass.

K

Katy Dear, p. 133: Compare the lyrics of this "Romeo and Juliet"-type tale with "East Virginia Blues" (p. 70) and "Silver Dagger."

Keep on the Sunnyside, p. 134: An old song the Carter Family adopted as their theme song. What better advice for life?

Knoxville Girl, p. 136: A murder ballad similar to "Banks of the Ohio" (p. 24) but perhaps even more gory and disturbing.

L

Late Last Night, p. 138: Also known as "Way Down Town," I first heard this from Doc Watson on the *Will the Circle be Unbroken* project from the early 1970s. That historic three LP set introduced traditional music and traditional and bluegrass musicians to the rock-oriented youth culture of the era.

Leave it There, p. 139: I heard this on a 1920s recording by Washington Phillips and it really grabbed me. Not only is it filled with great sentiment, I realized I recognized it from somewhere. Turns out it was from the old Baptist hymnal "Tabernacle Hymns."

Let Me Rest at the End of My Journey, p. 140: One of many cowboy-themed songs that ended up in the bluegrass repertoire.

Letter Edged in Black, The, p. 141: When I was a callow youth learning this repertoire from the older generation, songs like "The Letter Edged in Black" struck me as overly sentimental and dramatic. I was more drawn to the hot and fast material. I guess it was because I hadn't yet experienced the loss of a parent. Now, as I've gotten older and experienced more, I've come to love these songs and appreciate their eloquence in dealing with the life and death issues that we all face.

Life is Like a Mountain Railway, p. 142: See "Life's Railway to Heaven. (p. 142)

Life's Railway to Heaven, p. 142: Even if you're not religious, this song is an apt description of the journey of life.

Li'l Liza Jane, p. 144: Another folk song they taught us in grade school.

Little Annie, p. 145: I first heard this great song from Vern Williams, California's most important contribution to old time bluegrass. "Little Annie" marks the beginning of the massive "Little" section, the largest section in this book, which spans the old time musical horizon from "Annie" to "Willie." (One could argue that "Li'L Liza Jane" belongs here as well, but it's in the "Li'l" section, not the "Little.") For size, the "Old" section is a close rival.

Little Bessie, p. 146: As I mentioned above in "The Letter Edged in Black," my perception of these songs has changed with my age. Being the father of a beautiful twenty-one year old daughter (as of 2008), I find it impossible to sing "Little Bessie" without breaking down in tears.

Little Birdie, p. 148: This arrangement is simplified from the way it's typically performed. Singers usually stretch out syllables like the first "birdie..." an extra measure or longer. The band has to pay attention to the singer!

Little Georgia Rose, p. 168: See "My Little Georgia Rose." (p. 168)

Little Maggie, p. 150: As with "Little Birdie," (p. 148) singers often stretch lyrics beyond their written time values.

Little Old Log Cabin in the Lane, p. 152: If you can find it, listen to Fiddlin' John Carson's version. It was one of the first "country" or "hillbilly" recordings made in the early 1920s. It's just him singing, with his fiddle, and it's haunting.

Little Rosewood Casket, p. 153: Not about what you might think it's about. Compare with "I'll Be All Smiles Tonight" (p. 114) and "Wildwood Flower." (p. 246)

Little Sadie, p. 154: Both this and "Little Willie" (p. 155) are epic story songs where a lot goes on. Both have similarities to "Banks of the Ohio," (p. 24) "Knoxville Girl," (p. 136) and "Pretty Polly." (p. 188) May not be suitable for younger listeners.

Little Willie, p. 155: A brutal and graphic song but a true representation of real events.

Lonesome Reuben, p. 197: See "Reuben's Train." (p. 197)

Lonesome Road Blues, p. 80: See "Going Down This Road Feeling Bad." (p. 80)

Long Journey Home, p. 157: Check out the Monroe Brothers definitive version.

Lord, I'm Coming Home, p. 158: After hearing this for years by artists like the Stanley Brothers and loving it, I discovered "Lord, I'm Coming Home" in one of my worn old hymnals.

M

Mama Don't Allow, p. 159: A well-known and loved song that pops up in a variety of musical styles including jazz and country. It's a proven crowd pleaser.

Man of Constant Sorrow, p. 160: The most famous version of this song is from the film "O Brother, Where Art Thou?" sung by the mythical Soggy Bottom Boys. Their version is based on one recorded by the Stanley Brothers which features a repeat of each verse's last line as in "I have no friends to help me now/He has no friends to help him now."

McKinley, p. 242: See "White House Blues." (p. 242)

Methodist Pie, p. 162: Another tongue-in-cheek look at religion.

Midnight on the Stormy Deep, p. 164: The classic recording of this song is by Bill Monroe in the mid-1960s. Peter Rowan sings it in duet with Monroe.

Milwaukee Blues, p. 165: If you don't know the music of Charlie Poole, run to the store right now and buy one of the new CD box sets. He's one of the true pioneers of old time and bluegrass music with a repertoire and style that influenced all that came after him. Charlie Poole made great, entertaining music. In the last verse, "Santa Fe" rhymes with "be."

Molly and Tenbrooks, p. 166: One of the all-time hits of bluegrass based on much earlier sources.

More Pretty Girls Than One, p. 220: See "There's More Pretty Girls Than One." (p. 220)

Mrs. McCleod's Reel, p. 105: See "Hop High Ladies." (p. 105)

My Home's Across the Blue Ridge Mountains, p. 167: Sometimes sung as "My Home's Across the Smoky Mountains."

My Little Georgia Rose, p. 168: The true story behind this Bill Monroe composition can be found in his biography "*Can't You Hear Me Callin': The Life of Bill Monroe, Father of Bluegrass* by Richard D. Smith (Warner Books).

My Walking Cane, p. 88: See "Hand Me Down My Walking Cane." (p. 88)

My Wandering Boy, p. 34: See "Bring Back to Me My Wandering Boy." (p. 34)

N

Nellie Gray, p. 56: See "Darling Nellie Gray." (p. 56)

New River Train, p. 169: Another classic from the Monroe Brothers.

Nine Pound Hammer, p. 170: You gotta learn this one! It's one of the ten or twenty songs played by ALL Parking Lot Pickers.

Nobody's Business, p. 171: There are a variety of versions of this basic song in bluegrass, old time, blues, and jazz. It may be even more well-known in blues than in bluegrass. As far as I know, the Stanley Brothers brought it into the bluegrass lexicon.

O

Oh Death, p. 172: Another great song featured in the film "O Brother, Where Art Thou?" It's usually sung unaccompanied, with no instrumental backup, in a *rubato* (loose, drawn out rhythm) style. It's written here with backup chords, so you can hear the tonality, and in standard rhythm. The B7s in parenthesis are optional. Be sure to listen to Ralph Stanley's recording.

Oh! Didn't He Ramble, p. 173: Another old pop song appropriated by Charlie Poole. Also popular with dixieland jazz bands.

Old Dan Tucker, p. 174: One they taught us in grade school.

Old Joe Clark, p. 176: Check out the less than proper lyrics. Good taste is timeless! Fiddlers usually play this in the key of A.

Old Man at the Mill, p. 177: Also known as "Same Old Man," I first heard this old time song in a bluegrass context by the Dillards. The flatted seven chord, in this case an F natural, gives the song its modal flavor.

Old Paint, p. 178: See "I Ride an Old Paint." (p. 178) : It always gets back to just a cowboy and his horse. See also "Let Me Rest at the End of My Journey." (p. 140)

Old Rugged Cross, The, p. 179: The A diminished chord in measure one is a little unusual in old time and bluegrass music. Though it comes straight out of the hymnal, in practice it's often played as an Ab chord.

On and On, p. 181: Another very popular Monroe-penned classic of life on the road without your sweetheart.

Out in the Cold World, p. 34: See "Bring Back to Me My Wandering Boy." (p. 34)

Over in the Gloryland, p. 130: You'll hear this song in gospel, blues, and especially in the traditional jazz repertoire. It's interesting that so many songs end up as favorites in a variety of musical styles. I guess it's because so many types of American music share the same roots, often gospel. And, a good song is a good song, no matter where it comes from or who else sings it.

Over the Hills to the Poorhouse, p. 182: A pre-Social Security song that may have renewed resonance in the next few years, especially for baby boomer bluegrass musicians. It's a true song, if slightly dramatic.

P

Pass Me Not, p. 183: Beautiful melody, comforting lyrics.

Pig in a Pen, p. 185: Different versions of this song feature different combinations of the same basic lyrics. And you'll find verses from "Pig in a Pen" in a variety of other songs.

Poor Ellen Smith, p. 186: Sometimes this song is performed with the one line chorus "Nobody knows how I loved Ellen, nobody knows.

Poor Nellie Gray, p. 56: See "Darling Nellie Gray." (p. 56)

Poor Wayfaring Stranger, p. 231: See "The Wayfaring Stranger." (p. 231)

Precious Memories, p. 187: I love the dreamy imagery and moving poetry of this song. It's often mistaken for a gospel song though there's nothing overtly religious about it.

Pretty Polly, p. 188: Another murder ballad done so well by Ralph Stanley.

Put My Little Shoes Away, p. 190: The lyric "Won't he look so nice and cunning" always confused me. Webster's Dictionary of 1913 explains, "Pretty or pleasing; as, a cunning little boy."

R

Rabbit in a Log, p. 73: See "Feast Here Tonight." (p. 73)

Railroad Bill, p. 192: I learned this one from my brother-in-law Rick March when he was teaching me to fingerpick.

Rain and Snow, p. 193: This song has a kind of nebulous tonal center rocking between the Am and the D chord. That gives it a modal feel and the unresolved lyrics add to the song's sense of mystery.

Rank Strangers to Me, p. 194: One of the Stanley Brothers all-time hits that's become a bluegrass standard. The chorus is typically performed in a "call and response" format.

Red Rocking Chair, p. 195: Slightly unusual in that it has an Em or six minor chord in it.

Red Wing, p. 196: One of the most widely known tunes in American music. It's a pop tune from the early 1900s, part of a group of songs that idealized native Americans. Because of its popularity, the melody to "Red Wing" has been adapted again and again to other sets of lyrics. An anonymous writer used it as the basis for "Charlie Chaplin," a children's old time song about the famous tramp, and Woody Guthrie used it for his labor song "Union Maid." The main theme of "Red Wing" is based on Schumann's "The Happy Farmer" from 1849.

Reuben's Train, p. 197: This one shows up with many alternate titles including "Train 45," "Lonesome Reuben," and just plain old "Reuben."

Roll in My Sweet Baby's Arms, p. 199: You gotta know this one if you're going to play bluegrass. Especially for bluegrass bakers.

Roll on Buddy, p. 200: Another great one from the Monroe Brothers song bag. By the way, did you get one of the Monroe Brothers CD box sets yet?

Roving Gambler, p. 201: Another from the folk bag that's slipped into the bluegrass repertoire. Listen to the Country Gentlemen's version.

S

Sally Goodin, p. 203: Probably best known as a fiddle tune, "Sally Goodin" also has some funny lyrics, which are usually sung over the first part. The second part is played instrumentally.

Same Old Man, p. 177: See"Old Man at the Mill." (p. 177)

Seeing Nellie Home, p. 22: See "Aunt Dinah's Quilting Party." (p. 22)

Shady Grove, Bluegrass style, p. 204: "Shady Grove" is performed with a variety of arrangements and lyrics. Here's a version often played by bluegrass bands. An old time version follows. Lyrics are shared between the two and you'll notice one verse that's also in "Pig in a Pen." (p. 185)

Shady Grove, Old Time style, p. 205: See "Shady Grove, Bluegrass style." (p. 204)

Shall We Gather at the River, p. 206: Learned in church from "Tabernacle Hymns."

She's My Little Georgia Rose, p. 168: See "My Little Georgia Rose." (p. 168)

Short Life of Trouble, A, p. 207: Kind of a depressed look at life brought on by a failed love. The theme of verse six is common in traditional music: "You broke my heart, it killed me, plant some flowers on my grave so everybody'll know what a rat you are." Like that would happen!

Shortening Bread, p. 208: A very popular traditional song that fits well into the old time/bluegrass format.

Silver Threads Among the Gold, p. 209: A sentimental old parlor song dating from the late 1800s, if not earlier. I've collected several different sheet music versions of the song. Similar to "When You and I Were Young, Maggie," (p. 240) "Silver Threads" has beautiful, moving, and poetic lyrics about true love that seem all the more meaningful as I age.

Sitting on Top of the World, p. 210: From the blues repertoire.

Softly and Tenderly, p. 211: This one reminds me a bit of "Just as I Am," (p. 129) "Angel Band," (p. 14) and some of the other songs in this collection that offer a reassuring view of the inevitable.

Somebody Touched Me, p. 212: A great old gospel rouser.

Standing in the Need of Prayer, p. 213: Ditto "Somebody Touched Me." (p. 212)

Sugar Hill, p. 214: I learned this from the Goose Island Ramblers. Guitarist Wendy Whitford usually sang, "Shake them cinnamons down" instead of "Shake them 'simmons down."

Sweet Sunny South, p. 216: One of my absolute favorite songs with its serious and beautiful poetry that any one who's left home can relate to. I found it with a different melody and called "Take Me Home" (attributed to the composer "Raymond") in a book titled *Heart Songs* published in 1909. I also found other sources that credit W.L. Bloomfield, 1853. This is a slave song of sorts ("Where poor massa lies buried close by") but rather than idealize plantation life, it offers a bittersweet and universal portrait of aging and dying.

Swing Low, Sweet Chariot, p. 217: Another popular song that appears in many different genres from gospel to blues to country.

T

Take Me Home, p. 216: See "Sweet Sunny South." (p. 216)

Take This Hammer, p. 218: Similar in theme to "Nine Pound Hammer" (p. 170) and other mining songs, "Take This Hammer" has the added edge of forced labor and confinement. I love the verse: "If he asks you was I running/Tell him I's flying."

Take Your Burden to the Lord and Leave it There, p. 139: See "Leave it There." (p. 139)

Talk About Sufferin', p. 219: This is another song that's typically performed a capella. It's written here with accompaniment chords and fermatas.

Tenbrooks and Molly, p. 166: See "Molly and Tenbrooks." (p. 166)

That's the Way to Spell Chicken, p. 39: See "C-H-I-C-K-E-N." (p. 39)

There's More Pretty Girls Than One, p. 220: This song is also performed in 4/4. Check out Tony Rice and Ricky Skaggs' version on "Skaggs and Rice," one of the most beautiful duo recordings ever set to wax.

They Gotta Quit Kickin' My Dawg Aroun', p. 221: Another from the Goose Island Ramblers and a pop song from the early 1900s. I've collected the original sheet music, or at least most of it. The cover of my copy is missing. I borrowed the one shown.

This Little Light of Mine, p. 222: From Sunday school.

This Train, p. 223: Another one learned in grade school.

This World is Not My Home, p. 224: This book includes a lot of songs about death. I guess that's because, like love, it's a universally mysterious subject we all have difficulty dealing with. "This World is Not My Home" speaks to the fact that we're not here for a very long time; we're only passing through.

Train 45, p. 197: See "Reuben's Train."

Train That Carried My Girl From Town, The, p. 226: I suppose the singer's hate of the train, its engineer and fireman, is somewhat misplaced, but that's what makes the song interesting.

'Twas Midnight on the Stormy Deep, p. 164: See "Midnight on the Stormy Deep." (p. 164)

Two Dollar Bill, p. 157: See "Long Journey Home." (p. 157)

U

Unclouded Day, The, p. 227: This song would not be near as interesting if it had been titled "The Clear Day."

W

Wabash Cannonball, p. 228: This is one of the true classics of American folk music. There must be hundreds of variations. Some singers use the lyrics "rumor and roar" in the chorus. One of my favorite songs loosely based on "Wabash Cannonball" is Chuck Berry's "Promised Land."

Walk in Jerusalem Just Like John, p. 229: You'll notice the similarity of the last verse to one in "Swing Low, Sweet Chariot." (p. 217)

Walking in My Sleep, p. 230: "Walking in My Sleep" is a great old time song with wonderfully entertaining lyrics like verse one: "If you see that gal of mine tell her if you please/'Fore she goes to make my bread to roll up her dirty sleeves." That's art, man!

Way Downtown, p. 138: See "Late Last Night." (p. 138)

Wayfaring Stranger, The, p. 231: A beautiful standard played many different ways in a variety of genres.

What a Friend We Have in Jesus, p. 233: Learned in Sunday school from "Tabernacle Hymns."

When I Die, p. 234: Here's one I wrote. I was walking through the woods one day and suddenly felt the presence of my dear departed grandmother, the one who used to sing "The Church in the Wildwood" (p. 43) to me. The song puts words to my thoughts about the incident.

When I Lay My Burden Down, p. 235: Note the similarity of this melody to that of "Will the Circle Be Unbroken." (p. 247)

When My Race is Run, p. 236: Another of mine. I'll show her! Wait 'til I'll die!

When Springtime Comes Again, p. 145: See "Little Annie." (p. 145)

When the Roll is Called Up Yonder, p. 237: One more from the old Baptist hymnal.

When the Saints Go Marching In, p. 238: You're probably most familiar with this as a New Orleans jazz tune.

When the Work's All Done this Fall, p. 239: A cowboy song that's worked its way into the old time and bluegrass repertoire.

When You And I Were Young Maggie, p. 240: Another moving take on love and aging similar to "Silver Thread Among the Gold" (p. 209) and "Sweet Sunny South." (p. 216)

Where the Soul Never Dies, p. 241: I just had to write out both parts to this great duet. On the verses, the tenor sings the same lyrics as the lead adding "of man" into the phrase "Where the soul never dies." On the chorus the voices are in counterpoint to one another. You can hear it on the CD.

Whitehouse Blues, p. 242: Doctors are better now, especially with their bedside manner. The last verse made the rounds in the late 1960s.

Who Broke the Lock?, p. 243: Learned from Wendy Whitford of the Goose Island Ramblers.

Who Will Sing for Me?, p. 244: Another ponderous song about death.

Wild Bill Jones, p. 245: Another good "bully" song.

Wildwood Flower, p. 246: This song, probably the best known of all guitar melodies, has wonderful and poetic lyrics which so beautifully express the feelings of the composer. Compare the sentiments to "I'll Be all Smiles Tonight," (p. 114) and "Little Rosewood Casket." (p. 153) The Carter Family sings lyrics that are a bit different here and there. They may have "mis-heard" the names of some of the flowers mentioned.

Will the Circle Be Unbroken?, p. 247: One of the greatest hits of old time and bluegrass music.

Willie My Darling, p. 249: Beautiful song with bang-up, unexpected tear-jerker-ending. A classic of the "anti-flirting" genre.

Working on a Building, p. 116: See "I'm Working on a Building." (p. 116)

Worried Man Blues, p. 250: You may have heard the hit version of this in the early 1960s. It goes back much further than that, probably to slavery times.

Wreck of the Old 97, The, p. 251: You will need to know several train wreck songs if you intend to play bluegrass. Here's a good one that also happens to be quite popular.

You're a Flower Blooming in the Wildwood, p. 252: Lost love and death. A perfect summation of the main themes of this collection of songs. Not a word about taxes, politics, gas prices, or cell phones. If you ask me, the writers of all these songs knew what was important.

You're Drifting Too Far From the Shore, p. 69: See "Drifting Too Far From the Shore." (p. 69)

You've Got to Walk That Lonesome Valley, p. 156: See "Lonesome Valley." (p. 156)

Index by Artist

Hurst, Jim

Danny Boy, p. 54; Going Down this Road Feeling Bad, p. 80

Ickes, Rob

The Wayfaring Stranger, p. 231

Jim & Jesse

Blue Ridge Mountain Blues, p. 30; I Wonder How the Old Folks are at Home, p. 112; Just Over in the Gloryland, p. 130; Life's Railway to Heaven, p. 142; Long Journey Home, p. 157; Lord I'm Coming Home, p. 158; Nine Pound Hammer, p. 170; Old Time Religion, p. 180; Where the Soul Never Dies, p. 241; Worried Man Blues, p. 250

Johnson Mountain Boys

Don't This Road Look Rough and Rocky?, p. 63; Highway of Sorrow, p. 97; I'm Working on a Building, p. 116; Long Journey Home, p. 157; Standing in the Need of Prayer, p. 213

Kallick, Kathy

C-H-I-C-K-E-N, p. 39; Cotton-Eyed Joe, p. 46; Crawdad Song, p. 48; East Virginia Blues, p. 70; I Never Will Marry, p. 110; I'll Fly Away, p. 115; Little Rosewood Casket, p. 153; My Home's Across the Blue Ridge Mountains, p. 167

Keith, Bill

The Bully of the Town, p. 36; Don't Let Your Deal Go Down, p. 62

Kentucky Colonels

All the Good Times, p. 12; A Beautiful Life, p. 25; Bury Me Beneath the Willow, p. 38; Columbus Stockade Blues, p. 45; Cotton-Eyed Joe, p. 46; Don't Let Your Deal Go Down, p. 62; Fair and Tender Ladies, p. 71; Footprints in the Snow, p. 75; Going Down This Road Feeling Bad, p. 80; I Wonder How the Old Folks Are at Home, p. 112; I'm Working on a Building, p. 116; In the Pines, p. 118; John Hardy, p. 123; John Henry, p. 124; Jordan, p. 126; Just Over in the Gloryland, p. 130; Long Journey Home, p. 157; New River Train, p. 169; Nine Pound Hammer, p. 170; Old Joe Clark, p. 176; Roll on Buddy, p. 200; Shady Grove, p. 204; Wild Bill Jones, p. 245; Wildwood Flower, p. 246

Kincaid, Bradley

Footprints in the Snow, p. 75; Home Sweet Home, p. 103; The Letter Edged in Black, p. 141; Life's Railway to Heaven, p. 142; Methodist Pie, p. 162

King Wilkie

Little Birdie, p. 148

Krauss, Alison

Down in the Valley to Pray, p. 66; Wild Bill Jones, p. 245

Kruger Bros.

Red Rocking Chair, p. 195

Lawless, John

Aunt Dinah's Quilting Party, p. 22

Lawson, Doyle

A Beautiful Life, p. 25; Hallelujah! I'm Ready, p. 87; His Eye is on the Sparrow, p. 100

Lewis Family

Amazing Grace, p. 13; Honey in the Rock, p. 104; I Shall Not Be Moved, p. 111; In the Garden, p. 117

Lewis, Laurie & Kallick, Kathy

Little Annie, p. 145

Lewis, Laurie & Rozum, Tom

Old Dan Tucker, p. 174

Photo by Leigh Taylor

Above: Gerald Jones with Dale Morris, Sr. 1995.

Right: Gerald at a fiddle contest with his son Django Jones and Leigh Taylor, 1999.

bove: Gerald, 1967, in his cool Nehru cket, probably on his way to a gig.

ght: We all have a photo like this from 1980, don't we?

Photo by Bill Millet

CD Track Listing

CD #1:

1. All the Good Times :55
2. Amazing Grace :35
3. Angel Band :59
4. Angelina Baker :37
5. Angels Rock Me to Sleep :44
6. Are you From Dixie? 1:04
7. Are You Washed in the Blood of the Lamb? :38
8. Arkansas Traveller :25
9. Aunt Dinah's Quilting Party :37
10. Away in a Manger :35
11. Banks of the Ohio :56
12. Beautiful Life, A :48
13. Beautiful Star of Bethlehem 1:18
14. Bile Them Cabbage Down–Black Eyed Susie medley :39
15. Blue Ridge Mountain Blues :36
16. Bluebirds are Singing for Me :43
17. Bound to Ride :19
18. Bright Morning Stars :28
19. Bring Back My Wandering Boy :43
20. Buffalo Gals :23
21. Bully of the Town :36
22. Bury Me Beneath the Willow :50
23. C-H-I-C-K-E-N :40
24. Can't You Hear Me Callin'? :41
25. Careless Love :42
26. Children Go Where I Send Thee :50
27. Church in the Wildwood :42
28. Cindy :19
29. Columbus Stockade Blues :43
30. Cotton-Eyed Joe :22
31. Cowboy Jack :26
32. Crawdad Song, The :23
33. Cripple Creek :25
34. Crying Holy :37
35. Cuckoo, The :25
36. Daniel Prayed :51
37. Danny Boy 1:32
38. Darling Cory – Darling Nellie Gray medley 1:40
39. Darling Will You Ever Think of Me :43
40. Deep Elem Blues :27
41. Diamonds in the Rough :39
42. Do Lord :36
43. Don't Let Your Deal Go Down :35
44. Don't This Road Look Rough and Rocky? 1:02
45. Don't You Hear Jerusalem Moan? :29
46. Down Among the Budded Roses :53
47. Down in the Valley to Pray :33
48. Down in the Willow Garden :41
49. Down the Road :17
50. Drifting too Far from the Shore :51
51. East Virginia Blues :38
52. Fair and Tender Ladies :38
53. Fathers Have a Home Sweet Home :46
54. Feast Here Tonight :32
55. Foggy Mountain Top :24
56. Footprints in the Snow :45
57. Girl I Loved in Sunny Tennessee,
    The Give Me Oil in My Lamp medley 1:48
58. Give Me the Roses While I Live :38
59. Going Down this Road Feeling Bad
    – Grandfather's Clockmedley 1:23
60. Great Speckled Bird :36
61. Green Pastures :59
62. Groundhog :17
63. Hallelujah! I'm Ready :37
64. Hand Me Down My Walking Cane
    – Handsome Molly medley :52
65. Hard Times Come Again No More
    – Have Thine Own Way, Lord medley 1:39
66. He was a Friend of Mine :37
67. He Will Set Your Fields On Fire 1:05
68. High on a Mountain 1:00
69. Highway of Sorrow :34
70. Hills of Roane County :37
71. His Eye is on the Sparrow 1:22
72. Hold Fast to The Right :42
73. Hold to God's Unchanging Hand :56
74. Home Sweet Home :57
75. Honey in the Rock :26
76. Hop High Ladies :25
77. Hot Corn, Cold Corn :30
78. How Can You Treat Me So? :50
79. I Ain't Gonna Work Tomorrow :20
80. I Know You Rider :43
81. I Never Will Marry – I Shall Not Be Moved medley 1:12
82. I Wonder How the Old Folks are at Home :41
83. I'll Be all Smiles Tonight 1:01
84. I'll Fly Away :36
85. I'm Working on a Building :40
86. In the Garden :55
87. In the Pines :53
88. It's Mighty Dark to Travel – Jesse James medley 1:17
89. Jimmie Brown, the Newsboy :24
90. John Hardy :24
91. John Henry :26
92. Jordan 1:00
93. Just a Closer Walk With Thee :42
94. Just as I Am :30
95. Just Over in the Gloryland – Katy Cline medley 1:03
96. Katy Daley :36
97. Katy Dear :27
98. Keep on the Sunny Side – Knoxville Girl medley 1:22

D #2:

Late Last Night :38
Leave it There :51
Let Me Rest at the End of My Journey :47
Letter Edged in Black :28
Life's Railway to Heaven 1:00
Li'l Liza Jane :22
Little Annie :41
Little Bessie :25
Little Birdie :22
. Little Maggie – Little Old Log Cabin in the Lane medley 1:03
. Little Rosewood Casket :29
. Little Sadie :28
. Little Willie :26
. Lonesome Valley – Long Journey Home medley :45
. Lord I'm Coming Home 1:01
. Mama Don't Allow :21
. Man of Constant Sorrow :35
. Maple on the Hill :29
. Methodist Pie – Midnight on the Stormy Deep medley 1:15
. Milwaukee Blues :26
. Molly and Tenbrooks :28
. My Home's Across the Blue Ridge Mountains :23
. My Little Georgia Rose :38
. New River Train – Nine Pound Hammer medley 1:01
. Nobody's Business :23
. Oh Death :39
. Oh Didn't He Ramble – Old Dan Tucker medley 1:06
. Old Home Place :38
. Old Joe Clark :21
. Old Man at the Mill :17
. Old Paint :37
. Old Rugged Cross 1:10
. Old Time Religion :24
. On and On :43
. Over the Hills to the Poorhouse :39
. Pass Me Not 1:03
. Paul and Silas :21
. Pig in a Pen :21
. Poor Ellen Smith :24
. Precious Memories 1:04
. Pretty Polly :37
. Put My Little Shoes Away :44
. Railroad Bill :23
. Rain and Snow :37
. Rank Strangers to Me 1:21
. Red Rocking Chair :29
. Red Wing :42
. Reuben's Train :21
. Rocky Top :41
. Roll in My Sweet Baby's Arms :38
. Roll on Buddy :32
. Roving Gambler :19

53. Sailor on the Deep Blue Sea :26
54. Sally Goodin :27
55. Shady Grove, bluegrass :21
56. Shady Grove, old time :28
57. Shall We Gather at the River :41
58. Short Life of Trouble, A :22
59. Shortening Bread :26
60. Silver Threads Among the Gold :47
61. Sitting on Top of the World :24
62. Softly & Tenderly :58
63. Somebody Touched Me :35
64. Standing in the Need of Prayer :26
65. Sugar Hill :29
66. Sweet By and By :41
67. Sweet Sunny South :25
68. Swing Low, Sweet Chariot :35
69. Take This Hammer :30
70. Talk about Sufferin' :38
71. There's More Pretty Girls Than One :27
72. They Gotta Quit Kicking My Dawg Around :34
73. This Little Light of Mine :25
74. This Train :22
75. This World is Not My Home :44
76. Train, Train, Train 1:01
77. Train That Carried My Girl From Town, The :32
78. Unclouded Day, The :41
79. Wabash Cannonball :25
80. Walk in Jerusalem Just Like John :29
81. Walking in My Sleep :21
82. Wayfaring Stranger, The 1:06
83. Were You There When They Crucified My Lord?
– What a Friend We Have in Jesus medley 1:32
84. When I Die :31
85. When I Lay My Burden Down :28
86. When My Race is Run 1:09
87. When the Roll is Called Up Yonder
– When the Saints Go Marching In medley 1:02
88. When the Work's all Done This Fall :28
89. When You and I Were Young, Maggie :52
90. Where the Soul Never Dies :39
91. Whitehouse Blues – Who Broke the Lock? medley :57
92. Who Will Sing for Me? :52
93. Wild Bill Jones :22
94. Wildwood Flower :31
95. Will the Circle Be Unbroken
– Will There Be Any Stars in My Crown? medley 1:21
96. Willie My Darling :51
97. Worried Man Blues – Wreck of the Old 97 medley :59
98. You're a Flower Blooming in the Wildwood :41

Athens, TX, Black Eyed Pea Festival & Fiddle Contest, 2008.

Athens, TX, Black Eyed Pea Festival & Fiddle Contest, 2008.

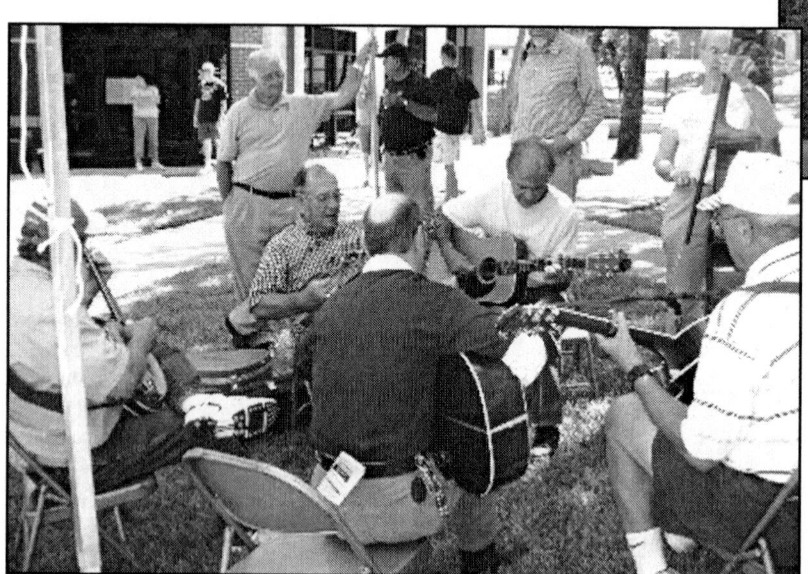

Photos by Gerald Jones

Bluegrass Heritage Foundation Festival, 2008